COMPLEMENTARITY, CATALYSTS, COMPLIANCE

Since its establishment at the turn of the century, a central preoccupation of the International Criminal Court (ICC) has been to catalyse the pursuit of criminal accountability at the domestic level. Drawing on ten years of research, this book theorizes the ICC's principle of complementarity as a transnational site and adaptive strategy for realizing an array of ambitious governance goals. Through a grounded, inter-disciplinary approach, it illustrates how complementarity came to be framed as a 'catalyst for compliance' and its unexpected effects on the legal frameworks and institutions of three different ICC 'situation countries' in Africa: Uganda, Kenya and the Democratic Republic of Congo. Linking complementarity's law and practice to contemporary debates in international law and relations, the book unsettles international law's dominant progressive narrative. It urges a critical rethinking of the ICC's politics and a reorientation towards international criminal justice as a project of global legal pluralism.

CHRISTIAN DE VOS is a senior advocacy officer with the Open Society Justice Initiative. He has worked for organizations including Amnesty International, the United States Institute of Peace, the War Crimes Research Office and Leiden University's Grotius Centre for International Legal Studies. He previously clerked for the United States Court of Appeals for the Second Circuit. He has published in a number of leading academic journals and was a coeditor of the volume *Contested Justice: The Politics and Practice of International Criminal Court Interventions* (with Sara Kendall and Carsten Stahn, 2015). A graduate of American University Washington College of Law (JD) and Leiden University (PhD), De Vos is a member of the New York Bar and was a term member of the Council on Foreign Relations.

'De Vos' careful, rich and well-informed study of the complementarity regime of the International Criminal Court shines by claiming neither too little nor too much. Illuminating how international justice interacts with national processes in three places, and how the first can catalyze the second, he concludes with a persuasive call to hopeful modesty about expectations.'

Samuel Moyn, Henry R. Luce Professor of Jurisprudence and Professor of History, Yale Law School

'Christian De Vos detoxes the ICC from its demons. He does so gently, respectfully, wisely and firmly. He delivers the most sophisticated, insightful and compelling assessment currently available about the ICC and its strained, awkward relationships with others. And De Vos builds, too, beautifully, by charting a path forward. His book stands tall. It has soul. It flows with roll, pitch and yaw: De Vos delivers a gleaming must-read.'

Mark A. Drumbl, Class of 1975 Professor of Law, Director, Transnational Law Institute, Washington and Lee University School of Law

'With an exquisite analysis of the ICC's catalytic impact in Uganda, the Democratic Republic of the Congo and Kenya, *Complementarity, Catalysts, Compliance* offers a brilliant analysis of the changes in complementarity as we know it. Christian De Vos' rethinking of complementarity's role in practice contributes a deeply insightful understanding of the transformation of international justice in the contemporary period. With breadth, depth and analytic innovation, this is a tour de force – a must read in international justice scholarship!'

Kamari Clarke, Professor of Anthropology, University of California–Los Angeles

'By following the strange trajectory of complementarity, Christian De Vos manages to capture the political dimensions of prosecution efforts for serious crimes as few have done before him. His study is a fascinating account of how complementarity has taken on multiple identities over the last decade. It plunges us into the meander of internal (mainly strategy changes in the Office of the Prosecutor) and external factors (resulting from the practice of state and non-state actors) that have successively influenced these multiple identities. The study reveals how each of these identities, in turn, influenced the behaviour of actors involved in the national prosecution efforts. The most original contribution of this study lies in the revelation of the versatility of complementarity. We have been conditioned to see complementarity as an intrinsically progressive doctrine – which explains why some find the term "positive complementarity" somewhat redundant. But, as the study reveals, local actors have used complementarity mechanisms and practices to frustrate national prosecutions. If complementarity allows the ICC to project its proverbial shadow, this book urges us to consider the source of its light.'

Pascal Kambale, Senior Advisor, Africa Regional Office – Open Society Foundations

CAMBRIDGE STUDIES IN INTERNATIONAL
AND COMPARATIVE LAW: 147

Established in 1946, this series produces high quality, reflective and innovative scholarship in the field of public international law. It publishes works on international law that are of a theoretical, historical, cross-disciplinary or doctrinal nature. The series also welcomes books providing insights from private international law, comparative law and transnational studies, which inform international legal thought and practice more generally.

The series seeks to publish views from diverse legal traditions and perspectives and of any geographical origin. In this respect, it invites studies offering regional perspectives on core *problématiques* of international law, and in the same vein, it appreciates contrasts and debates between diverging approaches. Accordingly, books offering new or less orthodox perspectives are very much welcome. Works of a generalist character are greatly valued, and the series is also open to studies on specific areas, institutions or problems. Translations of the most outstanding works published in other languages are also considered.

After seventy years, Cambridge Studies in International and Comparative Law sets the standard for international legal scholarship and will continue to define the discipline as it evolves in the years to come.

Series Editors

Larissa van den Herik
Professor of Public International Law, Grotius Centre for International Legal Studies, Leiden University

Jean d'Aspremont
Professor of International Law, University of Manchester and Sciences Po Law School

A list of books in the series can be found at the end of this volume.

COMPLEMENTARITY, CATALYSTS, COMPLIANCE

The International Criminal Court in Uganda, Kenya, and the Democratic Republic of Congo

CHRISTIAN M. DE VOS

Leiden University
Grotius Centre for International Legal Studies

CAMBRIDGE
UNIVERSITY PRESS

CAMBRIDGE
UNIVERSITY PRESS

University Printing House, Cambridge CB2 8BS, United Kingdom

One Liberty Plaza, 20th Floor, New York, NY 10006, USA

477 Williamstown Road, Port Melbourne, VIC 3207, Australia

314-321, 3rd Floor, Plot 3, Splendor Forum, Jasola District Centre, New Delhi - 110025, India

103 Penang Road, #05-06/07, Visioncrest Commercial, Singapore 238467

Cambridge University Press is part of the University of Cambridge.

It furthers the University's mission by disseminating knowledge in the pursuit of
education, learning and research at the highest international levels of excellence.

www.cambridge.org
Information on this title: www.cambridge.org/9781108459723
DOI: 10.1017/9781108560436

First published 2020
First paperback edition 2022

A catalogue record for this publication is available from the British Library

Library of Congress Cataloging in Publication data
Names: De Vos, Christian M., author.
Title: Complementarity, catalysts, compliance / Christian M. De Vos.
Description: New York : Cambridge University Press, 2020. | Series:
Cambridge studies in international and comparative law | Includes
bibliographical references and index.
Identifiers: LCCN 2019043874 | ISBN 9781108472487 (hardback) | ISBN
9781108459723 (ebook)
Subjects: LCSH: Complementarity (International law) | International crimes.
| International Criminal Court. | International criminal courts. |
Criminal law--International unification. | Criminal justice,
Administration of. | Compliance.
Classification: LCC KZ7379 .D48 2020 | DDC 345/.0122--dc23
LC record available at https://lccn.loc.gov/2019043874

ISBN 978-1-108-47248-7 Hardback
ISBN 978-1-108-45972-3 Paperback

For John, Rieve and Baird

CONTENTS

ACKNOWLEDGEMENTS

Like all books, this one has had a long journey with many debts acquired along the way. It began its life ten years ago when I took up a post as a PhD researcher at Leiden University's Grotius Centre for International Legal Studies and continued when I moved to the Open Society Justice Initiative. I count myself fortunate to have had the opportunity to work in both of these institutions, with colleagues whose intellect and passion have helped nourish and inspire my academic pursuits, as well as my commitment to advocacy and social change.

I want to first thank my many interlocutors – in Kenya, Uganda, the Democratic Republic of Congo and The Hague – without whose time and assistance this research would not have been possible. Their names do not all appear here or in the pages that follow, but the time they took to speak with me about their work, their achievements and their disappointments have helped shape this endeavour in ways both large and small.

I am also indebted to individuals whose insights and connections helped me to both develop my in-country networks and my thinking. My sincere thanks to Morten Bergsmo, Phil Clark, Judy Gitau, Kevin Jon Heller, Maria Kamara, George Kegoro, Patryk Labuda, Jacques Mbokani, Njonjo Mue, Sharon Nakhanda, Sarah Nouwen, Eva Nudd, Antonina Okuta, Stephen Oola, Rod Rastan, Carsten Stahn, Ruti Teitel, Larissa van den Herik, Muthoni Wanyeki and Marcel Wetsh'okonda Koso. Like many others who miss her, I am grateful for the wisdom of Chandra Lekha Sriram who offered helpful insights to me at a key moment in the project.

Members of my doctoral review committee also provided critical feedback, helping to guide the revisions that followed: I am grateful to Helen Duffy, Mark Drumbl, Robert Heinsch, William Schabas and Harmen van der Wilt. I owe particular thanks to Larissa for her steadfast encouragement over the years and to Mark, who summoned Matisse at the right moment. His support of this endeavour – and of me – has meant a great deal.

As a law student, I was fortunate to work with and learn from Susana SáCouto and Diane Orentlicher, whose scholarship drew me to the field of international criminal justice in the first place. Their influence on my thinking has been deep and lasting. Montserrat Carreras gave me my first job in international human rights when I landed at Amnesty International's Belgium chapter after college. My time working with her – just as the ICC was taking shape – helped shape my future pursuits, and I thank her for opening those doors for me. Finally, I am grateful to the Netherlands Organization for Scientific Research, which provided generous financial support to make this project possible; to Tom and Barbara Devine, who kindly let me commandeer their dining room table for several intense writing sojourns on Cape Cod; to Alex Foster, who proved a nimble and cheerful indexer; and to Pete Muller, for the permission to use his photograph as the book's cover image.

Friends and colleagues have been pillars of support. In particular, this work has benefited immeasurably from a conversation and friendship that began with Sara Kendall. She has been a travelling comrade, intellectual sounding partner and the best personal gift to emerge from this experience. Jennifer Easterday, Iavor Rangelov and Marieke Wierda have also been valued interlocutors and friends who came into my life through the course of this project.

It is my great fortune to work with outstanding, supportive colleagues at the Open Society Justice Initiative and the larger Open Society Foundations, which I joined in 2013. I owe particular thanks to the indomitable Betsy Apple, who patiently supported this extended juggling act (first as dissertation, then as book), as well as to Tracey Gurd, whose good cheer and big heart helped in innumerable ways as I transitioned to the Justice Initiative. Alpha Sesay and Eric Witte shared documents, contacts and insights with me generously both before and during my time at OSF; it is a delight to work with them now as colleagues. Conversations and collaborations with Yassir Al-Khudayri, Erika Dailey, Liliana Gamboa, James Goldston, Nina Ippolito, Pascal Kambale, Steve Kostas, Fiona McKay, Roger Mvita, Sharon Nakhanda (again), Mariana Pena, Taegin Reisman, Beini Ye and Ina Zoon have likewise enriched and challenged my thinking. That said, all views expressed (and any errors) in the pages that follow are my own. They do not represent those of OSF or the Justice Initiative.

As a long incubating effort, some parts of this book have appeared elsewhere in previously published forms. Portions of 'Investigating from Afar: The ICC's Evidence Problem', *Leiden Journal of International Law* 26(4) (2013) and "Magical Legalism" and the International Criminal Court: A Case Study of the Kenyan Preliminary Examination', in Morten Bergsmo and Carsten Stahn (eds.), *Quality Control in Preliminary Examination: Volume 1* (Torkel Opsahl Academic EPublisher, 2018) appear in a revised format in Chapter 4. Portions of the chapter 'All Roads Lead to Rome Implementation and Domestic Politics in Kenya and Uganda' from the edited volume *Contested Justice: The Politics and Practice of International Criminal Court Interventions* (Cambridge University Press, 2015) also appear in Chapter 5. This is my second opportunity to publish with Cambridge and, as before, I am grateful for their support and professionalism. My particular thanks go out to Finola O'Sullivan, Marianne Nield, Sarah Payne, Rebecca Jackaman, and Priyaa Menon.

This book would of course not be possible without the love and support of my parents, Christian De Vos and Marnie Whelan-De Vos. They raised me to believe that social justice is part of our work here on earth, but they also encouraged me to ask questions. I am forever grateful for their example. I am also fortunate to have been supported by a wonderful family of choice. Mary Baim and Michael Becker, in particular, have patiently encouraged this endeavour, while the memory of my late father-in-law, Robert Lance, is always with me. I miss him.

Above all, my greatest debt is to Abigail, who gave me the courage to take this leap and the gift of walking it together. She has endured living with this project – its scattered papers, endless Post-it Notes, late nights and too many foregone social outings – for longer than I had any right to ask. Every thought reflected in these pages is a tribute to her fine mind, her generous heart and her unwavering support. Marrying her is the best decision I ever made.

The completion of this project was marked by a number of life events, but three in particular loom large: the death of a dear friend and mentor, John Daniel, and the birth of my children, Rieve Francine Lance-De Vos and her brother, Baird Michael. John was a transformative educator and activist who committed his life to fighting the crime against humanity that was South African apartheid. For my children, this tragic, complicated, occasionally beautiful world is only beginning to take shape. As they steer their own paths in life, I hope that they will do so with the courage and integrity that helped guide John in his. This book is dedicated to them.

TABLE OF CASES AND PLEADINGS

The following cases and pleadings are ordered alphabetically by jurisdiction and then, where applicable, by situation and case name.

Democratic Republic of Congo

Affaire *Bongi* (*MP et PC c. Bongi Massaba*), Tribunal Militaire de Garnison de Ituri (24 March 2006)

Affaire *Songo Mboyo* (*MP et PC c. Bokila et consorts*), Tribunal Militaire de Garnison de Mbandaka (12 April 2006)

Affaire *Kibibi* (*MP et PC c. Daniel Kibibi et consorts*), Cour militaire de Bukavu (21 February 2011)

International Criminal Court
Situation in the Central African Republic

Decision Requesting Information on the Status of the Preliminary Examination of the Situation in the Central African Republic, ICC-01/05-06, PTC III (30 November 2006)

The Case of the Prosecutor *v.* Jean-Pierre Bemba Gombo

Judgment on the Appeal of Mr Jean-Pierre Bemba Gombo against the Decision of Trial Chamber III of 24 June 2010 entitled 'Decision on the Admissibility and Abuse of Process Challenges', ICC-01/05-01/08OA3, Appeals Chamber (19 October 2010)

The Case of the Prosecutor *v.* Jean-Pierre Bemba Gombo, Judgment on the Appeal of Mr Jean-Pierre Bemba Gombo against Trial Chamber III's 'Judgment Pursuant to Article 74 of the Statute', ICC-01/05-01/08 A, Appeals Chamber (8 June 2018)

Situation in the Republic of Côte d'Ivoire

Decision Pursuant to Article 15 of the Rome Statute on the Authorisation of an Investigation into the Situation in the Republic of Côte d'Ivoire, ICC-02/11, PTC III (3 October 2011)

The Case of the Prosecutor *v.* Laurent Gbagbo and Charles Blé Goudé

Decision on the Prosecutor's Application Pursuant to Article 58 for a Warrant of Arrest against Laurent Koudou Gbagbo, ICC-02/11-01/11, PTC III (30 November 2011)

Decision Adjourning the Hearing on the Confirmation of Charges Pursuant to Article 61(7)(c)(i) of the Rome Statute, ICC-02/11-01/11, PTC I (3 June 2013)

Decision on the '*Requeté relative a la recevabilité de l'affaire en vertu des Articles 19 et 17 du Statut*', ICC-02/11-01/11, PTC I (11 June 2013)

The Case of the Prosecutor *v.* Simone Gbagbo

Decision on Côte d'Ivoire's Challenge to the Admissibility of the Case against Simone Gbagbo, ICC-02/11-01/12, PTC I (11 December 2014)

Judgment on the Appeal of Côte d'Ivoire against the Decision of Pre-Trial Chamber I of 11 December 2014 entitled 'Decision on Côte d'Ivoire's Challenge to the Admissibility of the Case against Simone Gbagbo', ICC-02/11-01/12 OA, Appeals Chamber (27 May 2015)

Order to the Registrar to Request Information from the Competent National Authorities of the Republic of Côte d'Ivoire, ICC-02/11-01/12, PTC II (14 September 2018)

Situation in the Democratic Republic of Congo

Judgment of the Prosecutor's Appeal Against the Decision of Pre-Trial Chamber I Entitled 'Decision on the Prosecutor's Application for Warrants of Arrest, Article 58', ICC-01/04-169, Appeals Chamber (13 July 2006)

The Case of the Prosecutor *v.* Callixte Mbarushimana, Decision on the Confirmation of Charges, ICC-01/04-01/10-465-Red, PTC I (16 December 2011)

The Case of the Prosecutor *v.* Sylvestre Mudacumura, Decision on the Prosecutor's Application under Article 58, ICC-01/04-01/12, PTC II (13 July 2012)

The Case of the Prosecutor *v.* Bosco Ntaganda, Judgment, ICC-01/04-02/06, TC VI (8 July 2019)

The Case of the Prosecutor *v.* Thomas Lubanga Dyilo

The Case of the Prosecutor *v.* Germain Katanga and Mathieu Ngudjolo Chui

Situation in the Republic of Kenya

Request for Authorization of an Investigation Pursuant to Article 15, ICC-01/09, PTC II (26 November 2009)

Decision Pursuant to Article 15 of the Rome Statute on the Authorization of an Investigation into the Situation in the Republic of Kenya, ICC-01/09-19, PTC II (31 March 2010)

Request for Assistance on Behalf of the Government of the Republic of Kenya Pursuant to Article 93(10) and Rule 194, ICC-01/09 (21 April 2011)

Decision on the Request for Assistance Submitted on Behalf of the Government of the Republic of Kenya Pursuant to Article 93(10) of the Statute and Rule 194 of the Rules of Procedure and Evidence, ICC-01/09, PTC II (29 June 2011)

Decision on the Admissibility of the 'Appeal of the Government of Kenya against the "Decision on the Request for Assistance Submitted on Behalf of the Government of the Republic of Kenya Pursuant to Article 93(1) of the Statute and Rule 194 of the Rules of Procedure and Evidence"', ICC-01/09 OA (10 August 2011)

Victims' Request for Review of Prosecution's Decision to Cease Active Investigation, ICC-01/09, PTC II (3 August 2015)

The Case of the Prosecutor *v.* Francis Kirimi Muthaura and Uhuru Muigai Kenyatta

Corrigendum to the 'Document in Support of the "Appeal of the Government of Kenya against the Decision on the Application by the Government of Kenya Challenging the Admissibility of the Case Pursuant to Article 19(2)(b) of the Statute"', ICC-01/09-02/11 (21 June 2011)

Judgment on the Appeal of the Republic of Kenya against the Decision of Pre-Trial Chamber II of 30 May 2011 Entitled 'Decision on the Application by the Government of Kenya Challenging the Admissibility of the Case Pursuant to Article 19(2)(b) of the Statute', ICC-01/09-02/11 OA, Appeals Chamber (30 August 2011)

Decision on the Confirmation of Charges Pursuant to Article 61(7)(a) and (b) of the Rome Statute, ICC-01/09-02/11-382-Red, PTC II (23 January 2012)

Prosecution Notification of Withdrawal of the Charges Against Francis Kirimi Muthaura, ICC-01/09-02/11, TC V (11 March 2013)

Decision on Defence Application Pursuant to Article 64(4) and Related Requests, ICC-01/09-02/11, TC V (26 April 2013), Concurring Opinion of Judge Christine Van den Wyngaert

Leave to Submit Observations under Rule 103' Dated 5 November 2008,
ICC-02/04-01/05, PTC II (18 November 2008)
Decision on the Admissibility of the Case under Article 19(1) of the Statute, ICC-02/04-01/05, PTC II (10 March 2009)
Decision on the Confirmation of Charges Against Dominic Ongwen,
ICC-02/04-01/15/422, PTC II (23 March 2016)

Kenya

Francis Karioko Muruatetu and Another *v.* Republic of Kenya, Supreme Court
of Kenya, Pet. Nos. 15 & 16 (2015) (Judgment Delivered 14 December 2017)
Republic of Kenya *v.* Edward Kirui, High Court of Kenya (Nairobi), Criminal
Case no. 9 (Judgment Delivered 21 June 2010)
Republic of Kenya *v.* Stephen Kiprotich Leting and 3 Others, High Court of
Kenya (Nakuru), Criminal Case no. 34 (Judgment Delivered 30 April 2009)
Floriculture International Limited and Others, High Court Misc. Civil
Application no. 114 (1997)
Amwona & Others *v.* KBL, High Court Misc. Application no. 19 (2004)

Uganda

Thomas Kwoyelo Alias Latoni *v.* Attorney General, High Court (Civil Division),
HCT-00-CV-MC-0162-2011 (25 January 2012)
Uganda *v.* Thomas Kwoyelo Alias Latoni, Constitutional Court of Uganda,
Petition no. 036/11 (22 September 2011)
Uganda *v.* Thomas Kwoyelo, The Republic of Uganda in the Supreme Court of
Uganda at Kampala, Constitutional Appeal no. 1 of 2012 (8 April 2015)

Other

Handyside *v.* United Kingdom, European Court of Human Rights (1976)
International Criminal Tribunal for Rwanda, The Prosecutor *v.* Michel
Bagaragaza, Decision on Rule 11 *bis* Appeal, ICTR-05-86-AR11bis, Appeals
Chambers (30 August 2006)
Southern African Litigation Centre and Zimbabwe Exiles Forum *v.* National
Director of Public Prosecutions, High Court of South Africa (North
Gauteng), Case no. 77150/09, Judgment (8 May 2012)
African Commission on Human and Peoples' Rights, Communication no.
431/12 – Thomas Kwoyelo *v.* Uganda, 23 Extra-ordinary Session (12–22
February 2018)

TABLE OF STATUTES AND STATUTORY INSTRUMENTS

Democratic Republic of Congo

International Criminal Court

Kenya

Commission of Inquiry into Post-election Violence (Kenya) (15 October 2008)
The International Crimes Act, 2008
The National Accord and Reconciliation Act, 2008
The Special Tribunal for Kenya Bill, 2009
The Constitution of Kenya (Amendment) Bill

Uganda

Amnesty Act, 2000, Laws of Uganda
'Proposed New Part to ICC Bill; Part X – Alternate Proceedings' (proposed by
    MP Jacob Oulanyah, 12 December 2004)
Agreement on Cessation of Hostilities between the Government of the Republic
    of Uganda and Lord's Resistance Army Movement (Agenda Item no. 1), 26
    August 2006
Accountability and Reconciliation Agreement (Agenda Item no. 3), 29 June 2007
Annexure to the Agreement on Accountability and Reconciliation, 19 February 2008
Amnesty Commission, 'The Amnesty Act: An Act of Forgiveness' (August 2009)
Request for Parliament to Approve the Declaration of Named Individuals as
    Persons Not Eligible for Amnesty (13 April 2010)
International Criminal Court Act, 2010, *Uganda Gazette* no. 39, Vol. 103 (25
    June 2010) National Reconciliation Bill (Draft of 10 June 2011)
Statutory Instruments 2012 no. 34, The Amnesty Act (Declaration of Lapse
    of the Operation of Part II) Instrument, 2012 (issued by MP Hilary Onek,
    Minister of Internal Affairs, 23 May 2012)
Report of the Committee on Defence and Internal Affairs on the Petition on the
    Lapsing of Part II of the Amnesty Act (August 2013)

Other

Kampala Declaration, RC/Decl.1, para. 5 (Adopted 1 June 2010)
Kampala Declaration, Resolution RC/Res.1 – Complementarity (Adopted 8 June 2010)
Review Conference Resolution RC/Res.2 – The Impact of the Rome Statute
    System on Victims and Affected Communities (Adopted 8 June 2010)
United Nations Security Council Resolution 1503, S/RES/1503 (28 August 2003)
Draft Protocol on Amendments to the Protocol on the Statute of the African
    Court of Justice and Human Rights, STC/Legal/Min/7(I) Rev. 1 (15 May 2014)
Organic Law no. 11/2007 of 16 March 2007 Concerning Transfer of Cases to the
    Republic of Rwanda from the International Criminal Tribunal for Rwanda,
    Official Gazette of the Republic of Rwanda (19 March 2007)

ABBREVIATIONS

A&R	Accountability and Reconciliation Agreement (Uganda)
AC	Appeals Chamber (ICC)
ASF	*Avocats sans Frontières*
ASP	Assembly of States Parties
AU	African Union
CICC	Coalition for the International Criminal Court
CIPEV	Commission of Inquiry on Post-Election Violence (Kenya)
CMJ	*Comité Mixte de Justice* (DRC)
DPP	Director of Public Prosecutions
DRC	Democratic Republic of Congo
FARC	Revolutionary Armed Forces of Colombia
FDLR	Democratic Forces for the Liberation of Rwanda
FPA	Final Peace Agreement (Uganda)
HRW	Human Rights Watch
ICA	International Crimes Act (Kenya 2008)
ICC/Court	International Criminal Court
ICC Act	International Criminal Court Act (Uganda 2010)
ICD/Division	International Crimes Division (Uganda and Kenya)
I-CD	Inter-Congolese Dialogue
ICL	International Criminal Law
ICTJ	International Center for Transitional Justice
ICTR	International Criminal Tribunal for Rwanda
ICTY	International Criminal Tribunal for the Former Yugoslavia
JCCD	Jurisdiction, Complementarity and Cooperation Division
JLOS	Justice Law and Order Sector (Uganda)
JSC	Judicial Services Commission (Kenya)
KNHRC	Kenya National Human Rights Commission
KPTJ	Kenyans for Peace with Truth and Justice
LRA	Lord's Resistance Army
MONUSCO	United Nations Organization Stabilization Mission in the Democratic Republic of the Congo (formerly MONUC)
MP	Member of Parliament
NGOs	Non-Governmental Organizations

NILD	National Implementing Legislation Database
ODM	Orange Democratic Movement (Kenya)
OSF	Open Society Foundations
OTP	Office of the Prosecutor
PAJ	Political, Administrative and Judicial Committee (DRC)
PE	Preliminary Examination
PEV	Post-Election Violence
PGA	Parliamentarians for Global Action
PTC	Pre-Trial Chamber (ICC)
SCC	Special Criminal Court in the Central African Republic
STK	Special Tribunal for Kenya
TC	Trial Chamber (ICC)
UNDP	United Nations Development Programme
UPDF	Uganda People's Defence Force
UVF	Uganda Victims Foundation
VRWG	Victims' Rights Working Group
WCD	War Crimes Division (Uganda)

PREFACE

This book is about the International Criminal Court (ICC), the world's first permanent judicial body established to prosecute mass atrocity crimes, and the legal transformations its interventions have spawned in three 'situation countries' to date: Uganda, Kenya and the Democratic Republic of Congo (DRC). Its origins date back to the summer of 2010, a time that, in various ways, marked a turning point for the Court as well as the countries the book traverses.

In June, the first 'Review Conference of the Rome Statute' was held in Kampala, Uganda. Billed partly as a 'stock-taking' exercise of the ICC's founding treaty and of the Court's first eight years of operation, the conference was yet another illustration of international criminal justice's remarkable ascendance as a post-Cold War political project. The conference provided an opportunity for member states to finally establish an agreeable definition of aggression – the most contentious crime over which the ICC now has (partial) jurisdiction – and an occasion to issue a number of ambitious resolutions. One resolution extolled the impact of an emergent 'Rome Statute system' on victims and affected communities, while another noted the 'importance of States Parties taking effective domestic measures to implement the Statute' in their own legal systems (as the conference's host country, Uganda, had just done).[1] The final Kampala Declaration recalled the heady language of the Rome Statute's preamble – 'that all peoples are united by common bonds', whose 'delicate mosaic may be shattered at any time' – as it summoned 'the common bonds of our peoples, our cultures pieced together in a shared heritage'.[2]

---

[1] See RC/Res.2 The impact of the Rome Statute system on victims and affected communities and RC/Res.1 Complementarity, para. 4 (both adopted on 8 June 2010, by consensus), at https://asp.icc-cpi.int/en_menus/asp/reviewconference/resolutions%20and%20declarations/Pages/resolutions%20and%20declarations.aspx.
[2] See RC/Decl.1 Kampala Declaration (adopted on 1 June 2010, by consensus), at https://asp.icc-cpi.int/iccdocs/asp_docs/Resolutions/RC-Decl.1-ENG.pdf.

And yet, by 2010, these bonds were being sorely tested. After commencing its first investigations in both Uganda and the DRC (situations that were referred to the Court by those countries' own governments), the ICC had begun to navigate an increasingly rocky political terrain. Luis Moreno-Ocampo, the ICC's inaugural prosecutor, had initiated the Court's first, controversial *proprio motu* investigation in Kenya that spring, following the government's failure to establish a domestic tribunal for the post-election violence of late 2007. Shortly thereafter, ICC judges issued a second arrest warrant against former Sudanese President Omar Al Bashir, the first sitting head of state to then be charged by the Court. This time the charge was for genocide, the 'crime of crimes'.[3]

By late July, Kampala was again playing host, but this time to a different summit: the African Union's (AU) annual Assembly of Heads of State. At this convening, the focus was not on humanity's 'common bonds' but rather on charges of the ICC's racism and bias. Furious at what by then had increasingly come to be seen as a 'court for Africa' – neocolonial in design, imperial in ambition – the AU Assembly rejected the ICC's request to open a 'liaison office' in Addis Ababa (where the Union is headquartered) and accused Moreno-Ocampo personally of 'making egregiously unacceptable, rude and condescending statements' in relation to both the Al Bashir case and other situations on the continent. Already a source of animosity, the Court's relationship with the AU sank to a new low, one with which it continues to struggle.[4]

That same summer, I was packing up my apartment in New York City for a different, though related, destination: The Hague. Host city to an array of international courts and tribunals, including the ICC, my decision to move there was motivated by a desire to better understand an institution that both inspired and intrigued me. A young lawyer and aspiring academic at the time, I made the decision to join a new research project housed at Leiden University's Grotius Centre for International Legal Studies that sought to explore the Court's institutional evolution since first opening its doors on 1 July 2002, as well as the domestic legal effects that its interventions had 'catalysed', a concept I would come to interrogate closely over the coming years.

[3] See Prosecutor v. Kambanda (ICTR 97-23-S), International Criminal Tribunal for Rwanda, Trial Chamber I, Judgment 4 September 1998, para. 16.
[4] For a fuller accounting of the ICC's relationship with African politics, see Phil Clark, *Distant Justice: The Impact of the International Criminal Court on African Politics* (Cambridge: Cambridge University Press, 2019); Charles Chernor Jalloh and Ilias Bantekas (eds.), *The International Criminal Court and Africa* (Oxford: Oxford University Press, 2017); Kamari M. Clarke, Abel S. Knottnerus and Eefje de Volder (eds.), *Africa and the ICC: Perceptions of Justice* (Cambridge: Cambridge University Press, 2016).

Living and working in The Hague allowed me to regularly engage with an array of academics, jurists and human rights advocates from around the world, many of whom have made the creation and sustenance of the field called 'international justice' their life's work. Their often single-minded focus on the ICC was remarkable in its sophistication and ambition. Not only was it rooted in the vision of a global institution that could competently and fairly try those accused of international crimes (a formidable task in itself, as the Court's experience to date has made clear) but one that could also spark the domestic pursuit of accountability in countries around the world.

This book explores the belief in that spark – its origins, capacities and permutations – and offers an assessment of the ICC's ability to deliver upon it. It comes not only at a time when debates about the Court's performance and its 'catalytic effect' on states increasingly captivate scholars from a variety of disciplines but also at a moment when the ICC, international courts and the human rights project itself face a growing and possibly existential tide of political resistance.

At the centre of much of this discussion lies the principle of complementarity: the idea that the ICC is designed to supplement, not supplant, national jurisdictions.

This appealing idea is at once both straightforward and deeply complex. Originating as a technical admissibility rule for determining when the ICC can 'admit' a case within its jurisdiction, complementarity has since become the cornerstone for what is now commonly referred to as the 'Rome Statute System', one in which 'States remain responsible and accountable for investigating and prosecuting crimes committed under their jurisdiction'.[5] A related, core aspiration is that the ICC, through the principle of complementarity, will spur domestic jurisdictions to action. As put by two commentators, 'The [ICC] is intended to not only investigate and prosecute crimes under its jurisdiction but to act as a catalyst for genuine national justice by applying the principle of complementarity'.[6]

---

[5] 'Paper on some policy issues before the Office of the Prosecutor', ICC-OTP 2003 (September 2003), 5, at www.icc-cpi.int/nr/rdonlyres/1fa7c4c6-de5f-42b7-8b25-60aa962ed8b6/143594/030905_policy_paper.pdf.

[6] Jonathan O'Donohue and Sophie Rigney, 'The ICC Must Consider Fair Trial Concerns in Determining Libya's Application to Prosecute Saif al-Islam Gaddafi Nationally'. EJIL: Talk! (blog), *European Journal of International Law* (8 June 2012), at www.ejiltalk.org/the-icc-must-consider-fair-trial-concerns-in-determining-libyas-application-to-prosecute-saif-al-islam-gaddafi-nationally/.

Ultimately, my research led me to Uganda, Kenya and the DRC. Between 2011 and 2012, I travelled to each of these countries on multiple occasions to interrogate the idea of the ICC-as-catalyst further and to better understand what domestic legal transformations the Court's involvement in these early situations had augured. These 'field' trips – as well as my time living in The Hague – attempted to explore both the expectations that attended the Court's establishment and the effects of its interventions through interviews with international and domestic non-governmental organizations (NGOs), ICC staff, judges, human rights advocates and diplomatic representatives. In the course of those two years, I conducted over sixty interviews with actors based both in-country and The Hague. Three of these encounters are described in the following.

Uganda: 'We Have to Look Like
We Are Doing Something'

The International Crimes Division (ICD) – a special division of the Ugandan High Court's eight divisions – sits midway up a tall hill in the already hilly city of Kampala, Uganda's capital. The Division is not easy to reach. The easiest way, if you are without a car and unwilling to walk, is to grab one of the ubiquitous *matatus* that populate the city. I made three trips to the ICD in the course of my visits to Uganda, but on this sunny day in December 2011, my co-researcher and I were to meet with one of the judges of the Division who was part of the bench then overseeing early proceedings in the trial of former Lord's Resistance Army (LRA) commander, Thomas Kwoyelo, which had already been underway for nearly two years.[7] It was not the first time we were meeting this judge. Only several months prior, she and other colleagues from the Division had come to The Hague for a week-long training in international criminal law that Leiden supported, together with a leading transitional justice NGO.

As it happened, that morning we had also met with the legal counsel for Uganda's Amnesty Commission. The Commission had certified Kwoyelo's amnesty petition in January 2010 but was now engaged in a protracted battle with the Director of Public Prosecutions over its validity. Established by the Amnesty Act in 2000 as a way to incentivize defections from the LRA (as well as other rebel movements),

---

[7] Interviews with legal counsel to the Amnesty Commission and ICD judge (Kampala, 13 December 2011). My co-researcher refers to Dr Sara Kendall, with whom I conducted most interviews jointly.

the Commission was the Division's institutional opposite: it granted ex-combatants protection from prosecution, while the ICD was meant to be the putative forum for prosecuting them.[8] Curious, I asked the counsel what kind of impact he thought the ICC had in Uganda. 'A big one', he said soberly, 'The ICC has a lot of powers; it says some of these Africans need to behave'. I also asked the same of the ICD. 'It has increased international pressure', he replied, 'The donors have invested some money in that court, so we have to look like we are doing something'.

One long walk later, we sat before the judge who, over the course of an hour, answered a string of questions. How many judges sit on the Division? (Four, at that time.) When did it change from the War Crimes Division – its name when first established in 2008 – to the ICD? (In 2010.) What rules of procedure would they use? (The rules were not yet created at the time but would have to be originated by the Division, and they would have to 'reflect the best practices in the world'.) The judge indicated that ICD colleagues had received multiple trainings in subjects ranging from substantive international criminal law and procedure to organized crime and the laws of war. On the subject of the ICC, the judge expressed disappointment that the Division itself did not have any interactions with the Court and stressed the need for more 'positive complementarity' – for instance, a proper witness protection program, judicial trainings, even perhaps 'attaching' the Division to other 'courts of complementarity' in countries like Australia or Canada. 'I wish the ICC could help with that, but I think it prefers to keep safe', the judge said, with evident disappointment.

---

[8] For a more detailed history of the Ugandan conflict, the following texts offer useful background context: Tim Allen, *Trial Justice: The International Criminal Court and the Lord's Resistance Army* (London: Zed Books, 2006); Matthew Green, *The Wizard of the Nile: The Hunt for Africa's Most Wanted* (London: Portobello Books, 2009); Tim Allen and Koen Vlassenroot (eds.), *The Lord's Resistance Army: Myth and Reality* (London: Zed Books, 2010); Aili Mari Tripp, *Museveni's Uganda: Paradoxes of Power in a Hybrid Regime* (Boulder: Lynne Rienner Publishers, 2010); Adam Branch, *Displacing Human Rights: War and Intervention in Northern Uganda* (Oxford: Oxford University Press, 2011). Sverker Finnström's *Living with Bad Surroundings: War, History, and Everyday Moments in Northern Uganda* (Durham: Duke University Press, 2008) is an excellent anthropological account of the conflict in northern Uganda; see also Sverker Finnström, 'Reconciliation Grown Bitter? War, Retribution, and Ritual Action in Northern Uganda', in Rosalind Shaw and Lars Waldorf, with Pierre Hazan (eds.), *Localizing Transitional Justice: Interventions and Priorities after Mass Violence* (Stanford: Stanford University Press, 2010), 135–156.

Democratic Republic of Congo:
la poursuite de la 'pérennité'

Kinshasa, the Democratic Republic of Congo's dense and sprawling capital city, is known as 'Kin la belle', although the description is at times difficult to appreciate. Even as it sits far from the violence that grips the east of the country (where the ICC has concentrated its work), the city's chaotic rhythms seemed to vibrate with its dense, complex history. Stretching back to the 'First Congo War', when Rwandan and Ugandan troops backed Congolese rebel forces in the overthrow of then President Mobutu Sésé Seko, the DRC has remained at the epicentre of one of the world's most enduring conflicts.[9]

Given this, it was not hard to appreciate the daunting challenge that a country like the DRC posed for a young institution like the ICC. Nor was the Congo's violent legacy of colonialism ever far from my mind. I thought frequently of my Belgian family's own particular story with the country (my grandfather worked for many years in the shipyards and rail stations of pre-independence Belgian Congo; my aunt and father were born there), as I engaged in earnest conversations with expats about how to 'end impunity' for the atrocities that civilians continued to endure. I wrestled with the idea that a court situated thousands of miles away could do this and about the complicated donor economies that encircled its intervention. Many of the same European countries that were now financing the ICC and other judicial reform projects in the country were the same ones that had been divvying up this continent not so long ago.

Our arrival in June 2011 preceded the DRC's second presidential elections by several months, although it was clear that their imminence was already consuming most of the diplomatic community's energies. These elections were the first to follow the arrest of one of the country's leading politicians, Jean-Pierre Bemba, whose trial before the ICC (for crimes committed in

---

[9] See, for example, Kris Berwouts, *Congo's Violent Peace: Conflict and Struggle since the Great African War* (London: Zed Books, 2017). There is a vast literature on the conflict in the DRC. Useful texts consulted for this research are Filip Reyntjens, *The Great African War: Congo and Regional Geopolitics, 1996–2006* (Cambridge: Cambridge University Press, 2009); Jason K. Stearns, *Dancing in the Glory of Monsters: The Collapse of the Congo and the Great War of Africa* (New York: PublicAffairs, 2011); Michael Deibert, *The Democratic Republic of Congo: Between Hope and Despair* (London: Zed Books, 2013); and David van Reybrouck, *Congo: The Epic History of a People* (London: Fourth Estate, 2014). Notably, the ICC's presence in the DRC is barely mentioned (or mentioned only in passing) in most of these texts; of them, Deibert engages most with Court developments in the context of the continued fighting in eastern DRC.

the neighbouring Central African Republic) had begun in November 2010. On our first day, an interview that had been scheduled with the European Union (EU) delegation provided us, fortuitously, with an opportunity to meet two Congolese human rights advocates whose NGO had been engaged around the ICC's intervention for several years.[10] Much of their work focused on facilitating the participation of victims in Court proceedings, as well as advocating for the passage of Rome Statute implementing legislation. As they explained, their mandate was to 'simplify' the Statute and make it understandable to people – in French, *la vulgarisation* ('popularizing work'). The advocates were there to brief the EU delegation's Working Group on Human Rights, a monthly gathering of donor states, but with elections then looming, the long table they were meant to address was almost empty. Except for one representative, no one had shown up.

The Working Group's loss was our gain: over coffee, we seized the opportunity for a conversation. It quickly became apparent that despite our interlocutors' support for the ICC's work in the DRC, they were deeply critical of its performance. They spoke of the poor quality of investigations and of the investigator one of them met who had never even been to the DRC before. How were they selected? How were they vetted? They recalled that the best years for contact with the Court were probably between 2002 and 2005 – the early years of its intervention – and expressed frustration with the many ICC staff changes since then. 'People leave, and you don't know where they go', one remarked. *Il faut que le peu qui est fait, soit bien fait* ('the little that is done must be done well') said the other, but, in her view, too much had not been done well. Although there was 'a lot of hope' amongst victims in the beginning, it was not as strong now, and people could not understand why the first trial in The Hague (that of Thomas Lubanga, for the recruitment of child soldiers) had gone on for so long.

Towards the end, the discussion turned to the prospects for domestic accountability in the DRC. What about the prospect of a mixed chamber for these serious crimes, of the sort that was then being proposed? They were sceptical. 'It is not just about the judges – it is about the prisons, the personnel, the system at large', one replied. It was the need for long-term sustainability within the criminal justice system that concerned them – in French, *la poursuite de la pérennité*. A special chamber would only deal with one category of crimes: it would be an 'itinerant' court unconnected to the domestic judiciary. What, they asked, about the rest of the country?

---

[10] Interview with Congolese human rights advocates (Kinshasa, 20 June 2011).

Kenya: 'One Long Game'

On my third trip to Nairobi, I met again with the director of the Kenyan Country Office for a prominent international NGO. Shortly after my last visit, the Office of the Prosecutor (OTP) had issued its summons for the defendants that came to be known as the 'Ocampo Six'. On this visit, two of those accused, Uhuru Kenyatta and William Ruto, had just announced a new political ticket forged out of the ICC's accusations: the Jubilee Alliance.[11] At the time, however, the Court was riding relatively high. From my very first visit to Nairobi, the sophistication of Kenyan civil society was quickly apparent, as was the jolt that the ICC's intervention had brought to the human rights community there.[12] As the same director said at our first meeting, Kenya had a long history of impunity for political violence, such that, when the Court first arrived, many Kenyans embraced it. 'They were so used to seeing people get away with things', he said.[13]

Indeed, the ICC's arrival brought with it, for a time, great hope. Members of Kenyan civil society set about supporting the Court's work in a variety of ways: registering and interviewing victims, supporting an 'underground' witness protection system, conducting outreach in conflict-affected communities, gathering evidence and, later, pushing for the establishment of a special domestic tribunal.[14] In Kenya, as elsewhere, national NGOs came to serve as a kind of shadow network for the Court. They were its eyes and ears on the ground.

By the time of our second meeting in late 2012, however, that hope had dimmed considerably.[15] Two of the 'Ocampo Six' had not had their charges confirmed, and there was fear – well founded, as it would soon

[11] On shifts in the Kenyan political order, see Sara Kendall, '"UhuRuto" and Other Leviathans: The International Criminal Court and the Kenyan Political Order', *African Journal of Legal Studies* 7(3) (2014); Gabrielle Lynch, 'Electing the "Alliance of the Accused": The Success of the Jubilee Alliance in Kenya's Rift Valley', *Journal of Eastern African Studies* 8(1) (2014).

[12] On the emergence and accomplishments of modern civil society in East Africa, see Makau Mutua (ed.), *Human Rights NGOs in East Africa: Political and Normative Tensions* (Kampala: Fountain Publishers, 2009).

[13] Interview with Kenyan NGO director (Nairobi, 17 June 2011).

[14] These examples were offered through interviews with Kenyan civil society advocates (Nairobi, June 2011 and January 2012). See also Njonjo Mue and Judy Gitau, 'The Justice Vanguard: Kenyan Civil Society and the Pursuit of Accountability', in Christian De Vos, Sara Kendall and Carsten Stahn (eds.), *Contested Justice: The Politics and Practice of International Criminal Court Interventions* (Cambridge: Cambridge University Press, 2015).

[15] Second interview with Kenyan NGO director (Nairobi, 3 December 2012).

turn out – that the other cases would also collapse.[16] Kenyatta and Ruto were on the political rise, it seemed, with ominous implications for the trials that awaited them; indeed, Kenyatta would go on to win the presidency the following year. I asked my interlocutor what kind of impact he thought the ICC had had, despite its mistakes. What had it catalysed? The answer came in two parts. On the one hand, 'the only time you hear about something being set up [in Kenya] is when the ICC moves'. That was what led Parliament to attempt to set up a domestic tribunal in 2009, to the creation of a special 'task force' within the Director of Public Prosecutions office to investigate the post-election violence cases and later to talk about the creation of a special judicial division to try international crimes. But none of that, apparently, mattered. 'All that has supposedly been done for complementarity', he said with a long sigh, 'It has just been one long game'.

***

Much has changed in the years since these encounters took place. The ICC bench is now populated with new judges, while, in 2012, a new prosecutor, Fatou Bensouda, succeeded (and inherited) Moreno-Ocampo's tumultuous tenure; a third prosecutor will follow her in 2021.[17] The last of the 'Ocampo Six' cases was dismissed in early 2016, following a damaging series of missteps by the OTP and significant interference in the proceedings by the Kenyan government itself. In Uganda, one trial of the original five accused members of the LRA has moved forward (following the surprise arrest and transfer of former child soldier Dominic Ongwen in 2015), but the group's leader, Joseph Kony, remains at large and no new warrants have been issued since. And while the DRC remains the greatest source of the ICC's judicial activity to date, the OTP's increasingly fragile record of successful prosecutions has done little to deter ongoing violence in the region, as many had hoped. Meanwhile, amidst the Court's increasingly uneven performance, new situations crowd the Prosecutor's docket, spanning countries as diverse as Georgia, Palestine, the Philippines and Myanmar. Repeated threats by African countries to initiate a mass

---

[16] Following the confirmation of charges decisions, the ICC prosecutor announced in March 2013 that her office was withdrawing the charges against Francis Muthaura. The charges against Kenyan President Uhuru Kenyatta were subsequently withdrawn in March 2015.
[17] See, for example, David Kaye, 'Who's Afraid of the International Criminal Court? Finding the Prosecutor Who Can Set It Straight', *Foreign Affairs* 90(3) (May/June 2011).

withdrawal from the Statute have largely not come to pass, but the situation remains tense and uncertain.[18] After the promise of Rome, the threat of state withdrawal is perpetual.

Much has changed for me in these years as well. Though the dissertation on which this book is based was completed in early 2016, I made the decision to move towards practice-based work when I joined the Open Society Justice Initiative, part of the Open Society Foundations (OSF), in 2013. In that process, the methodology and investments I made in this project have necessarily shifted. For one, I became a member of the same transnational 'community of practice' described in the pages that follow, as both the Justice Initiative and OSF more broadly are significant actors in the international and transitional justice landscape. Furthermore, although my work for the Justice Initiative has not directly involved any of the three countries addressed herein, I myself now advocate in support of the ICC and its work. I also engage in other countries where the Court's intervention is sought. In the course of doing so, several of my former interlocutors have since become valued colleagues and friends. In short, I sit in the privileged, if complicated, position of having become a participant in my own research.

Thus, while this book began its journey as a scholarly pursuit and its insights draw principally from my PhD research, it is also now, inevitably, a personal analytical account. It is not only multi-sited in the geographies it traverses but also multi-positioned in the professional identities I have inhabited.[19] In his influential ethnography of development practice, the anthropologist David Mosse, himself a former consultant for the United Kingdom's Department for International Development (DFID), aptly describes such research as 'both social investigation and lived experience'.[20] While Mosse's research first drew on his insights as a participant-insider with DFID, for me, the reverse is true: my role as a 'participant-insider' in the field of international criminal justice has

---

[18] At the time of writing, only two states have withdrawn from the Rome Statute (Burundi, which announced its withdrawal in October 2017, and the Philippines, which deposited notification of its intention to withdraw in March 2018), but many others have threatened to do so, including the three countries examined here. For an analysis of threatened African withdrawals, see Christian De Vos, 'The Politics of Departure: Africa and the International Criminal Court' (3 November 2016), at https://theglobalobservatory.org/2016/11/international-criminal-court-south-africa-burundi-gambia/.

[19] See, for example, George E. Marcus, 'Ethnography in/of the World System: The Emergence of Multi-Sited Ethnography', *Annual Review of Anthropology* 24 (1995).

[20] David Mosse, *Cultivating Development: An Ethnography of Aid Policy and Practice* (London: Pluto Press, 2005), ix.

evolved over time. This experience has itself influenced the conclusions I draw from my research. As Mosse writes, 'Mine is an interested interpretation not a scientific judgment; it adds interpretations to those of actors whose experience I share'.[21]

Similarly, my experience as a human rights advocate and practitioner has expanded my own interpretations. I have come to see with new eyes and greater appreciation the campaign that was waged to not only successfully establish a permanent international criminal court – a political dream harboured by so many, for so many years – but to also then help transform the meaning and understanding of complementarity itself. These are advocacy victories to celebrate and learn from; they were hard fought and hardly imaginable today. But, as I hope this book illustrates, they have exacted a certain price as well. The expectations these victories ushered in, as well as the ambitions that animated them, appear almost impossibly large in retrospect. Implementation of a catalytic 'complementarity norm' has been a challenge for the ICC and its supporters to realize as they struggle, increasingly, to reconcile a political dream amidst a host of growing practical, political and fiscal constraints. This book is a partial exploration into what that dream has looked like in practice and an effort to suggest what should come next.

[21] Ibid., 14.

1

Introduction

Since its establishment at the early turn of the century, the International Criminal Court (ICC) has been both a symbol of and vehicle for the ascendance of a global accountability norm. Central to that ascendance has been a preoccupation with the nature of the ICC's relationship to national jurisdictions. As a permanent body intended to investigate and adjudicate crimes conceivably without geographical restriction, the ICC is structurally designed to work at the intersection of the international and the domestic. Complementarity – the idea that the court is intended to supplement, not supplant, national jurisdictions – has been the dominant juridical logic through which this relationship has been expressed, but, as this book's preface suggests, this principle occupies a charged space in the political imaginary, replete with tensions and ambiguity. To a domestic judge in Uganda, it suggests that the ICC might serve as a kind of 'big brother' court to its domestic counterparts, while to a human rights advocate in Kenya, it represents little more than a 'long game' by a government determined to evade The Hague.

Meanwhile, for many of the court's supporters, complementarity is now commonly invoked as the 'cornerstone of the Rome Statute': it represents the very future of an international criminal justice system. In the words of the International Center for Transitional Justice, 'How the complementarity principle is put into practice will be the key to the fight against impunity and thus the future of international justice will largely turn on these efforts'.[22] So understood, complementarity is no longer a legal concept confined to the courtroom – an organizing principle for the regulation of concurrent jurisdiction – but a policy tool for catalysing progressive change in post-conflict countries' legal frameworks and institutions. There is by now a well-developed (and still rapidly proliferating)

---

[22] International Center for Transitional Justice, 'The Future of International Justice: National Courts Supported by International Expertise', at www.ictj.org/news/future-international-justice-national-courts-supported-international-expertise.

literature that frames its inquiries around the ICC's catalytic potential
through the principle of complementarity.[23]
Whereas the dominant approach of many of these texts has taken the
catalytic potential of the ICC as a given, this book examines how complementarity and, by extension the court came to be framed as 'catalysts'
for domestic investigations and prosecutions in the first place. It then
explores what effects this framing has had in three distinct country contexts where the ICC has intervened. In particular, it asks how both state
and non-state actors in Uganda, Kenya and the Democratic Republic
of Congo (DRC) have relied upon the principle of complementarity as
the logic through which the court's catalytic potential can be realized,
as well as a transnational site and adaptive strategy for entrenching the
norm of international criminal accountability domestically. In tracing
these steps, the book addresses three principal questions. First, how has
the understanding of complementarity evolved since the ICC's inception,
and what role have non-state actors, in particular, played in this evolution? Second, how have ICC judges understood and interpreted complementarity in the courtroom, and how has the Office of the Prosecutor

[23] One of the earliest articles to employ the phrase was Jonathan Charney, 'International
Criminal Law and the Role of Domestic Courts', *American Journal of International
Law* 95(1) (2001), 120 (viewing the effective success of the ICC as 'having first served as
a catalyst, and then as a monitoring and supporting institution'). See further Jo Stigen,
*The Relationship between the International Criminal Court and National Jurisdictions:
The Principle of Complementarity* (Leiden: Martinus Nijhoff, 2008); Jann K. Kleffner,
Complementarity in the Rome Statute and National Criminal Jurisdictions (Oxford:
Oxford University Press, 2008); Géraldine Mattioli and Anneke van Woudenberg, 'Global
Catalyst for National Prosecutions? The ICC in the Democratic Republic of Congo', in
Nicholas Waddell and Phil Clark (eds.), *Courting Conflict? Justice, Peace and the ICC in
Africa* (London: Royal African Society, March 2008); Nidal Nabil Jurdi, *The International
Criminal Court and National Courts: A Contentious Relationship* (Farnham: Ashgate,
2011); Carsten Stahn and Mohamed M. El Zeidy (eds.), *The International Criminal Court
and Complementarity: From Theory to Practice* (Cambridge: Cambridge University
Press, 2011); Amrita Kapur, 'The Value of International-National Interactions and Norm
Interpretations in Catalysing National Prosecution of Sexual Violence', *Oñati Socio-
Legal Series* 6(1) (2016), 62–90; Ovo Catherine Imoedemhe, *The Complementarity Regime
of the International Criminal Court: National Implementation in Africa* (Cham: Springer
International, 2017). See also Janine Natalya Clark, 'Peace, Justice and the International
Criminal Court: Limitations and Possibilities', *Journal of International Criminal Justice*
9 (2011), 521–545 (arguing that 'through the implementation and practice of complementarity, the Court can potentially have a significant catalytic effect'), 538. The best
work to date is Sarah M. H. Nouwen, *Complementarity in the Line of Fire: The Catalysing
Effect of the International Criminal Court in Uganda and Sudan* (Cambridge: Cambridge
University Press, 2013).

sought to implement it as a matter of policy? Finally, how have the ICC's interventions in Uganda, Kenya and the DRC affected these countries' normative legal and institutional frameworks for carrying out domestic criminal proceedings, and to what extent have such proceedings, indeed, been catalysed by the court itself?

1   Framing the ICC as a Catalyst

Framing international legal institutions as catalysts for progressive domestic reform dominates much of a growing literature on their effects and impact at the national level. While the ICC represents a more recent iteration of this scholarship, the presumption that other institutions – from regional human rights courts to United Nations (UN) human rights mechanisms – would have or have had a salutary effect on state behaviour has drawn the interest of legal scholars and political scientists alike.[24] The political scientist Kathryn Sikkink writes that '[w]ell before the creation of the ICC, the Inter-American Commission on Human Rights and the Inter-American Court of Rights … played a catalytic role in pushing for individual criminal accountability'.[25] Sikkink contends that these courts were part of an array of actors and norm entrepreneurs, 'including NGOs, regional human rights organizations, and members of transnational governments', who collectively contributed to the rise and legitimation of individual criminal accountability as a new international norm.[26]

Describing this new norm as part of a 'justice cascade', Sikkink argues that 'states and non-state actors worked to build a firm streambed of international human rights law and international humanitarian law that fortified the legal underpinnings of the cascade, culminating in the Rome Statute of the ICC in 1998'.[27] The prosecutions of several

---

[24] See, e.g., Kathryn Sikkink, *The Justice Cascade: How Human Rights Prosecutions Are Changing World Politics* (New York: W. W. Norton & Company, 2011); Ted Piccone, *Catalysts for Change: How the UN's Independent Experts Promote Human Rights* (Washington, DC: Brookings Institution Press, 2012), 269.

[25] Sikkink, *The Justice Cascade*, 105.

[26] Ibid., 245. The concept of 'norm entrepreneur' has a long history explored in the next chapter. Cass Sunstein is first believed to have introduced the phrase in a 1996 article, wherein he defines entrepreneurs simply as 'people interested in changing social norms'. See Cass R. Sunstein, 'Social Norms and Social Roles', *Columbia Law Review* 96(4) (May 1996), 903–968.

[27] Ibid., 97.

high-level political figures, which drew legal scholars to examine the domestic effects that such efforts might augur, illustrate the fortification of this cascade.[28] These developments followed the establishment and evolution of the *ad hoc* tribunals for Rwanda and the former Yugoslavia. There, too, the trope of 'catalyst' has been summoned: William Burke-White argues that 'the ICTY has encouraged the development of domestic courts in [Bosnia and Herzegovina] and catalysed the activation of domestic judicial institutions'. Similarly, in her authoritative study of the International Criminal Tribunal for the former Yugoslavia (ICTY), Diane Orentlicher concludes that the tribunal became a key catalyst for ramping up Bosnia's (and, to a lesser extent, Serbia's) domestic capacity to prosecute wartime atrocities.[29] Yuval Shany likewise observes that the 'practical importance of international criminal proceedings is mainly symbolic and catalytic', insofar as they 'may trigger or nurture domestic and international legal and political processes'.[30]

Interest in the capacity of international courts and prosecutions to serve as 'catalysts' at the national level has strong affinities with an

[28] See, e.g., Ellen L. Lutz and Caitlin Reiger (eds.), *Prosecuting Heads of State* (Cambridge: Cambridge University Press, 2009). Naomi Roht-Arriaza, noting the 'burgeoning field of transnational prosecutions' that followed the attempted extradition of former Chilean General Augusto Pinochet from the United Kingdom in 1998 (the same year as the Rome Statute's adoption), argues that the case 'played a catalytic role in stimulating and accelerating judicial investigations' in countries like Chile and Argentina. See Naomi Roht-Arriaza, 'Of Catalysts and Cases: Transnational Prosecutions and Impunity in Latin America', in Madeleine Davis (ed.), *The Pinochet Case: Origins, Progress and Implications* (London: Institute of Latin American Studies, 2003), 210; Naomi Roht-Arriaza, *The Pinochet Effect: Transnational Justice in the Age of Human Rights* (Philadelphia: University of Pennsylvania Press, 2005).
[29] William W. Burke-White, 'The Domestic Influence of International Criminal Tribunals: The International Criminal Tribunal for the Former Yugoslavia and the Creation of the State Court of Bosnia & Herzegovina', *Columbia Journal of Transnational Law* 46 (2008), 282; Diane F. Orentlicher, *Some Kind of Justice: The ICTY's Impact in Bosnia and Serbia* (New York: Oxford University Press, 2018), 323–425. More recent scholarship has focused on the Special Court for Sierra Leone's contributions to domestic justice advancements as well. See, e.g., Sigall Horovitz, 'How International Courts Shape Domestic Justice: Lessons from Rwanda and Sierra Leone', *Israel Law Review* 46(3) (2013), 339–367.
[30] Yuval Shany, 'The Legitimacy Deficit of Exceptional International Criminal Jurisdiction', in Fionnuala Ni Aolain and Oren Gross (eds.), *Guantanamo and Beyond: Exceptional Courts and Military Commissions in Comparative Perspective* (Cambridge: Cambridge University Press, 2013), 370.

expanding scholarship on the socializing power of international law and legal institutions and their role in shaping state behaviour.[31] Seminal texts like the *Power of Human Rights*[32] and the early work of such scholars as Abram and Antonia Handler Chayes[33] opened up a new literature amongst legal scholars and social scientists on compliance with international norms and institutions, one that has proliferated rapidly in the last two decades. To that end, focusing on the ICC as a catalyst for domestic criminal proceedings reflects a converging interest of two distinct, though interconnected, disciplines – international relations and international law – in how legal institutions can influence state behaviour and, more particularly, how they can encourage 'rule-consistent' behaviour.[34] Interest in complementarity thus parallels a larger political project wherein supranational judicial bodies are increasingly scrutinized in

---

[31] See, e.g., Karen Alter, *The New Terrain of International Law: Courts, Politics, Rights* (Princeton: Princeton University Press, 2014); Ryan Goodman and Derek Jinks, *Socializing States: Promoting Human Rights Through International Law* (Oxford: Oxford University Press, 2013); Beth A. Simmons, *Mobilizing for Human Rights: International Law in Domestic Politics* (Cambridge: Cambridge University Press, 2009). Goodman and Jinks, in particular, have advanced a theory of 'acculturation as a distinct mode of social influence', arguing that this model best accounts for changes in state behaviour, in part, 'because 'conforming' and 'belonging' themselves confer substantial affective returns', 30–31.

[32] Drawing on quantitative and qualitative case studies, *The Power of Human Rights* suggested that a five-phase 'spiral model' explains the socialization process of states with human right norms; the model links interactions amongst governments, domestic opposition groups and transnational human rights networks. See Thomas Risse, Stephen C. Ropp and Kathryn Sikkink (eds.), *The Power of Human Rights: International Norms and Domestic Change* (Cambridge: Cambridge University Press, 1999); see also Thomas Risse, Stephen C. Ropp and Kathryn Sikkink (eds.), *The Persistent Power of Human Rights: From Commitment to Compliance* (Cambridge: Cambridge University Press, 2013).

[33] The Chayes' scholarship forms part of – and was an early contribution to – an important strand in compliance literature focusing on 'managerial' compliance, suggesting that limitations on the capacity of states and the absence of domestic regulatory apparatuses, rather than the ability to sanction, better explains why states comply with international law. See Abram Chayes and Antonia Handler Chayes, 'On Compliance', *International Organization* 47(2) (1993).

[34] See, e.g., Jeffrey L. Dunoff and Mark A. Pollack (eds.), *Interdisciplinary Perspectives on International Law and International Relations: The State of the Art* (Cambridge: Cambridge University Press, 2013); Michael Barnett and Martha Finnemore, *Rules for the World: International Organizations in Global Politics* (Ithaca: Cornell University Press, 2004); Anne-Marie Slaughter, Andrew S. Tulumello and Stepan Wood, 'International Law and International Relations Theory: A New Generation of Interdisciplinary Scholarship', *American Journal of International Law* 92 (1998), 367–397.

terms of their effects on state compliance with international norms, rules and judgments.[35] As part of a larger but increasingly contested moment in global governance, these scholars ask not only whether international legal institutions can influence state behaviour but also why and how they do so.[36]

Importantly, these developments in scholarship and the rise of the accountability norm described by Sikkink resonate with a larger understanding of international law and its institutions as progressive, catalytic forces on states. As a discursive structure, characterizing these institutions as 'catalysts' recalls what Thomas Skouteris has called the notion of progress in public international law discourse, one that looms particularly large in international criminal law. In the context of the 'new tribunalism', of which the ICC is perhaps the most emblematic, this 'vocabulary of progress' becomes a 'legitimizing language' – a narrative of evolution and disciplinary progress.[37] In Skouteris' words, 'It is

---

[35] On compliance, see Dinah Shelton (ed.), *Commitment and Compliance: The Role of Non-Binding Norms in the International Legal System* (Oxford: Oxford University Press, 2003); Sonia Cardenas, *Conflict and Compliance: State Responses to International Human Rights Pressure* (Philadelphia: University of Pennsylvania Press, 2007); Courtney Hillebrecht, *Domestic Politics and International Human Rights Tribunals: The Problem of Compliance* (Cambridge: Cambridge University Press, 2014). For an account of the rise of global governance through international institutions, see Mark Mazower, *Governing the World: The History of an Idea, 1815 to the Present* (New York: Penguin Books, 2013); Mikkel Jarle Christensen, 'Reunited Europe and the Internationalization of Criminal Law: The Creation and Circulation of Criminal Law as an International Governance Tool', in Mikkel Jarle Christensen and Ron Levi (eds.), *International Practices of Criminal Justice: Social and Legal Perspectives* (London: Routledge, 2017), 17–32.

[36] Attendant with this turn has also been a growing interest in identifying 'indicators' for measuring compliance. See, e.g., Sally Engle Merry, 'Measuring the World: Indicators, Human Rights, and Global Governance', *Current Anthropology* 52(3) (April 2011), 83–93; Sally Engle Merry, *The Seductions of Quantification: Measuring Human Rights, Gender Violence, and Sex Trafficking* (Chicago: University of Chicago Press, 2016). A growing attention to the 'effectiveness' and 'efficiency' of international courts appears to mark a further shift in this direction, wherein judicial institutions are increasingly measured by the satisfaction of certain performance indicators and/or other quantifiable metrics. See, e.g., Yuval Shany, *Assessing the Effectiveness of International Courts* (Oxford: Oxford University Press, 2014); Theresa Squatrito, Oran R. Young, Andreas Follesdal and Geir Ulfstein (eds.), *The Performance of International Courts and Tribunals* (Cambridge: Cambridge University Press, 2018).

[37] Thomas Skouteris, *The Notion of Progress in International Law Discourse* (Leiden: Proefschrift, 2008), 187. On the discourse of progress as a dominant narrative of modern

a compelling story about how international law may finally be able to travel the coveted distance from a power-oriented approach to a rule-oriented approach, from indeterminacy to determinacy, from impunity to accountability'.[38] Thus figured, international tribunals are 'not only the latest addition to the repertoire of international legal action: they are also the catalyst for coping with the realist challenges of the 21st century'.[39] Established at the dawn of that new century, the ICC was a critical addition to this repertoire.

2 Complementarity as a Catalyst for Compliance

Most writing about the ICC's power to catalyse domestic investigations and prosecutions has interpreted complementarity as a matter of compliance with legal rules. As stated in the ICC Prosecutor's first policy paper: '[T]he system of complementarity is principally based on the recognition that the exercise of national criminal jurisdiction is not only a right but also a duty of States'.[40] In this duty-based understanding, these 'rules' include a legal obligation on states to implement the Rome Statute within their domestic penal code; to ensure that their courts are capable of accommodating prosecutions for international crimes and, as the Statute's preambular language affirms, to investigate and prosecute those responsible.[41] A number of legal scholars, notably Jann Kleffner's pioneering work on complementarity, have sought to locate these duties

international law, see also David Koller, '... and New York and The Hague and Tokyo and Geneva and Nuremberg and ...: The Geographies of International Law', *European Journal of International Law* 23(1) (February 2012); Gerry Simpson, 'The Sentimental Life of International Law', *London Review of International Law* 3(1) (2015), 4; Barrie Sander, 'International Criminal Justice as Progress: From Faith to Critique', in Morten Bergsmo, Cheah Wui Ling, Song Tianying and Yi Ping (eds.), *Historical Origins of International Criminal Law: Volume 4* (Brussels: Torkel Opsahl Academic EPublisher, 2015), 749–834.
[38] Skouteris, *The Notion of Progress in International Law Discourse*, 137.
[39] Ibid.
[40] OTP, 'Paper on some policy issues before the Office of the Prosecutor' (September 2003), at www.icc-cpi.int/nr/rdonlyres/1fa7c4c6-de5f-42b7-8b25-60aa962ed8b6/143594/030905_policy_paper.pdf.
[41] Rome Statute, Preamble, para. 10; see also Kampala Declaration, RC/Decl.1, para. 5 ('Resolve to continue and strengthen effective domestic implementation of the Statute, to enhance the capacity of national jurisdictions to prosecute the perpetrators of the most serious crimes of international concern in accordance with internationally-recognized fair trial standards, pursuant to the principle of complementarity'.).

within the text of the Rome Statute itself.[42] For Kleffner, complementarity is understood as 'aiming to induce and facilitate the compliance of States with their obligation "to exercise [their] criminal jurisdiction over those responsible for international crimes," which underlies the Rome Statute'.[43] Furthermore, he argues, 'The detailed content of the obligation imposed by the [Rome] Statute, as derived from the complementarity requirements, demands that State Parties conduct effective, genuine, independent and impartial investigations into allegations of ICC crimes without unjustified delays'.[44]

I argue that this duty-based approach has entailed two key strategies for complementarity. On the one hand, complementarity signals the Court's potential to stimulate national prosecutorial activity through threatened intervention (a coercive relationship); on the other, it signals the ICC's ability to serve a more supportive, managerial function, wherein it supports or, literally, 'complements' national jurisdictions (a cooperative relationship). While these divergent approaches have important implications for the strategies by which complementarity is realized and the domestic forms it has taken in the three countries studied here, both share a vision in which the ICC's metaphorical 'shadow' can precipitate or spur

---

[42] See, e.g., Jann K. Kleffner, 'Complementarity as a Catalyst for Compliance', in Jann K. Kleffner and Gerben Kor (eds.), *Complementary Views on Complementarity: Proceedings of the International Roundtable on the Complementary Nature of the International Criminal Court, Amsterdam, 25/26 June 2004* (The Hague: TMC Asser Press, 2006). See also Jo Stigen, *The Relationship between the International Criminal Court and National Jurisdictions*, 473–478; Jann K. Kleffner, 'The Impact of Complementarity on National Implementation of Substantive International Criminal Law', *Journal of International Criminal Justice* 1 (2003), 113 (noting that 'complementarity provides for a supervision of national criminal courts, supported by the threat that they relinquish the primary right to exercise jurisdiction if they fail to meet the relevant requirements'); Florian Jessberger and Julia Geneuss, 'The Many Faces of the International Criminal Court', *Journal of International Criminal Justice* 10 (2012), 1088 ('The ICC's possible intervening looming over the affected states' reputation serves as a tool to trigger domestic prosecution and is a "catalyst for compliance"'.); Sigall Horovtiz, Gilad Noam and Yuval Shany, 'The International Criminal Court', in *Assessing the Effectiveness of International Courts*, 235 ('[T]he principle of complementarity, which limits the jurisdiction of the ICC to cases in which states fail to properly fulfil their duty to investigate and prosecute international crimes, serves as a catalyst for states to comply with their obligation to investigate and prosecute international crimes'.). See also Heike Krieger (ed.), *Inducing Compliance with International Human Rights Law: Lessons from the African Great Lakes Region* (Cambridge: Cambridge University Press, 2018).

[43] Kleffner, 'Complementarity as a Catalyst for Compliance', 80.

[44] Kleffner, *Complementarity in the Rome Statute and National Criminal Jurisdictions*, 307.

progress in conducting investigations and prosecutions at the domestic level.[45] This understanding of complementarity was actively developed under the tenure of the Court's first prosecutor, who identified 'positive' complementarity – defined as the active encouragement of 'genuine national proceedings' – as a principal pillar of the Office's strategy.[46] It remains a significant pillar today.[47]

Yet, as this books shows, complementarity's evolution and framing as compliance inducement has predominantly cast the domestic forms and possibilities for post-conflict justice in Uganda, Kenya and the DRC within a retributive model, furthering 'the criminal trial, courtroom, and jailhouse as the preferred modalities to promote justice for atrocity'.[48] Domestic accountability is commonly understood as requiring, for instance, the establishment of exceptional courts that confirm with, or mimic, the ICC's structures rather than prosecutions enabled through the 'regular' criminal justice system. Prosecutions, too, are typically thought to necessitate adjudication as international crimes

---

[45] The 'shadow of the ICC' has become a commonplace description of the Court's beneficial effects, popularized by former UN Secretary General Ban Ki-moon. See Ban Ki-moon, 'With the International Criminal Court, a New Age of Accountability', *Washington Post* (29 May 2010) ('Those who thought the court would be little more than a paper tiger have been proved wrong. To the contrary, the ICC casts an increasingly long shadow. Those who would commit crimes against humanity have clearly come to fear it'.). Prosecutor Bensouda has summoned similar imagery, see, e.g., Statement of the Prosecutor of the International Criminal Court, Fatou Bensouda, at first arria-formula meeting on UNSC-ICC relations (6 July 2018), at www.icc-cpi.int/Pages/item.aspx?name=180706-otp-statement-arria-formula ('[The ICC's] work is having an impact on the ground, and cultivating norms. Reverberations of such work are also felt beyond the jurisdictional limits of the ICC, where the shadow of the Court, is ever-present. The demobilisation of countless children in Nepal on the heels of the Lubanga case is just one such example'.).

[46] 'The Office of the Prosecutor – Report on Prosecutorial Strategy' (14 September 2006), II.2.a, at www.icc-cpi.int/NR/rdonlyres/D673DD8C-D427-4547-BC69-2D363E07274B/143708/ProsecutorialStrategy20060914_English.pdf.

[47] See ICC Office of the Prosecutor, 'Strategic Plan: 2016–2018', paras. 55, 57, 100–106, at www.icc-cpi.int/iccdocs/otp/EN-OTP_Strategic_Plan_2016-2018.pdf. The OTP's most recent strategic plan, for 2019–2021, also maintains 'contributing to the effective functioning of the Rome Statute system' as one of its six strategic goals. See ICC Office of the Prosecutor, Strategic Plan: 2019–2021 (17 July 2019) (on-file).

[48] Mark A. Drumbl, *Atrocity, Punishment, and International Law* (Cambridge: Cambridge University Press, 2007), 5. Ruti Teitel similarly refers to the growing 'enforcement of international human rights norms through judicial proceedings', in particular through international criminal law. Ruti G. Teitel, 'The Universal and the Particular in International Criminal Justice', in *Globalizing Transitional Justice: Contemporary Essays* (Oxford: Oxford University Press, 2014).

rather than 'ordinary' crimes, while justice itself is increasingly understood and prioritized as the exclusive domain of criminal accountability, rather than the plural approaches more commonly associated
with transitional justice policy and practice.[49] Indeed, the ICC itself is
now often referred to as a 'transitional justice mechanism'.[50] Domestic
accountability is thus increasingly understood and measured in retributive, outcome-oriented terms.

Judged by these terms, the ICC may appear to have done little in
Uganda, Kenya or the DRC.[51] In Kenya, no senior official or political
leader has been held to account for crimes committed during the 2007–8
elections. While there have been a handful of scattered domestic prosecutions, they have been charged as 'ordinary' crimes, in the ordinary
Kenyan criminal justice system (most of these already limited proceedings also stalled once the ICC's investigation commenced).[52] Efforts to
establish a domestic special tribunal in Kenya have repeatedly failed,
and despite the appointment of various working groups and a domestic 'task force' to review hundreds of PEV case files, the vast majority
of them have been deemed unfit for prosecution due to an alleged lack
of evidence.[53] There have been more, but still limited, prosecutions in

---

[49] See, e.g., Lisa J. Laplante, 'Outlawing Amnesty: The Return of Criminal Justice in
Transitional Justice Schemes', *Virginia Journal of International Law* 49(4) (2009),
915–984. On the persistence (and necessity) of amnesties, see Mark Freeman, *Necessary
Evils: Amnesties and the Search for Justice* (Cambridge: Cambridge University Press,
2009).

[50] See, e.g., Obiora Chinedu Okafor and Uchechukwu Ngwaba, 'The International Criminal
Court as a "Transitional Justice" Mechanism in Africa: Some Critical Reflections',
International Journal of Transitional Justice 9(1) (2015), 90 ('Much scholarly writing on
the International Criminal Court (ICC) gives the impression that the Court can function
effectively as one of the primary transitional justice mechanisms on the African continent,
and that it should, indeed, be deployed more or less frequently, liberally and robustly as
such.').

[51] Nouwen's 'most striking' finding in her commanding study of the Court's interventions
in Uganda and Sudan was that the relevant compliance sought – an increase in domestic
proceedings for crimes within the ICC's jurisdiction – was 'barely observable in either
state'. She is careful to note, however, that an absence of domestic proceedings did not
mean that complementarity was without catalytic effect. See Nouwen, *Complementarity
in the Line of Fire*, 10, 33.

[52] See, e.g., Irene Wairimu, 'Kenya: First Life Sentence in Local PEV Trial', *The Star* (12
June 2012); Human Rights Watch, '"Turning Pebbles": Evading Accountability for
Post-Election Violence in Kenya' (December 2011), at www.hrw.org/report/2011/12/09/
turning-pebbles/evading-accountability-post-election-violence-kenya.

[53] In June 2008, Kenya's Attorney General constituted a 'task force' within the Director of
Public Prosecutions (then subordinate to the Attorney General's Office) to undertake a

the DRC through domestic military courts; however, as I argue, these are primarily due to the efforts of human rights advocates who summon complementarity as a principle of burden-sharing and cooperation (rather than admissibility) to animate their work. The ICC itself is barely present. Finally, in Uganda, there has been only one attempted prosecution to date of a former Lord's Resistance Army (LRA) member before its International Crimes Division (ICD), a proceeding which itself has been beset with fair trial violations.

Yet, from a process-oriented perspective, the 'idea of the ICC' has been deeply alive in domestic politics, and there has been considerable national-level activity pursued in complementarity's name. The absence of domestic proceedings has not meant that states are inactive, but nor has it meant that compliance with legal rules necessarily produces greater accountability. Furthermore, an approach defined principally by outcome rather than process underscores the extent to which legalism animates the catalyst/compliance framework. More particularly, it underscores the dominance of what Bronwyn Leebaw has called 'human rights legalism', which 'not only insists upon the promotion of *law* and courts in general, but on the centrality of *criminal* law in the aftermath of atrocities and political violence'.[54]

Scholars have noted for some time the dominance of legalism – defined by the political theorist Judith Shklar as 'the ethical attitude that holds moral conduct to be a matter of rule following, and moral relationships to consist of duties and rights determined by legal rules'[55] – in transitional justice literature. Kieran McEvoy notes, for instance, that

---

nationwide review of the PEV cases; it later released two reports on domestic investigations and prosecutions, in 2009 and 2011. For a more detailed assessment of these figures, see Sosteness Francis Materu, *The Post-Election Violence in Kenya: Domestic and International Legal Responses* (The Hague: T.M.C. Asser Press, 2015), 102–111. The Attorney General also established a 'Working Committee on the International Criminal Court' in 2012, following the government's failed admissibility challenges. See 'Report of Government's Working Committee on the International Criminal Court' (16 March 2012) (on-file).

[54] Bronwyn Leebaw, *Judging State-Sponsored Violence, Imagining Political Change* (Cambridge: Cambridge University Press, 2011), 6 (emphasis in original). For a more recent exploration of the centrality of criminal punishment in addressing human rights violations, see Karen Engle, Zinaida Miller and D. M. Davis (eds.), *Anti-Impunity and the Human Rights Agenda* (Cambridge: Cambridge University Press, 2016).

[55] Judith N. Shklar, *Legalism: Law, Morals, and Political Trials* (Cambridge: Harvard University Press, 1964), 1.

'a strongly positivistic trend of scholarship and practice persists in the legal understanding of transitional justice'.[56] This, he suggests, is the product of the 'institutionalization of transitional justice in major legal edifices', including the ICC.[57] In McEvoy's view, legalism is seductive, for it 'encourages a notion of a rational and ordered place based on universal understandings'.[58] Similarly, Shklar notes the influence of legalism as a 'matter of rule following', one that seeks to separate legal analysis from politics, as well as other disciplines. She writes:

> The urge to draw a clear line between law and non-law has led to the constructing of ever more refined and rigid systems of formal defini-tions. This procedure has served to isolate law completely from the social context within which it exists. Law is endowed with its own 'science', and its own values, which are all treated as a single 'block' sealed off from general social history, from general social theory, from politics, and from morality.[59]

Legalism thus shares with compliance an emphasis on rule abidance, wherein political problems are often subordinated to legal categories. In Shklar's words, 'Politics is regarded not only as something apart from law, but as inferior to law'.[60]

By contrast, this book underscores the primacy of process, and of political context, in understanding both how complementarity has evolved as a concept over time and the ways in which domestic actors have shaped and negotiated ICC interventions at the national level. Building on Leebaw's insight, I argue that these interventions and the legal transformations they seek to achieve have not transcended 'the influence of local politics or the impact of global asymmetries' but are, in fact, constituted by them.[61] In taking this approach, I make five principal arguments.

---

[56] Kieran McEvoy, 'Letting Go of Legalism: Developing a "Thicker" Version of Transitional Justice', in Kieran McEvoy and Lorna McGregor (eds.), *Transitional Justice from Below: Grassroots Activism and the Struggle for Change* (Portland: Hart Publishing, 2008), 15–45, 19.

[57] Ibid.

[58] Ibid., 20. For a qualified defence of legalism and international criminal tribunals, see Gary Jonathan Bass, *Stay the Hand of Vengeance: The Politics of War Crimes Tribunals* (Princeton: Princeton University Press, 2000).

[59] Shklar, *Legalism: Law, Morals, and Political Trials*, 2–3.

[60] Ibid., 111. For a contemporary critique from a conservative legal scholar, see Eric Posner, *The Perils of Global Legalism* (Chicago: The University of Chicago Press, 2009).

[61] Leebaw, *Judging State-Sponsored Violence, Imagining Political Change*, 179. Leebaw empha-sizes instead the importance of political judgment in the examination of systematic

First, complementarity contains multiple meanings: it is both a rule of admissibility and an instrument of policy. This policy, often referred to as 'positive' complementarity, is one that promotes the ICC and the 'Rome Statute System' as proactive agents for domestic accountability. The ascendance of this more ambitious articulation of the ICC's relationship to national jurisdictions reflects the innovations of norm entrepreneurs and the efforts of a transnational 'community of practice' – international human rights NGOs and their national counterparts, academics and scholars, influential donors and private philanthropists – that constructed, over a short but immensely productive period of time, a broad array of policy goals through the principle of complementarity. Indeed, while ICC case law and the Rome Statute are both sources of legal authority, it has often been these entrepreneurs who play the most active role in mediating complementarity's normative content and in framing the Court as a catalyst.[62]

Second, in both its jurisprudence and prosecutorial practice, the ICC has struggled to accommodate this more expansive understanding of complementarity. A catalyst/compliance framework typically privileges the ICC as the institutional locus for triggering domestic change, wherein rules and practices devised in The Hague radiate outwards. ICC

atrocities, which 'informs the ways in which clashing local and international standards will be treated', 178. Sarah Nouwen and Wouter Werner have also called for an evaluation of the ICC's activities that acknowledge and understand its political dimensions; however, their framework of analysis emanates from the friend/enemy framing advanced by the political theorist Carl Schmitt. See Sarah M. H. Nouwen and Wouter G. Werner, 'Doing Justice to the Political: The International Criminal Court in Uganda and Sudan', *European Journal of International Law* 21(4) (2010), 941–965.

[62] For a similar conclusion, see Geoff Dancy and Florencia Montal, 'Unintended Positive Complementarity: Why International Criminal Court Investigations May Increase Domestic Human Rights Prosecutions', *American Journal of International Law* 111(3) (2017), 712–713 (concluding that there is a statistical correlation between ICC investigations and domestic human rights prosecutions but that 'ICC investigations are, like domestic human rights prosecutions, a byproduct of domestic reform, rather than an independent catalyst'); Xinyuan Dai, 'The Conditional Effects of International Human Rights Institutions', *Human Rights Quarterly* 36 (2014), 589 (arguing that IHRIs 'in and of themselves, do not directly impact states' policies or behaviors'; rather, 'others – interested stakeholders and human rights activists – may (or may not) use them to gain additional leverage to push for improvement in human rights practices'); Patrice C. McMahon and David P. Forsythe, 'The ICTY's Impact on Serbia: Judicial Romanticism Meets Network Politics', *Human Rights Quarterly* 30 (2008), 433 (arguing that 'the court's effects must be considered in the context of the networked order in Europe').

judges, for instance, have articulated a complex set of rules that states must satisfy in order to successfully challenge the admissibility of cases before the Court, leaving little room (or the perception of little room) for agency or political discretion. This vertical approach, however, places a heavy burden on the ICC itself: its catalytic power depends on safeguarding its perception as a credible threat to states. The OTP has struggled in this respect with its record of confirmations and convictions to date, requiring it to balance awkwardly between complementarity's coercive and cooperative dimensions. At the same time, the Court and its political stakeholders (notably, the Assembly of States Parties) have struggled to reconcile complementarity's policy goals with its legal dimensions.

Third, although complementarity was initially seen as a mechanism to primarily influence the choices of state actors, its effects on non-state actors appear to have been far more profound. Indeed, while the threat of ICC intervention itself has not been a catalyst for domestic criminal proceedings (limited as they are), it has arguably had a far more consequential effect on the global and domestic private actors who orbit the Court, as well as their respective policy agendas. This assemblage of global civil society actors, technical advisors and international consultants who attend Court interventions are, in turn, often the critical agents who spur domestic reform agendas and seek to influence political priorities with respect to accountability.[63] They summon the ICC to advance their causes, even as the Court itself remains at a distance.

[63] Recent work has drawn attention to the vital role played by these actors in the ICC's establishment and functioning. Nouwen, for instance, points out that, '[i]n practice, most catalysing effects are not the result of direct ICC-state interaction'. *Complementarity in the Line of Fire*, 22. See also Milli Lake, 'Ending Impunity for Sexual and Gender-Based Crimes: The International Criminal Court and Complementarity in the Democratic Republic of Congo', *African Conflict & Peacebuilding Review* 4(1) (Spring 2014), 4 (concluding that 'many of the developments within the Congolese justice sector have been propelled not by the ICC, but by the work of international and domestic NGOs'). On the significance of civil society's role in the ICC's creation and evolution, see Marlies Glasius, *The International Criminal Court: A Global Civil Society Achievement* (New York: Routledge, 2006); Johan D. Van Der Vyver, 'Civil Society and the International Criminal Court', *Journal of Human Rights* 2(3) (2003), 425–439; Fanny Benedetti, Karine Bonneau and John L. Washburn, *Negotiating the International Criminal Court: New York to Rome, 1994–1998* (Leiden: Martinus Nijhoff, 2014); Heidi Nichols Haddad, *The Hidden Hands of Justice: NGOs, Human Rights, and International Courts* (Cambridge: Cambridge University Press, 2018). See also Julie Mertus, 'Considering Nonstate Actors in the New Millennium: Toward Expanded Participation in Norm Generation and Norm Application', *NYU Journal of International Law and Politics* 32 (2000), 554.

Fourth, complementarity has largely been interpreted in a manner that privileges (even when it does not legally require) a mirroring of the ICC's normative and institutional frameworks. Borrowing the concept of a 'meme' as a cultural replicator and unit of imitation first popularized by the evolutionary biologist Richard Dawkins, I suggest that this 'justice meme' is a function of the predominant framing of complementarity as a catalyst for compliance with international standards and 'best practices'.[64] Again, however, the perpetuation of the ICC's mirroring effect is not only the work of Court actors. It is the result of private actors and norm entrepreneurs who have powerfully and deliberately sought to shape the public understanding of justice-as-accountability in the ICC's image.

Finally, the effects of ICC interventions in Uganda, Kenya and the DRC underscore how global asymmetries, and the patronage networks they produce and sustain, are deeply entwined with the catalytic project. The focus on 'compliance' with ICC standards and procedures is partially a function of these asymmetries: it belies the outsized influence that external constituencies can hold over what activities states undertake in the name of complementarity, as well as the political interests that motivate them. For these reasons, the ICC's 'catalytic effect' on state behaviour is better understood as part of a complex political process, rather than a singular desired outcome, for example, as criminal accountability.

3   Country Selection, Methodology and Terminology

This book draws upon a wide variety of primary and secondary sources, including the early doctrinal literature on complementarity to more recent books and articles that have begun to explore the practical effects of ICC interventions on a range of questions, from its impact on domestic and regional politics in Africa to its effect on the relationship between accountability and conflict resolution.[65] It also draws heavily on news

---

[64] Richard Dawkins, *The Selfish Gene*, 4th ed. (Oxford: Oxford University Press, 2016), 249.
[65] See, e.g., Kamari Clarke, *Fictions of Justice: The International Criminal Court and the Challenge of Legal Pluralism in Sub-Saharan Africa* (Cambridge: Cambridge University Press, 2009); Adam Branch, *Displacing Human Rights: War and Intervention in Northern Uganda* (Oxford: Oxford University Press, 2011); Sarah M. H. Nouwen, *Complementarity in the Line of Fire*; Lionel Nichols, *The International Criminal Court and the End of Impunity in Kenya* (Springer International Publishing, 2015); Patrick S. Wegner, *The International Criminal Court in Ongoing Intrastate Conflicts: Navigating the Peace-Justice*

articles, NGO reports, official ICC documents and speeches, parliamentary debates and international and domestic jurisprudence. The primary approach is thus textual. Through discourse analysis, I seek to trace how complementarity has been understood and portrayed by different actors and stakeholders as a shifting, protean principle, one that does not admit of a singular understanding.

In addition, while not a work of legal ethnography, the ideas reflected herein are informed by several field research trips carried out in Nairobi, Kenya; Kampala, Uganda; and Kinshasa, DRC, over the course of 2011 and 2012, as well as the two and a half years I spent living and working in The Hague (between 2010 and 2012).[66] The book thus adopts a 'multi-sited' focus, one that shares an interest in using ethnographic methods as useful tools for 'accessing the complex ways in which law, decision-making and legal regulations are embedded in wider social processes'.[67] It is rooted in legal analysis but seeks to contribute to a growing field of interpretive social science that uses interdisciplinary, qualitative methods to capture a wider, more situated perspective on the value and impact of global legal institutions.[68] My situated perspective has come to include, as the prologue highlights, more recent practice-based experience with the ICC and international justice community as well. Although I have not directly engaged with any of the three countries studied here in the course of my professional work, my position has afforded me the opportunity to engage more deeply, and understand more fully, both the internal dimensions

Divide (Cambridge: Cambridge University Press, 2015); Mark Kersten, *Justice in Conflict: The Effects of the International Criminal Court's Interventions on Ending War and Building Peace* (Oxford: Oxford University Press, 2016); Phil Clark, *Distant Justice: The Impact of the International Criminal Court on African Politics* (Cambridge: Cambridge University Press, 2019). For a perspective outside of the ICC, see Jelena Subotić, *Hijacked Justice: Dealing with the Past in the Balkans* (Cornell: Cornell University Press, 2009).

[66] Research trips were conducted in the periods of June 2011 (four weeks), December 2011 (two weeks), January 2012 (one week) and November–December 2012 (ten days). A fourth trip to Nairobi, in July 2017, allowed me to pursue follow-up interviews with several original interlocutors. All interviews were conducted in French or English.

[67] See George E. Marcus, 'Ethnography in/of the World System: The Emergence of Multi-Sited Ethnography', *Annual Review of Anthropology* 24 (1995), 95–117; see also June Starr and Mark Goodale, 'Introduction', in June Starr and Mark Goodale (eds.), *Practicing Ethnography in Law* (New York: Palgrave Macmillan, 2002), 2.

[68] On methodologies, see Hugo van der Merwe, Victoria Baxter and Audrey R. Chapman (eds.), *Assessing the Impact of Transitional Justice: Challenges for Empirical Research* (Washington, DC: USIP Press, 2009).

of the ICC, including the Office of the Prosecutor, and the efforts of the Court's supporters to magnify and deepen its impact at the national level. Understanding the theatre of the ICC's work outside of its institutional centre in The Hague also afforded me the opportunity to better understand the complex circumstances in which its interventions unfold. At the time that the project began in mid-2010, the ICC had five situations (all on the African continent), which had advanced to an investigatory stage: Uganda, DRC, the Central African Republic (CAR), Sudan (Darfur) and Kenya. In the light of my desire to engage meaningfully with field-informed research, I made a deliberate decision to limit my choice of countries to those countries that had at least advanced to this stage and to choose from amongst them. On the spectrum of Court engagement, then, 'intervention' as defined here has entailed, at the least, active deployment of ICC personnel to the countries in question, as well as a substantial (if developing) body of case law ranging from questions of admissibility and victim participation to individual criminal responsibility and reparations.[69] (Colombia, discussed at some length in Chapter 4, is a notable example where the Court's engagement has been longstanding and substantial but has yet to pass this threshold.)

Security concerns, resource constraints and the sheer complexity of each of these five situations required further selectivity. On this basis, I excluded Sudan and the CAR: Sudan principally because of the political difficulty of conducting such research inside the country at the time and CAR because of the apparently limited scope of the ICC's investigations and the substantial implications that those proceedings, while formally part of the CAR referral, have had in the DRC.[70] Subsequent developments in other ICC situation countries inform parts of my analysis, but they are not addressed in depth here.

---

[69] This focus on direct Court engagement is not meant to dismiss, however, more 'indirect' forms of intervention, including the use of preliminary examinations (explored further in Chapter 4) or the evolving, normative impact of the Rome Statute on national legal frameworks. Nevertheless, such forms of intervention demand considerably less of the ICC's financial and material resources, and the connection between its work and national-level change is even more difficult to delineate.

[70] To date, only one arrest warrant has been issued for the first CAR situation and that was for the (now acquitted) former vice-president of the DRC, Jean-Pierre Bemba. After opening its investigation in 2007, the Prosecutor initiated a second investigation into the Central African Republic (known as 'CAR II'), in September 2014, following renewed violence. Both situations were 'referred' to the Court by the CAR government itself.

The research trips allowed me to undertake interviews with a wide array of actors engaged in ICC-related work: Court officials working (either long-term or on mission) in Kampala, Kinshasa and Nairobi; practitioners in the field of human rights and transitional justice, either in the national offices of international NGOs or for national or local organizations; domestic lawyers, judges and bar associations; government officials and an extensive community of international diplomats and donors. In addition, I was able to gather numerous documents – court judgments, parliamentary debates, draft laws, and brochures – that were generally not available outside of the countries and occasionally not publicly available within. On several occasions, I also attended and observed private meetings and public programs convened by NGOs working in country.

Informants were initially approached through personal contacts that my co-researcher and I had developed prior to the first research trip in June 2011, on the basis of their expertise in some aspect of the ICC's intervention at a national level, as well as their engagement in domestic political or legal aspects of the Court's work.[71] Following a 'snowball' approach, these initial meetings became important points of connection to other interlocutors: we relied on referrals from initial informants to identify additional interview subjects.[72] Despite the debt that this work owes to those individuals who gave of their time, I reference these interviews relatively sparingly in the chapters that follow. Because of the sensitivity of the subject matter, many interlocutors only spoke with the express understanding that their views were not for attribution. While others imposed no such restrictions, the sensitive nature of their work and its

---

[71] Interviews were formal but followed a semi-structured format: questions were prepared in advance, although the discussions frequently evolved to accommodate unexpected insights or new lines of inquiry.

[72] Given that the risk of selection bias is always present (particularly so for the snowball approach; the technique has been criticized for reducing the likelihood that the sample of informants represent a representative cross-section of the population), I generally had greater success in speaking with – and accessing representatives of – international and national NGOs, although in all three countries my colleague and I were at least able to meet with several senior representatives from the domestic judicial sector, in-country ICC staff (from the OTP, as well as the Registrar) and individuals engaged in donor work on behalf of the diplomatic community. It should be noted, however, that this study did not use interviews as a means of sampling the country populations or determining the factual accuracy of their views; rather, as noted, the interviews provided important contextual information for the claims that I develop herein. On snowball interviewing, see Paula Pickering, *Peacebuilding in the Balkans: The View from the Ground Floor* (Ithaca: Cornell University Press, 2007).

attendant security risks compel caution in identifying them. For these reasons, references to interview subjects occur only where the assertions provide explicit, additional validation of claims central to my analysis.[73]

Finally, defined as 'a person or thing that causes a change', I employ catalyst here in its literal meaning: as a causal agent. The etymology of 'catalyst' is chemical: it was introduced in the mid-nineteenth century by a Swedish chemist as 'change caused by an agent which itself remains unchanged'.[74] While other treatments of the ICC have taken a more elastic approach to the term (for instance, describing the ICC's 'catalytic effect' rather than the institution itself as a catalyst), my choice to take a more limited framing here is deliberate given the ambitious, often overly eager claims to validate Court interventions as the cause of domestic change. My intent is thus two-fold: to clarify to what extent the ICC's interventions, as opposed to the influence of mediating actors and events, have catalysed domestic change and to better understand the nature of this mediated relationship as a catalytic force in itself.

As a methodological approach to understanding the relationship between the ICC's engagement and change at the domestic level, I rely on process tracing. As defined by Bennett, 'Process tracing involves looking at evidence within an individual case, or a temporally and spatially bound instance of a specified phenomenon, to derive and/or test alternative explanations of that case'.[75] Further, as a method, it uses 'histories, archival documents, interview transcripts, and other sources to see whether the causal process a theory hypothesizes or implies in a case is in fact evidence in the sequence and values of the intervening variables in that case'.[76] The challenge of understanding whether the relationship

[73] Needless to say, my interlocutors do not necessarily endorse the conclusions advanced herein.

[74] Oxford Dictionary. The etymology of 'catalyst' is chemical: it was introduced in the mid-nineteenth century by a Swedish chemist as 'change caused by an agent which itself remains unchanged'.

[75] Andrew Bennett, 'Process Tracing: A Bayesian Perspective', in Janet M. Box-Steffensmeier, Henry E. Brady and David Collier (eds.), *The Oxford Handbook of Political Methodology* (Oxford: Oxford University Press, 2008), 704. For a useful exploration of process tracing's origins in the field of cognitive psychology, and its application in the study of international institutions, see also Jeffrey T. Checkel, 'Mechanisms, Process, and the Study of International Institutions', in Andrew Bennett and Jeffrey T. Checkel (eds.), *Process Tracing: From Metaphor to Analytic Tool* (Cambridge: Cambridge University Press, 2015).

[76] Alexander L. George and Andrew Bennett, *Case Studies and Theory Development in the Social Sciences* (Cambridge: MIT Press, 2005), 6.

between relevant national-level events – the establishment of a domestic war crimes court, the passage of domestic Rome Statute legislation or the initiation of a criminal case – and the ICC's actions is indeed causal rather than contributory is thus crucial. As this book illustrates, more than one factor contributes to change.

A final note on terminology: formally, the ICC is an institution and complementarity a principle of limitation, one which governs the priority of the Court's jurisdiction. Yet regardless of formal ICC intervention in a country, complementarity is also invoked as a duty of member states. For instance, the 'complementarity principle' can be said to catalyse the passage of implementation legislation merely as a precaution against the threat of ICC intervention and to facilitate prosecutions domestically. In the context of Kenya, Uganda and the DRC, however, where the Court itself has formally intervened, the operation and invocation of complementarity is fundamentally intertwined with the work of the ICC itself. Thus, in Uganda, a dedicated unit for adjudicating international crimes was seen as a necessary step to (potentially) displace the ICC, but complementarity was the principle that justified its creation. I have sought to make this conceptual distinction clear throughout but occasionally use the terms 'ICC' and 'complementarity' interchangeably.

4   Structure of the Book

The book is structured in two parts. The first part addresses the evolution, interpretation and implementation of complementarity by state and non-state actors, as well as Court actors (specifically, ICC judges and the Office of the Prosecutor) in The Hague.[77] The second part is broadly empirical: it illustrates the effects of this (changed) interpretation and the interaction of the ICC with the normative and institutional accountability frameworks in Uganda, Kenya and the DRC. Three aspects are explored in particular: the passage of Rome Statute implementation

---

[77] Another important ICC actor is the Office of the Registry, which defines itself as 'a neutral organ of the Court that provides services to all other organs so the ICC can function and conduct fair and effective public proceedings'. See ICC Registry, at www.icc-cpi.int/about/registry. While the Registry performs roles relevant to some of the discussion here, e.g., outreach to affected communities, it plays a less significant role in interpreting or applying the complementarity principle as such or in developing the Court's prosecutorial strategy.

legislation in the legal frameworks of each country; the establishment of specialized domestic courts or justice mechanisms as part of the institutional architecture for prosecuting grave crimes domestically and the initiation of actual, atrocity-related proceedings that have ensued in the wake of ICC action.

Chapter 2 examines how complementarity has evolved from a legal rule of admissibility – an organizing principle for the regulation of concurrent jurisdiction – to an instrument of policy. This policy, often referred to as 'positive complementarity', is one that promotes the ICC and the 'Rome Statute System' as proactive agents for domestic accountability. Drawing on constructivist international relations literature, the chapter traces this more ambitious articulation of the ICC's relationship to national jurisdictions and argues that its ascendance reflects the work of norm entrepreneurs and transnational civil society networks who, through a duty-based reading of the Statute, have progressively sought to articulate a more catalytic vision for the Court and, with it, a broader array of policy goals. At the same time, the chapter explores how this duty-based interpretation has contributed to an increasingly disciplinary approach to implementation, one that privileges a mirroring of the Rome Statute's content and the ICC's form. It concludes that complementarity's evolution in this regard is testament to the significant influence of non-state actors at both the transnational and local levels and of a growing effort on their part to route the entrenchment of domestic human rights norms through the framework and standards of international criminal law.

This discursive project runs alongside the Court's jurisprudence, which, thus far, has shown little interest in incorporating positive complementarity into its interpretive framework for determining admissibility under Article 17 of the Rome Statute. To that end, Chapter 3 offers a detailed review of the Court's admissibility jurisprudence to date. In so doing, it argues that the ICC has developed a body of case law that requires states to largely mirror the same conduct (and even the same factual incidents) that the OTP investigates as a precondition for rendering a case inadmissible. While this approach is consistent with the coercive dimension of complementarity, insofar as it seeks to pull states towards compliance with the Rome Statute framework, it can also place a heavy burden on states, one that they may be unprepared (or unwilling) to meet. At the same time, the judicial treatment of Article 93(10), which provides the statutory basis for a 'positive complementarity' policy, has been scant insofar as the Court has chosen to separate its treatment of requests for

ICC cooperation from admissibility challenges. Complementarity thus appears less as a space for constructive engagement and dialogue than a set of unifying criteria with which states must comply. While Court officials and some commentators have defended the ICC's approach, suggesting that it is technically consistent with the wording of Article 17, others have advocated a more flexible approach. The chapter thus illustrates the tensions that arise between complementarity's policy goals and the ICC's more narrow, judicial remit. It further suggests that such tension is symptomatic of legalism: it relies on an artificial division between the Court as a legal and political actor.

Chapter 4 turns from complementarity's juridical framework to address its policy dimensions as engaged by the Office of the Prosecutor. Situated between the ICC's institutional centre in The Hague and the various country contexts in which it operates, the Office not only shapes the overall work of the Court but can also have a significant influence on the contours of domestic accountability efforts. The chapter thus queries in what ways the OTP has sought to influence state behaviour through two key areas of its work: preliminary examinations and investigations. Returning to complementarity's dual properties as both coercive and cooperative, the chapter first examines the OTP's use of preliminary examinations as a key tool in its efforts to prod national jurisdictions into action. Turning to the country studies, the chapter offers a detailed review of the Kenyan preliminary examination, wherein the Office, under Moreno-Ocampo's tenure, took a largely coercive approach as it sought to push the government to establish a national accountability mechanism in the wake of its post-election violence (PEV). (By contrast, in other countries like Colombia, the Office has pursued a more cooperative, managerial approach to complementarity.) The chapter then considers the Office's early investigatory practices, focusing on Uganda and the DRC in particular. It argues that, particularly in cases of 'self-referred' states, investigations could be a material site where a positive, cooperative approach to complementarity might have been more meaningfully enacted, but for the most part, it was not. This has not only been to the detriment of the OTP's relationship with national-level actors but also, arguably, to its disappointing record of confirmed charges and convictions, which itself imperils the Court's catalytic potential.

The book's second half examines the interaction of the ICC with the normative and institutional accountability frameworks in Uganda, Kenya and the DRC, moving from legislative frameworks to domestic judicial institutions to actual criminal proceedings and related litigation. Chapter 5 first explores the relationship between ICC intervention and efforts to reform the normative legal frameworks in each country with respect to atrocity crimes. It argues that it was less the Court's intervention or the desire of state actors to undertake domestic prosecutions that catalysed the passage of national implementation legislation; rather, implementation of the Statute was undertaken at certain political moments in order to 'perform' complementarity, typically for international audiences. But while the power of external constituencies was largely responsible for driving the implementation process in Uganda and Kenya, in particular, it often glossed over deeper concerns about the desirability of international criminal law as a framework for accountability. The chapter also illustrates how the near identical importation of the Rome Statute's substantive and procedural provisions – at the expense of other, possible forms of accountability – reflects an increasingly disciplinary approach to implementation. By contrast, in the DRC, political mistrust in international judicial intervention not only thwarted the passage of comprehensive implementing legislation for many years but has also appeared to encourage a more syncretic approach to implementation later on. Indeed, while much commentary has focused on 'misapplication' of the Rome Statute in the DRC, I suggest that political contestation within the DRC was itself a catalyst that allowed other implementation strategies to take root, including, notably, the direct application of the Rome Statute by Congolese military judges in domestic proceedings.

Chapter 6 turns to the institutional effects of complementarity: it examines the emergence and attempted establishment of specialized domestic courts or chambers for the prosecution of serious crimes as one of the most frequently cited outcomes of ICC interventions. In so doing, it highlights the shifting, adaptive nature of complementarity as the basis for transforming and reforming domestic judicial systems, even though the link between these efforts and the ICC itself is often quite tenuous. In describing these various courts, the chapter highlights how, in certain contexts like Uganda and Kenya, the threat of the Court's jurisdiction was used to prompt the setting up (or attempted setting up) of domestic legal bodies and to buttress putative admissibility challenges. By contrast, more recent descriptions of these bodies have depicted them literally as institutional extensions of the ICC: rather than displacing the Court, they are meant to complement, and even 'complete', its work. Non-state actors in the DRC have invoked complementarity in a similar manner, even though the limited domestic proceedings there through military courts are not connected in any material way to – nor the direct result of – the ICC's undertakings. In tracing these shifts, the chapter further considers complementarity's dualities: its impulse towards conformity (between the design of specialized domestic courts and the ICC) and towards competition (between the exceptionalism that underwrites such courts and their relationship to the ordinary domestic criminal justice system). I suggest here the concept of a 'justice meme' as one way in which such conformity/compliance with ICC structures and practices is transmitted and replicated.

The book's penultimate chapter turns, finally, to the question of national proceedings and queries to what extent ICC interventions have catalysed these proceedings. As further evidence of the catalysing effect that the ICC's engagement has had on non-state actors, the chapter highlights the efforts that Kenyan civil society has had in their efforts to pursue other forms of litigation as part of the logic of complementarity. Similarly, in the DRC, the use of mobile military courts supported by international NGOs and donors has been a civil society innovation, often invoked as 'complementary' to ICC intervention. While not connected to the Court in a formal way, these proceedings constitute the largest number of domestic trials for international crimes undertaken by an ICC situation country to date. Finally, the procedural history of the sole trial to thus far come before Uganda's ICD in relation to the LRA conflict – that of former commander (and child soldier) Thomas Kwoyelo – is examined. In so doing, I highlight the vexed relationship between state power and complementarity, demonstrating how formal 'compliance' can lead to outcomes that are themselves at odds with human rights norms.

The final, concluding chapter summarizes the book's key findings and concludes that the ICC's interventions and complementarity are better understood as axes around which advocacy for a global accountability norm has turned. Rather than a catalyst in itself, it is the Court's mediated relationship with non-state actors that has had the greatest 'catalytic effect' on domestic accountability efforts. In this sense, civil society organizations are both object and subject of this effect: they seek to expand complementarity's normative influence, while having themselves been transformed by it. In concluding, the book offers a number of recommendations for future inquiry and practice.

PART I

The ICC and Complementarity: Evolutions,
Interpretations and Implementation

2

Tracing an Idea, Constructing a Norm

Complementarity as a Catalyst

Since the signing of the Rome Statute in 1998, complementarity has grown from a legal rule to an instrument of policy. This policy sees the International Criminal Court (ICC) not only as a forum for prosecution where states fail to undertake criminal investigations and prosecutions themselves, but also as a means to enable or encourage proceedings at the national level. As stated by former prosecutor Moreno-Ocampo in a 2004 speech to the ICC's Assembly of States Parties, one of his office's 'core policies' would be to pursue a 'positive approach to cooperation and to the principle of complementarity'. This meant, in his words, 'encouraging genuine national proceedings where possible, relying on national and international networks, and participating in a system of international cooperation'.[78]

Such a description of complementarity might now seem commonplace; however, the expansion of its definition, and of its popular understanding, was neither obvious nor ordained. Furthermore, while the vision of 'positive' complementarity outlined by Moreno-Ocampo may have been 'an inherent concept of the [Rome] Statute', it was also a policy invention. As Carsten Stahn notes, 'In court policy, complementarity was slowly discovered as a virtue, ... as an instrument to foster legitimacy and enhance the efficiency of justice'.[79] This discovery was chiefly driven by non-state actors – international and national NGOs, human rights advocates, academics and donors – many of whom had initially sought a stronger role for the court vis-à-vis national courts (primacy, rather than complementarity); had themselves served in previous leadership positions with other criminal

---

[78] Third session of the Assembly of States Parties to the Rome Statute of the International Criminal Court, address by prosecutor Luis Moreno-Ocampo (The Hague, 6 September 2004), 2, at www.icc-cpi.int/iccdocs/asp_docs/library/asp/LMO_20040906_En.pdf.
[79] Carsten Stahn, 'Taking Complementarity Seriously: On the Sense and Sensibility of "Classical", "Positive" and "Negative" Complementarity', in *The International Criminal Court and Complementarity*, 235.

tribunals and, in certain cases, came to occupy important leadership positions in the early years of the ICC itself. These 'norm entrepreneurs' have persuasively advanced the conception of complementarity as a catalyst, while typically framing it as a series of obligations upon states to legislate, prosecute and adjudicate international crimes at the national level.

This chapter traces complementarity's transformational evolution – its meaning and purpose as a catalyst – and queries how it came to dominate so much of the ICC's early discursive space. It first offers a brief overview of the Rome Statute's drafting history, emphasizing how the predominant understanding of complementarity amongst states at the time was as a principle of constraint. Unlike the *ad hoc* tribunals for Rwanda (ICTR) and the former Yugoslavia (ICTY), the drafters of the Statute chose not to grant the ICC primacy over national jurisdictions. This issue was deeply contested in the negotiations over the court and reflected a delicate process that sought to balance supranational jurisdiction with an enduring concern for state sovereignty. Furthermore, in line with this process, a deliberate choice was made to permit states substantial leeway in their prosecution of international crimes, including, for instance, their ability to prosecute Rome Statute crimes as 'ordinary' crimes.

Despite these careful negotiations, the second section of the chapter examines the evolution of complementarity from a technical rule of admissibility crafted by states towards a more catalytic vision driven by private actors. In so doing, it traces complementarity's growth as a policy concept, which was embraced early on by the Office of the Prosecutor (OTP) as a way of encouraging national accountability for grave crimes. The intellectual history of complementarity is also considered, including the experiences of the ICTR and ICTY, whose completion strategies vis-à-vis the states of the former Yugoslavia and Rwanda played an important role in academic writing on the concept of positive complementarity and, in turn, influenced early ICC practice. Finally, the role of non-state actors in advancing the normative content of this concept is examined. Through this discourse analysis, the chapter demonstrates how the carefully negotiated compromises that informed the Rome Statute's drafting have been progressively constructed and reshaped through the principle of complementarity.

The final section attempts to better understand the means by which complementarity's polysemy (its meaning both as a rule of admissibility and as a catalyst) evolved with such apparent speed. Indeed, rather than complementarity's 'slow discovery' as a virtue, the pace of this discovery – given the degree to which it might alter the perceived obligations of states, and the extent to which states at least initially ratified that perception – is more notable for its swiftness.[80] One reason for this swiftness, I suggest, is that the framing of complementarity as a catalyst benefited from the unprecedented and influential role that non-state actors played in the establishment of the ICC itself. Consistent with constructivist approaches to international relations, the success of private actors in this transformation underscores how a new complementarity norm was 'discovered and learned' through an interactional process, one in which 'actors generate shared knowledge and shared understandings that become the background for subsequent interactions'.[81] I also suggest that constructivist literature on transnational 'communities of practice', a concept developed by Etienne Wenger and advanced by the political scientist Emanuel Adler, offers a helpful lens through which to understand how this new complementarity norm – as an expectation of 'what ought to be done' – proliferated.[82] In highlighting this dynamic interplay between practice and discourse, complementarity emerges as an evolving, adaptive principle rather than a static legal concept.

1 Complementarity as Constraint

While negotiations around the ICC's establishment inaugurated a wave of interest in complementarity, the principle itself is not new. As Mohamed El Zeidy notes, 'the conditions or the parameters of [complementarity's] operation developed over a lengthy period of time until the adoption of the 1998 Rome Statute'.[83] The principle was the subject of much debate around the creation and operation of a United Nations (UN) War Crimes

---

[80] For instance, the successful negotiation of duty-based language in the resolutions that emerged out of the Rome Statute Review Conference was seen as significant victories by civil society. See, e.g., Kampala Declaration, RC/Decl.1, para. 5 (adopted 1 June 2010) ('Resolve to continue and strengthen effective domestic implementation of the Statute, to enhance the capacity of national jurisdictions to prosecute the perpetrators of the most serious crimes of international concern in accordance with internationally recognized fair trial standards, pursuant to the principle of complementarity'.); Resolution RC/Res.1 – Complementarity (adopted 8 June 2010), para. 2 ('Emphasizes the principle of complementarity as laid down in the Rome Statute and *stresses* the obligations of States Parties flowing from the Rome Statute'.).

[81] Jutta Brunnée and Stephen J. Toope, *Legitimacy and Legality in International Law: An Interactional Account* (Cambridge: Cambridge University Press, 2010), 13.

[82] See Andrew Hurrell, 'Norms and Ethics in International Relations', in Walter Carlsnaes, Thomas Risse and Beth Simmons (eds.), *Handbook of International Relations* (London: Sage, 2002), 137–154, 143 (defining norms as 'prescribed patterns of behavior that give expectations as to what ought to be done').

[83] Mohamed El Zeidy, 'The Genesis of Complementarity', in *The International Criminal Court and Complementarity*, 77.

Commission during World War II, where the role of the commission vis-à-vis allied states played an 'antecedent role' to the Rome Statute.[84] Still, most academic commentary on the subject did not emerge until the early 1990s, spurred on by the end of the Cold War and, relatedly, the International Law Commission's (ILC) efforts to study the question of international criminal jurisdiction.

The International Law Commission: 1990–1994

Trinidad and Tobago first requested that the UN General Assembly consider the question of establishing an international criminal court in 1989.[85] In its initial report responding to that request, the commission presaged much of the debate that would follow by emphasizing that the main questions to resolve in establishing such a court were whether it was intended to 'replace, compete with or complement national jurisdictions'.[86] The general assembly subsequently requested that the commission prepare a formal draft Statute for an international court as a matter of priority. It did so, culminating in the ILC's 1994 Draft ICC Statute, which proposed jurisdiction over genocide, aggression, war crimes and crimes against humanity.

Of note in that 1994 draft was Article 42, which drew upon the principle of *ne bis in idem* (the principle that a person should not be prosecuted more than once for the same criminal conduct) as embodied in the ICTY and ICTR Statutes.[87] As proposed, a person could be retried under the proposed court's jurisdiction if the offence for which he or

---

[84] Mark S. Ellis, *Sovereignty and Justice: Balancing the Principle of Complementarity between International and Domestic War Crimes Tribunals* (Newcastle upon Tyne: Cambridge Scholars Publishing, 2014), 19. Operating from 1943 to 1948, part of the UN War Crimes Commission's task was to assist national governments in the prosecution of Axis personnel, prefiguring much of the modern discourse around complementarity and the role of the ICC.

[85] Notably, this initial request focused on a court with far narrower subject matter jurisdiction: drug trafficking. After the prime minister drafted a motion (with the assistance of former Nuremberg prosecutor Benjamin Ferencz and law scholar M. Cherif Bassiouni) proposing that the International Law Commission study the idea, the general assembly adopted it in 1989. Crucially, the language of that motion was to consider a court with jurisdiction to try crimes including, but not limited to, illicit drug trafficking. See, e.g., Benjamin N. Schiff, *Building the International Criminal Court* (Cambridge: Cambridge University Press, 2008), 37–38.

[86] El Zeidy, 'The Genesis of Complementarity', 111.

[87] Draft Statute for an International Criminal Court with commentaries (1994), at http://legal.un.org/ilc/texts/instruments/english/commentaries/7_4_1994.pdf.

she had been tried by another court was 'characterized as an ordinary crime', or if the proceedings 'were not impartial or independent or were designed to shield the accused from international criminal responsibility or the case was not diligently prosecuted'.[88]

Support for this provision was far from unanimous, with substantially differing views as to the ICC's relationship with national jurisdictions. As Kleffner notes:

> Some members of the ILC envisaged the court as supplementing rather than superseding national jurisdiction, while others envisaged it as an option for prosecution in case the state concerned was unwilling to unable to do so. A third group of members suggested providing the court with limited inherent jurisdiction for a core of the most serious crimes, thus presumably envisaging exclusive jurisdiction of the International Criminal Court for these crimes.[89]

Although no final decision was taken on a specific model at the time, the draft Statute presented by the ILC endorsed the proposed court being 'complementary to national criminal justice systems in cases where such trial procedures may not be available or may be ineffective'.[90] The ILC further proposed, in Article 35, a regime according to which jurisdiction would be allocated based on a determination of the admissibility of a case.[91]

In the commentary to this paragraph, the commission explained to the General Assembly that the international court was 'intended to operate in cases when there is no prospect of [the suspect] being duly tried in national courts'.[92] Thus, 'the emphasis is … on the court as a body which will complement existing national jurisdictions and existing procedures for international judicial cooperation in criminal matters and which is not intended to exclude the existing jurisdiction of national courts [.]'[93] With respect to a situation where a person had already been tried by another

---

[88] Draft Statute, Article 42(2)(a); see also James Crawford, 'Current Developments: The ILC's Draft Statute for an International Criminal Tribunal', *American Journal of International Law* 80 (1994).

[89] Kleffner, *Complementarity in the Rome Statute and National Criminal Jurisdictions*, 73.

[90] Draft Statute for an International Criminal Court with commentaries (1994), *Yearbook of the International Law Commission 1994*, Vol. II, A/CN.4/SER.A/1994/Add.1, Preamble ('ILC Draft Statute').

[91] Ibid., Article 35 ('Issues of Admissibility'). The Rome Statute retains this provision: admissibility assessments are case-specific.

[92] ILC Draft Statute, 27 (commentary 1).

[93] Ibid.

(domestic) court, the 1994 draft retained the provision that subsequent trial by the ICC would not be barred where the initial trial had been for an ordinary crime, or in the case of sham, i.e., non-genuine, proceedings.[94] The ILC report thus reflected the 'classical' conception of complementarity as a limiting jurisdictional principle. In Stahn's words, it was a 'concept to regulate potential conflicts as between the (primary) jurisdiction of national courts and the residual jurisdiction of the ICC'.[95]

The Ad Hoc and Preparatory Committees: 1995–1998

Whereas complementarity appeared only in passing in the ILC's earlier draft, it featured prominently in the discussions of the Ad Hoc Committee that was set up by the General Assembly to discuss the ILC's report, in advance of the assembly's 1995 session.[96] The topic appeared under three general headings in the committee's 1995 report: the 'significance' of the principle, its jurisdictional implications and the role of national jurisdictions.[97] As the report noted, many state delegations 'stressed that the principle of complementarity should create a strong presumption in favour of national jurisdictions'.[98] In so doing, a number of advantages were highlighted, including that 'evidence and witnesses would be readily available', 'language problems would be minimized' and the 'applicable law would be more certain and developed'.[99] Furthermore, states had a 'vital interest in remaining responsible and accountable for prosecuting violations of their laws – which also served the interest of the international community'.[100] An additional point of debate was whether the principle should be reflected in the preamble of the Statute or its operative part.[101]

---

[94] See ILC Draft Statute, Article 42(2).
[95] Carsten Stahn, 'Complementarity: A Tale of Two Notions', *Criminal Law Forum* 19 (2008), 90.
[96] Kleffner, *Complementarity in the Rome Statute and National Criminal Jurisdictions*, 76.
[97] Report of the Ad Hoc Committee on the Establishment of an International Criminal Court, A/50/22 (1995), at www.legal-tools.org/uploads/tx_ltpdb/doc21168.pdf. See generally paras. 29–37.
[98] Ibid., para. 31.
[99] Ibid., paras. 31, 129.
[100] Ibid., para. 31.
[101] Ibid., paras. 35–37.

Other delegations expressed support for national courts retaining current jurisdiction with the proposed ICC, but insisted that 'the latter should also have primacy of jurisdiction'.[102] A particular point of contention remained the principle of *ne bis in idem*, as it was seen by some delegations as 'incompatible with what they considered to be the intention of the ILC not to establish a hierarchy between the ICC and national courts or to allow the ICC to pass judgment on the operation of national courts'.[103] To that end, the suggestion was made to delete the distinction between ordinary crimes and international crimes that had survived previous drafts. In particular, 'It was stressed that the standards set by the Commission were not intended to establish a hierarchy between the international criminal court and national courts, or to allow the international criminal court to pass judgement on the operation of national courts in general'.[104]

A Preparatory Committee ('PREPCOM'), whose task it was to further develop the draft Statute replaced the Ad Hoc Committee in 1996, with the idea that a plenipotentiary conference would follow. Over the course of the next three years, 'the original 43-page 1994 ILC draft Statute expanded into a draft Statute of 173 pages replete with bracketed options, alternative phrasing, and footnotes for consideration at the Rome Conference'.[105] John Holmes, the head of the Canadian delegation that was asked to coordinate informal consultations on what became Article 35, produced a draft that, for the first time, introduced the terms 'unwilling', 'unable' and 'genuine' into the text of the proposed Statute, along with a set of conditions for determining where those conditions would render a case admissible.[106]

---

[102] Ibid., paras. 32, 218.
[103] Kleffner, *Complementarity in the Rome Statute and National Criminal Jurisdictions*, 77.
[104] Ad Hoc Committee Report, para. 43.
[105] Schiff, *Building the International Criminal Court*, 70. See also Immi Tallgren, 'Completing the "International Criminal Order": The Rhetoric of International Repression and the Notion of Complementarity in the Draft Statute for an International Criminal Court', *Nordic Journal of International Law* 67 (1998), 107–137. Tallgren offers a compelling account of the PREPCOM negotiations through the analogy of 'Master' and 'Butler', the latter 'see[ing] complementarity as a means of restricting the role of the ICC and its scope of jurisdiction' (i.e., constraint) and the former 'represent[ing] the process of internationalization', 124.
[106] See J. T. Holmes, 'The Principle of Complementarity', in R. Lee (ed.), *The International Criminal Court – The Making of the Rome Statute* (The Hague: Kluwer Law International, 1999).

According to Holmes, inability was not controversial in principle: relevant agreed upon factors were the 'total or partial collapse' of a state's national judicial system, the state being unable to secure the accused, or being 'otherwise unable to carry out its proceeding'.[107] Unwillingness, however, proved more contentious, 'as some delegations had concerns with regard to state sovereignty and constitutional guarantees in domestic systems against double jeopardy'.[108] To assuage concerns about the subjectivity inherent in such a test, the word 'genuinely' was inserted, as it was thought to carry a more objective connotation.[109] Debates around the *ne bis in idem* principle also persisted, leading to the deletion of the ordinary crimes exception that had survived previous drafts.[110] The Statute instead refers to the 'same conduct' of an accused, 'to make clear that a national prosecution of a crime – international or ordinary – did not prohibit ICC retrial for charges based on different conduct'.[111]

The Rome Statute: Article 17 and the Substance of the Principle

The term 'complementarity' itself does not appear in the Rome Statute. The Statute only notes, in its tenth preambular recital and in Article 1, that the ICC 'shall be complementary to national criminal jurisdictions'.[112] Article 17 sets out the substantive criteria for determining the admissibility of a case, but it does not use the term 'complementarity' as such. The article instead states that 'a case is inadmissible where ... [it] is

[107] Ibid., 45–49.
[108] Kleffner, *Complementarity in the Rome Statute and National Criminal Jurisdictions*, 85.
[109] In addition to concern that sham proceedings might be used to shield an accused, two other forms of unwillingness were agreed upon: undue delay inconsistent with an intent to bring the person to justice and lack of independence or impartiality.
[110] Holmes, 'The Principle of Complementarity', 57–58. Stigen also confirms that the 'ordinary crime' criterion, initially endorsed by the [ILC], 'was proposed but rejected [in the negotiations] as it met too much resistance'. Stigen, *The Relationship between the International Criminal Court and National Jurisdictions*, 335.
[111] Kevin Jon Heller, 'A Sentence-Based Theory of Complementarity', *Harvard International Law Journal* 53(1) (2012), 224. For a similar conclusion, see Nouwen, *Complementarity in the Line of Fire*, 50; Rod Rastan, 'What Is "Substantially the Same Conduct"? Unpacking the ICC's "First Limb" Complementarity Jurisprudence', *Journal of International Criminal Justice* 15(1) (2017), 1–29. Article 93(10), discussed in the following chapter, further supports this interpretation, as it refers to the court providing assistance to a state party 'conducting an investigation into or trial in respect of conduct which constitutes a crime within the jurisdiction of the court or which constitutes a serious crimes under the national law of the requesting State'.
[112] Rome Statute Preamble, tenth recital. Article 1 of the Statute also states that the ICC 'shall be complementary to national criminal jurisdictions'.

being investigated or prosecuted by a state which has jurisdiction over it, unless the state is *unwilling or unable* genuinely to carry out the investigation or prosecution'.[113] A case will also be inadmissible when 'the state has decided not to prosecute, unless the decision resulted from the *unwillingness or inability* of the state to genuinely prosecute', or when the person 'has already been tried for conduct which is the subject of the complaint, and a trial by the court is not permitted under Article 20, paragraph 3'.[114]

The Statute thus sets forth a two-step test, 'the first explicit question of which is whether a state is investigating or prosecuting the case or has done so'.[115] Where there are no such proceedings evident at the national level – which under ICC case law requires, as the following chapter discusses, similar charges of conduct – the case is admissible. The more difficult assessment to be made is the second step: whether a state, even where proceedings are underway, is 'unwilling or unable genuinely to carry out the investigation or prosecution'. This prong of the test has generated significantly more controversy, as it invites the ICC to scrutinize the quality and standard of national proceedings.[116] It involves a more subjective assessment of the standards by which such proceedings should be judged.

As discussed further below, several interpretive controversies have also arisen with respect to the test itself. For instance, Darryl Robinson (the drafter of the text that became Article 17) notes that rather than the two-step test that the text sets forth, a 'slogan version' of complementarity has instead come to exercise a 'powerful grip on popular imagination'.[117] In this 'slogan' version, complementarity is effectively reduced to a 'one-step test' that omits the predicate question of whether a state is investigating or prosecuting – the proceedings requirement – by focusing instead on the 'unwilling/unable' prong as the entirety of the test.[118] This 'hermeneutic

---

[113] Rome Statute, Article 17 ('Issues of Admissibility').
[114] To determine whether a state is 'unwilling' to prosecute after an investigation, the court will look to see whether the proceedings shielded the person concerned, whether the proceedings were unjustifiably delayed 'inconsistent with an intent to bring the person concerned to justice' or whether the proceedings were not conducted impartially or independently and 'in a manner which, in the circumstances, is inconsistent with an intent to bring the person concerned to justice'. Ibid., Arts 17(2)(a–c).
[115] Darryl Robinson, 'The Mysterious Mysteriousness of Complementarity', *Criminal Law Forum* 21(1) (2010), 68. As the following chapter examines further, the court has only rarely entered into questions of ability or willingness, finding instead an absence of domestic proceedings in almost all of its admissibility decisions to date.
[116] Ibid., 67–102.
[117] Ibid., 68.
[118] Ibid., 69.

"blind spot"', as Robinson puts it, has since become ubiquitous in popular descriptions of the ICC, which routinely state that it is a court of 'last resort', or that it only intervenes where a state 'is unable or unwilling'.[119] Supportive of Robinson's analysis, the text of Article 17 makes clear that complementarity is a case-based assessment. The question is not whether a 'situation' in general is or has been the subject of domestic investigations or prosecutions, despite the frequent shorthand of inability or unwillingness.[120] To that end, commentators and court documents alike have noted that 'complementarity does not require an assessment of [a] state's overall justice system ... merely that is it capable of conducting genuine proceedings in the particular case'.[121] While the condition of that system

---

[119] The so-called 'slogan' version of complementarity has raised the ire of other commentators as well. See, e.g., Paul Seils, *Handbook on Complementarity: An Introduction to the Role of National Courts and the ICC in Prosecuting International Crimes* (International Center for Transitional Justice, 2016), 43 ('The slogan version [of complementarity] does not understand the importance of the two-step process. Only if you understand how the test works will you understand the right questions to ask about complementarity'.). On the occasion of International Justice Day, the ICTJ released the cited handbook alongside an invitation to test viewers on 'how well [they] understand the ins and outs' of complementarity. See ICTJ, 'Quiz: How Much Do You Know About Complementarity?' (13 July 2016), at www.ictj.org/news/complementarity-quiz.

[120] As defined by Pre-Trial Chamber I, cases 'comprise specific incidents during which one or more crimes within the jurisdiction of the court seem to have been committed by one more identified suspects [and] entail proceedings that take place after the issuance of a warrant of arrest or a summons to appear'. Situations, by contrast, are 'generally defined in terms of temporal, territorial and in some cases personal parameters'. *Situation in the Democratic Republic of Congo*, Decision on the applications for participation in the proceedings of VPRS 1, VPRS 2, VPRS 3, VPRS 4, VPRS 5 and VPRS 6, ICC-01/04-101, PTC I (17 January 2006), para. 65. See also The Prosecutor *v.* Francis Kirimi Muthaura, Uhuru Muigai Kenyatta and Mohammed Hussein Ali, judgment on the appeal of the Republic of Kenya against the decision of Pre-Trial Chamber II of 30 May 2011 entitled 'Decision on the application by the government of Kenya challenging the admissibility of the case pursuant to Article 19(2)(b) of the Statute', ICC-01/09-02/11 OA, Appeals Chamber, 30 August 2011, paras. 38–39 ('Kenyatta Admissibility Appeals Judgment') and The Prosecutor *v.* William Samoei Ruto, Henry Kiprono Kosgey and Joshua Arap Sang, Judgment on the appeal of the Republic on Kenya against the decision of Pre-Trial Chamber II of 30 May 2011 entitled 'Decision on the Application by the Government of Kenya Challenging the Admissibility of the Case Pursuant to Article 19(2)(b) of the Statute', Appeals Chamber (30 August 2011), paras. 39–40 ('Ruto et al. Admissibility Appeals Judgment') (stating that the specificity of the term 'case' will depend on the stage at which admissibility is challenged). For further on the distinction, see Rod Rastan, 'Situation and Case: Defining the Parameters', in *The International Criminal Court and Complementarity*, 421–459.

[121] Nouwen, *Complementarity in the Line of Fire*, 74, 106.

can undoubtedly influence the ability to investigate or prosecute a particular case, it is not a determinative basis for admissibility. As explained later, however, arguments have since emerged to the effect that a national system should be considered 'available' only when it 'incorporates the entire spectrum of substantive and procedural safeguards enshrined in the Statute and by which the ICC is to abide'.[122]

Complementarity also combines optional and mandatory features. Article 17 provides that the 'court *shall* determine that a case is inadmissible' in response to a challenge lodged by a state or individual.[123] States, however, may also 'refer' cases to the ICC, as both Uganda and the Democratic Republic of Congo (DRC) (and other states subsequently) have done.[124] El Zeidy has termed this 'optional complementarity' and notes that it is the 'reversed scheme of 'mandatory complementarity', in that it is not due to the court's determination that a state was inactive, unwilling or unable, but rather that the 'state itself voluntarily decided to renounce the exercise of its jurisdiction in favour of the [ICC]'.[125]

This practice has also generated a significant literature amongst commentators who contend that such so-called 'self-referrals' are unsupported by the Statute and the intention of the drafters.[126] Robinson again persuasively contests this view, noting that Article 14 expressly provides for state party referrals and that they were a 'recurring and explicit topic of deliberation throughout the negotiations, from the first to the final discussion'.[127] Not unlike the one-step 'slogan version' of complementarity, he notes that, 'a reconstructed history appears to have eclipsed the actual drafting history'.[128] Indeed, despite the

---

[122] See Federica Gioia, 'State Sovereignty, Jurisdiction, and "Modern" International Law: The Principle of Complementarity in the International Criminal Court', *Leiden Journal of International Law* 19 (2006), 1113.

[123] Three states have raised such challenges to date: Kenya, Libya and the Ivory Coast.

[124] See Rome Statute, Article 14 ('Referral of a situation by a State Party').

[125] El Zeidy, 'The Genesis of Complementarity', 137.

[126] See, e.g., William Schabas, 'Prosecutorial Discretion v. Judicial Activism', *Journal of International Criminal Justice* 6 (2008).

[127] Darryl Robinson, 'The Controversy over Territorial State Referrals and Reflections on ICL Discourse', *Journal of International Criminal Justice*, 9(2) (2011), 364. See, e.g., Max du Plessis and Jolyon Ford (eds.), *Unable or Unwilling? Case Studies on Domestic Implementation of the ICC Statute in Selected African Countries* (Pretoria: Institute for Security Studies, 2008). Du Plessis and Ford argue, '[T]he ICC is, by design, a "court of last resort" – with the main responsibility for dealing with alleged offenders resting with domestic justice systems', 8.

[128] Robinson, 'The Controversy over Territorial State Referrals and Reflections on ICL Discourse', 380.

frequency with which the ICC is referred to as a court of 'last resort', states may, and have, voluntarily referred situations on their territory to the court's attention.

Articles 18 and 19, in turn, set out the procedural framework for complementarity. The former sets out a notification requirement of one month for the OTP when a situation has been referred, or where the office initiates an investigation. States may also pre-empt an OTP investigation by invoking Article 18. Doing so obligates the requesting state to initiate an investigation, but compels the prosecutor to 'defer' to the domestic jurisdiction.[129] (Notably, however, this procedure has been rarely, if ever, invoked.[130]) Where the OTP has decided to prosecute, Article 19 grants the right to challenge admissibility to an accused, as well as to 'a state which has jurisdiction over a case'. Such challenges may be brought only once – and, for states, 'at the earliest opportunity' – and 'prior to or at the commencement of the trial'.[131]

Taken together, the Rome Statute's complementarity criteria establish a 'horizontal relationship between national and international courts: they constitute jurisdictional alternatives to one another with right of way normally given to national courts'.[132] This 'horizontal paradigm' in turn, appeared to affirm a preference for domestic prosecution. Added to this were the decisions on the part of the drafters to explicitly depart from the primacy that characterized the *ad hoc* tribunals for Rwanda and the former Yugoslavia, to not include the absence of domestic due process rights as a condition for admissibility, and, relatedly, to reject the distinction between international and ordinary crimes as a basis for the *ne bis in idem* provision.

---

[129] It should be noted that while this procedure applies to situations that are referred to the OTP or where the prosecutor has opened an investigation *proprio motu*, it does not apply in situations referred by the Security Council.

[130] Carsten Stahn, 'Admissibility Challenges before the ICC: From Quasi-Primacy to Qualified Deference?' in Carsten Stahn (ed.), *The Law and Practice of the International Criminal Court* (Oxford: Oxford University Press, 2015), 240 (describing deferral has having 'largely remained a dead letter'). Articles 89 and 94 also provide for consultation between a state and the court in cases where an ICC request conflicts with domestic investigation of prosecution (or conviction), but this regime has also been little used to date. Article 17 is thus the dominant juridical avenue through which the court's complementarity case law has been developed to date.

[131] Rome Statute, Article 19(4)–(5). Article 19(4) foresees the possibility of an additional challenge ('In exceptional circumstances, the court may grant leave for a challenge to be brought more than once or at a time later than the commencement of the trial'.).

[132] Yuval Shany, *Regulating Jurisdictional Relations between National and International Courts* (Oxford: Oxford University Press, 2007), 35.

Unsurprisingly, those who had sought a stronger role for the court as it was being developed viewed some of these compromises with dismay. Federica Gioia argues, for instance, that 'despite the ambitious objectives set forth in the preamble of the Statute, the ICC still pays too great a tribute to state sovereignty',[133] while Frédéric Mégret notes that human rights NGOs, in particular, found the Statute's 'compromises' to 'have been fundamentally unrepresentative of the state of international law, or at least at variance with the better objectives of international criminal justice'.[134] In the end, many in the NGO community came to embrace complementarity, but largely as a strategic concession: by supporting it as a mechanism that could curtail the ICC, political support could be marshalled for other critical proposals (for instance, the granting of powers to the prosecutor to initiate investigations *proprio motu*, i.e., on her own accord).[135] Ultimately though, the Statute was a 'bargained document', one in which the complementarity principle emerged less as a catalytic instrument than as protector of a classical principle of international law: sovereignty.[136]

[133] Gioia, 'State Sovereignty, Jurisdiction, and "Modern" International Law', 1096; see also Mohamed El Zeidy, 'The Principle of Complementarity: A New Machinery to Implement International Criminal Law', *Michigan Journal of International Law* 23 (2001–2002), 869.

[134] Frédéric Mégret, 'Implementation and the Uses of Complementarity', in *The International Criminal Court and Complementarity*, 374. For a similar characterization of the negotiations, see Gerry Simpson, '"Throwing a Little Remembering on the Past": The International Criminal Court and the Politics of Sovereignty', *University of California Davis Journal of International Law and Policy* 5(2) (1999).

[135] Even if opinion was more divided earlier in the earlier period of negotiations, by the time of the PREPCOM in 1997 many of the principal NGOs engaged in negotiations were largely supportive of complementarity. See, e.g., Human Rights Watch, 'Justice in the Balance: Recommendations for an Independent and Effective International Criminal Court' (June 1998) (noting that 'codification and application of the Statute's complementarity principle … is key to the functioning of the [ICC]' and that 'one by-product of an effective and independent court should be to encourage national authorities themselves to investigate the crimes within the jurisdiction of the court, and the consequent strengthening of national judicial systems'), 69. Michael Struett also notes that, while debate on the meaning of complementarity became 'more complex and sophisticated' during the course of PREPCOM negotiations, NGOs 'hammered away at the importance of designing the complementarity jurisdiction in such a way that it would not permit states to shield accused persons for political reasons', 98. See Michael Struett, *The Politics of Constructing the International Criminal Court: NGOs, Discourse, and Agency* (Palgrave Macmillan, 2008).

[136] Schiff, *Building the International Criminal* Court, 79, 85. See also Markus Benzing, 'The Complementarity Regime of the International Criminal Court: International Criminal Justice between State Sovereignty and the Fight against Impunity', *Max Planck Yearbook of United Nations Law* 7 (2003), 591–632, 595 ('The most apparent underlying interest that the complementarity regime of the court [was] designed to protect and serve is the *sovereignty* both of state parties and third states'.) (emphasis in original).

2   From Constraint to Catalyst: The Evolution of Complementarity

The drafting history recounted above affirms that the Rome Statute was the result of extensive negotiation and compromise. The decision to vest the ICC with jurisdiction secondary to that of domestic courts was critical: states insisted upon it, even if many advocates had, at least initially, hoped that the new institution would possess the same jurisdictional primacy enjoyed by the ICTY and ICTR. So understood, complementarity was thought to primarily be an instrument of limitation, a 'technical term of art for a priority rule set out in Article 17 of the Rome Statute'.[137]

Early ICC Policy: The Office of the Prosecutor

Notwithstanding these earlier compromises, a 'thicker' notion of the complementarity principle grew swiftly in the wake of the ICC coming formally into existence in the summer of 2002. While the court did not start functioning until late the following year – after prosecutor Moreno-Ocampo had been elected and other key staff appointed – a 'start-up team' within the OTP suggested that an expert consultation process on complementarity be convened early on, to consider the 'potential legal, policy and management challenges which are likely to confront the OTP as a consequence of the complementarity regime of the Statute'.[138] Comprised of experts drawn from a range of state, academic and NGO backgrounds – many of whom were part of the same epistemic community that had been engaged in early debates around the ICC and complementarity – the 'informal expert paper' that emerged from this process reflects the early seeds of a broader approach to complementarity. In its words, 'The principle of complementarity can magnify the effectiveness of the ICC beyond what it could achieve through its own prosecutions, as it prompts a network of over 90 states parties and other states to carry out consistent and rigorous national proceedings'.[139]

---

[137] Nouwen, *Complementarity in the Line of Fire*, 14.
[138] 'Informal expert paper: The principle of complementarity in practice', ICC-OTP (2003), 2, at www.icc-cpi.int/iccdocs/doc/doc654724.PDF. For a detailed accounting of the history behind this exercise, see Morten Bergsmo and SONG Tianying, 'The Principle of Complementarity in Practice', in Morten Bergsmo, Klaus Rackwitz and SONG Tianying (eds.), *Historical Origins of International Criminal Law: Volume 5* (Brussels: Torkel Opsahl Academic EPublisher, 2017), 739–798.
[139] Ibid., 4.

As a matter of 'respect for the primary jurisdiction of states' and of the limits on the number of prosecutions the ICC could 'feasibly conduct', the paper took as its premise that the complementarity regime 'serves as a mechanism *to encourage and facilitate* the compliance of states with their primary responsibility to investigate and prosecute core crimes'.[140] The report argued that two principles should guide this approach: (1) partnership, which may include 'possibly provid[ing] advice and certain forms of assistance to facilitate national efforts', as well as situations where the OTP and a state 'agree that a consensual division of labour is in the best interest of justice'; and (2) vigilance, which 'marks the converse principle ... that where there is an indicia that a national process is not genuine, the prosecutor must be poised to take follow-up steps, leading if necessary to an exercise of jurisdiction'.[141]

The distinction between partnership and vigilance indexed an emergent distinction between complementarity as a contentious, coercive principle and as the framework for a more consensual, managerial relationship between the court and national jurisdictions. For the latter, the paper envisioned a range of direct assistance and advice functions, including 'exchang[ing] information and evidence to facilitate a national investigation or prosecution', providing technical advice (the OTP would, it was presumed, 'build up a unique and unparalleled in-house expertise') and training.[142] As to its 'vigilance function', the paper noted that 'certain background contextual information ... may be gathered in order to inform an admissibility assessment under either the 'unwillingness' or 'inability' branches' of the Statute. Such contextual information might include a state's legislative framework '(offences, jurisdiction, procedures, defences)'; 'specific jurisdictional regimes (military tribunals)'; and the 'legal regime of due process standards'.[143] Factors affecting the inability test could include a 'lack of judicial infrastructure', as well as a 'lack of substantive or procedural penal legislation rendering [the criminal justice] system "unavailable"'.[144]

In this indexing, the expert paper articulated a number of possible indicia that have assumed a more determinative character over time in the course of their uptake in scholarship and a range of advocacy

---

[140] Ibid., 3.
[141] Ibid., 4.
[142] Ibid., 5–6.
[143] Ibid., 13–14; 28–31.
[144] Ibid., 15. At the same time, the paper noted that "The standard for showing inability should be a stringent one, as the ICC is not a human rights monitoring body, and its role is not to ensure perfect procedures and compliance with all international standards'. Ibid.

materials developed by NGOs. Furthermore, it painted an early picture of both the coercive and cooperative dimensions of complementarity and of the OTP's wide-ranging and discretionary role in its application. To that end, the office's first policy paper, also published in 2003, emphasized that a 'major part of [its] external relations and outreach strategy ... [would] be to encourage and facilitate states to carry out their primary responsibility of investigating and prosecuting crimes'.[145] The paper further developed the idea of a division-of-labour relationship between the court and national jurisdictions, noting that it 'will encourage national prosecutions, where possible for the lower-ranking perpetrators, or work with the international community to ensure that the offenders are brought to justice'.[146] Such an approach suggested a two-tiered arrangement between the ICC and states, with those 'most responsible' being prosecuted in The Hague. Architecturally, the OTP reflected the prioritization of this policy as well. The establishment of a separate division responsible for jurisdiction and complementarity issues (the Jurisdiction, Complementarity and Cooperation Division, JCCD) underscored the importance attached to this aspect of the office's work.[147]

Emergent Theories: Complementarity as Cooperation and Coercion

From the outset, then, complementarity's potential was understood as more than a tool for regulating jurisdiction, but also, as 'a forum for managerial interaction between the court and states'.[148] This 'systemic dimension' of complementarity, Stahn argues, 'institutes a legal system under which the court and domestic jurisdictions are meant to complement and reinforce each other in their mutual efforts to institutionalize accountability for mass crimes'.[149] Scholars have offered different descriptions to explain this imagined relationship. The ICC as 'backstopping' national courts has been a more passive iteration, while the court as a 'reinforcement' mechanism has been another.[150]

---

[145] 'Paper on some policy issues before the Office of the Prosecutor', 5.
[146] Ibid., 3.
[147] The JCCD's function is discussed further in Chapter 4. Notably, the establishment of the division was not without controversy, as some critics saw it as unduly politicizing OTP's role. See, e.g., Schiff, *Building the International Criminal Court*, 113–115.
[148] Stahn, 'A Tale of Two Notions', 88.
[149] Ibid., 91.
[150] Anne-Marie Slaughter and William Burke-White, 'The Future of International Law Is Domestic (or, The European Way of Law)', *Harvard International law Journal* 47(2) (Summer 2006), 122.

By contrast, a catalytic relationship is more active in its design. Burke-White, for instance, has argued that 'international and domestic institutions are engaged in complex interactions whereby the international level, and particularly the ICC's complementarity regime, may catalyse changes at the national level'.[151] Likewise, referencing complementarity's dynamic component, Stahn has written that 'complementarity serves as a catalyst for compliance by virtue of the construction of Articles 17 and 19 of the Rome Statute'.[152] And, as previously noted, Kleffner argues that complementarity should be a 'catalyst for compliance', insofar as it is 'understood as aiming to induce and facilitate the compliance of states with their obligation "to exercise [their] criminal jurisdiction over those responsible for international crimes", which underlies the Rome Statute'.[153]

Cooperation: Technical Assistance, Burden Sharing and Capacity-Building

Kleffner's reference to inducement and facilitation again suggests two different models for the court's role as a catalyst for compliance: one coercive, the other cooperative.[154] In the latter, the ICC's relationship with domestic jurisdiction is compliance-driven, but fundamentally beneficent. The court and national jurisdictions complement each other not only in a 'negative' dynamic, wherein the ICC's competences are engaged by the absence (or non-genuineness) of state action, but 'also

---

[151] William W. Burke-White, 'Complementarity in Practice: The International Criminal Court as Part of a System of Multi-level Global Governance in the Democratic Republic of Congo', *Leiden Journal of International Law* 18 (2005), 568. See also William W. Burke-White, 'Proactive Complementarity: The International Criminal Court and National Courts in the Rome System of International Justice', *Harvard International Law Journal* 49(1) (Winter 2008). Burke-White argues, 'As a strategy for encouraging national governments to undertake their own prosecutions of international crimes, proactive complementarity would allow the court to catalyze national judiciaries to fulfill their own obligations to prosecute international crimes', 57.
[152] Stahn, 'A Tale of Two Notions', 92.
[153] Kleffner, 'Complementarity as a Catalyst for Compliance', 80.
[154] Stigen echoes this two-sided approach, noting that 'The complementarity principle seeks to enhance national jurisdictions partly by stimulating and partly by applying pressure', 17. See also Rod Rastan, 'Complementarity: Contest or Collaboration', in Morten Bergsmo (ed.), *Complementarity and the Exercise of Universal Jurisdiction for Core International Crimes* (Oslo: Torkel Opsahl Academic EPublisher, 2010). Rastan contends that 'limiting complementarity to a contest paradigm will prevent the realization of the statutory goal to put an end to impunity and thereby contribute to the prevention of crimes', 84.

in a positive fashion, i.e., through mutual assistance and interaction'.[155] This policy of 'positive' complementarity received early endorsement from the OTP. As Stahn argues, however, 'positive' complementarity is not only a policy invention; it is also an 'inherent concept of the Statute', reflected, for instance, in its cooperation regime.[156] Thus, 'positive' complementarity is 'focused on problem-solving, i.e., the ability of the court to strengthen domestic jurisdictions and to organize a division of labour based on "comparative advantages"'.[157]

Even if it was 'hardly … contemplated by all the [Rome Statute] negotiators', numerous commentators and jurists have endorsed this approach to complementarity.[158] Former ICC judge Mauro Politi, for instance, notes that there is 'no doubt' that one important goal of complementarity 'is to establish a division of labour between national jurisdictions and the ICC, under which the court should essentially concentrate on those who have major responsibility for the crimes involved'.[159] Cherif Bassiouni likewise identified that an 'important ancillary function of the ICC is to prod national jurisdictions to assume their international legal obligations', which may extend to the court providing technical assistance and capacity-building support to national criminal justice systems.[160] Cooperation also animates complementarity's affinity with a 'managerial model of compliance', or a 'global compliance system for the enforcement of international criminal law',[161] wherein the ICC and states participate in a 'cooperative venture to ensure accountability of perpetrators'.[162] Gioia

[155] Stahn, 'Taking Complementarity Seriously', 260. As discussed further in the following chapter, this dimension of complementarity also finds statutory support in Article 93(10) of the Statute.
[156] Ibid., 236. Nouwen similarly contends that the Statute's cooperation regime is what effectuates a policy of assisting domestic jurisdictions; in her view, 'such a policy of assisting domestic jurisdictions is not inherent in complementarity'. *Complementarity in the Line of Fire*, 97–98.
[157] Ibid., 260–261.
[158] Stigen, 476.
[159] Mauro Politi, 'Reflections on Complementarity at the Rome Conference and Beyond', in *The International Criminal Court and Complementarity*, 145.
[160] M. Cherif Bassiouni, 'The ICC – *Quo Vadis?*', *Journal of International Criminal Justice* 4 (2006), 422.
[161] Rastan, 'Complementarity', 131. See also Emilie Hunter, 'Using "Managerial Compliance" to Strengthen the International Criminal Court Cooperation Regime', in Olympia Bekou and Daley J. Birkett (eds.), *Cooperation and the International Criminal Court: Perspectives from Theory and Practice* (Brill Nijhoff, 2016), 366–395.
[162] Kleffner, *Complementarity in the Rome Statute and National Criminal Jurisdictions*, 311.

likewise writes that 'A "friendly" version of complementarity relies on the assumption that the ICC is not meant to act as a censor of national jurisdictions, but rather to allow for the most efficient sharing of competencies between the national and international level'.[163]

Burke-White's scholarship is amongst the most well-known and influential articulation of the ICC's relationship to national jurisdictions, casting it explicitly in catalytic terms. A 2005 article on the influence of the ICC in the DRC posited that the court was not merely an institution acting against domestic states, but rather part of a 'multi-level global governance model', one that also 'participates in the domestic process, altering political as well as legal outcomes'.[164] As part of such a multi-level system, his elaboration of a 'Rome system of justice' is rooted in a 'virtuous circle in which the court stimulates the exercise of domestic jurisdiction through the threat of international intervention'.[165] This invocation of the ICC as the apex of an organic judicial chain (the 'virtuous circle'), while also recognizing its coercive properties (the 'threat of international intervention'), comes together in the idea of 'proactive complementarity', in which the ICC 'can and should encourage, and perhaps even assist, national governments to prosecute international crimes'.[166]

Burke-White's writing – part of a growth of scholarly interest on the impact of the ICTY's proceedings on domestic jurisdictions more generally – also drew heavily on the introduction of a completion strategy for the tribunal to support the notion of shared responsibility between national and international courts.[167] Characterizing the completion strategy as a catalytic force for domestic accountability in states like Bosnia and Serbia, he argued that such an approach could be instructive for the ICC's complementarity regime. In his words, 'The structural changes in the ICTY's jurisdiction and mandate undertaken as part of the completion strategy essentially shifted the governance structure from one of absolute international primacy toward a new relationship with incentives similar to those of complementarity'.[168] These changes occurred in the

---

[163] Federica Gioia, 'Complementarity and "Reverse Cooperation"', in *The International Criminal Court and Complementarity*, 817.
[164] Burke-White, 'Complementarity in Practice', 559.
[165] Burke-White, 'Proactive Complementarity', 57.
[166] Ibid., 56.
[167] See, e.g., Burke-White, 'The Domestic Influence of International Criminal Tribunals'.
[168] Ibid., 320.

same period as the ICC's operations began to take shape, contributing to the developing concept of 'positive' complementarity.[169] Under the completion strategy the ICTY's Rules of Procedure and Evidence were amended, such that the tribunal could effectively incentivize domestic institutions by referring cases back to national jurisdictions, monitoring proceedings and ultimately taking cases back to the international forum if certain targets of due process were not met.[170] UN Security Council Resolution 1503, issued in August 2003, endorsed the tribunal's strategy and called upon the international community to 'assist national jurisdictions, as part of the completion strategy, in improving their capacity to prosecute cases transferred from the ICTY'.[171] Coordinating mechanisms initially set out in the 1996 Rome Agreement, which governed the relationship between the ICTY and local courts, were likewise strengthened under the so-called 'rules of the road', with the tribunal, after years of delay, fulfilling its obligation to review locally initiated cases before an arrest warrant could be issued by domestic authorities.[172]

---

[169] For a trenchant critique of Rule11*bis* analogies to the ICC, see Padraig McAuliffe, 'Bad Analogy: Why the Divergent Institutional Imperatives of the Ad Hoc Tribunals and the ICC Make the Lessons of Rule 11*bis* Inapplicable to the ICC's Complementarity Regime', *International Organizations Law Review* 11 (2014), 345–427.

[170] There is an abundant literature on the so-called Rule 11*bis* 'referrals' and their impact on domestic jurisdictions in former Yugoslavia. For further discussion, see Fausto Pocar, 'Completion or Continuation Strategy? Appraising Problems and Possible Developments in Building the Legacy of the ICTY', *Journal of International Criminal Justice* 6 (2008), 655–665; David Tolbert and Aleksandar Kontic, 'The International Criminal Tribunal for the Former Yugoslavia and the Transfer of Cases and Materials to National Judicial Authorities: Lessons in Complementarity' and Fidelma Donlon, 'Positive Complementarity in Practice: ICTY Rule11*bis* and the Use of the Tribunal's Evidence in the Srebrenica Trials before the Bosnian War Crimes Chamber', both in *The International Criminal Court and Complementarity*, 888–954. For a more sober assessment of the ICTY's engagement with domestic institutions, see Yaël Ronen, 'The Impact of the ICTY on Atrocity-Related Prosecutions in the Courts of Bosnia and Herzegovina', *Penn State Journal of Law & International Affairs* 3(1) (2014), 113–160.

[171] United Nations Security Council Resolution 1503, S/RES/1503 (28 August 2003) at www.refworld.org/cgi-bin/texis/vtx/rwmain?docid=3f535ca64.

[172] For a thorough discussion of these developments and the ICTY's role on domestic war crimes prosecutions, see Lara J. Nettelfield, *Courting Democracy in Bosnia and Herzegovina: The Hague Tribunal's Impact in a Postwar State* (Cambridge: Cambridge University Press, 2010). For an early assessment of the 'rules of the road', see also Mark S. Ellis, 'Bringing Justice to an Embattled Region – Creating and Implementing the "Rules of the Road" for Bosnia-Herzegovina', *Berkeley Journal of International Law* 17(1) (1999), 1–25.

This approach found early endorsement in OTP policy. 'Positive' complementarity was described as a deliberate way to promote national proceedings through the provision of information to states, advice and the development of legal tools to empower domestic criminal jurisdictions.[173] The metaphor of catalyst was also embraced by those affiliated with the office. In the words of Juan Mendez, the OTP's then special advisor on crime prevention, 'Under its policy of positive complementarity, the OTP can act as a catalyst for national action'.[174]

The division-of-labour approach to cooperation as a means towards this end was also closely linked to the OTP's policy of 'invited' referrals under Article 14. The 2006 report of the office stated, for instance, that, over the course of the first three years (2003–2006), it had adopted a formal policy 'of inviting and welcoming voluntary referrals by territorial states as a first step in triggering the jurisdiction of the court'.[175] As described in detail in Chapter 6, such a division of labour was the explicit basis for seeking the DRC government's referral, where it was made clear that the OTP's role was to prosecute senior leaders and those 'most responsible', while domestic authorities would handle other responsible actors. More recent statements by Prosecutor Bensouda suggest a similar approach to other situations. After the OTP did not contest the Libyan state's admissibility challenges, for instance, Bensouda told the UN Security Council that 'Joint complementary efforts of both the government of Libya and the ICC, strongly and actively supported by the international community, are … crucial for ending impunity in the country'.[176] She further added that her office would 'prioritise its investigations and prosecution of those who are outside the territory of Libya and who are thus largely inaccessible to the Libyan authorities', while the government would focus on those suspects within Libyan territory.

---

[173] Office of the Prosecutor, 'Report on the activities performed during the first three years (June 2003–June 2006)', ICC-OTP (12 September 2006), 22–23.
[174] Juan Méndez, 'Justice and Prevention', in *The International Criminal Court and Complementarity*, 33.
[175] OTP Report 2003–2006, 7.
[176] To that end, the OTP and the Libyan government 'concluded a burden-sharing memorandum of understanding, the purpose of which is to facilitate our collaborative efforts to ensure that individuals allegedly responsible for committing crimes in Libya as of 15 February 2011 are brought to justice either at the ICC or in Libya itself'. See 'Statement of the Prosecutor of the International Criminal Court, Fatou Bensouda, to the United Nations Security Council on the situation in Libya, pursuant to UNSCR 1970 (2011)' (remarks delivered in New York, 14 November 2013).

Coercion: Complementarity as Duty and Threat

Coercion, in which the threat of ICC intervention is meant to function as a leveraging device on national jurisdictions, has arguably been the more predominant iteration of complementarity, rooted as it is in a compliance-oriented model of state interaction with the Court. Stigen, for instance, has posited that the court's catalytic effect is fundamentally one of ICC avoidance. In his words, 'An ICC finding that the territorial state or the suspect's home state is unwilling or unable to proceed genuinely may well be perceived as a considerable stigma that states will seek to avoid'.[177] In order to avoid such stigma, states would be compelled to act. Similarly, in his early work, Bruce Broomhall suggested that the ICC would 'spur' on national prosecutions in order to avoid 'adverse attention, the diplomatic entanglements, the duty to cooperate and other consequences of ICC activity'.[178]

Kleffner's work on complementarity also explored the principle's coercive potential, 'as a mechanism through which states parties are induced to and facilitated in complying with [the] obligation [to investigate and prosecute ICC crimes]'.[179] In his view,

> [T]he novelty of complementarity lies in the fact that, for the first time in the history of international criminal law, states parties have agreed ex ante that this failure [to investigate and prosecute] will entail a concrete legal consequence: states forfeiting the claim to exercise jurisdiction, including over their own nationals and officials.[180]

Kleffner's conception of the court's role is similarly compliance oriented. In his words, the ICC 'can generate a pull-effect towards complying with the obligation to investigate and prosecute'.[181] One reason for this anticipated effect is, he contends, the court's 'high degree of legitimacy', and its potential as a vehicle to 'bestow legitimacy on national

---

[177] At the same time, Stigen correctly notes that the auto-referrals of Uganda and the DRC to the ICC suggest that, at least in some cases, 'being labelled as unable is something that some states can live well with', 475.

[178] Bruce Broomhall, *International Justice and the International Criminal Court: Between Sovereignty and the Rule of Law* (Oxford: Oxford University Press, 2003), 84, 87.

[179] Kleffner, *Complementarity in the Rome Statute and National Criminal Jurisdictions*, 309.

[180] Ibid., 319–320.

[181] Ibid., 311; see also Patricia Soares, 'Positive Complementarity and the Law Enforcement Network: Drawing Lessons from the Ad Hoc Tribunals' Completion Strategy', *Israel Law Review* 46(3) (2013), 320–322 (characterizing 'positive complementarity' as 'a "binding policy" or a "quasi legal" imposition insofar as it gives effect to core principles of the ICC Statute').

proceedings', which further 'generates a pull towards compliance'.[182] Additionally, in his view, the 'procedural setting of complementarity contains elements of an interaction between the court and national criminal jurisdictions, which may serve to induce states to carry out investigations and prosecutions'.[183] A final reason is the threat of sanction, which 'finds support in the largely *antagonist premise* on which the regime of complementarity is based'.[184]

As with 'positive' complementarity, the experience of the tribunals in Rwanda and the former Yugoslavia also played an influential role in elaborating the catalytic potential of 'jurisdictional forfeiture'. The ICTR, like the ICTY, amended its Rules of Procedure and Evidence in 2004 under pressure from the UN Security Council, in order to allow the referral of cases from the tribunal to 'competent national jurisdictions, as appropriate, including Rwanda'.[185] Notably, the requirement of a fair trial was explicitly included amongst the conditions that had to be satisfied for such referrals, which contributed in turn to the 2007 passage of a national law in Rwanda that sought to implement the ICTR's due process standards (including abolition of the death penalty).[186] Notwithstanding this accommodation,

---

[182] Ibid., 313. Kleffner sees the ICC as carrying both procedural and substantive legitimacy, insofar as it 'is based on the *specific consent of states* to the Rome Statute', while also safeguarding the sovereignty of states, 'in as much as it reaffirms rather than encroaches upon their primary role in the investigation and prosecution of core crimes', 311, 314. Further, complementarity 'benefits from a large degree of determinacy' and 'leaves no doubt' that 'the sole role of the ICC is to supply the deficiencies of national criminal jurisdictions', 315.

[183] Kleffner, 'Complementarity as a Catalyst for Compliance', 82.

[184] Kleffner, *Complementarity in the Rome Statute and National Criminal Jurisdictions*, 320.

[185] UNSC Resolution 1503, preambular para. 8; Rule11*bis* of the ICTR's rules was so amended in April 2004. As with the ICTY, there is a similarly abundant literature on the ICTR's referral process and its impact at the national and local level in Rwanda. For a fuller treatment see L. J. van den Herik, *The Contribution of the Rwanda Tribunal to the Development of International Law* (Leiden: Martinus Nijhoff, 2005); Jesse Melman, 'The Possibility of Transfer(?): A Comprehensive Approach to the International Criminal Tribunal for Rwanda's Rule 11*bis* to Permit Transfer to Rwandan Domestic Courts', *Fordham Law Review* 79(3) (2011), 1271–1332.

[186] See Organic Law no. 11/2007 of 16 March 2007 Concerning Transfer of Cases to the Republic of Rwanda from the International Criminal Tribunal for Rwanda, Official Gazette of the Republic of Rwanda, 19 March 2007; the law has subsequently been amended. For a fuller exploration of the 2007 law and domestic accountability in Rwanda, see Phil Clark, *The Gacaca Courts, Post-Genocide Justice and Reconciliation in Rwanda: Justice without Lawyers* (Cambridge: Cambridge University Press, 2010). For an incisive reading of the death penalty's abolition as more than the result of top-down pressure from the ICTR, see Audrey Boctor, 'The Abolition of the Death Penalty in Rwanda', *Human Rights Review* 10 (2009), 99–118.

the tribunal denied the first five requests for transfer to Rwanda, using the antagonist premise on which the primacy regime was based to strengthen, ostensibly, fair trial guarantees at the domestic level.[187]

Under this threat-based approach, complementarity's catalytic potential rests on several presumptions. One presumption is that states would necessarily want to avoid the ICC, or that the political costs of pursuing domestic prosecutions will necessarily prevail over the desire to keep the court at bay. The cooperative dimensions of complementarity might also stifle its coercive potential, insofar as a state could seek the ICC's assistance (as was initially the case in Uganda and the DRC), or may seek to 'offload' complex cases to another judicial forum. Robinson makes a similar point when he acknowledges that 'an over-strong regime might resist ICC intervention as a *threat to* government, [while] an under-strong government might welcome impartial and effective intervention as a *reinforcement of governance*'.[188] Here again, then, the ICC may not be a court of 'last resort' as it is so often described, but rather a *forum conveniens* for a government who might turn to the court to bolster its own authority.

The ICC's coercive capacities have been taken up as part of the OTP's approach to complementarity. In his first address to the Assembly of States Parties (ASP), the ICC prosecutor noted that 'due to the dissuasive effect that the mere existence of the court generates, the possibility of presenting a case at the International Criminal Court could convince some states with serious conflicts to take the appropriate action'.[189] Furthermore, one sees in the office's approach to certain situation countries a more adversarial approach towards domestic jurisdictions. In Uganda, for instance, later attempts by the government to negotiate with the Lord's Resistance Army clashed with the ICC's outstanding arrest warrants. Similarly, in Kenya, the prosecutor adopted a threat-based approach to complementarity in an attempt to force the government to establish a domestic tribunal to prosecute its post-election violence. These histories are examined more fully in later chapters.

---

[187] See 'Complementarity in Action: Lessons Learned from the ICTR Prosecutor's Referral of International Criminal Cases to National Jurisdictions for Trial', International Criminal Tribunal for Rwanda (February 2015), para. 43, at www.unictr.org/sites/unictr.org/files/legal-library/150210_complementarity_in_action.pdf. For a critical analysis of the ICTR's referral jurisprudence, see Nicola Palmer, 'Transfer or Transformation: A Review of the Rule 11*bis* Decisions of the International Criminal Tribunal for Rwanda', *African Journal of International and Comparative Law* 20(1) (2012).
[188] Robinson, 'The Controversy over Territorial State Referrals and Reflections on ICL Discourse', 383.
[189] Press Release, 'ICC – Election of the Prosecutor, Statement by Mr. Moreno- Ocampo', ICC-OTP-20030502-10 (22 April 2003).

3   A Catalyst for Compliance: The 'Duties' of Complementarity

Complementarity's power to advance domestic accountability relies upon a duty-based reading of the Rome Statute. These duties have commonly been understood to encompass not only the prosecution of serious crimes through national criminal fora, but also the domestic implementation of the Rome Statute's substantive and procedural provisions. Most commentators root these duties in a purposive reading of the Statute, particularly its pre-ambular language, which recalls 'that it is the duty of every state to exercise its criminal jurisdiction over those responsible for international crimes'.[190] As Padraig McAuliffe has noted, 'the open-ended and aspirational language of the preamble', in particular, supports a 'teleological impulse to apply expansive modes of interpretation to admissibility provisions in the interest of maximizing the impact of its main institution, the ICC'.[191] Much of the literature cited above exemplifies this teleological impulse.

In fact, as its drafting history illustrates, there is no provision on states parties' prosecutorial duties in the operative part of the Statute.[192] While states may be obliged to investigate or prosecute crimes based on *other* rules of international law, the Statute itself obliges states only to cooperate with the court (as part IX of the treaty enumerates), to ensure that its

---

[190] Para. 6, Rome Statute. See, e.g., Gioia, 'State Sovereignty, Jurisdiction, and "Modern" International Law', 1113. Gioia states that only investigations and prosecutions that 'abide by the highest standards of fair trial' can be regarded as 'proper implementation of the obligations at stake [in the Rome Statute]', and that 'failure to comply with such standards should be construed as tantamount to failing to perform the obligation and result in the court legitimately stepping in'.

[191] Padraig McAuliffe, 'From Watchdog to Workhorse: Explaining the Emergence of the ICC's Burden-sharing Policy as an Example of Creeping Cosmopolitanism', *Chinese Journal of International Law* 13 (2014), 294. See also Darryl Robinson, 'The Identity Crisis of International Law', *Leiden Journal of International Law* 21 (2008), 944–946 (noting that, through 'victim-focused teleological reasoning aggravated by utopian aspirations', ICL seeks to 'end' crime rather than merely manage it); Nouwen, *Complementarity in the Line of Fire*, 241 ('Many members of the international-criminal-justice movement interpreted the Statute on the basis more of their functional biases than of the international rules of interpretation as codified in the Vienna Convention on the Law of Treaties. The biases of international experts stem from their background in international fora and favour the international: an international court, international crimes and international standards'.).

[192] See, e.g., Payam Akhavan, 'Whither National Courts? The Rome Statute's Missing Half', *Journal of International Criminal Justice* 8(5) (2010); Anja Seibert-Fohr, 'The Relevance of the Rome Statute of the International Criminal Court for Amnesties and Truth Commissions', in A. von Bogdandy and R. Wolfrim (eds.), *Max Planck Yearbook of United Nations Law* 7 (Koninklijke Brill, 2003), 559.

domestic law facilitates cooperation with the ICC and that offences against the 'administration of justice' be criminalized domestically.[193] Furthermore, as a matter of treaty interpretation, the preambular recital was deliberately not made part of the Statute's operative text; rather, it merely 'recalls' a suggested pre-existing duty, not one arising from the treaty itself.[194] As Nouwen notes, the recital itself 'merely reflects an aspiration, just like many of the other preambular considerations'.[195]

With respect to implementation, there is also no positive obligation on member states to implement the Rome Statute's substantive (or procedural) provisions.[196] Alain Pellet (himself a member of the ILC that authored the 1994 draft Statute) states, 'neither the signatory states nor even the states parties have any clear obligations to bring their domestic legislation into harmony with the basic provisions of the Rome Statute'.[197] Indeed, as noted during the drafting of Article 20(3) on *ne bis in idem*,

---

[193] Such rules may arise under relevant human rights treaties that impose a duty to criminalize and investigate, see, e.g., UN Convention Against Torture (Articles 4, 5 and 7) and the International Convention for the Protection of all Persons from Enforced Disappearance (Arts. 4, 6, 9 and 11). Regional human rights treaties may also impose such obligations: the Inter-American Court on Human Rights has held that '[t]he state has a legal duty ... to use the means at its disposal to carry out a serious investigation of violations committed within its jurisdiction, to identify those responsible, to impose the appropriate punishment and to ensure the victim adequate compensation'. *Velásquez Rodriguez v. Honduras* (29 July 1988), para. 174; the European Court of Human Rights has affirmed a similar line of jurisprudence, see, e.g., *Al-Skeini and others v. U.K.*, Grand Chamber Judgment (7 July 2011), para. 167. See also Diane Orentlicher, 'Settling Accounts: The Duty to Prosecute Human Rights Violations of a Prior Regime', *Yale Law Review* 100 (1991), 2539–2615. Arguably, customary international law may also impose a duty to investigate and prosecute. See, e.g., International Law Commission, *Second Report on the Obligation to Extradite or Prosecute*, para. 26, UN Doc. A/CN.4/585 (11 June 2007); but see Kieran McEvoy and Louise Mallinder, 'Amnesties in Transition: Punishment, Restoration, and the Governance of Mercy', *Journal of Law and Society* 39(3) (2012), 419 ('[I]n relation to international crimes regulated by international customary law, it appears that the best that can be argued at present is that the duty to prosecute is *permissive*, rather than mandatory, which leaves more discretion for states to explore alternative approaches to truth and accountability'.).
[194] Robinson, 'The Mysterious Mysteriousness of Complementarity', 94–95.
[195] Nouwen, *Complementarity in the Line of Fire*, 39.
[196] Article 88, Rome Statute.
[197] Alain Pellet, 'Entry Into Force and Amendment of the Statute', in Antonio Cassese, Paola Gaeta and John R. W. D. Jones (eds.), *The Rome Statute of the International Criminal Court: A Commentary, Vol. 1* (Oxford University Press, 2002), 153; see also Alexander K. A. Greenawalt, 'The Pluralism of International Criminal Law', *Indiana Law Journal* 86 (2011), 1128 ('[T]he ICC's complementarity process need not require domestic courts prosecuting ICL offenses to incorporate the entirety of the Rome Statute's law'.).

states explicitly rejected a proposal that would have made a case admissible before the ICC where the national proceeding failed to consider the international character or grave nature of a crime. Instead, the Statute refers to the 'same conduct' of an accused, 'to make clear that a national prosecution of a crime – international or ordinary – did not prohibit ICC retrial for charges based on different conduct'.[198]

In a related vein, the difference between 'ordinary' and international crimes has also been advanced as a basis for domestic implementation. In the context of the ICC, Kleffner has again been one of the strongest proponents of this position. He argues that:

> Implementation can only be considered satisfactory if it comprehensively and effectively covers the entire range of conduct criminalized by the Rome Statute, without adversely affecting pre-existing obligations under international law that go beyond the Rome Statute, and while taking into account the need to fill gaps in the legislation that may lead to impunity, such as those resulting from the absence of universal jurisdiction.[199]

Key ICC actors also endorsed this view early on. Silvana Arbia, the court's former registrar, writes:

> Without [implementing legislation], states could be left in the position of prosecuting only for some of the constitutive acts of the crimes, such as murder and rape. This could undermine the basis of national prosecutions and may invite the ICC's Judges to take jurisdiction where this might not be needed.[200]

Arbia's qualification that the ICC might 'take jurisdiction' grants that such an outcome is not mandatory, but the language of both she and Kleffner is threat based: failure to conform with the Rome Statute risks forfeiture at the national level.

Influential non-state actors have advanced similarly expansive interpretations. Of particular relevance are individuals whose organizations often act as a bridge between academic or policy communities and advocacy-oriented organizations engaged in accountability work. For instance, Mark Ellis, who serves as executive director of the International Bar Association

---

[198] Heller, 'A Sentence-Based Theory of Complementarity', 224. That said, as Robinson notes, it may be 'prudent to ensure that [a state's] criminal laws are at least as broad as the subject matter jurisdiction of the ICC'. It is not, however, required. See Darryl Robinson, 'Three Theories of Complementarity: Charge, Sentence, or Process?', *Harvard International Law Journal*, 53 (April 2012), 169, fn. 25.

[199] Kleffner, *Complementarity in the Rome Statute and National Criminal Jurisdictions*, 112.

[200] Silvana Arbia and Giovanni Bassy, 'Proactive Complementarity: A Registrar's Perspective and Plans', in *The International Criminal Court and Complementarity*, 65.

(described as 'the world's leading organisation of international legal practitioners, bar associations and law societies'[201]), is unequivocal that state
failure to 'effectively incorporate the Rome Statute into its domestic body of
criminal and procedural law' would trigger a finding of 'inability' under the
Rome Statute.[202] In his view,

> [A] state party must incorporate the Rome Statute's substantive criminal
> law provisions into its domestic body of law. This is the complementarity
> part of the test. It requires states parties to take steps such as criminalizing
> all offences contained in the Statute, ensuring that the principle of com-
> mand responsibility is incorporated into domestic legislation, removing
> any statute of limitations for Rome Statute offences, and perhaps most
> importantly, denying immunity to heads of state.[203]

Similarly, David Donat Cattin, secretary-general of Parliamentarians for
Global Action (PGA) (a 'non-profit, non-partisan international network'
of legislators whose 'vision is to contribute to the creation of a rules-based
international order for a more equitable, safe and democratic world'[204]),
argues that the principle of complementarity 'implies that states shall
fully implement the Rome Statute in their domestic legal orders in order
to comply with their primary responsibility to realize the object and purpose of the treaty (and [Rome Statute] system)', which is to put an end to
impunity and deter future crime.[205] The PGA, in turn, describes complementarity as follows:

> Complementarity means that states have the primary obligation to inves-
> tigate and prosecute those responsible for international crimes, but also
> that the court will only intervene when states do not have the genuine
> will or the capacities to do so. ... To this effect, the first and minimal

---

[201] International Bar Association, 'About the IBA', at www.ibanet.org.

[202] Ellis, *Sovereignty and Justice*, 123.

[203] Ibid., 125. Curiously, later in his text, Ellis nevertheless appears to endorse the Libyan
government's admissibility challenge on the grounds that it is 'irrelevant' if the acts are
charged as 'ordinary crimes' pursuant to the Libyan criminal code. In so doing, he avers
that his 'position is supported by a number of jurists who have argued that the prosecution of international crimes using ordinary domestic law would satisfy a state's obligations under the Rome Statute', 211.

[204] Parliamentarians for Global Action, 'About Us – Overview', at www.pgaction.org/about/
overview.html.

[205] David Donat Cattin, 'Approximation or Harmonisation as a Result of Implementation of
the Rome Statute', in Larissa van den Herik and Carsten Stahn (eds.), *The Diversification
and Fragmentation of International Criminal Law* (Leiden: Martinus Nijhoff, 2012),
361–362. For a similar analysis, see Roberto Bellelli, 'Obligation to Cooperate and Duty
to Implement', in Roberto Bellelli (ed.), *International Criminal Justice: Law and Practice
from the Rome Statute to Its Review* (UK: Ashgate, 2010), 221.

condition enabling states to abide to this obligation of accountability for genocide, crimes against humanity, war crimes and crime of aggression is the existence of legislation that incorporates in their national law the crimes and general principles of law contained in the Rome Statute.[206]

As Chapter 5 illustrates, the PGA was amongst those international NGOs who played a crucial role in the implementation of the Statute in Uganda and Kenya, as well as the DRC.

Other views of complementarity encompass even more ambitious policy goals, including that domestic criminal justice systems satisfy 'international standards'.[207] Linking these goals to the juridical foundation of complementarity, Ellis contends that 'inability' as set forth in Article 17(3) should encompass states that 'lack the type of judicial systems that is required under the international standard of legal fairness, or have failed to incorporate implementing legislation necessary to cooperate with the court, or have failed to ensure fair trial proceedings'.[208] To that end, he has proposed the establishment of an international advisory group that could, at the request of the ICC or a state party, provide an 'objective, impartial and non-political evaluation regarding a state's ability to carry out judicial proceedings with international standards'.[209] In his view, questions this group should ask in making its assessments would include the following:

> Does the domestic court have extensive backlogs resulting in long pretrial detention? Does the state have a sufficient number of trained defence lawyers and an effective legal aid program for indigent defendants? Are there sufficient guarantees against outside pressure on the judiciary?

[206] 'Implementing Legislation on the Rome Statute', at www.pgaction.org/programmes/ilhr/icc-legislation.html.

[207] As with investigations and prosecutions, it is clear that the absence of due process and/or the failure to meet such standards is not grounds for admissibility under Article 17. For a convincing articulation of this view, see Kevin Jon Heller, 'The Shadow Side of Complementarity: The Effect of Article 17 of the Rome Statute on National Due Process', *Criminal Law Forum* 17 (2006), 255–280.

[208] Ellis, *Sovereignty and Justice*, 113. Elsewhere, Ellis has also argued that 'If [s]tates desire to retain control over prosecuting nationals charged with crimes under the ICC Statute, they must ensure that their own judicial systems meet international standards. At a minimum, states will have to adhere to standards of due process found in international human rights instruments, particularly as they relate to the rights of defendants'. See Mark S. Ellis, 'The International Criminal Court and Its Implication for Domestic Law and National Capacity Building', *Florida Journal of International Law* 15 (2002), 241.

[209] Mark S. Ellis, 'International Justice and the Rule of Law: Strengthening the ICC through Domestic Prosecutions', *Hague Journal on the Rule of Law* 1 (2009), 84. In the same article, Ellis also calls for the creation of an international technical assistance office, whose purpose would be to 'provide technical and unbiased assistance to domestic war crimes courts', 82.

Does the state impose the death penalty? Can the court provide witnesses and victims with medical, psychological and material support during and after trial through a witness and victim support office? Can the court provide these same witnesses and victim security protection prior to, during and after the trial? Is there ongoing political strife and repression in the country? Does the state have detention facilities that meet international standards?[210]

While such ambitious criteria could be asked of any country's criminal justice system, here the language of complementarity animates them. 'Positive' complementarity is also summoned by many human rights and rule-of-law actors in their efforts to engage criminal justice sector reform more broadly. For instance, at a 2011 workshop on witness protection held in Uganda, a paper prepared by the UN's Office of the High Commissioner for Human Rights drew explicitly on the ICC, noting that the court has 'emphasized the importance of witness protection in recent decisions, demonstrating that [it] is a key concern'. To that end, and 'in line with the doctrine of positive complementarity, the application of witness protection standards by the court will serve a great role in demonstrating adequate capacity, competence and credibility' of Ugandan courts.[211] Similarly, a report of the Institute for Security Studies argues that Uganda 'must now consider *the requirements* of ICC complementarity'.[212] In its words, 'the creation of a witness protection programme is a critical element of ICC complementarity considerations', as it 'may well be a future driver of African protection mechanisms'.[213] A July 2018 paper from the International Bar Association likewise insists that under Article 17, the assessment of national proceedings should, 'de minimis, cover ... [an] evaluation of compliance with principles of due process recognised by international law'.[214]

---

[210] Ibid., 85.
[211] This quoted material was included in OHCHR's concept note for the victim and witness protection workshop, held in August 2011 (on-file).
[212] Chris Mahony, 'The justice sector afterthought: Witness protection in Africa' (Pretoria: Institute for Security Studies, 2010), xi (emphasis added).
[213] Ibid. Other commentators have gone further, suggesting that the failure to provide 'gender sensitive' witness protection could also be a form of inability that might invite the ICC's involvement'. See Louise Chappell, Rosemary Grey and Emily Waller, 'The Gender Justice Shadow of Complementarity: Lessons from the International Criminal Court's Preliminary Examinations in Guinea and Colombia', *International Journal of Transitional Justice* 7(3) (2013), 455–475.
[214] International Bar Association, 'Analysis of overcrowded and under-examined areas, following a mapping of organisations' work on ameliorating domestic capacity to try serious international crimes' (July 2018), 5.

The 'requirements' of complementarity, as rendered in these and other documents, underscores the centrality of compliance to the ICC's catalytic framing. Materials that domestic NGOs circulate in countries like Kenya, Uganda and the DRC further reinforce this discourse. The Ugandan Coalition for the ICC, for instance, urges Uganda's 'compliance with the Rome Statute',[215] while a study on the DRC prepared by Protection International (an international NGO dedicated to the protection of human rights defenders) notes that the passage of domestic implementing legislation would 'enable the DRC to comply with its obligation … to integrate the Rome Statute in its internal legislation'.[216] A convening of government officials throughout southern Africa (supported by the University of Pretoria's Centre for Human Rights, International Criminal Legal Services and the Konrad Adenauer Foundation) even notes in its workshop report that the '[p]erception that [Rome Statute] crimes *can* be prosecuted as ordinary crimes'[217] – itself a correct statement of the law – is an 'obstacle' for promoting greater domestication of the Statute.

Framing complementarity as a duty for states, and the bridge that this builds to compliance, offers a way to route broader governance objectives through the authority of the ICC. Indeed, Ellis's suggested questions are themselves reflected in the views of the Ugandan government, which opined at a United Nations conference in 2011 that 'Complementarity is … envisioned and approached more broadly in Uganda, encompassing the adoption of relevant institutional, legal and judicial measures to strengthen the rule of law institutions and the administration of justice more generally'.[218] Rather than a constraint on the court, then, complementarity became a means of extending the ICC's authority.

---

[215] Uganda Coalition for the International Criminal Court (UCICC), 'Strategic Plan 2011–2013', 6. The plan adds that 'Uganda being the host ought to be a good example in implementing the [Kampala] Declaration that was passed'.

[216] Isabelle Fery, 'Executive Summary of a Study on the Protection of Victims and Witnesses in D. R. Congo' (Brussels: Protection International, July 2012), 11.

[217] Workshop Report, 'Expert Workshop: Giving Effect to the Law on War Crimes, Crimes Against Humanity and Genocide in Southern Africa', Workshop Report (University of Pretoria: 13–14 June 2011) (emphasis added), at www.iclsfoundation.org/wp-content/uploads/2012/02/final-workshop-report-english.pdf.

[218] 'The Role of Specialised Courts in Prosecuting International Crimes and Transitional Justice in Uganda', Remarks of the honourable minister of state and deputy attorney general at the United Nations Development Programme (UNDP) policy dialogue on 'complementarity' and transitional justice (New York: 12–13 October 2011), at www.jlos.go.ug/old/index.php/document-centre/news-room/archives/item/213-the-role-of-specialised-courts-in-prosecuting-international-crimes-and-transitional-justice-in-uganda.

4   Constructivism and the Social Production of a (New) Norm

In her seminal analysis of complementarity's 'catalytic effect' in Uganda and Sudan, Nouwen focuses on the efforts of norm entrepreneurs, whom she defines as 'activists, often foreigners working in cooperation with local actors, who promote the adoption of international norms (or what in their view should be international norms) at the domestic level'.[219] Driven by what she describes as a 'pro-ICC ideology', Nouwen argues that these activists have in turn sought to build a network of actors – ICC officials, diplomats, rule-of-law and development experts – who increasingly understand complementarity not as a rule of admissibility, but as a normative ordering principle.[220] Nouwen characterizes these actors not merely as entrepreneurs, however, but also as 'hijackers', whom she accuses of 'misrepresentation' and 'distortion' when invoking complementarity in the literal sense – to endorse, for instance, a certain standards and benchmarks for domestic proceedings that 'are laudable from a human rights perspective, but do not fit complementarity'.[221]

As noted, the transformation that Nouwen describes represents a significant evolution from the negotiated compromises that informed the Rome Statute's drafting. Rooted in the language of compliance, this evolution is noteworthy both for the relative speed with which it has evolved (given the greater burden it arguably imposes on states parties) and the degree to which it has come to dominate the public discourse about complementarity. But how should the uptake and proliferation of this new norm be understood?

Rather than focusing on norm 'distortion' or 'misrepresentation' by a select group of international elites, I suggest that constructivism – with its emphasis on the norm-shaping and socializing role of international law – offers a better window through which to understand not only complementarity's evolving meaning, but also the popular traction that particular interpretations of it came to command.[222] As

---

[219] Nouwen, *Complementarity in the Line of Fire*, 23.

[220] Nouwen defines this ideology as based on three interrelated beliefs: (1) that international courts 'mete out better justice than domestic systems'; (2) that international crimes must be prosecuted as such; and (3) because, 'at a minimum, once the ICC is involved the fledgling court must be seen to succeed'. She further suggests that this ideology has been 'at times more powerful than complementarity', to the detriment of its catalysing effect. See *Complementarity in the Line of Fire*, 13.

[221] Ibid., 192, 241. For a similar critique, see McAuliffe, 'From Watchdog to Workhorse'.

[222] See, e.g., Emanuel Adler, 'Seizing the Middle Ground: Constructivism in World Politics', *European Journal of International Relations* 33(3) (1997), 319–363; Alexander Wendt, 'Constructing International Politics', *International Security* 20(1) (Summer 1995), 77–81.

noted, these interpretations range from the view that self-referrals were never contemplated by the Rome Statute's drafters, to the popular 'shorthand' version of complementarity (i.e., that the ICC will act only 'when a state is unable or unwilling'), to the view that complementarity imposes an obligation on states to prosecute and legislate Rome Statute crimes domestically. The power of these interpretations is consistent with the evolution of complementarity itself, wherein a principle that was once meant to affirm a limitation on the ICC's power was instead reinterpreted in ways that sought to magnify its influence. These reinterpretations have, in turn, circulated to a broader epistemic community that generates and maintains new collective understandings of the principle.

Norm Entrepreneurs

A rich literature on network analysis and norm diffusion helpfully illustrates the means by which the broader understanding of complementarity – one that imposes certain duties upon states – has acquired such currency. By focusing on the role that non-state actors have played as agents of this new discourse, the significance of the transnational network of ICC supporters, rather than the court as an institution in itself, comes more clearly into focus. Aaron Boesenecker and Leslie Vinjamuri note that 'International human rights NGOs are quintessential [norm] facilitators; they both participate in global networks and discussions on justice and accountability and work locally in conflict and post-conflict situations to diffuse norms through a power of socialization'.[223] Many of these organizations, ranging from Human Rights Watch to *Avocats sans Frontieres*, Amnesty International to the International Center for Transitional Justice, also maintain national offices in key ICC situation countries (including the three studied herein), creating a nodal network between those sites where international criminal law is produced – The Hague, Brussels, Geneva, New York – and enacted.

The motivations of these influential 'trans-sovereign entrepreneurs' – the epistemic community they inhabit – are informed not only by NGOs, but through a wider network of private actors, ranging from journalists

---

[223] Aaron P. Boesenecker and Leslie Vinjamuri, 'Lost in Translation? Civil Society, Faith-Based Organizations and the Negotiation of International Norms', *International Journal of Transitional Justice* 5 (2011), 359.

and media professionals, to donor organizations, professional and civic associations and legal experts.[224] Indeed, the views advanced by an array of scholars like Burke-White, Kleffner and Stahn (to name a few) have sought to expand the earlier consensus around complementarity and explore more deeply the policy dimensions of this new ordering principle. In part, these efforts offered new readings of the Rome Statute through systematic and teleological interpretations, but their purpose in doing so was the same as those working within the ICC: to magnify the court's influence.

These 'teleological impulses' matched well with the community of NGOs and advocates engaged in developing the 'cascading' international accountability norm that scholars like Sikkink have described. As she and Martha Finnemore note, norm entrepreneurs bring actors to embrace new norms and, in so doing, displace existing standards or understandings by establishing a different 'logic of appropriateness' as a basis for decision making.[225] In their words, 'Ideational commitment is the main motivation when entrepreneurs promote norms or ideas because they believe in the ideals and values embodied in the norms'. In so doing, actors construct new 'cognitive frames', which, when successful, 'resonate with broader public understandings and are adopted as new ways of talking about and understanding issues'.[226]

---

[224] Peter Haas defines an epistemic community as a 'network of professionals with recognized expertise and competence in a particular domain and an authoritative claim to policy-relevant knowledge within that domain or issue-area'. See 'Introduction: Epistemic Communities and International Policy Coordination', *International Organization* 46(1) (1992), 3; see also Mikael Risk Madsen and Mikkel Jarle Christensen, 'Global Actors: Networks, Elites, and Institutions', *Oxford Research Encyclopaedia of Politics* (October 2016).

[225] Martha Finnemore and Kathryn Sikkink, 'International Norm Dynamics and Political Change', *International Organization* 52(4) (Autumn 1998), 897–898. Elsewhere, Haas has described entrepreneurs as 'cognitive baggage handlers as well as gatekeepers governing the entry of new ideas into institutions', ibid., 27. On 'logic of appropriateness', see James G. March and Johan P. Olsen, *Rediscovering Institutions* (New York: Free Press, 1989) and 'The Institutional Dynamics of International Political Orders', *International Organizations* 52 (1998).

[226] Finnemore and Sikkink, 'International Norm Dynamics and Political Change', 897–898. In a more recent article, Finnemore examines the role of norm entrepreneurship in the context of cybersecurity, highlighting incentives, persuasion and socialization as three 'discrete tools' that successful norm promoters may draw upon for 'promoting the progressive development and spread of norms', 449. See Martha Finnemore and Duncan B. Hollis, 'Constructing Norms for Global Cybersecurity', *American Journal of International Law* 110 (3) (July 2016), 425–478. For another similar study of norm entrepreneurship in international law, see Peter Hilpold, 'Intervening in the Name of Humanity: R2P and the Power of Ideas', *Journal of Conflict & Security Law* 17(1) (2012).

Here, the desire to diffuse and entrench more deeply an ideational commitment to international accountability dovetailed with the need to construct complementarity as a normative ordering principle, rather than a narrow admissibility test. Thus, while many of the entrepreneurs advancing this new, more ambitious norm may have initially wished more for the ICC vis-à-vis national jurisdictions – that it, too, might be a court of primacy – this shortcoming was progressively reinvented in the post-Rome period. Complementarity as a 'catalyst' marked the arrival of a new cognitive frame.

Transnational Advocacy Networks and 'Communities of Practice'

Emanuel Adler's scholarship on transnational 'communities of practice', building on the work of Etienne Wenger, is also instructive in understanding complementarity's evolution, as it points to the dense array of ICC-engaged actors who helped advance the complementarity-as-catalyst framework.[227] Adler's work is illuminating insofar as it examines the social construction of shared norms and ideas, as well as how a group of actors 'develops a common body of knowledge and common practices by engaging in their field in relation with each other'.[228] Building on Adler, Brunnée and Toope have advanced a concept of 'interactional international law', one in which 'shared understandings' are 'created through communities of practice that shape the mutual engagement of various actors in international society'.[229] This dynamic of socialization is practice based: 'For such a community to exist, participants must be engaged in interactions of a certain density and specificity'.[230]

---

[227] Wenger's theory of communities of practice was rooted in his observation that people develop knowledge socially, i.e., through others who are engaged in similar activities and motivated by shared concerns. Wenger defined the term as 'groups of people informally bound together by shared expertise and passion for a joint enterprise'. See Etienne Wenger and William M. Snyder, 'Communities of Practice: The Organizational Frontier', *Harvard Business Review* (2000); Etienne Wenger, *Communities of Practice: Learning, Meaning, and Identity* (Cambridge University Press, 1998).
[228] Elena Baylis, 'Function and Dysfunction in Post-Conflict Judicial Networks and Communities', *Vanderbilt Journal of Transnational Law* 47 (2014), 643. See also Julie Mertus, 'From Legal Transplants to Transformative Justice: Human Rights and the Promise of Transnational Civil Society', *American University International Law Review* 14(5) (1999), 1335–1389.
[229] Brunnée and Toope, *Legitimacy and Legality in International Law*, 86.
[230] Ibid., 70.

Extrapolating this insight to the transnational, Adler suggests that 'we can take the international system as a collection of communities of practice' – diplomats, human rights advocates, legal experts, progressive donors – who may share 'a sense of joint enterprise that is constantly being renegotiated', as well as shared practices, which 'are sustained by a repertoire of communal resources, such as routines, words, tools, ways of doing things, stories, symbols, and discourse'.[231] In a similar vein, Margaret Keck and Sikkink point to the role of 'transnational advocacy networks', which can be understood as one component of Adler's communities of practice. They define such a network as 'those actors working internationally on an issue, who are bound together by shared values, a common discourse, and dense exchanges of information and services'.[232] Pertinent to complementarity, they note that such networks are 'most prevalent in issue areas characterized by high value content and informational uncertainty'. Thus, even where information may be technically inaccurate (as with the depiction of complementarity as imposing a set of prosecutorial duties), or represent a departure from previously settled understandings, it is through participation in these relationships that such information is not only transmitted, but also where meaning itself develops. These relationships and repertoires underscore, in Adler's view, 'the role of knowledge communities, communities of discourse, and, more generally, "communities of the like-minded" in the structuration and dynamic evolution of social reality'.[233]

The density, frequency and specificity of interaction amongst entrepreneurs and network members resonate particularly strongly in the context of international criminal law, which remains a specialized field (if one that enjoys significant influence), and in the context of a singular judicial institution like the ICC, popularly seen as the institutional apex of

---

[231] Emanuel Adler, 'Communities of Practice in International Relations', in *Communitarian International Relations: The Epistemic Foundations of International Relations* (Abingdon: Routledge, 2005), 15. For a provocative analysis of transnational communities of practice in the context of international peacekeeping, see Séverine Autesserre, *Peaceland: Conflict Resolution and the Everyday Politics of International Intervention* (Cambridge: Cambridge University Press, 2014).

[232] Margaret E. Keck and Kathryn Sikkink, *Activists Beyond Borders: Advocacy Networks in International Politics* (Ithaca, NY: Cornell University Press, 1998), 2. For an insightful reflection on this landmark text, see Peter Evans and César Rodríguez-Garavito (eds.), *Transnational Advocacy Networks: Twenty Years of Evolving Theory and Practice* (Dejusticia Series, 2018), at www.dejusticia.org/wp-content/uploads/2018/11/Transnational-Advocacy-Networks-1.pdf.

[233] Adler, *Communitarian International Relations*, 4.

the international justice 'movement'. ICC staff not only share a sense of joint enterprise (to combat impunity), but so do the transnational communities of human rights NGOs, advocates and academics that played a pivotal role in the court's establishment. As Gerry Simpson notes of the Rome Statute's negotiations, 'Never before had non-state actors played such a prominent role in bringing a treaty into existence. NGOs such as Amnesty International, No Peace Without Justice and Human Rights Watch were highly influential – providing expertise and advice, drafting and circulating proposals and cajoling delegates'.[234]

Marlies Glasius's monograph on the establishment of the ICC captures well the development of these network ties and the sense of community amongst them. Describing the 'organization of national and international conferences, expert meetings, public debates, seminars, symposia, and workshops' that were organized in the years leading up to the Rome conference, she writes that the conferences were 'characterized by an intermingling of officials with the NGO and the activist communities, and by high-level legal debates, rather than political confrontations'.[235] International, regional and national meetings alike 'often boasted one or more international guests drawn from the ranks of the NGO coalition, the Yugoslavia and Rwanda tribunals, or from the academic community'.[236]

This intermingling of communities, focused on the normative and institutional growth of the ICC has endured post-Rome, concomitant

---

[234] Gerry Simpson, *Law, War and Crime: War Crimes Trials and the Reinvention of International Law* (Cambridge: Polity, 2007), 36. For detailed profiles of key actors and organizations, see Benedetti, Bonneau and Washburn, *Negotiating the International Criminal Court: New York to Rome, 1994–1998*, 68–117.

[235] Glasius, *The International Criminal Court: A Global Civil Society Achievement*, 39. More recent iterations of such intermingling includes the series of 'Greentree retreats' supported over the course of 2010–2012 by the ICTJ, UNDP and various donor governments; these retreats were designed to 'bring together high-level actors from three different sectors: international justice, rule of law assistance, and development'. See Synthesis Report on 'Supporting Complementarity at the National Level: From Theory to Practice' (Greentree III, 25–26 October 2012), as well as International Law Association's 'Committee on Complementarity in International Law', which was created in November 2013. Its mandate is to 'consider the question of how the concept of complementarity, particularly positive complementarity, should be interpreted and applied both in the context of admissibility proceedings of the International Criminal Court and in the domestic jurisdictions of states parties (and beyond)'. See ILA Johannesburg Conference 2016, Complementarity in International Law Discussion Report; ILA Sydney 2018, Complementarity in International Criminal Law.

[236] Glasius, *The International Criminal Court*, 39.

with the expansion in complementarity's definition and meaning.[237] Examples abound of personnel from state delegations and NGOs who were involved in setting up the ICC having since swapped roles – former delegates leaving political service to join civil society and vice versa. Likewise, a number of ICC staff and judges in the court's early years were drawn from the same pool of people who had been involved in drafting the Statute, either as part of state delegations or as NGO representatives. Edited volumes about the court regularly include contributions from ICC officials and human rights advocates alike, while academic institutions house a number of legal training projects that seek to enhance the impact of the 'Rome Statute System'. Key organizations like the Coalition for the International Criminal Court (CICC), which serves as a global coalition of local and international NGOs, is another critical node in this thickly webbed network.[238] Likewise, many former staff members of the *ad hoc* tribunals were themselves part of the initial vanguard within the ICC (later moving to academia themselves).[239] To an unusual degree, then, 'network ties and communal identity exist within and across organizational boundaries' in the field of international criminal law.[240] In Elena Baylis' words, 'in the ICL tribunal context, [networks] are acting as the framework for a transnational community that conceives of itself as building the field of ICL'.[241]

The dominant framing of complementarity as a catalyst for compliance/ rule-following amongst these transnational communities is also significant in illuminating the vertical engagement between international actors and civil society organizations at the national or local levels. Returning

[237] See, e.g., Mikkel Jarle Christensen, 'The Creation of an Ad Hoc Elite: And the Value of International Criminal Law Expertise on a Global Market', in Kevin Jon Heller, Frédéric Mégret, Sarah Nouwen, Jens Ohlin and Darryl Robinson (eds.), *The Oxford Handbook of International Criminal Law* (Oxford University Press, 2019); Baylis, 'Function and Dysfunction in Post-Conflict Judicial Networks and Communities', 633.

[238] For a more detailed history of the CICC, see Heidi Nichols Haddad, 'After the Norm Cascade: NGO Mission Expansion and the Coalition for the International Criminal Court', *Global Governance* 19(2) (2013), 187–206; Claude E. Welch, Jr. and Ashley F. Watkins, 'Extending Enforcement: The Coalition for the International Criminal Court', *Human Rights Quarterly* 33 (2011), 927–1031.

[239] See, e.g., Philipp Ambach and Klaus U. Rackwitz, 'A Model of International Judicial Administration? The Evolution of Managerial Practices at the International Criminal Court', *Law and Contemporary Problems* 76(3&4) (2013), 148–153.

[240] Baylis, 'Function and Dysfunction in Post-Conflict Judicial Networks and Communities', 633.

[241] Ibid., 649. See also David S. Koller, 'The Faith of the International Criminal Lawyer', *NYU Journal of International Law and Politics* 40 (2008), 1060 ('The ultimate value of international criminal law may rest … in its role in identity construction, in particular in constructing a cosmopolitan community embracing all of humankind'.).

to Adler, 'learning means redefining reality by means of "contextual" community knowledge, from which [practitioners] borrow in order to get their bearings'.[242] This borrowing is again part of a process, wherein the transmission of information has helped redefine the meaning of complementarity away from a technical rule of admissibility to a normative ordering principle, one that emphasizes fidelity and conformity with the Rome Statute. The pursuit of this framework was predominantly forged through practice, including, notably, a growth in 'capacity-building' projects amongst ICC member states, northern NGOs and advocates in ICC situation countries. A number of such projects were highlighted at the ICC Review Conference in 2010: from *Avocats sans Frontieres'* 'Integrated Project on Fighting Impunity and the Reconstruction of the Legal System in the DRC' to 'Danish Support to the War Crimes Court and the Judiciary in Uganda', these efforts have collectively furthered the cognitive framing of complementarity as a catalyst for accountability.[243]

The actors engaged in this transnational learning community thus advanced a vision for complementarity – as catalyst, rather than constraint – that appears different than it did at the time of the Rome Statute's drafting. But this was not merely the result of innate 'pro-ICC ideology'; rather, the coercive and cooperative dimensions of complementarity were discovered, learned and transmitted over a period of time to a broader community and network of actors. As Brunnée and Toope explain, 'through interaction and communication, actors generate shared knowledge and shared understandings that become the background for subsequent interaction'.[244] These shared understandings, in turn, become structures that shape 'how actors perceive themselves and the world',

---

[242] Adler, *Communitarian International Relations*, 20. Writing in another context, the legal scholar Annelise Riles's description of a discourse community is equally apt. As she notes, '"language" is quoted and reprinted from one conference document to the next and as states begin to conform their practices, or at least their discourse, to the norms expressed therein, some of what is agreed upon at global conferences gradually will become rules of "customary international law"'. Annelise Riles, *The Network Inside Out* (University of Michigan Press, 2001), 8.

[243] For descriptions of these (and other) projects, see 'Focal points' compilation of examples of projects aimed at strengthening domestic jurisdictions to deal with Rome Statute Crimes', RC/ST/CM/INF.2, 30 May 2010 (see examples D and I).

[244] Brunnée and Toope, *Legitimacy and Legality in International Law*, 13; see also Lisbeth Zimmerman, *Global Norms with a Local Face: Rule-of-Law Promotion and Norm Translation* (Cambridge: Cambridge University Press, 2017) (underlining 'the desirability of an international and deliberative approach to norms that stresses mutual processes of construction as a condition for the legitimacy of global norms in local contexts'), 6.

as well as how they form interests and set priorities.[245] This process of interest formation and priority setting constructed an expanded understanding of the ICC's purpose and of the complementarity principle, one that increasingly came to dominate its public persona.

As an evolving norm, then, complementarity was not so much 'hijacked', as it was built over time. Constructivism's attention to interactional processes and knowledge generation is critical to understanding the evolution and plural understandings that animate the discourse around complementarity. It also points to the contingent nature of norm generation, as well as the 'constantly shifting ground on which precarious paths to validity, power, or legitimacy must be constructed'.[246] Indeed, while the history described in this chapter explains complementarity's evolution towards a magnification of the ICC's influence, more recent discourse from some member states has begun to contest this interpretation and pushback on the degree of influence that NGOs have previously enjoyed in the expansion of the concept. The ICC's recent performance challenges have, for instance, heightened the insistence of some states that the court should focus on its 'core mandate' and leave 'positive complementarity' to other actors.

Other states (several of which have been the subject of early preliminary examinations) have also now found it politically convenient to question what mandate the court has to engage in 'positive complementarity' or what the legal basis for such a policy would be. One NGO report notes, for instance, that while the term 'positive complementarity' appears in the OTP's 2013 policy paper (and still in its latest strategy), those within the office now 'prefer to avoid using the term', as it 'could be interpreted to indicate that the OTP applies this as a "policy" in every situation or that it has earmarked funds to support such activities'.[247] To that end, the OTP's 2019–2021 strategy now states:

> Although capacity building or technical assistance are important elements that can speed up the office's completion strategy in a given situation, the office recalls that this is a role for development agencies and other actors; the office's role is more limited to encouraging engagement by such partners, to make its standards, lesson learned and best practices available for use, and to contributing participants, where possible and

[245] Ibid., 65.
[246] Frédéric Mégret, 'The Anxieties of International Criminal Justice', *Leiden Journal of International Law* 29(1) (March 2016), 221.
[247] Human Rights Watch, 'Pressure Point: The ICC's Impact on National Justice – Lessons from Colombia, Georgia, Guinea, and the United Kingdom' (2018), 157, n. 561.

within its means, to the expert-level meetings, trainings and seminars organised by others. In the office's assessment, which it invites states to provide continuous feedback on, all these activities flow from the Statute and draw from the mutually-reinforcing cooperating framework it establishes.[248]

This pushback may be temporary, or it may signal a larger retrenchment from the scope and ambition that animated complementarity's early evolution. It is a reminder, however, that just as a new complementarity norm was constructed, it can also be whittled back.

5 Conclusion

Over the past decade, complementarity has become the normative site and an adaptive strategy for realizing a broad array of goals, wherein the ICC is meant to not only complement national forums, but to actively encourage domestic proceedings as well. As mediated by a dense, interconnected web of actors – NGOs, ICC officials, human rights advocates, academics, donors and receptive state officials – complementarity has thus become increasingly polysemous, imbued with multiple meanings (admissibility rule, as well as catalyst) and dimensions (cooperative, as well as coercive).

Furthermore, in the travel towards a more 'positive', policy-based vision for complementarity, new interpretive meanings have arisen. One such interpretation holds that states have not only the right to investigate and prosecute international crimes, but also, under the Rome Statute, the duty to do so in a manner consistent with fair trial standards. As with the 'slogan' version of complementarity, the dominance of this popular understanding of the principle is another example of how international obligations – here, complementarity as compliance – are created and learned, and how 'shared understandings can be successfully promoted by non-state actors, be they groups or influential individuals'.[249]

Rather than a concession to sovereignty, then, complementarity-as-compliance might now be considered a condition of sovereignty, i.e., a test that states must satisfy in order to successfully challenge the ICC's control over a case. The following chapter examines the juridical nature of these challenges in greater detail and the tensions that arise in negotiating these plural understandings in the work of the court itself.

---

[248] OTP Strategic Plan 2019–2021, para. 51.
[249] Brunnee and Toope, *Legitimacy and Legality in International Law*, 61.

3

Mirror Images? Complementarity
in the Courtroom

The previous chapter explored complementarity's discursive shifts, tracing its ascension from an admissibility principle to a more expansive norm
focused on the International Criminal Court's (ICC) ability to catalyse
accountability efforts at the national level. In the light of this ambitious
and expanding norm, it might be expected that states would have been
granted a relatively broad discretion over the contours of their domestic
criminal proceedings. Indeed, several commentators, expressing concern
at the risk of an overly permissive admissibility regime, have previously
suggested that the ICC's 'institutional bias' might 'give too much deference to national proceedings'.[250] Other scholars, by contrast, have coun-
selled in favour of a more flexible approach, suggesting that would be a
'smart way of stimulating national proceedings'.[251]

This chapter argues that, rather than encouraging such flexibility, the
court has largely endorsed a strict approach to admissibility in its Article
17 jurisprudence to date. Most notable amongst these is an emphasis on
whether proceedings initiated by the Office of the Prosecutor (OTP)
and a state that would seek to successfully challenge admissibility are
sufficiently the same. As described by the Appeals Chamber, 'What is
required is a judicial assessment of whether the case that the state is

---

[250] See, e.g., Lars Waldorf, '"A Mere Pretense of Justice": Complementarity, Sham Trials,
and Victor's Justice at the Rwandan Tribunal', *Fordham International Law Journal*
33(4) (2011), 1270. See also Drumbl, *Atrocity, Punishment, and International Law*, 206
(positing that 'the ICC shall approach complementarity determinations with some
restraint').
[251] Stigen, *The Relationship between the International Criminal Court and National
Jurisdictions*, 18; see also Michael Newton, 'The Complementarity Conundrum: Are
We Watching Evolution or Evisceration?' *Santa Clara Journal of International Law*
8(1) (2010), 164 (concluding that 'the ICC should work with states to enhance their
domestic capacity and defer to domestic investigations or prosecutions in any feasible
conditions').

investigating sufficiently mirrors the one that the prosecutor is investi-gating'.[252] While this interpretation has provoked perhaps the most con-troversy amongst academics and practitioners, other procedural aspects have also contributed to a narrow reading of admissibility. In particular, when faced with competing claims about domestic proceedings (notably challenges brought by an individual accused), ICC judges have under-taken a relatively superficial review of domestic proceedings, while set-ting a high evidentiary bar for challengers to satisfy. The court has also effectively narrowed the opportunity to bring admissibility challenges by restricting the scope of review for pre-trial chambers when determin-ing whether to issue an arrest warrant.

Although much of the ICC's early complementarity jurisprudence unfolded in the context of individual defendants who raised admissi-bility challenges following the referral of situations to the court by the state itself (as in Uganda and the Democratic Republic of Congo, DRC), more recent decisions have been triggered at the behest of states, notably in Kenya, Libya and the Ivory Coast. This chapter explores the evolution of the ICC's admissibility jurisprudence and identifies its key elements as developed and articulated by the court to date. Particular attention is paid to the Appeals Chamber's 2009 and 2011 decisions in the challenges brought by Germain Katanga and the Kenyan government, as well as the challenges filed by the Libyan government to the cases brought against Saif Gaddafi and Libya's former chief of intelligence, Abdullah al-Senussi. To date, the challenge filed on behalf of al-Senussi has been the only one to succeed. Attention is also paid to the judicial treatment of Article 93(10), which provides a statutory basis for the policy of 'positive' complementar-ity. Here, too, however, the court has taken a broadly restrictive approach, explicitly separating its treatment of requests for ICC cooperation – a core tenet of 'positive' complementarity – from admissibility challenges.[253]

---

[252] The Prosecutor v. Saif Al-Islam Gaddafi and Abdullah Al-Senussi, Judgment on the appeal of Libya against the decision of Pre-Trial Chamber I of 21 May 2013 entitled 'Decision on the admissibility of the case against Saif Al-Islam Gaddafi', ICC-01/11-01/11 OA 4, Appeals Chamber (21 May 2014) ('Gaddafi Admissibility Appeals Judgment'), para. 73; see also The Prosecutor v. Saif Al-Islam Gaddafi and Abdullah Al-Senussi, Judgment on the appeal of Mr. Abdullah Al-Senussi against the decision of Pre-Trial Chamber I of 11 October 2013 entitled 'Decision on the admissibility of the case against Abdullah Al-Senussi', ICC-01/11-01/11 OA 6, Appeals Chamber (24 July 2014) ('Al Senussi Admissibility Appeals Judgment'), para. 119.
[253] Situation in the Republic of Kenya, Decision on the request for assistance submitted on behalf of the government of the Republic of Kenya pursuant to Article 93(10) of the Statute and Rule 194 of the Rules of Procedure and Evidence, ICC-01/09, PTC II (29 June 2011) ('PTC Article 93(10) Decision').

In reviewing this body of case law, the ICC appears to have followed a strict approach to complementarity, adopting, as other scholars have noted, standards for admissibility that would require domestic proceedings to be framed in much the same way as the OTP's cases – in effect, to mirror them. As discussed in the chapter's third section, it also places a burden on states that they may be unprepared (or unwilling) to meet. Rather than catalysing domestic proceedings, then, the court's admissibility regime could instead thwart them. Some commentators have responded to this apparent paradox by insisting that the juridical operation of complementarity can be bifurcated from its treatment outside of the courtroom (a position that the OTP and Assembly of States Parties, ASP, have also endorsed); however, I suggest that this attempted partition is itself symptomatic of legalism: it relies on an artificial division between the court as a legal and political actor. Indeed, while such a bifurcated approach to complementarity may be appealing insofar as it allows both ICC officials and supporters to summon different versions of the principle for different purposes and audiences, it fails to recognize that the policy goals of complementarity and the court's judicial function cannot be easily uncoupled.

1   Complementarity as Admissibility Rule

'Same Case' Test: Person, Conduct and Incident?

The application of the 'same case' test dates back to the ICC's investigations in the DRC, following the government's referral to the court in April 2004. Thomas Lubanga Dyilo was the first accused to be surrendered to the ICC and also the first to be found guilty: in March 2012, he was convicted on the sole charge of recruiting, conscripting and enlisting child soldiers.[254] Three other former rebel leaders have also been tried (Mathieu Ngudjolo Chui, acquitted in December 2012; Germaine Katanga, convicted in March 2014; Bosco Ntganda, convicted in July 2019), as well as former DRC vice-president, Jean-Pierre Bemba, who was surrendered in the context of the first situation in the Central African Republic (Bemba was convicted in March 2016, but acquitted in

---

[254] The Prosecutor v. Thomas Lubanga Dyilo, Judgment pursuant to Article 74 of the Statute, ICC-01/04-01/06, TC I (14 March 2012).

a controversial appellate decision in June 2018).[255] Notably, as these were cases in a situation that the government itself had referred to the prosecutor, they raised little opposition with Kinshasa. Indeed, at the time that the OTP lodged its application, Lubanga had been in the custody of Congolese authorities since March 2005, where he was being held on several charges, including genocide and crimes against humanity.[256] An arrest warrant for Lubanga was first sought in January 2006 and issued under seal by the Pre-Trial Chamber the following month.[257] In its application, the prosecutor acknowledged that proceedings against Lubanga were underway in the DRC; however, it argued that this was not a bar to admissibility since, at the time of the Congolese government's referral to the ICC in March 2004, the government had stated that it was not able to prosecute crimes falling within the court's jurisdiction.[258]

In deciding whether to approve the requested warrant, Pre-Trial Chamber I actively examined whether the case was admissible since, in its view, such a determination had to necessarily precede the issuance of a warrant. The chamber rejected the OTP's argument that the Congolese government's referral of the situation rendered the case admissible *per se*. Importantly, it noted that for the purpose of the admissibility analysis, the DRC national judicial system 'ha[d] undergone certain changes since March 2004, particularly in the region of Ituri', where Lubanga's alleged crimes had been committed and where the OTP had opted to begin its investigations.[259] As a result, the court found the prosecutor's 'general

---

[255] The Prosecutor *v.* Mathieu Ngudjolo, Judgment pursuant to Article 74 of the Statute, ICC-01/04-02/12, TC II (18 December 2012) ('Ngudjolo Judgment'); The Prosecutor *v.* Germain Katanga, Judgment pursuant to Article 74 of the Statute, ICC-01/04-01/07,TC II (7 March 2014); The Prosecutor *v.* Jean-Pierre Bemba Gombo, Judgment on the appeal of Mr. Jean-Pierre Bemba Gombo against Trial Chamber III's 'Judgment pursuant to Article 74 of the Statute', ICC-01/05-01/08 A, Appeals Chamber (8 June 2018); The Prosecutor *v.* Bosco Ntaganda, Judgment, ICC-01/04-02/06, TC VI (8 July 2019). Although President Kabila initially refused to transfer Ntaganda to The Hague (and later expressed an intention for the DRC to prosecute him domestically), no admissibility challenge in those proceedings was filed.
[256] See The Prosecutor *v.* Thomas Lubanga Dyilo, Decision on the prosecutor's application for a warrant of arrest, Article 58, ICC-01/04-01/06, PTC I (10 February 2006) ('Lubanga Arrest Warrant Decision'), para. 36.
[257] Ibid.
[258] The Prosecutor *v.* Thomas Lubanga Dyilo, Prosecutor's application for warrant of arrest, ICC-01/04-01/06-8 (13 January 2006), para. 186.
[259] Lubanga Arrest Warrant Decision, para. 36.

statement that the DRC national judicial system continues to be unable in the sense of article 17 ... of the Statute [did] not wholly correspond to ... reality any longer'.[260]

The Pre-Trial Chamber nevertheless determined that the case was admissible. In so doing, it concluded that 'it is a condition sine qua non for a case arising from the investigations of a situation to be inadmissible that national proceedings encompass both the person and the conduct which is the subject of the case before the court'.[261] Drawing on its earlier definition of a case in the context of victim participation, the chamber noted that the word 'case' referred to 'specific incidents during which one or more crimes within the jurisdiction of the court seem to have been committed by one or more identified suspects'.[262] Because Lubanga was charged with crimes other than those related to the recruitment of child soldiers – even where those crimes were broader in scope than those charged by the ICC – the case was not being investigated or prosecuted by the DRC within the ambit of Article 17(1)(a).[263] There was thus no bar to admissibility.

In decisions reviewing other arrest warrants, the court has subsequently applied the 'same person, same conduct' test.[264] In these instances, the relevant pre-trial chambers have acted proprio motu under the discretionary power provided under Article 19(1) of the Rome Statute, leading them to conclude that while the proceedings in question concerned the same person, they did not concern the same conduct. In several cases, the prosecutor advanced an even narrower test, arguing in subsequent

---

[260] Ibid.
[261] Ibid., para. 31. As commentators have noted, the 'same conduct' language was added to the chapeau of Article 20(3) during the Rome Statute's drafting to ensure that the principle of ne bis in idem would be respected, without prohibiting ICC retrial for charges based on different conduct. See Heller, 'A Sentence-Based Theory of Complementarity'; Robinson, 'Three Theories of Complementarity', 175–182.
[262] Ibid. (citing The Prosecutor v. Thomas Lubanga Dyilo, Decision on the application for participation in the proceedings of VPRS-1, VPRS-2, VPRS-3, VPRS-4, VPRS-5 and VPRS-6 (18 January 2006), para. 65).
[263] Lubanga Arrest Warrant Decision, paras. 39–40.
[264] See, e.g., The Prosecutor v. Germain Katanga, Decision on the evidence and information provided by the prosecution for the issuance of a warrant of arrest for Germain Katanga, ICC-01/04-01/07-4, PTC I, 6 July 2007 (finding the case admissible before the ICC because the proceedings against Katanga in the DRC 'did not encompass the same conduct' that was the subject of the Article 58 application); The Prosecutor v. Ahmad Muhammad Harun and Ali Muhammad Ali Abd-Al-Rahman, Decision on the prosecution application under Article 58(7) of the Statute, ICC-02/05-01/07-I-Corr, PTC I (27 April 2007).

motions that the 'same conduct' test required domestic proceedings to involve not only the same acts, but also the same incidents, i.e., the same factual allegations.[265] While there has been no explicit judicial endorsement of these additional requirements, Pre-Trial Chamber III, in the case of former Cote d'Ivoire President Laurent Gbagbo, indicated that a case encompasses 'specific incidents during which one or more crimes within the jurisdiction of the court seem to have been committed by one or more identified suspects'.[266]

Katanga was the first accused to challenge the admissibility of his case. In March 2009, before Trial Chamber II, he filed an application under Article 19(2)(a) on the basis that, inter alia, the same conduct test was overly strict and constituted 'flawed' precedent.[267] Instead, he argued that the court should adopt a more flexible approach to admissibility, one based on a 'comparative gravity' or 'comprehensive conduct' standard.[268] While there was 'no mathematic formula' for such a standard, Katanga averred, 'Only when the ICC prosecutor's scope of investigation is significantly more comprehensive than the scope of national investigations, would there be a basis for admissibility'.[269] Furthermore, even if the same conduct test did apply, Katanga argued that he was being investigated by the DRC at the time the ICC issued its arrest warrant, and that these investigations encompassed crimes committed on or about 24 February 2003 in the village of Bogoro, which was the basis of the ICC's case as well.

---

[265] See, e.g., The Prosecutor v. Ahmad Muhammad Harun ('Ahmad Harun') and Ali Muhammad Ali Abd-Al-Rahman ('Ali Kushayb'), Prosecutor's application under Article 58(7), ICC-02/05-56, 27 February 2007, paras. 266–267; The Prosecutor v. Germain Katanga, Public redacted version of the 19th March 2009 prosecution response to motion challenging the admissibility of the case by the defence of Germain Katanga, pursuant to Article 19(2)(a), ICC-01/04-01/07-1007 (30 March 2009) ('The term "case" should … be understood as being constituted by the underlying event, incident, and circumstances – i.e. in the criminal context, the conduct of the suspect in relation to a given incident').

[266] The Prosecutor v. Laurent Gbagbo, 'Decision on the prosecutor's application pursuant to Article 58 for a warrant of arrest against Laurent Koudou Gbagbo', ICC-02/11-01/11, PTC III (30 November 2011), para. 10. The chamber did not, however, specify what would be encompassed by the notion of 'incident'.

[267] The Prosecutor v. Germain Katanga, Motion challenging the admissibility of the case by the defence of Germain Katanga, pursuant to Article 19(2)(a), ICC-01/04-01/07-949 (11 March 2009) ('Katanga Admissibility Challenge').

[268] Ibid., paras. 46–47, 51.

[269] Ibid., para. 47. The defence also proffered a 'comparative gravity/comprehensive conduct' test, para. 51.

The trial chamber dismissed the challenge, but rather than opine on the validity of the same conduct test (around which Katanga's motion had primarily been framed), it found that the DRC authorities were unwilling to prosecute Katanga.[270] The chamber implicitly affirmed the validity of the test, however, insofar as it rejected Katanga's claim that the prosecutor had failed to produce documents about the attack on Bogoro relevant to admissibility, on the grounds that they were not 'decisive'.[271] The presumption that domestic proceedings had to encompass the same conduct (the attack on Bogoro) was thus implicit in the court's dismissal. The Appeals Chamber clarified this determination on review – finding that inaction at the domestic level, not unwillingness, rendered the case admissible – but it did not address the alternative standard ('comprehensive conduct') that Katanga had proposed.[272]

Other defendants before the ICC have raised similar challenges. In the case of Laurent Gbagbo, the chamber was also asked to 'interpret "conduct" in a flexible manner, focusing on the general conduct of the suspect in relation to the context in which the crimes were committed'. The petition noted that the 'short-sighted view of complementarity' endorsed by the court 'fails to take account of the wider goals of international criminal justice, in particular, the need for national jurisdictions to build capacity to try such crimes domestically … as part of the overall

---

[270] The Prosecutor v. Germain Katanga, Reasons for the oral decision on the motion challenging the admissibility of the case (Article 19 of the Statute), ICC-01/04-01/07, TC II (16 June 2009), para. 95 ('Katanga Admissibility Decision') ('In light of these statements, and without the need to rule on the 'same conduct test' which the defence for Germain Katanga sought to challenge in its motion, the chamber cannot but note the clear and explicit expression of unwillingness of the DRC to prosecute this case.').

[271] Ibid., para. 72. In arriving at this determination, the chamber noted that one of the documents – a request by the Kinshasa High Military Court to extend Katanga's provisional detention – 'does not specify the exact date of the acts allegedly committed in Bogoro', and that it was not 'conclusive as to whether the acts allegedly committed there could be attributed to Germain Katanga', paras. 68, 70.

[272] Prosecutor v. Germain Katanga and Mathieu Ngudjolo Chui, Judgment on the appeal of Mr. Germain Katanga against the oral decision of Trial Chamber II of 12 June 2009 on the admissibility of the case, ICC-01/04-01/07-OA8, AC (25 September 2009), para. 81 ('Katanga Admissibility Appeals Judgment') ('In light of the above, the Appeals Chamber does not have to address in the present appeal the correctness of the 'same-conduct' test used by the pre-trial chambers to determine whether the same "case" is the object of domestic proceedings'.).

process of reconciliation and peace building'.[273] The chamber declined to address this argument, however, finding instead that while the evidence submitted showed that a domestic prosecution for economic crimes may have been initiated – 'and that some initial procedural steps may have been undertaken' – prior to his surrender to the ICC in November 2011, there had been no apparent domestic activity since that date. Thus, on that basis alone, it had 'not been demonstrated that Mr. Gbagbo "[was] being prosecuted" in Côte d'Ivoire, within the meaning of article 17(l)(a) of the Statute'.[274]

Significantly, the context for these cases was one in which the state had supported the ICC's intervention (at least initially) and relinquished its jurisdiction through self-referral. In effect, 'state authorities sided with the ICC, rather than the defence, since they had an interest in seeing the case being tried internationally'.[275] By contrast, the proceedings in Kenya and Libya presented an alternative picture, as those challenges were both brought by governments under Article 19(2)(b). In Kenya, the government disputed the correctness of the test on the basis that the 'same person' element of the test was flawed. Instead, national investigations should cover 'the same conduct in respect of persons at the same level in the hierarchy being investigated by the ICC'.[276] It also offered a 'proposed timetable for investigative processes' at the national level, including a report on post-election violence (PEV) investigations under a new director of public prosecutions (one that would 'extend up to the highest levels') and, by September 2011, a 'report on progress made with investigations and readiness for trials in light of judicial reforms'.[277] The Pre-Trial Chamber rejected the state's challenge within

---

[273] The Prosecutor v. Laurent Gbagbo, Decision on the 'Requeté relative a la recevabilité de l'affaire en vertu des Articles 19 et 17 du Statut', ICC-02/11-01/11, PTC I (11 June 2013), paras. 11–12 ('Gbagbo Admissibility Decision'). Notably, the national proceedings that Gbagbo alleged were underway related to economic crimes (see para. 8), over which the Rome Statute has limited subject matter jurisdiction.

[274] Ibid., para. 28.

[275] Stahn, 'Admissibility challenges before the ICC', 234.

[276] The Prosecutor v. William Samoei Ruto, et al., Application on behalf of the government of the Republic of Kenya pursuant to Article 19 of the ICC Statute, ICC-01/09-01/11 and ICC-01/09-02/11, PTC II (31 March 2011), para. 32.

[277] Ibid., para. 79.

two months, finding that the proposed measures '[fell] short of any concrete investigative steps regarding the ... suspects in question'.[278]

On appeal, the government continued to press its view that 'it cannot be right that in all circumstances in every situation and in every case that may come before the ICC the persons being investigated by the prosecutor must be exactly the same as those being investigated by the state'; rather, '[t]here simply must be a leaway [sic] in the exercise of discretion in the application of the principle of complementarity'.[279] To that end, it averred, much as Katanga did, that a better test should query whether national proceedings capture the 'same conduct in respect of the persons at the same level in the hierarchy being investigated by the ICC'.[280]

By a majority, the Appeals Chamber affirmed the Pre-Trial Chamber's decision. It clarified that 'where summonses to appear have been issued, the question is no longer whether suspects at the same hierarchical level are being investigated by Kenya, but whether the same suspects are the subject of investigation by both jurisdictions for *substantially* the same conduct'.[281] The majority further rejected Kenya's appeal to domestic discretion, noting that the only purpose of admissibility proceedings under Article 19 is to determine if there is a jurisdictional conflict. While complementarity might favour national jurisdictions, the chamber noted, 'it does so only to the extent that there actually are, or have

---

[278] See The Prosecutor v. William Samoei Ruto, Henry Kiprono Kosgey and Joshua Arap Sang, Decision on the application by the government of Kenya challenging the admissibility of the case pursuant to Article 19(2)(b) of the Statute, PTC II, ICC-01/09-01/11 (30 May 2011), para. 65 ('Ruto et al. Admissibility Decision'). The chamber noted further that it 'lack[ed] information ... as to the conduct, crimes or the incidents for which the three suspects are being investigated or questioned for', para. 69; see also paras. 56, 60–61 in the parallel Kenyan cases.

[279] The Prosecutor v. Francis Kirimi Muthaura, Uhuru Muigai Kenyatta and Mohammed Hussein Ali, Corrigendum to the 'Document in support of the "appeal of the government of Kenya against the decision on the application by the government of Kenya challenging the admissibility of the case pursuant to Article 19(2)(b) of the Statute"', ICC-01/09-02/11 (21 June 2011), para. 43.

[280] Ibid. Kenya further averred that, in conducting preliminary investigations with respect to other situations, the prosecutor should consider the 'operation and capability of the national system as a whole as being determinative of whether he should intervene', para. 89.

[281] Ruto et al. Admissibility Appeals Judgment, paras. 42, 47; see also paras. 41, 46 in the parallel Kenyan cases. Arguably, the chamber opened the door to a potentially less demanding standard by its reference to 'substantially', but it did not elaborate on the implication of this qualification.

been, investigations and/or prosecutions at the national level'.[282] Finally, it specified that a successful challenge required concrete investigative steps: 'mere preparedness' to take such steps would not suffice.[283]

Like Kenya, the Libyan government also contended in its challenges to the Gaddafi and Al-Senussi cases that the 'same case' test should be broadened, recognizing that 'the state is to be accorded a margin of appreciation as to the contours of the case to be investigated and the ongoing exercise of the national authorities' prosecutorial discretion as to the focus and formulation of the case'.[284] Further, domestic authorities should not be 'unduly restrained in pursuing a national accountability agenda by being compelled to conduct an investigation and prosecution that mirrors precisely the factual substance' of the OTP's investigation.[285] Conformity to ICC practice should instead yield to a more flexible standard, the newly installed government argued, 'with a policy of giving the benefit of doubt to states exercising jurisdiction'.[286]

While not discarding the test, Pre-Trial Chamber I took a noticeably broader approach in both cases than in previous admissibility decisions. In each challenge, it rejected the suggestion that 'conduct' must be understood as 'incident specific',[287] but it affirmed that domestic investigations must be 'case-specific', meaning that:

> [I]t must be demonstrated that: a) the person subject to the domestic proceedings is the same person against whom the proceedings before the court are being conducted; and b) the conduct that is subject to the national investigation is substantially the same conduct that is alleged in the proceedings before the court.[288]

---

[282] Ruto et al. Admissibility Appeals Judgment, para. 44; see para. 43 in the parallel Kenyan cases.

[283] Ibid., para. 41; ibid., para. 40.

[284] The Prosecutor v. Saif Al-Islam Gaddafi and Abdullah Al-Senussi, Application on behalf of the government of Libya relating to Abdullah Al-Senussi pursuant to Article 19 of the ICC Statute, ICC-01/11-01/11 (2 April 2013), para. 88, 43 ('Al-Senussi Admissibility Application'); see also application on behalf of the government of Libya pursuant to Article 19 of the ICC Statute, ICC-01/11-01/11-130-Red (1 May 2012) ('Gaddafi Admissibility Application').

[285] Al-Senussi Admissibility Application, para. 88.

[286] Ibid., para. 97; Gaddafi Admissibility Application, para. 92.

[287] The Prosecutor v. Saif Al-Islam Gaddafi and Abdullah Al-Senussi, Decision on the admissibility of the case against Saif Al-Islam Gaddafi, ICC-01/11-01/11, PTC I (31 May 2013), paras. 73, 76–77 ('Gaddafi PTC Decision'); Decision on the admissibility of the case against Abdullah Al-Senussi, ICC-01/11-01/11, PTC I (11 October 2013), para. 66 ('Al-Senussi PTC decision').

[288] Al-Senussi PTC Decision, para. 66(i).

As to the question of what constitutes 'substantially' the same conduct, the chamber found that will 'vary according to the concrete facts and circumstances of the case, and, therefore, requires a case-by-case analysis'.[289] Significantly, contrary to duty-based arguments over the need to implement Rome Statute legislation domestically, the chamber took the opportunity in both decisions to clarify that 'the question of whether domestic investigations are carried out with a view to prosecuting "international crimes" is not determinative of an admissibility challenge'.[290] In its words, 'the decision to exclude reference to the ordinary crimes exception [of the International Criminal Tribunal for the Former Yugoslavia, ICTY, and International Criminal Tribunal for Rwanda, ICTR Statutes] was a deliberate decision that followed extensive discussions during the negotiating process'.[291]

Pre-Trial Chamber I nevertheless rejected the challenge brought on behalf of Gaddafi – chiefly because the Zintan militia was holding him, thus making the state 'unable' to obtain him for purposes of trial – but it found al-Senussi's case inadmissible.[292] It did so, in part, on the determination that 'it is not required that domestic proceedings concern each of those

---

[289] Gaddafi PTC Decision, para. 77; Al-Senussi PTC Decision, paras. 48, 66(iii).

[290] Gaddafi PTC Decision, para. 85; Al-Senussi PTC Decision, para. 66(iv). Similarly, adopting a significantly more permissive posture than it had under previous Article 19 challenges, the OTP supported most of these claims, noting that 'There is no requirement that the crimes charged in the national proceedings have the same "label" as the ones before this Court'. See The Prosecutor v. Saif Al-Islam Gaddafi and Abdullah Al-Senussi, Prosecution response to application on behalf of the government of Libya pursuant to Article 19 of the ICC Statute, ICC-01/11-01/11 (5 June 2012), para. 23.

[291] Gaddafi PTC Decision, paras. 87–88 ('It is the chamber's view that Libya's current lack of legislation criminalising crimes against humanity does not per se render the case admissible before the court'.).

[292] Though the chamber found that Libya had 'fallen short of substantiating [its submission], by means of evidence of a sufficient degree of specificity and probative value', the gravamen of its opinion fell on its finding that the national system was 'unavailable' within the meaning of Article 17(3) because it was unable to 'obtain' the accused as well as necessary witnesses or testimony and because it could not 'overcome the existing difficulties in securing a lawyer for [Gaddafi]'. See Gaddafi PTC Decision, paras. 135, 206–208, 215. The Appeals Chamber, however, only affirmed the PTC's finding that Libya had not satisfied the 'same conduct' first step; it did not consider 'inability'. Gaddafi Admissibility Appeals Judgment, para. 86. In June 2018, Gaddafi filed another admissibility challenge before the (now reconstituted) PTC I under Article 17(1)(c) and the ne bis in idem principle, contending that his 2015 trial and conviction in Libya was for the same conduct as the case still pending against him in the ICC (Gaddafi was subsequently released in 2016, ostensibly pursuant to an amnesty law adopted the year prior). See The Prosecutor v. Saif Al-Islam Gaddafi, Admissibility challenge by Dr. Saif Al-Islam Gaddafi pursuant to Articles 17(1)(c), 19 and 20(3) of the Rome Statute, ICC-01/11-01/11, PTC I (5 June 2018).

events [mentioned in the ICC arrest warrant] at the national level'; rather, whether 'all or some of the "incidents" or "events"' encompassed constitute a 'relevant indicator' that the cases are the same.[293] After an extensive assessment of evidence submitted to that effect, the pre-trial judges were satisfied that Libyan authorities 'are taking concrete and progressive steps directed at ascertaining the criminal responsibility of Mr Al-Senussi for substantially the same conduct as alleged in the proceedings before the court'.[294]

The Appeals Chamber affirmed both of the Pre-Trial Chamber's rulings though, in so doing, it walked back some of the latter's more flexible language on the degree of required 'sameness'. Indeed, while concurring with the lower chamber's evidentiary assessment of the domestic case against Al-Senussi, the chamber insisted that 'incidents' were of relevance as a basis for comparison. In its words:

> What is required is a judicial assessment of whether the case that the state is investigating sufficiently mirrors the one that the prosecutor is investigating. The Appeals Chamber considers that to carry out this assessment, it is necessary to use, as a comparator, the underlying incidents under investigation both by the prosecutor and the state, alongside the conduct of the suspect under investigation that gives rise to his or her criminal responsibility for the conduct described in those incidents.[295]

Notably, however, Judge Anita Ušacka took issue with the court's continued fidelity to the 'same case' test. In dissent, she argued:

> Establishing such a rigid requirement would oblige domestic authorities to investigate or prosecute exactly or nearly exactly the conduct that forms the basis for the 'case before the court' at the time of the admissibility proceedings, thereby being obliged to 'copy' the case before the court. Instead of complementing each other, the relationship between the court and the state would be competitive, requiring the state to do its utmost to fulfill the requirements set by the court.[296]

The Pre-Trial Chamber rejected that request in April 2019, principally on the grounds that the decision of the Tripoli court – which was still subject to appeal and conducted in absentia – was not sufficiently 'final' within the meaning of Article 20(3) to have res judicata effect. See The Prosecutor v. Saif Al-Islam Gaddafi, Decision on the 'Admissibility Challenge by Dr. Saif Al-Islam Gaddafi pursuant to Articles 17(1)(c), 19 and 20(3) of the Rome Statute', ICC-01/11-01/11, PTC I (5 April 2019), paras. 38–48.

[293] Al-Senussi PTC Decision, paras. 79, 165.
[294] Ibid., para. 167.
[295] Gaddafi Admissibility Appeals Judgment, para. 73.
[296] Gaddafi Admissibility Appeals Judgment, Dissenting Opinion of Judge Anita Ušacka, para. 52; see also Al Senussi Admissibility Appeals Judgment, Separate Opinion of Judge Anita Ušacka, para. 14 (finding that the PTC 'may have been too demanding when it considered whether Libya was able genuinely to investigate and prosecute in

Echoing Judge Ušacka, Kevin Jon Heller has also been a forceful critic of the 'same conduct' test. In his view, 'the same-conduct requirement expects states to be mind-readers: if [states] do not accurately anticipate the precise conduct that will draw the ICC's attention—no small task, given the "universe of criminality in atrocity-crime situations"—they will be deemed "inactive" with regard to the international proceedings and the court will admit the case'.[297]

Despite such criticism, the 'same case' test has become an interpretive mainstay of the court's jurisprudence. It was most recently applied in the Appeals Chamber's May 2015 judgment rejecting the Ivory's Coast challenge to the ICC's proceedings against Simone Gbagbo, notwithstanding the fact that she had already been convicted and sentenced to 20 years imprisonment, on different charges, by a domestic court in March of that year.[298] Subsequently, following reports that she had been charged with crimes against humanity in a 2017 trial, the Pre-Trial Chamber issued a proprio motu order for information from the

relation to Mr. Gaddafi'). Payam Akhavan has argued that the time difference between the two filings – the challenge to Gaddafi's case was filed in May 2012, al-Senussi's in April 2013 – was critical to the competing outcomes. Although both cases 'covered essentially the same facts', based as they were on a common criminal plan to attack civilians, the later filing of the Al-Senussi challenge meant that the national investigation was considerably more advanced than it was at the time of Gaddafi's challenge. See Payam Akhavan, 'Complementarity Conundrums: The ICC Clock in Transitional Times', *Journal of International Criminal Justice* 14(5) (2016), 1043–1059. For further criticism of the Gaddafi decision, see Nidal Nabil Jurdi, 'The Complementarity Regime of the International Criminal Court in Practice: Is It Truly Serving the Purpose? Some Lessons from Libya', *Leiden Journal of International Law* 30(1) (2017), 219 (arguing that the PTC's reasoning was flawed because it confused a situation of inability with 'a law enforcement problem').

[297] Heller, 'A Sentence-Based Theory of Complementarity', 241. Heller has advanced a 'sentencing based heuristic', wherein any national prosecution of an ordinary crime would satisfy the principle of complementarity as long as it results in a sentence equal to, or longer than, the sentence the perpetrator would receive from the ICC. In later work, he has advocated what he calls 'radical complementarity – the idea that as a long as a state is making a genuine effort to bring a suspect to justice, the ICC should find his or her case inadmissible regardless of the conduct the state investigates or the prosecutorial strategy the state pursues', 664. See Kevin Jon Heller, 'Radical Complementarity', *Journal of International Criminal Justice* 14(3) (2016), 637–665. For a defence of the test's application, see Rastan, 'What Is "Substantially the Same Conduct?"'.

[298] The Prosecutor *v.* Simone Gbagbo, Judgment on the appeal of Cote d'Ivoire against the decision of Pre-Trial Chamber I of 11 December 2014 entitled 'Decision on Cote d'Ivoire's challenge to the admissibility of the case against Simone Gbagbo', ICC-02/11-01/12 OA, AC (27 May 2015).

OTP concerning any acts taken by Ivorian authorities since December 2014 that could affect the admissibility of her case.[299] Noting that the admissibility of a case is 'not static', the chamber requested 'all pertinent judicial decisions … to determine whether the admissibility of the case ought to be reviewed'.[300] As this example attests, while defensible as a matter of statutory interpretation, the 'same case' test has the potential of placing the ICC in awkward disjuncture with national jurisdictions. Indeed, rather than encouraging flexibility in the manner and method by which states pursue domestic accountability, the test has often promoted the opposite.[301]

Admissibility Challenges and Timing

In addition to the substantive constraints imposed by the same conduct requirement, the ICC has also applied procedural limitations on admissibility challenges that can frustrate a more probative review. As noted, most ICC pre-trial chambers have addressed admissibility challenges pursuant to Article 19(1), which the court interprets with broad discretion to determine proprio motu the admissibility of a case.[302] In July 2006, however, the Appeals Chamber narrowed the scope of such review, holding that 'the Pre-Trial Chamber should exercise its discretion [with respect to admissibility] only when it is appropriate in the circumstances

---

[299] The Prosecutor v. Simone Gbagbo, Order to the registrar to request information from the competent national authorities of the Republic of Cote d'Ivoire, ICC-02/11-01/12, PTC II (14 September 2018). It appears that Ms. Gbagbo was charged with crimes against humanity, and acquitted following a domestic trial in 2017; however, the Supreme Court later overturned her acquittal. Subsequently, as of August 2018, she was released from prison following an amnesty from President Ouattara. See Ange Aboa, 'Ivory Coast's Simone Gbagbo leaves detention after amnesty', *Reuters* (8 August 2018).

[300] Ibid., paras. 5–6.

[301] Sharon A. Williams and William A. Schabas, 'Article 17: Issues of Admissibility', in Otto Triffterer (ed.), *Commentary on the Rome Statute of the International Criminal Court: Observers' Notes, Article by Article* (Portland: Hart, 2008), 616. For an alternative view, see Diane Bernard, 'Beyond Hierarchy: Standard of Review and the Complementarity of the International Criminal Court', in Lukasz Gruszczynski and Wouter Werner (eds.), *Deference in International Courts and Tribunals: Standard of Review and Margin of Appreciation* (Oxford: Oxford University Press, 2014), 372–386.

[302] See, e.g., The Prosecutor v. Joseph Kony et al., Decision on the admissibility of the case under Article 19(1) of the Statute, ICC-02/04-01/05, PTC II (10 March 2009) ('Uganda Admissibility Decision').

of the case, bearing in mind the interests of the suspect'.[303] Such exceptional circumstances, the chamber noted, 'may include instances where a case is based on the established jurisprudence of the court, uncontested facts that render a case clearly inadmissible or an ostensible cause impelling the exercise of proprio motu review'; otherwise, it would constitute an abuse of discretion.[304] While conceding that, in this instance, such discretion had in fact benefited the accused, that 'advantage [was] only marginal and could be attained through other procedures', since admissibility challenges could be lodged after an arrest warrant had been issued, but prior to the accused's arrest or surrender.[305] In the Appeals Chamber's view, it was thus 'not necessary for a Pre-Trial Chamber to "come to the aid" of a suspect by making an initial determination of a case before a warrant of arrest has been issued'.[306]

This early decision has attracted significant criticism. As Gilbert Bitti and Mohamed El Zeidy note, the decision ignores the fact that admissibility is 'a general principle in the Rome Statute which does not need to be reiterated in every single provision'.[307] Furthermore, the chamber's decision would appear to ignore, or overlook, the practical context of most ICC arrest warrants, many of which have been issued under seal and ex parte.[308] In practice, this effectively prevents a defendant from challenging admissibility prior to his or her surrender to the ICC. As the Katanga Trial Chamber noted, '[T]he DRC did not challenge the admissibility of the case when this warrant of arrest was communicated to it and ... as soon as said warrant was unsealed, Germain Katanga's transfer to The Hague was ordered immediately'.[309]

---

[303] *Situation in the Democratic Republic of Congo*, Judgment of the prosecutor's appeal against the decision of Pre-Trial Chamber I entitled 'Decision on the Prosecutor's Application for Warrants of Arrest, Article 58', ICC-01/04-169, AC (13 July 2006), para. 52. The impugned portion of the Pre-Trial Chamber's decision concerned its denial of the prosecutor's ex parte application under Article 58 for a warrant of arrest against Bosco Ntganda, in part, because the chamber determined that the case was inadmissible.
[304] Ibid.
[305] Ibid., para. 51.
[306] Ibid.
[307] Gilbert Bitti and Mohamed M. El Zeidy, 'The *Katanga* Trial Chamber Decision: Selected Issues', *Leiden Journal of International Law* 23 (2010), 323.
[308] The surrender of Alfred Yekatom in the CAR II situation (also a self-referred situation) by CAR authorities was also made pursuant to a sealed arrest warrant. See www.icc-cpi.int/Pages/item.aspx?name=pr1418.
[309] Katanga Admissibility Decision, para. 95.

The logic of the Appeals Chamber's decision suggests a circular approach to assessing prosecutorial or judicial activity at the national level, particularly in situations where the state itself has relinquished jurisdiction. In Katanga's admissibility decision, for instance, the chamber affirmed that the case was inadmissible, but the grounds of its determination focused on the first-prong of the admissibility test: inactivity.[310] Specifically, the chamber found that there were no proceedings against Katanga at the time he raised his challenge because the DRC had closed them upon his transfer to The Hague.[311] This approach to the admissibility provision thus subordinated the presence of domestic proceedings to a narrow question: Were proceedings ongoing 'at the time of' the court's actual determination of the admissibility of the case?[312]

The chamber appeared untroubled by the potentially chilling effect that such relinquishment of jurisdiction might have on the duty of states to exercise their criminal jurisdiction. In its words, 'It is purely speculative to assume that a state that has refrained from opening an investigation into a particular case or from prosecuting a suspect would do so, just because the [ICC] has ruled that the case is inadmissible'.[313] While the chamber's reasoning is consistent with the plain language of Article 17, it suggests that judicial inquiry into the broader context of domestic proceedings (at least with respect to Article 17(1)(a)–(b)) would be immaterial. As other chambers have similarly ruled, the nature of any past investigations – who initiated them,

---

[310] As noted, the Appeals Chamber corrected the Trial Chamber and held that complementarity comprised a two-part test: '(1) whether there are ongoing investigations or prosecutions, or (2) whether there have been investigations in the past, and the state having jurisdiction has decided not to prosecute the persons concerned. It is only when the answers to these questions are in the affirmative that … one has to examine the question of unwillingness and inability'. See Katanga Admissibility Appeals Judgment, para. 78.

[311] Ibid., para. 82.

[312] Ibid., para. 75. One commentator, acknowledging this apparent catch-22, describes it as follows: '[O]nce transferred, if the domestic investigation is terminated then this means that Article 17(1)(a) does not render the case inadmissible; and the decision to transfer, reflecting a decision that the person should be brought to justice, means that the case is also not inadmissible under Article 17(1)(b)'. See Ben Batros, 'Evolution of the ICC Jurisprudence on Admissibility', in *The International Criminal Court and Complementarity*, 601.

[313] Katanga Admissibility Appeals Judgment, para. 86.

for what crimes, based on what evidence – is irrelevant in assessing domestic judicial activity.[314]

The insistence that concrete investigative steps must be underway at the time the court makes a determination on an admissibility challenge is further compounded by Article 19(5) of the Statute, which stipulates that such challenges be made 'at the earliest opportunity'.[315] The Appeals Chamber has clarified such opportunity as 'the earliest point in time after [a] conflict of jurisdictions has actually arisen', not (as Kenya unsuccessfully argued) when a summons to appear is issued.[316] Still, this interpretation may be difficult to meet for states that have a genuine desire to conduct domestic proceedings, but suffer from the challenges common to many post-conflict states, e.g., collapsed (or compromised) judicial systems, limited capacity or inadequate national legal frameworks. Indeed, it was on this basis that the Libyan government averred in its admissibility challenge that 'no state emerging from conflict could ever benefit from the complementarity principle'.[317]

Similarly, in the Kenyan government's admissibility challenge, the government averred that the Pre-Trial Chamber had erred by failing to give it sufficient time to submit additional evidence before ruling on the application. The Appeals Chamber rejected this argument, concluding that a two-month period was sufficient between the receipt of

---

[314] For similar outcomes, see The Prosecutor v. Jean-Pierre Bemba Gombo, Judgment on the appeal of Mr. Jean-Pierre Bemba Gombo against the decision of Trial Chamber III of 24 June 2010 entitled 'Decision on the Admissibility and Abuse of Process Challenges', ICC-01/05-01/08OA3, AC (19 October 2010), para. 74 (recalling that a 'decision not to prosecute' in terms of Article 17(1)(b) 'does not cover decisions of a state to close judicial proceedings against a suspect because of his or her surrender to the ICC'); Gbagbo Admissibility Decision, paras. 21, 27 (noting that 'national authorities chose to refrain' from opening an investigation into Gbagbo for 'violent crimes', while his prosecution for economic crimes 'has been impaired since his surrender to the court').

[315] Rome Statute, Article 19(5). Article 19(4) articulates a further deadline, requiring that the challenge be filed prior to the commencement of the trial. The Katanga Trial Chamber further held that the 'commencement of trial' is actually the moment of the constitution of the Trial Chamber, rather than the start of the trial per se; the Appeals Chamber did not pronounce on the merits of this interpretation, but noted that its decision to do so 'does not necessarily mean that it agrees with the Trial Chamber's interpretation of the term'. See Katanga Admissibility Appeals Judgment, para. 38.

[316] Ruto et al. Admissibility Appeals Judgment, paras. 46, 100.

[317] Gaddafi Admissibility Application, para. 101. For a similar argument, see also Akhavan, 'Complementarity Conundrums' (contending that 'admissibility determinations must reasonably accommodate the unpleasant realities of national judicial systems in the wake of such calamities'), 1057.

an admissibility challenge and a ruling upon it. Further, relying on the two-stage test articulated in the Katanga judgment, the chamber reiterated that the admissibility challenge must be 'sufficiently substantiated' at the time the motion is filed. States cannot expect to be allowed to make further submissions.[318]

Evidentiary Thresholds

Another limitation of some Article 17 decisions has been the uneven scrutiny with which ICC chambers have assessed claims of ongoing domestic proceedings. In this regard, Katanga's proceedings illustrate the negative consequences of the Appeals Chamber's 2006 judgment narrowing the scope of proprio motu review, which resulted in the Pre-Trial Chamber conducting a 'very limited review' of the admissibility of the case against him.[319] As a result, when Katanga brought his admissibility challenge before the Trial Chamber, the chamber was thrust into the 'difficult position of trying to respect the 13 July 2006 Appeals Chamber judgment and to guess the Pre-Trial Chamber's attitude if it had been engaged in a detailed review of the admissibility of the case during the issuance of the arrest warrant'.[320]

The Trial Chamber's reasoning in Katanga's challenge is noteworthy for its approach to the question of state 'willingness', which has otherwise yet to be addressed by the court. Notably, the Trial Chamber did not address the activity or inactivity of the DRC authorities (as the Appeals Chamber later did); rather, it proceeded directly to what Robinson has termed the 'slogan' version of the test, i.e., it proceeded directly to an unwillingness/inability assessment.[321] It examined the intent of the DRC to bring Katanga to justice and considered that the evidence presented to date supported the 'clear and explicit expression of unwillingness of the DRC to prosecute [the] case'.[322] Echoing an argument that had initially

---

[318] On this point, it should be noted that the Libyan government was offered the opportunity to submit a second challenge after the Appeals Chamber affirmed the PTC's ruling finding Gaddafi's case admissible. See Gaddafi Admissibility Appeals Judgment, para. 44.

[319] Bitti and El Zeidy, 'The *Katanga* Trial Chamber Decision', 324.

[320] Ibid.

[321] See Robinson, 'The Mysterious Mysteriousness of Complementarity'; see also Robinson, 'The Inaction Controversy: Neglected Words and New Opportunities', in *The International Criminal Court and Complementarity*, 460–502.

[322] Katanga Admissibility Decision, para. 95.

been rejected by the Pre-Trial Chamber in Lubanga, the Trial Chamber held that because the Congolese authorities had wilfully surrendered him to the court, the national system must be deemed 'unwilling' within the meaning of Article 17.[323]

In arriving at this conclusion, the trial judges uncritically accepted the DRC's submissions that it had voluntarily relinquished jurisdiction. The chamber cited to a letter from the government, which stated the DRC's 'official position' that the ICC must reject Katanga's admissibility challenge because, in so doing, the ICC would be 'doing justice' to 'His Excellency Mr. Joseph Kabila, President of the DRC, [who] has demonstrated to the world his determination to fight resolutely against impunity by making the DRC to date an unequalled model of cooperation with the ICC'.[324] The court further appeared to accept as dispositive a letter submitted to the OTP by the director of the immediate office of the chief prosecutor of the High Military Court in Kinshasa, which stated that 'the military prosecuting authority had not initiated any investigation against Germain Katanga in relation to the attack on Bogoro on 24 February 2003'.[325] Such 'clear and explicit' expressions of unwillingness, according to the chamber, meant that the 'DRC clearly intend[ed] to leave it up to the court' to prosecute Katanga for the attack in Bogoro.[326]

Yet, by the chamber's own admission, disagreement did exist as to whether domestic criminal proceedings against Katanga had been initiated and whether there was unwillingness to prosecute. One of the threshold questions was defence counsel's claim that the prosecutor had 'inadvertently or negligently' failed to provide the Pre-Trial Chamber with information on the existence of domestic proceedings against Katanga at the time the arrest warrant was issued.[327] These documents included a request filed by the Kinshasa High Military

---

[323] Ibid., para. 77. ('This second form of unwillingness, which is not expressly provided for in Article 17 of the Statute, aims to see the person brought to justice, but not before national courts. The chambers considers that a state which chooses not to investigate or prosecute a person before its own courts, but has nevertheless every intention of seeing that justice is done, must be considered as lacking the will referred to in Article 17'.)

[324] Ibid., para. 94.

[325] Ibid., para. 93.

[326] Ibid., para. 95.

[327] The Prosecutor v. Germain Katanga, Document in support of appeal of the defence for Germain Katanga against the decision of the Trial Chamber 'Motifs de la décision Oral Relative a l'exception d'irrecevabilité de l'affaire', ICC-01/04-01/07 (8 July 2009), paras. 42–51.

Court in March 2007 to extend Katanga's provisional detention, which contained reference to Bogoro 'as one of the ten locations where people had allegedly been killed in the course of systematic attacks against the civilian population'.[328] In the light of this submission, the chamber even acknowledged that the document contained 'objective information indicating that Germain Katanga was one of several persons under investigation for crimes ... between 2002 and 2005 in, among other locations, Bogoro'.[329]

The awkward posture in which the Trial Chamber found itself – effectively second guessing the issuance of Katanga's arrest warrant, following the Pre-Trial Chamber's limited review – likely contributed to its cursory analysis of the documents that had allegedly not been provided.[330] These documents suggest, at the least, discrepancies between the DRC government's representation and the situation on the ground at the time, but the chamber declined the opportunity to query the matter further. In particular, the judges found 'no need to answer the question' as to whether the materials would have led the Pre-Trial Chamber to exercise its discretion differently because, in its view, the document did not contain 'decisive information' on the question of whether there had been domestic proceedings, nor was it 'conclusive as to whether the acts allegedly committed there could be attributed to Germain Katanga'.[331] As with the court's later decisions, this apparent endorsement of a 'conclusive' and/or 'decisive' standard sets a high threshold for evidence of domestic activity.

The Trial Chamber's conclusions also appeared to rest on a prima facie acceptance of the representations of the Congolese executive. In effect, it treated the state as a unitary actor, overlooking evidence that there had been apparent disagreement *within* the state on the status of Katanga's case, as well as on the ability to try cases at the sub-state,

---

[328] Katanga Admissibility Decision, para. 68.
[329] Ibid., para. 70.
[330] In Bitti and El Zeidy's words, rather than undertaking a more robust inquiry into whether proceedings had been underway, the Trial Chamber 'used a clever legal argument to overcome a practical problem', 324. See also Matthew E. Cross and Sarah Williams, 'Recent Developments at the ICC: Prosecutor v. *Germain Katanga and Mathieu Ngudjolo Chui* – A Boost for "Co-operative Complementarity"?' *Human Rights Law Review* 10(2) (2010), 342 ('On the facts, the decision rested on a delicate, and perhaps somewhat strained, definition of "inactivity"'.)
[331] Katanga Admissibility Decision, paras. 70–73.

i.e., provincial, level.[332] Phil Clark, for instance, notes that the ICC's Ituri-only focus at the time of Katanga's challenge had raised concerns amongst senior judicial officials given that Ituri had one of the better functioning local judiciaries in the DRC.[333] While other ICC officials have contested the veracity that DRC authorities were pursuing an investigation against Lubanga, the fact that there were competing claims received scant attention from the court.[334]

The 'conclusive' threshold apparently adopted by the Trial Chamber in Katanga is heightened by the fact that a state challenging the admissibility of a case 'bears the burden of proof to show that the case is inadmissible'; further, to 'discharge that burden', the state 'must provide the court with evidence of a sufficient degree of specificity and probative value that demonstrates that it is indeed investigating the case'.[335] Thus, as the Appeals Chamber clarified in the Kenyan admissibility challenge, concrete evidence must be submitted that points to 'specific investigative steps', including, inter alia, 'interviewing witnesses or suspects, collecting documentary evidence, or carrying out forensic analyses'.[336] Despite these requirements, the Pre-Trial Chamber refused to grant the Kenyan government's requests to submit additional evidence or to present its argument in an oral hearing, where it had wanted the state police commissioner to testify concerning the progress of national proceedings (the chamber did allow evidence from the commissioner to be filed in writing, but the government declined to so submit). While the Appeals Chamber conceded that 'there might have been reasons to hold an oral hearing', it concluded that the PTC's decision not to do so was not an abuse of discretion.[337]

---

[332] See Phil Clark, 'Chasing Cases: The Politics of State Referral', in *The International Criminal Court and Complementarity*, 1194–1195. In a similar vein, another commentator has noted that 'We have little sense of how the ICC measures willingness. Is willingness determined according to what a country's executive branch says? By the judicial system's choice of cases'? See 'The ICC on the Ground: Complementarity at work in Colombia and the DRC', International Center for Transitional Justice (May 2010), at www.ictj.org/sites/default/files/ICTJ-Global-Newsletter-May-2010-English.pdf.

[333] Clark, 'Chasing Cases'. Clark quotes Chris Aberi, the state prosecutor in Bunia: 'When the ICC first came here, we showed them the dossiers we had already assembled on Lubanga and others. We were ready to try those cases here'. Clark expands upon this argument in *Distant Justice*, 176–181.

[334] See, e.g., Rastan, 'What Is "Substantially the Same Conduct?"' 27.

[335] Kenyatta Admissibility Appeals Judgment, para. 61.

[336] Ibid., para. 40.

[337] Ibid., para. 108.

Judge Ušacka again dissented from this view. She criticized the Pre-Trial Chamber for not seeking submission on such 'pivotal matters' as the 'definition of investigation and prosecution, standard of proof, and the type of evidence that was required to meet the burden, even though the appellant had requested a hearing on those matters'.[338] She further argued that the Pre-Trial Chamber abused its discretion in failing to consider Kenya's submissions that investigations were underway (it had, for instance, included a case file referring to Ruto as a suspect with information on the scope of the investigation) or about their prospective nature, i.e., the possibility that, while in an early stage, the investigations might satisfy Article 19's standards at some point in the near future since 'the assessment of complementarity is the outcome of an ongoing process'.[339] In her view, the Kenyan government should have been allowed more time to submit further evidence; moreover, the Pre-Trial Chamber could (and should) have used its authority to request additional documentation.

The court's approach in both the Katanga and Kenya's admissibility challenges suggests that the level of scrutiny applied to investigations and prosecutions at the national level has been less than thorough and that a desire for speed or 'efficiency' – or quite simply a lack of faith in the veracity of those challenges – has overwhelmed the opportunity for more careful analysis and dialogue with national- (or local)-level courts and prosecutors.[340] Notably, however, the court appeared to adjust this approach in the course of Libya's admissibility challenges. In those challenges, it requested further clarifications on a variety of issues to obtain 'concrete, tangible and pertinent evidence that proper investigations are

---

[338] Ibid., Dissenting Opinion of Judge Anita Ušacka, 20 September 2011, para. 25; see also para. 8.

[339] Ibid., para. 20; see also para. 27 ('The court should not circumvent [the high threshold] created by unwillingness or inability by requiring a state to prove, e.g., the existence of a full-fledged investigation or prosecution of a case in order to establish that there is no situation of inactivity'.) For a similar view, see Charles Cherner Jalloh, 'Kenya vs. The ICC Prosecutor', *Harvard International Law Journal* 53 (August 2012), 242 ('the judges' strict application of the same person/substantially same conduct test arguably does not respect and nurture the growth of complementarity and the anti-impunity work of national jurisdictions upon which the Rome Statute was predicated').

[340] One commentator has also suggested that the Pre-Trial Chamber's imposition of a 'high legal burden of proof' on the Kenyan challenge was because of its lack of faith in the government's intentions: 'The real issue is that it simply did not believe that Kenya was acting in good faith'. See Clare Brighton, 'Avoiding Unwillingness: Addressing the Political Pitfalls Inherent in the Complementarity Regime of the International Criminal Court', *International Criminal Law Review* 12 (2012), 658.

currently ongoing in Libya'.[341] While this additional information did not alter the Pre-Trial Chamber's admissibility determination with respect to Gaddafi, it did sway the court as it pertained to Al-Senussi's challenge. To that end, the breadth of the additional information it sought and the additional time taken to review the proffered evidence (the Libya admissibility proceedings 'stretched for the longest period' of all challenges to date) suggest the possibility of a more probing approach to future challenges.[342]

Due Process: Domestic Legal Systems on Trial

Following the two-stage test for dealing with admissibility challenges, states are not first evaluated as to their willingness and ability to prosecute. This determination comes second and has only rarely been dealt with in the complementarity case law to date. When it has, however, the legal framework applied suggests a similarly exacting approach to admissibility determinations. In Uganda, for instance, the Pre-Trial Chamber invoked its proprio motu powers to examine the continued admissibility of the case against Lord's Resistance Army (LRA) leader Joseph Kony, following the creation of the then War Crimes Division, a new special division within the Ugandan High Court meant to prosecute serious crimes. In finding that it nonetheless remained properly seized of the case, the

---

[341] The Prosecutor v. Saif Al-Islam Gaddafi and Abdullah Al-Senussi, Decision requesting further submissions on issues related to the admissibility of the case against Saif Al-Islam Gaddafi, ICC-01/11-01/11, PTC I (7 December 2012), para. 9. These documents included: (1) issues relating to the status of domestic proceedings (including what investigative steps have been taken, whether evidence has been collected and of what type); (2) issues relating to the subject-matter of the domestic investigations (including the 'anticipate contours' of the case at the national level); (3) issues of Libyan national law (including progress made in relation to law reform and the incorporation in Libyan law of international crimes as defined under the Rome Statute, and whether such reform would impact on the proceedings against Gaddafi); (4) issues relating to Gaddafi's exercise of his rights under Libyan national law; and (5) issues relating to the capacity of Libyan authorities to investigate and prosecute (including questions of resource allocation, witness protection and custody). Ibid., paras. 14–47.

[342] Akhavan, 'Complementarity Conundrums', 1050. Notably, Pre-Trial Chamber I did not seize a similar opportunity in rejecting the admissibility challenge to the case against Simone Gbagbo; it concluded that, despite evidence suggesting national proceedings had been initiated, the document provided was 'contrary, sparse and disparate'. Further clarification was not sought. See The Prosecutor v. Simone Gbagbo, Decision on Cote d'Ivoire's challenge to the admissibility of the case against Simone Gbagbo, ICC-02/11-01/12, PTC I (11 December 2014), para. 65.

chamber suggested a strict approach to complementarity, consistent with the expanded concept of it as a tool for compliance. In its words, 'Pending the adoption of *all* relevant texts and the implementation of *all* practical steps, the scenario ... remains therefore the same as at the time of the issuance of the warrants, that is one of *total inaction* on the part of the relevant national authorities'.[343]

The court considered the adequacy of a state's domestic legal framework most extensively in the context of Libya, where the fairness of domestic proceedings and the adequacy of the country's national criminal code were central issues. Whereas the Kenyan accused were aligned with the government's admissibility challenges, in Libya, both Gaddafi and al-Senussi sought transfer to The Hague on the basis that they would not be afforded a fair trial domestically. These challenges have presented perhaps the most complex set of questions for the court to consider, in a political environment marked by little desire to cooperate with the ICC's warrants, but where genuine political transition offered (at least for a time) greater prospects for domestic accountability.[344] Put differently, the concern was not that Libyan authorities were unwilling to prosecute Gaddafi and al-Senussi, but rather that they were too willing.

In its challenge to the case against Gaddafi, Libya submitted that an active investigation – broader than, but including the same incidents and conduct as those contained in the ICC warrant – was ongoing since the date of Gaddafi's capture, and that it was willing and able genuinely to carry out the proceedings.[345] The government focused on efforts made

---

[343] Uganda Admissibility Decision, para. 52 (emphasis added).

[344] Illustrative of the challenge facing the court is the wealth of academic commentary that the Libyan situation has spawned. See, e.g., Elinor Fry, 'Between Show Trials and Sham Prosecutions: The Rome Statute's Potential Effects on Domestic Due Process Protections', *Criminal Law Forum* 23 (2012) (advocating a 'modified approach' focusing on 'core fair trial elements ... without turning the ICC into a traditional human rights body'); Frédéric Mégret and Marika Giles Samson, 'Holding the Line on Complementarity in Libya: The Case for Tolerating Flawed Domestic Trials', *Journal of International Criminal Justice* 11 (2013), 585 ('we would suggest that the litmus test is not whether the right to a fair trial has been violated in itself, but whether the degree to which it has been violated is such that one cannot realistically say that there has been a trial at all, thus revealing an unwillingness or inability'); H. J. van der Merwe, 'The Show Must Not Go On: Complementarity, the Due Process Thesis and Overzealous Domestic Prosecutions', *International Criminal Law Review* 15(1) (2015), 40–75 (contending that the conjunctive requirements of Article 17(2)(c) 'should be interpreted to establish the risk of losing [a conviction] as a sine qua non for state willingness'); Heller, 'Radical Complementarity'.

[345] Gaddafi Admissibility Application, para. 101.

to strengthen judicial capacity building and to improve the security situation, but argued that 'It is not the function of the ICC to hold Libya's national legal system against an exacting and elaborate standard beyond that basically required for a fair trial'.[346] Similar arguments were made in the challenge to the al-Senussi case, with Libya asserting that an appropriate courtroom complex and prison facilities would be available.[347] It noted, however, that due process need not 'ensure that the domestic proceedings accord with a particular ideal as determined by the ICC'.[348] In this case, the prosecutor agreed.[349]

As noted, the court issued divided rulings. In the case of Gaddafi, the chamber rejected Libya's challenge both on the grounds of 'inability' (insofar as it was unable to 'obtain' both the accused as well as testimony from witnesses who were being held in detention facilities not yet under the government's control), and because there was insufficient evidence to 'discern the actual contours of the case against [Gaddafi] such that the scope of the domestic investigation could be said the cover the same case [as the ICC]'.[350] A third line of reasoning, however, was that *national* due process standards were relevant to the principle of complementarity. Specifically, the chamber found that the failure to provide Gaddafi with a defence attorney, despite the guarantee of counsel under Libyan law, was 'an impediment to the progress of proceedings', as it meant that 'a trial cannot be conducted in accordance with the rights and protections of the Libyan national justice system'.[351] In short, while a state's failure to satisfy international standards of due process might not render a case inadmissible, the failure to respect national due process standards – 'in the context of the relevant national systems and procedures' – could.[352]

The chamber, however, granted the state's later challenge to the admissibility of al-Senussi's case. While that case was different than Gadaffi's in

---

[346] Ibid., para. 99.
[347] Al-Senussi Admissibility Application, paras. 176, 181, 193.
[348] Ibid., para. 111.
[349] OTP Response to Libya Application, para. 28 ('The Statute requires that the state with jurisdiction must establish a genuine willingness and ability, but it need not also establish that its domestic procedural protections comport with the ICC Statute and Rules of Procedure and Evidence'.).
[350] Gaddafi PTC Decision, paras. 135, 206–211.
[351] Ibid., para. 214.
[352] Ibid., 200.

that al-Senussi was in the custody of the Libyan government, the national proceedings for both accused were closely related.[353] Here, however, the court's approach suggested a modified approach to due process questions.[354] In affirming the decision, the Appeals Chamber,

> recall[ed] that, in the context of admissibility proceedings, the court is not primarily called upon to decide whether in domestic proceedings certain requirements of human rights law or domestic law are being violated. Rather, what is at issue is whether the state is willing genuinely to investigate or prosecute.[355]

The chamber concluded that, even accepting the fair trial violations that would flow from lack of access to a lawyer during the investigation stage of proceedings, 'such violations would not reach the high threshold for finding that Libya is unwilling genuinely to investigate or prosecute Mr. Al-Senussi'.[356] In its view, such a high threshold meant proceedings that would 'lead to a suspect evading justice . . . in the equivalent of sham proceedings that are concerned with that person's protection'.[357]

The court's decision in Al-Senussi was not without criticism: several human rights NGOs expressed concern with the high threshold that the chamber set for the consideration of due process rights as part of the complementarity assessment.[358] But the ICC's general approach in both of

---

[353] Unlike Gaddafi's challenge, however, both the PTC and Appeals Chamber found that the 'same conduct' test was satisfied as it pertained to al-Senussi. As previously noted, the difference in time between the filing of the two challenges may well explain the different outcomes. See Akhavan, 'Complementarity Conundrums', 1044 (arguing that 'judicial appreciation of time in transitional contexts produced two different outcomes').

[354] The Pre-Trial Chamber's apparent emphasis on the fact that al-Senussi's lack of counsel 'at the present time' was not dispositive of 'inability' (as it appeared to be in the case of Gaddafi), suggests a more permissive temporal approach by the court as well. Ibid., paras. 307–308.

[355] Al-Senussi Admissibility Appeals Judgment, para. 190.

[356] Ibid.

[357] Ibid., para. 218.

[358] Civil society reaction to the court's decision was decidedly mixed. The only international NGO to explicitly welcome the ruling was No Peace Without Justice, which considered it 'a positive answer to Libyans' aspirations to see the alleged perpetrators of crimes against them face justice where those crimes were committed'. See 'Libya: NPWJ and NRPTT welcome ICC ruling on the Al-Senussi case' (24 July 2014), at www.npwj.org/ICC/Libya-NPWJ-and-NRPTT-welcome-ICC-ruling-Al-Senussi-case-which-heralds-new-potential-justice-and-. For criticisms of the decision, see Jennifer Trahan, 'A Complementarity Challenge Gone Awry. The ICC and the Libya Warrants', *OpinioJuris* (4 September 2015), at http://opiniojuris.org/2015/09/04/guest-post-a-complementarity-challenge-gone-awry-the-icc-and-the-libya-warrants/; Mark Ellis,

the Libyan cases suggests that there may be a loosening of other admissibility doctrines – or a willingness to engage in more probative review – particularly where, in an environment of political transition, the desire of state authorities to investigate and prosecute is not in question.[359] Complementarity-as-admissibility in that context thus hewed more closely to the goals of complementarity-as-catalyst. At the same time, the Appeals Chamber's effective rejection of the 'due process' thesis, as well as its explicit affirmation that conduct need not be charged as international crimes, suggests that there may be a greater margin for discretion in future admissibility assessments.

2   'Positive' Complementarity in the Courtroom

The ascendance of the concept of 'positive' complementarity within the OTP and amongst non-state actors seeking to maximize the ICC's catalytic properties is partly rooted, as the previous chapter argued, in a cooperative spirit of mutual assistance and interaction. Article 93 sets forth the ways in which states parties are obligated to cooperate with the court and also the way in which the court *may* cooperate with states

---

'Beyond a Flawed Trial: ICC Failures to Ensure International Standards of Fairness in the Trials of Former Libyan Regime Members', *American University International Law Review* 33(1) (2017), 143 ('It seems clear that the ICC has exhibited a tendency to focus more on its role in catalyzing domestic prosecutions than it has in ensuring international standards of fairness at the domestic level'.). In February 2017, the United Nation's (UN) Office of the High Commissioner for Human Rights also issued a report concluding that the Libyan trial of Gaddafi, in absentia, and 36 other members of his father's regime, including Al-Senussi, 'represented significant progress' by the Libyan judiciary, but ultimately failed to meet international fair trial standards. See United Nations Support Mission in Libya/OHCHR, 'Report on the Trial of 37 Former Members of the Qadhafi Regime (Case 360/2012)' (21 February 2017), at https://unsmil.unmissions.org/sites/default/files/regime-trial-report-english.pdf. Amongst the report's recommendations was that Libya, 'Adhere to the Rome Statute of the International Criminal Court and core international human rights treaties'. Ibid., 55.

[359] Indeed, in April 2016, the ICC presidency issued a decision approving the DRC's request to prosecute Germain Katanga before the High Military Court in Kinshasa for war crimes and crimes against humanity, following his release from ICC custody. The presidency concluded that the proposed prosecution did not 'undermine fundamental procedures of the Rome Statute', including the principle of ne bis in idem. Citing the Libya admissibility challenges, it further affirmed that the ICC 'is not an international court of human rights, sitting in judgment over domestic legal systems to ensure that they are compliant with international standards of human rights'. The Prosecutor v. Germain Katanga, Decision pursuant to article 108(1) of the Rome Statute, ICC-01/04-01/07, The Presidency (7 April 2016), para. 31.

(both state and non-state parties). Article 93(10), in particular, provides the legal basis for such cooperation. It authorizes (but does not require) the ICC to, upon request:

> [C]ooperate with and provide assistance to a state party conducting an investigation into or trial in respect of conduct which constitutes a crime within the jurisdiction of the court or which constitutes a serious crime under the national law of the requesting state.[360]

While a broad array of information can be provided – ranging from the 'transmission of statements, documents or other types of evidence obtained in the course of an investigation or trial conducted by the court', to 'the questioning of any person detained by order of the court' – the Statute provides certain safeguards for the provision of such information, including if the documents or information sought were provided by another state, or a witness or expert.[361]

But while the court has endorsed, as in Katanga, certain division-of-labour relationships between the prosecutor and national jurisdictions that positive complementarity proponents have similarly encouraged,[362] direct assistance under Article 93(10) in the context of admissibility has commanded little judicial support to date.[363] It was raised directly in the course of the Kenyan litigation when the government filed, along with

---

[360] Rome Statute, Article 93(10)(a). As noted, non-state parties may also be granted requests for assistance as well. Ibid., Article 93(10)(c). Other commentators have referred to the Statue's 93(10) function as 'proactive complementarity' and the perspective from which 'the catalytic effect of the ICC should be conceptualized', see Ovo Catherine Imoedemhe, *The Complementarity Regime of the International Criminal Court*, 47–50; another has referred to it as 'reverse cooperation', see Frederica Gioia, 'Complementarity and "Reverse Cooperation"', in *The International Criminal Court and Complementarity*, 807–829.

[361] Ibid., Article 93(10)(b)(i)–(ii). Christopher Hall urges an added set of safeguards, namely, that the OTP develop criteria for determining whether, consistent with Article 21(3), the assistance the office might provide could have 'a seriously detrimental impact on human rights', for instance, through application of 'the death penalty, torture or other ill-treatment, unfair trial or other human rights violations'. See Christopher Hall, 'Positive Complementarity in Action', in *The International Criminal Court and Complementarity*, 1032–1033.

[362] As the Appeals Chamber noted, '[T]here may be merit in the argument that the sovereign decision of a state to relinquish its jurisdiction in favour of the court may well be seen as complying with the "duty to exercise [its] criminal jurisdiction" as envisioned in the … preamble'. Katanga Appeals Admissibility Judgment, para. 85.

[363] For similar conclusions, see Nidal Nabil Jurdi, 'Some Lessons on Complementarity for the International Criminal Court Review Conference', *South African Yearbook of International Law* 34 (2009), 36 ('No traces of positive complementarity can be found in either the *Lubanga*, *Katanga* and *Ntaganda* cases, or in the Ugandan situation'.);

its admissibility challenge, a request for assistance from the court seeking the 'transmission of all statements, documents, or other types of evidence obtained by the court and the prosecutor in the course of the ICC investigations'.[364]

The only previous occasion in which such a request appears to have been raised in the course of litigation was in Katanga's challenge, where defence counsel pointed to 'evidence that the DRC was keen on investigating this case at the national level' and noted that the government had 'submitted a request for legal assistance to the prosecutor, making use of the mechanism in Article 93(10)'.[365] Counsel stated that it was 'unaware of the fate of that request', but, two weeks later, the OTP's reply suggested a significantly more restrained approach to the policy goals of positive complementarity. It stated:

> The ICC was not created to be an international investigative bureau with resources to support national authorities. It is instead a judicial body with jurisdiction over the most serious crimes of international concern and established to be complementary to national criminal jurisdictions. Furthermore, Article 93(10), which addresses requests for cooperation from states to the court, does not impose an obligation on the ICC to render assistance to states. Compliance with a request is discretionary

Nouwen, *Complementarity in the Line of Fire*, 101; Karolina Wierczynska, 'Deference in the ICC Practice Concerning Admissibility Challenges Lodged by States', in *Deference in International Courts and Tribunals*, 369 ('At the moment the complementarity principle, as interpreted by the ICC, seems mainly focused on the mechanism of control'.).

[364] *Situation in the Republic of Kenya*, Request for assistance on behalf of the government of the Republic of Kenya pursuant to Article 93(10) and Rule 194, ICC-01/09 (21 April 2011), para. 2.

[365] Katanga Admissibility Challenge, para. 50. It should be noted that the OTP receives requests under 93(10), which have not been the subject of judicial review. For instance, in the court's 2017 report, it notes that 'the office shared relevant material with national judicial authorities in answer to 10 requests sent pursuant to article 93(10) and continued assisting national judicial authorities in their own investigations wherever possible'. Assembly of States Parties, 'Report on activities and programme performance of the International Criminal Court for the year 2017', ICC-ASP/17/2 (1 August 2018), para. 84. Rod Rastan (the OTP's legal advisor) and Pascal Turlan (its head of judicial cooperation) have also noted that 'the court has received a number of incoming requests for judicial assistance from situation countries', including requests from Uganda and DRC. Rastan and Turlan, 'International Cooperation and Judicial Assistance', in Adejoke Babington-Ashaye, Aimee Comrie and Akingbolahan Adeniran (eds.), *International Criminal Investigations: Law and Practice* (The Hague: Eleven International Publishing, 2018); see also Turlan, 'The International Criminal Court Cooperation Regime', 58–79. As discussed in Chapter 6, however, the degree to which such assistance was satisfactorily provided to DRC authorities remains in doubt.

and dependent on the fulfilment of the factors listed therein, including considerations of witness protection and the principle of originator consent.[366]

Subsequent proceedings indicate no judicial determination as to the outcome of Katanga's request. The court's assessment of the Kenyan government's 93(10) application, considered in June 2011, preceded the onset of its more overtly hostile relationship with the state (President Kenyatta himself was not elected until two years later), as well as serious allegations of witness intimidation and interference.[367] While these subsequent developments raise legitimate questions about the good faith of the government's application, the court was nonetheless unwilling to entertain the state's request. First, it explicitly stated that any requests for assistance under 93(10) should be formally separated from admissibility challenges: in the Pre-Trial Chamber's words, 'a determination on the inadmissibility of a case pursuant to Article 17 of the Statute does not [necessarily] depend on granting or denying a request for assistance under Article 93(10) of the Statute'.[368] Then, in a subsequent, short opinion, the chamber formulated strict conditions for such requests. In its words:

> [The] requesting state part must have, at least, either conducted an investigation, or be doing so with respect to 'conduct which constitutes a crime within the jurisdiction of the court or which constitutes a serious crime under the national law of the requesting state'. This entails that the requesting state party must show that is it at a minimum investigating or has already investigated one or more of the crimes referred to in Article 5 and defined in Articles 6–8 of the Statute. Alternatively, the state party

---

[366] Prosecutor v. Germain Katanga and Mathieu Ngudjolo Chui, Public redacted version of the 19 March 2009 prosecution response to motion challenging the admissibility of the case by the defence of Germain Katanga, pursuant to Article 19(2)(a), ICC-01/04-01/07, TC II (30 March 2009), paras. 100–101 ('OTP Response to Katanga Admissibility Challenge'). Notably, when the OTP and DRC signed a 2004 cooperation agreement (in the absence of national implementation legislation), a provision was included, consistent with Article 93(10), that the OTP 'could cooperate with national jurisdictions and provide them with assistance in their investigations, prosecutions and eventual trials for crimes committed within the ICC's subject matter jurisdiction'. See Judicial Cooperation Agreement between the Democratic Republic of Congo and the Office of the Prosecutor of the International Criminal Court, para. 39 (on-file).

[367] See, e.g., Open Society Justice Initiative, 'Briefing Paper: Witness Interference in Cases before the International Criminal Court' (November 2016), at www.opensocietyfoundations.org/sites/default/files/factsheet-icc-witness-interference-20161116.pdf.

[368] Ruto et al. Admissibility Decision, para. 34.

must demonstrate that it is either doing or has done so with respect to conduct constituting a 'serious crime under the national law'.[369]

Referring only to the cooperation request – not the information provided in the government's admissibility challenge – the chamber concluded that 'The government submitted...a two-page [request], which lack[s] any documentary proof that there is or has been an investigation, as required pursuant to Article 93(10)(a) of the Statute'.[370]

The relationship between a state's admissibility challenge and a related Article 93(10) request is difficult to ignore, particularly where the need to satisfy a high admissibility standard may well depend on information in the court or prosecutor's possession.[371] Indeed, interpreted alongside the 'same case' jurisprudence highlighted above, the chamber's fleeting treatment of Kenya's cooperation request establishes a potential paradox: in order for states to demonstrate they merit assistance, they may lack the very evidence for which they seek assistance. As Stahn has argued, 'This approach leaves limited space to take into account emerging justice efforts under domestic jurisdiction'.[372]

Judge Ušacka was again a dissenting voice on this issue. In the Kenyan cases, her dissent correctly suggests that the Pre-Trial Chamber 'did not take into account that ... [it] has the power to adapt the admissibility proceedings to ... changing circumstances', or on how it could

---

[369] *Situation in the Republic of Kenya*, Decision on the request for assistance submitted on behalf of the government of the Republic of Kenya pursuant to Article 93(10) of the Statute and Rule 194 of the Rules of Procedure and Evidence, ICC-01/09, PTC II (29 June 2011), para. 33.

[370] Ibid., para. 34. As noted by Judge Ušacka, however, the government had submitted evidence that investigations were underway at the time of the admissibility challenge. See Dissenting Opinion of Judge Anita Ušacka, 20 September 2011, para. 8.

[371] On appeal, Kenya insisted on the 'inter-relationship' between its Article 93(10) request and its Article 19 application (and thus appealable as a matter of right under Article 82(1)(a)), noting that a state 'may simply not have evidence available to the prosecutor of the ICC or may even be deprived of such evidence', further complicating the state's ability to pursue 'an identical cohort of individuals' as those of the ICC. *Situation in the Republic of Kenya*, Decision on the admissibility of the appeal of the government of Kenya against the 'Decision on the request for assistance submitted on behalf of the government of the Republic of Kenya pursuant to Article 93(1) of the Statute and Rule 194 of the Rules of Procedure and Evidence', ICC-01/09 OA (10 August 2011). The Appeals Chamber rejected the government's request, finding that it did not constitute a 'decision with respect to admissibility', pursuant to Article 82(1)(a).

[372] Stahn, 'Admissibility Challenges before the ICC', 237; see also Akhavan, 'Complementarity Conundrums', 1059 (illustrating how the Libya case 'directly addresses the extent to which the ICC should accommodate the time and resource constraints of transitional situations').

'facilitate the appellant by asking for more information or awaiting additional evidence on the start of investigations'.[373] Furthermore, in her dissent from the Appeals Chamber's affirmation that Gaddafi's case was admissible, she specifically endorsed that the court 'is in an ideal position to actively assist domestic authorities in conducting [investigations and prosecutions], be it by the sharing of materials and information collected or of knowledge and expertise'.[374] Thus, the Office of the Prosecutor and states should endeavour to 'work in unison – by complementing each other – in reaching the Statute's overall goal, i.e., to fight against impunity'.[375] Such explicit approval of the ICC's role in encouraging domestic accountability has yet to find wider endorsement from other judges.

3 Complementarity as Policy and Law

Complementarity's evolution in both legal and policy discourse underscores the dynamic, shifting nature of the principle. Given the ambitious goals that animate 'positive' complementarity in particular, one desirable approach is to conceive of it as, in Frédéric Mégret's words, 'primarily a device to accommodate diversity'.[376] Under this view, a broader conception of the interpretive principles that underwrite admissibility would likely be necessary if the court is indeed to play a catalytic role in a world of multiple, complex states. Furthermore, if the ICC is to genuinely encourage national investigations and prosecutions, then it will likely have to do so in a way that preserves greater political discretion and flexibility to states.

This approach, however, rests uneasily with the ICC's complementarity jurisprudence to date and, perhaps, with the Rome Statute itself. Indeed, notwithstanding the ambitious vision that animates complementarity as a catalyst, commentators have defended the court's 'refusal to import the policy aspects of positive complementarity into the admissibility regime', contending that it 'does not detract from the existence and importance' of

[373] Kenyatta Admissibility Appeals Judgment, Dissenting Opinion of Judge Anita Ušacka, para. 28.
[374] Gaddafi Admissibility Appeals Judgment, Dissenting Opinion of Judge Anita Ušacka, para. 65.
[375] Ibid., para. 19.
[376] Frédéric Mégret, 'Too Much of a Good Thing? Implementation and the Uses of Complementarity', in *The International Criminal Court and Complementarity*, 390.

such a policy; rather, 'It is simply to say that this decision of complementarity is not one which is enforced by judicial decisions'.[377] The ASP has endorsed a similar partition of the juridical approach to complementarity from its policy goals as a catalyst, suggesting that the aspirations of the latter should not be undertaken by the court itself. As the 2010 'stocktaking' report on complementarity made clear:

> While positive complementarity could take many forms, for the purposes of this paper, [it] refers to all activities/actions whereby national jurisdictions are strengthened and enabled to conduct genuine national investigations and trials of crimes included in the Rome Statute, without involving the court in capacity building, financial support and technical assistance, but instead leaving these actions and activities for states, to assist each other on a voluntary basis.[378]

Similarly, states parties have insisted that the ICC is not a 'development organization or an implementing agency': any 'positive' practical assistance that can be offered 'is limited by the court's core judicial mandate'.[379] The Assembly's 2012 report on complementarity is even more explicit:

> As stressed in the court's first report, two aspects of the term 'complementarity' have to clearly be separated. The first aspect is the question of admissibility as provided for in the Rome Statute, this being a judicial issue to be ultimately determined by the judges of the court. The second aspect of complementarity relates to the complementary roles of the court and national jurisdictions in contributing toward ending

---

[377] Ben Batros, 'The *Katanga* Admissibility Appeal: Judicial Restraint at the ICC', *Leiden Journal of International Law,* 23 (2010), 360. Batros argues that the chamber 'took the facts as they existed at the time, rather than trying to use the judgment to create new facts which might have been more in line with the ideals of complementarity', 361. See also Batros, 'Evolution of the ICC Jurisprudence on Admissibility', 600. Other commentators have suggested that the criticism of the court's 'same conduct' test is misplaced. See, e.g., Robinson, 'Three Theories of Complementarity' (defending the test, and pointing to the Statue's consultation mechanisms and the 'interests of justice' test as alternative means to defer a case); Rastan, 'What Is "Substantially the Same Conduct?"' (defending the test and suggesting that criticism should be directed at the exercise of prosecutorial discretion over case selection).

[378] Assembly of States Parties, 'Report of the bureau on stocktaking: Complementarity', ICC-ASP/8/51 (18 March 2010), para. 16. In this vein, the paper notably describes the ICC as 'a catalyst for assistance, helping to bridge the divide between donors and potential partner countries', para. 45.

[379] Ibid., para. 42. The stocktaking paper concedes that there 'may be scope for the Office of the Prosecutor to engage in certain capacity building activities within existing resources and without compromising its judicial mandate', but the implication is clear that such scope should be both limited and resource-neutral. Ibid., para. 44.

impunity. Within this second aspect, the term 'positive complementarity' is sometimes used to refer to the active encouragement of and assistance to national prosecutions where possible.[380]

The OTP has also ratified this dichotomy, stating that complementarity has two dimensions: '(i) the admissibility test, i.e. how to assess the existence of national proceedings and their genuineness, which is a judicial issue; and (ii) the positive complementarity concept, i.e. a proactive policy of cooperation aimed at promoting national proceedings'.[381]

Such a bifurcated approach may be appealing insofar as it allows stakeholders to summon different versions of complementarity, for different purposes and audiences. Whereas the Office of the Prosecutor took a dim view of cooperation in Katanga and the Kenyan cases, it has otherwise championed (at least rhetorically) such a relationship outside of the courtroom. And while states parties have elsewhere trumpeted the ambitious norms upon which 'positive' complementarity rests – that there is a statutory duty to investigate and prosecute ICC crimes domestically – reports from the ASP's committee on budget and finance suggest a far more modest vision, one that does not corrupt the court's 'core judicial mandate'.

But the goal of promoting national proceedings and questions of judicial admissibility are linked; they cannot be 'clearly separated'. Indeed, while the court's apparent endorsement of a burden-sharing component to 'positive' complementarity lends support to its more cooperative dimensions, it simultaneously 'downplays the significance of the national duty to investigate and prosecute'.[382] As noted in a 2009 report on the DRC:

> Despite the intention spelled out in the ICC Rome Statute to complement and give precedence to investigations and prosecutions in national courts, the national justice sector seems to use the ICC as an excuse for not pursuing such cases. UN officials working to strengthen national capacities have been frustrated when, in at least one case, a judge insisted he should not take up a case if there were a chance that the ICC might prosecute it.[383]

---

[380] Assembly of States Parties, 'Report of the Court on Complementarity', ICC-ASP11/39, 16 October 2012, para. 2.

[381] OTP Prosecutorial Strategy, 2009–2012 (1 February 2010), para. 16.

[382] Cross and Williams, 'Recent Developments at the ICC', 343. See also Susana SáCouto and Katherine Cleary, 'The Katanga Complementarity Decisions: Sound Law but Flawed Policy', Leiden Journal of International Law 23 (2003).

[383] Laura Davis and Priscilla Hayner, Difficult Peace, Limited Justice: Ten Years of Peacemaking in the DRC (ICTJ, March 2009), 30.

Thus, just as ICC prosecutions can create an incentivizing environment for states consistent with the complementarity-as-catalyst framework, they may also have a chilling effect.

Furthermore, even if judicial proceedings must, as a matter of statutory interpretation, 'mirror' those of the ICC, that requirement cannot be easily reconciled with broader goals for the court to function as a catalyst for domestic accountability. As Drumbl notes, 'Should [such] trials become the expected baseline of post-conflict justice, the result may be the universalization of a methodology that is unaffordable to nearly all states or would only remain affordable if the justice narrative were limited to a tiny subsection of perpetrators'.[384] Evidence of such 'universalization' – or 'mirroring', as the Appeals Chamber termed it – is explored further in Chapters 5 and 6, but can be seen in countries like Uganda, where, in the absence of clear precedents for challenging complementarity, the 'safer' route appeared to be following ICC practice as closely as possible. Nouwen quotes the former principal judge of the Ugandan High Court as follows, 'The ICC wants us to do everything the way they did it: we must use the same Statute and the same standards'.[385]

The ICC's reluctance thus far to develop a more flexible approach to its admissibility jurisprudence suggests that the court has been reluctant to incorporate explicit policy considerations into its admissibility jurisprudence. An attempt to bifurcate the two suggests that the policy imperative of complementarity-as-catalyst can be separated from – or subordinated to – the legal tests of complementarity-as-admissibility, but this partition is itself symptomatic of legalism, insofar as it seeks to 'isolate law … from the social context within which it exists'.[386] Indeed, as the following chapters illustrate, ICC interventions – and the admissibility challenges they necessarily produce – have produced a range of political and legal consequences, neither of which can be neatly separated. Similarly, the ICC cannot at once be perceived by state actors as a jealous guardian of cases, while also presenting itself as a catalytic force for domestic proceedings. As one commentator has sharply put it, 'In terms of jurisprudence, ICC practice has shown a patchy approach that lacks a consistent and clear vision with respect to its relationship with domestic jurisdictions'.[387]

---

[384] Drumbl, *Atrocity, Punishment, and International Law*, 210.
[385] Nouwen, *Complementarity in the Line of Fire*, 205.
[386] Shklar, 2.
[387] Jurdi, 'The Complementarity Regime of the International Criminal Court in Practice', 218.

The goals of complementarity as policy, then, and the body of case law that is meant to guide the judicial operation of the principle cannot be easily uncoupled. Each informs the other, while both have an influence on the ability, and the political willingness, of state actors to pursue accountability at the domestic level.

4   Conclusion

Despite the ascension of the complementarity-as-catalyst norm, ICC judges have appeared noticeably more reticent to incorporate this goal as part of their interpretive framework. Rather, the weight of Article 17 jurisprudence has seen the ICC emerge as the privileged forum for prosecution. Under the court's case law, in order for a state to successfully challenge admissibility, domestic proceedings must be conducted in relation to the same 'case' as that of the ICC, such that they concern the same person, conduct and the same factual incidents. This substantial threshold is even more pronounced in the case of 'self referrals', where the practical value of individuals contesting admissibility appears increasingly unclear.

Furthermore, when faced with competing claims about the existence of national-level proceedings, the ICC has undertaken a relatively superficial level of review, while setting a high evidentiary threshold for challengers to satisfy. And despite otherwise endorsing the 'burden sharing' model that has accompanied the policy of 'positive' complementarity, as a cooperation regime under Article 93(10), such a policy has barely registered in the ICC's case law. Complementarity thus appears less as a space for constructive engagement and dialogue than a set of unifying criteria with which states must comply.[388] The Libyan admissibility challenges may signal a partial loosening of the court's interpretive commitment to the 'mirror' test, but it remains to be seen whether this approach will prevail in the long term.

---

[388] Stahn similarly gestures towards the 'possibility of adopting a dialogue-based understanding of complementarity which would promote continued interaction with domestic jurisdictions in deference of cases'. See 'Admissibility Challenges before the ICC', 245.

4

Leveraging The Hague

Complementarity and the Office of the Prosecutor

The previous chapter focused on complementarity within the International Criminal Court's (ICC) juridical framework; this chapter addresses its policy dimensions as engaged by another crucial court actor: the Office of the Prosecutor (OTP). As the organ responsible for investigating the situations and prosecuting the cases brought before the court, the OTP is a critical participant in the complementarity landscape. Situated at once between the ICC's institutional centre in The Hague and the various country contexts in which it operates, the office – through the exercise of prosecutorial discretion and its access to local actors working on the ground – not only shapes the overall work of the court, but can also have a significant influence on the contours of domestic accountability efforts. Indeed, as a material site for engagement and cooperation with national-level actors, the OTP is uniquely positioned to undertake a variety of activities that could further its goal of 'encouraging states to carry out their primary responsibility to investigate and prosecute international crimes'.[389]

This chapter focuses on two key aspects of the OTP's work relevant to the ICC's potential for catalysing domestic proceedings: preliminary examinations and investigations. Returning to complementarity's duality as a coercive or cooperative stimulus on national jurisdictions, it first considers the office's use of preliminary examinations as an example of complementarity's coercive, catalytic power, wherein the threat of prosecutorial action might stimulate domestic efforts at accountability. As the only country of the three studied here to have been the subject of a prolonged preliminary examination (in the context of a coercive intervention), a case study of Kenya is offered in order to understand how the office, under the leadership of prosecutor Moreno-Ocampo, sought to use the potential leveraging power of this period to push for the establishment

---

[389] OTP, 'Policy Paper on Preliminary Examinations' (November 2013), para. 100.

of a domestic criminal tribunal. Ultimately unsuccessful in this respect, the Kenyan experience highlights both the context-specific nature of the preliminary examination phase and the diverse political dynamics in which ICC interventions unfold. This section also highlights some of the office's later preliminary examinations under the tenure of Prosecutor Bensouda, where it has appeared to pursue a more cooperative, managerial approach.

The second half of the chapter addresses the office's early investigatory practices, which, I argue, are a material site where a positive, cooperative approach to complementarity could have been enacted in Democratic Republic of Congo (DRC) and Uganda, but was not. Indeed, during the height of the office's investigations in both countries, the OTP largely eschewed such an approach, choosing not to base any of its investigators in situation-countries, not to proactively pursue information and evidence-sharing with national authorities and not to develop a more sustained field-based presence, thereby diminishing the investigatory phase's potential to enact a more 'positive', cooperative posture with national jurisdictions. Instead, its reliance on relationships with local information providers, known as 'intermediaries', became the source of increasing judicial approbation, while underscoring the challenges the office faced in operating at a distance.

A focus on investigations is also critical as it has become increasingly clear that the ICC has an investigations problem, one that threatens to imperil the court's ability to serve as a credible threat should a state fail to pursue proceedings at the national level.[390] The withdrawal of charges against Kenyan President Uhuru Kenyatta and the acquittals of former DRC vice-president, Jean-Pierre Bemba, and former Ivory Coast president, Laurent Gbagbo (the latter based on a no case to answer motion), are the most recent, though undoubtedly the most damaging, in a series

---

[390] See, e.g., Christian De Vos, 'The ICC's Evidence Problem', *Leiden Journal of International Law* 26(4) (2013), 1009–1024; Nadia Carine Fornel Poutou and Lucie Boalo Hayali, 'A Belief Shattered: The International Criminal Court's Bemba Acquittal', *Just Security* (25 June 2008), at www.justsecurity.org/58386/belief-shattered-international-criminal-courts-bemba-acquittal/. As one report on OTP investigations concluded, the ICC has faced 'a substantially higher rate of dismissal than the acquittal rate seen at other international criminal bodies following a full trial, even though the standard at trial – beyond a reasonable doubt – is higher than the burden at the confirmation stage'. See War Crimes Research Office, *Investigative Management, Strategies, and Techniques of the International Criminal Court's Office of the Prosecutor* (2012), 9 ('WCRO Report').

of setbacks for the court.[391] If the ICC is to safeguard its potential as a threat-based catalyst, ensuring effective investigations and prosecutions are thus essential.

1 Preliminary Examinations

The OTP is made up of three divisions: jurisdiction, complementarity and cooperation (JCCD); investigations; and prosecutions.[392] Led by Phakiso Mochochoko since February 2011, the JCCD is the 'division that heavily influences policy decisions and the prosecutor's selective choices originate there'.[393] Its situation analysis section is primarily responsible for conducting preliminary examinations, which include evaluating information the office receives and making recommendations as to whether an investigation has a sufficient basis to proceed. Meanwhile, its international cooperation section is broadly regarded as the office's 'diplomatic' arm: it carries out external relations activities, including negotiating cooperation agreements, providing legal advice on complementarity and cooperation and 'liais[ing] with external actors

---

[391] In May 2014, the prosecutor withdrew charges against President Uhuru Kenyatta on the basis of insufficient evidence; in so doing, she noted the Kenyan government's lack of cooperation and non-compliance with the OTP's investigation, as well as the deaths of several important potential witnesses and the recanting of earlier testimony by other key witnesses. In March 2013, the prosecutor was also granted permission to withdraw charges against Francis Muthaura, on the basis that 'serious investigative challenges, including a limited pool of potential witnesses' led her to the conclusion that there was no longer a reasonable prospect of conviction. See The Prosecutor v. Francis Kirimi Muthaura and Uhuru Muigai Kenyatta, Prosecution notification of withdrawal of the charges against Francis Kirimi Muthaura, ICC-01/09-02/11, TC V (11 March 2013), para. 11. The Gbagbo acquittal, the written opinion of which was finally released in July 2019, is particularly withering in its criticism of the Office of the Prosecutor's case. See The Prosecutor v. Laurent Gbagbo and Charles Blé Goudé, Reasons of oral decision of 15 January 2019 on the Requête de la Défense de Laurent Gbagbo afin qu'un jugement d'acquittement portant sur toutes les charges soit prononcé en faveur de Laurent Gbagbo et que sa mise en liberté immédiate soit ordonnée, and on the Blé Goudé Defence no case to answer motion, ICC-02/11-01/15, TC I (16 July 2019) (Public redacted version of reasons of Judge Geoffrey Henderson; Opinion of Judge Cuno Tarfusser).

[392] See Regulations of the Office of the Prosecutor, ICC-BD/05-01-09 (23 April 2009) ('OTP Regulations'), Regulations 7–9. The OTP also has an executive committee, which is responsible for strategic, policy and budgetary decisions. Ibid., Regulation 4(1).

[393] Ignaz Stegmiller, The Pre-Investigation Stage of the ICC (Berlin: Duncker and Humblot, 2011), 457.

to implement the complementarity policy'.[394] Notably, the division's role has not been without controversy, with sceptics suggesting that the role of the JCCD – 'defined by diplomatic (external relations and complementarity) expertise', in the words of one commentator – could be perceived as inconsistent with the OTP's independence, and others expressing concern over how the division's functions were elevated over other parts of the office during the first prosecutor's tenure.[395] Other commentators, by contrast, have described it as 'an inspired institutional choice'.[396]

Legal Framework

The preliminary examination is a unique pre-investigative stage within the statutory framework of the ICC. While the scope and length of the examination falls within the discretion of the OTP, Article 15 of the Rome Statute mandates the prosecutor to first determine, regardless of the manner in which a situation comes before the court, whether there is a 'reasonable basis to proceed' with an investigation.[397] As noted by the court, 'reasonable basis' is the lowest evidentiary standard in the Statute; as compared to evidence gathered during the investigation stage, the standard is neither 'comprehensive' nor 'conclusive'.[398] At a minimum, however, the

---

[394] Gregory Townsend, 'Structure and Management', in Luc Reydams, Jan Wouters and Cedric Ryngaert (eds.), *International Prosecutors* (Oxford: Oxford University Press, 2012), 289. The JCCD is broadly responsible for the following: '(a) the preliminary examination and evaluation of information pursuant to Articles 15 and 53, ... and the preparation of reports and recommendations to assist the prosecutor in determining whether there is a reasonable basis to proceed with an investigation; (b) the provision of analysis and legal advice to [the executive committee] on issues of jurisdiction and admissibility at all stages of investigations and proceedings; (c) the provision of legal advice to [the executive committee] on cooperation, the coordination and transmission of requests for cooperation made by the office under Part 9 of the Statute. Regulation 7, OTP Regulations.

[395] Schiff, *Building the International Criminal Court*, 114. For similar criticism in the context of the Kenyan situation, see 'Executive Summary of the Report of the External Independent Experts' (2018), available as Annex 1 at https://www.icc-cpi.int/itemsDocuments/261119-otp-statement-kenya-eng.pdf (E14: 'JCCD appeared to exceed its mandate in these cases, exerting too much control and influence over operational matters to the detriment of effective investigation and prosecution'.).

[396] Jens Meierhenrich, 'The Evolution of the Office of the Prosecutor at the International Criminal Court: Insights from Institutional Theory', in Martha Minow, C. Cora True-Frost and Alex Whiting (eds.), *The First Global Prosecutor: Promise and Constraints* (University of Michigan Press, 2105), 108.

[397] Rome Statute, Article 15 ('Prosecutor').

[398] *Situation in the Republic of Kenya*, Decision pursuant to Article 15 of the Rome Statute on the Authorization of an Investigation into the Situation in the Republic of Kenya, ICC-01/09-19, PTC II (31 March 2010), para. 27 ('Kenya Article 15 Decision'); *Situation in*

preliminary examination involves assessing whether the jurisdictional and admissibility requirements are met in order to open a formal investigation, and whether, 'taking into account the gravity of the crime and the interests of victims, there are nevertheless substantial reasons to believe than an investigation would not serve the interests of justice'.[399]

Once a situation is identified, Article 53(1)(a)–(c) establishes the legal framework for a preliminary examination.[400] Seeking, in part, to provide clarity on its approach to the process, the OTP first published a policy paper on the subject in October 2010 (revised as of November 2013).[401] The office identified three general principles – independence, impartiality and objectivity – that guide preliminary examination practice and set forth a four-phase procedure:

> Phase 1: During this phase, the office conducts an 'initial assessment' of all information and communications on alleged crimes received under Article 15. As an initial filtering exercise, the initial purpose is both to exclude information that is outside the ICC's jurisdiction and to analyse the seriousness/gravity of information that 'appears to fall within the jurisdiction of the court'.
>
> Phase 2: The second phase represents the 'formal commencement' of an examination: it includes all communications not rejected in phase 1, as well as referrals by states parties or the Security Council. The purpose at this stage is to ascertain whether the pre-conditions for the exercise of jurisdiction under Article 12 are satisfied and 'whether there is a reasonable basis to believe' that

the Republic of Cote d'Ivoire, Decision pursuant to Article 15 of the Rome Statute on the authorisation of an investigation into the situation in the Republic of Côte d'Ivoire, ICC-02/11, PTC III (3 October 2011). In both decisions, the chamber further noted that this standard reflected the prosecutor's more limited powers during the examination stage as compared to the investigation stage under Article 54.

[399] These criteria are enumerated in Article 53(1)(a)–(c) of the Rome Statute ('Initiation of an Investigation'). Notably, the term 'interests of justice' is not defined in the Rome Statute. A brief (and less than persuasive) policy paper produced by the Office of the Prosecutor in 2007 construed the provision narrowly, stating that it should be invoked only in 'exceptional circumstances', with a 'presumption in favour of investigation or prosecution'. See OTP, 'Policy Paper on the Interests of Justice' (September 2007).

[400] Rule 104 of the Rules of Procedure and Evidence and Regulation 27 of the OTP's Regulations also govern preliminary examinations. Regulation 27 requires the office to make a 'preliminary distinction' amongst information that pertains to matters that are either manifestly outside the court's jurisdiction, related to an ongoing examination or unrelated to an existing situation.

[401] OTP, 'Policy Paper on Preliminary Examinations'.

the crimes fall within the ICC's subject matter jurisdiction. This phase thus entails not only a 'thorough factual and legal assessment' of the crimes allegedly committed to ascertain potential cases falling within the court's jurisdiction, but it also includes 'gather[ing] information on relevant national proceedings if such information is available at this stage'.

Phase 3: The third phase focuses on the admissibility of potential cases in terms of complementarity and gravity ('the scale, nature, manner of commission of the crimes and their impact').

Phase 4: The final phase involves examining whether any 'interests of justice' – a 'countervailing consideration' – should apply before making a final recommendation to the prosecutor on whether there is a reasonable basis to initiate an investigation. Once the prosecutor is satisfied that there is a reasonable basis to open an investigation into a situation, the authorization of the Pre-Trial Chamber must be sought.

In following this procedure, the prosecutor has broad discretion as to the means by which to assess the 'seriousness' of the information the office receives. In particular, 'he or she may seek additional information from states, organs of the United Nations (UN), intergovernmental or non-governmental organization or other reliable sources that he or she deems appropriate, and may receive written or oral testimony at the seat of the court'.[402]

The discretion afforded the OTP during the preliminary examination stage is significant. Unlike investigations, where the prosecutor must obtain the authorization of the Pre-Trial Chamber to proceed, judicial oversight of preliminary examinations is limited, nor are Article 17's admissibility requirements applicable at this stage.[403] Furthermore, there is no prescribed time limit for conducting preliminary examinations nor any guidance as to what constitutes a 'reasonable time' to conclude one.

---

[402] Rome Statute, Article 15(2). The office 'does not enjoy investigative powers' at the preliminary examination stage, however, 'other than for the purpose of receiving testimony at the seat of the court'.

[403] Pre-Trial Chamber I's decision under Article 53(3)(a), ordering the OTP to reconsider the decision not to investigate the situation referred to it by the Union of Comoros (on the grounds that the prosecutor committed material errors in her determination of the gravity of the potential cases) marked the first time that a decision by the prosecutor not to investigate was successfully challenged. See *Situation on the Registered Vessels of the Union of the Comoros, the Hellenic Republic and the Kingdom of Cambodia*, Decision on the request of the Union of Comoros to review the prosecutor's decision not to initiate an investigation, ICC-01/13, PTC I (16 July 2015) ('Comoros Decision').

In the first situation in the Central African Republic, Pre-Trial Chamber III noted that preliminary examinations were to be conducted 'within a reasonable time regardless of its complexity' and, to that end, requested the prosecutor to provide it with a report containing information on the current status of the preliminary examination, as well as an estimate of when it would be concluded.[404] In reply, however, the OTP stated its view that 'there is no obligation under the Statute or the rules to provide such an estimate or to give such a date'.[405] In the office's view, this was intentional on the part of the drafters, to accommodate such factors as the degree of state cooperation, the availability of information and the scale of the alleged crimes.[406] Notably, more recent Pre-Trial Chamber (PTC) decisions have been (increasingly) critical of the length of preliminary examinations, urging the prosecutor to complete them 'within a reasonable time [...] regardless of [their] complexity'.[407]

The temporal dimension of preliminary examinations – for instance, the setting of deadlines for the establishment of domestic proceedings or other, similar benchmarks to demonstrate 'willingness' – also allows the office to engage in potentially wide-ranging dialogue with a state. The Colombian experience, which has remained within the examination phase for more than ten years, is instructive in this regard as it has not only influenced the government's approach to accountability, but also helped

---

[404] See *Situation in the Central African Republic*, Decision requesting information on the status of the preliminary examination of the situation in the Central African Republic, ICC-01/05, PTC III (30 November 2006) ('CAR Preliminary Examination Decision').

[405] See 'Prosecution's report pursuant to Pre-Trial Chamber Ill's 30 November 2006 decision requesting information on the status of the preliminary examination of the situation in the Central African Republic', 15 December 2006. The office nevertheless stated that it was 'committed to completing its analysis of the CAR situation as expeditiously as possible and informing the relevant parties in a timely fashion in accordance with the Rules and Regulations of the court'. Ibid.

[406] By contrast, Olasolo has argued that the office is required to close preliminary examinations within a reasonable period of time and is obliged to inform information providers if it decides not to initiate an investigation. Hector Olasolo, *The Triggering Procedure of the International Criminal Court* (Leiden: Martinus Nijhoff, 2005), 62.

[407] See Request under Regulation 46(3) of the Regulations of the court, 'Decision on the "prosecution's request for a ruling on jurisdiction under Article 19(3) of the statute"', ICC-RoC46(3)-01/18, PTC I, 6 September 2018, paras. 85–86 (stating that 'an investigation should in general be initiated without delay and be conducted efficiently in order for it to be effective'); Comoros Decision, para. 50 (requesting the prosecutor to 'reconsider her decision not to initiate an investigation' and ordering she 'do so as soon as possible').

shape the contours of its protracted peace negotiations.[408] As the Kenyan case illustrates, domestic political developments can also have a significant influence on the timing or duration of preliminary examinations. Importantly, however, while the OTP has stated that its examination activities are conducted in the same manner regardless of how a situation comes before the court – in its words, 'no automaticity is assumed'[409] – it would appear that, in practice, different standards may well apply. For instance, while several proprio motu examinations have lasted for years or more (Colombia, Kenya), UN Security Council referred situations (as in Libya) have remained in examination status for a matter of days.[410]

While the outcome of a preliminary examination depends on the circumstances of each situation, three options are ultimately available to the OTP. It may first decline to initiate an investigation, or it may alternatively choose to proceed.[411] According to Seils, 'By the time the process of preliminary examination reaches its conclusion, there should almost always be substantial clarity on the type of the alleged criminal conduct, the numbers of incidents and victims of that conduct and related matters concerning aggravation or impact.'[412] A third approach is to keep a situation under preliminary examination, in order to 'collect information in order to establish a sufficient factual and legal basis' for a final determination. Seils has, in fact, argued for a more open-ended approach to examinations as an exercise in 'creative ambiguity'.[413]

---

[408] See, e.g., Alejandro Chehtman, 'The ICC and Its Normative Impact on Colombia's Legal System' (DOMAC/16, October 2011); Kai Ambos, 'The Colombian Peace Process (Law 975 of 2005) and the ICC's Principle of Complementarity', in *The International Criminal Court and Complementarity*, 1071–1096; Courtney Hillebrecht, Alexandra Huneeus with Sandra Borda, 'The Judicialization of Peace', *Harvard International Law Journal* 59(2) (Summer 2018), 279–330.

[409] OTP, 'Policy Paper on Preliminary Examinations', para. 28; see also 'Report on Preliminary Examination Activities 2013' (November 2013), para. 10.

[410] On this point, see David Bosco, 'Discretion and State Influence at the International Criminal Court: The Prosecutor's Preliminary Examinations', *American Journal of International Law* 111(2) (2017), 395–414.

[411] Closed examinations where the OTP made public its decision not to proceed to investigation include the situations in Comoros, the Republic of Korea, Honduras and the 2006 examination of Venezuela (though a new examination has since opened as of 2018). An examination of Iraq, which concerns allegations of abuses committed by British soldiers, was reopened following an earlier decision to close the examination.

[412] Seils, 'Making Complementarity Work', 993.

[413] Paul Seils, 'Putting Complementarity in Its Place', in Carsten Stahn (ed.), *The Law and Practice of the International Criminal Court*, 326. Other commentators have taken a different view, suggesting that the duration of examinations should be limited. See, e.g., Anni Pues, 'Towards the "Golden Hour"? A Critical Exploration of the Length of Preliminary Examinations', *Journal of International Criminal Justice* 15(3) (2017), 435–453.

Preliminary Examinations and Complementarity

Until recently, there has been little empirical examination of the effects of preliminary examinations, and whether they have indeed catalysed national accountability efforts.[414] Early anecdotal accounts support the contention that the preliminary examination procedure has had a deterrent effect in some instances. Juan Mendez, for instance, argues that the court's examination of Cote d'Ivoire (which later became an investigation and prosecution) played an important role in deterring a further escalation of violence, following a rise in ethnic hate propaganda that was being broadcast on national radio and television in the wake of a failed attempt to overthrow then President Laurent Gbagbo.[415] Colombia is also frequently cited as an example of the OTP's 'positive' complementarity approach, insofar as the passage of the so-called Justice and Peace Law – meant to establish a criminal accountability process for violence committed during the country's long-running armed conflict – was an outcome, in part, of the OTP's public scrutiny of the situation there.[416] The office also had a similar impact, discussed further below, on the content and terms of the final 2015 agreement negotiated between the Colombian government and the Revolutionary Armed Forces of Colombia (FARC), the country's largest guerrilla group, having interjected itself through various public speeches, correspondence with authorities and amicus briefs into the domestic process.[417]

These examples also illustrate the OTP's adoption of a progressively more public approach to preliminary examinations. While earlier examinations were largely confidential, their potential virtue as a

---

[414] See, e.g., Hillebrecht, Huneeus with Borda, 'The Judicialization of Peace'; Human Rights Watch, 'Pressure Point'; Morten Bergsmo and Carsten Stahn (eds.), *Quality Control in Preliminary Examination, Vols. 1–2* (Torkel Opsahl Academic Epublisher, 2018). For a detailed overview of all OTP examinations to date, see Sara Wharton and Rosemary Grey, 'The Full Picture: Preliminary Examinations at the International Criminal Court', *The Canadian Yearbook of International Law* 56 (2019), 1–57.

[415] See Juan E. Mendez and Jeremy Kelley, 'Peace Making, Justice, and the ICC', in *Contested Justice: The Politics and Practice of International Criminal Court Interventions*, 490–491.

[416] See Chehtman, 'The ICC and Its Normative Impact on Colombia's Legal System'; Ambos, 'The Colombian Peace Process (Law 975 of 2005) and the ICC's Principle of Complementarity'.

[417] See, e.g., René Urueña, 'Prosecutorial Politics: The ICC's Influence in Colombian Peace Processes, 2003–2017', *American Journal of International Law* 111(1) (2017), 104–125; Priscilla Hayner, *The Peacemaker's Paradox: Pursuing Justice in the Shadow of Conflict* (New York: Routledge, 2018), 194–214.

tool to prompt states into action has, like complementarity itself, been discovered over time. As Human Rights Watch notes, 'This increased publicity is closely tied to the OTP's policy of using preliminary examination to promote two aims at the heart of the Rome Statute: spurring national justice officials to pursue their own rigorous investigations (complementarity) and signalling to would-be rights violators that the international community is watching (deterrence)'.[418] Compliance with these norms is thus reinforced in the approach to preliminary examinations as well.

To that end, the office now often publicizes, where confidentiality and security considerations permit, when it initiates an examination and provides periodic updates of its activities.[419] These measures include publishing, as of 2011, an annual summary of activities performed during the course of the year (presented with increasing fanfare in the margins of the annual Assembly of States Parties, ASP) and, for a time, including information in the office's weekly bulletin, which it began distributing in 2009.[420] OTP policy documents also provide that it may 'disseminate statistics on information on alleged crimes under Article 15; make public the commencement of a preliminary examination through press releases and public statements; publicize events, such as OTP high-level visits to the concerned countries, so that information can be factored in by relevant departments within states and [international organizations] and issue periodic reports on the status of its preliminary examination'.[421] Collectively, these measures seek to bring greater transparency to the examination process, but also greater scrutiny to those states under review.

[418] Human Rights Watch, 'ICC: Course Correction – Recommendations to the Prosecutor for a More Effective Approach to "Situations under Analysis"' (16 June 2011).
[419] Regulation 28 governs the publicity of activities taken under Article 15. While the office is required to 'send an acknowledgement in respect of all information received on crimes to those who provided the information', it is within the prosecutor's discretion to 'make public such acknowledgement', and 'to make public the office's activities in relation to the preliminary examination of information on crimes under Article 15', or a determination that there is no reasonable basis to proceed with an investigation. See Regulation 28, OTP Regulations.
[420] See, e.g., OTP, 'Report on Preliminary Examination Activities 2017' (4 December 2017) (detailing three 'phase 2' examinations in Gabonese Republic, Palestine, Ukraine and four 'phase 3' examinations in Colombia, Guinea, Iraq/UK and Nigeria).
[421] ICC-OTP, 'Prosecutorial Strategy 2009–2012' (1 February 2010), paras. 38–39; see also OTP, 'Policy Paper on Preliminary Examinations', paras. 89–90 and Annual Report 2014, para. 95.

The OTP's investment in the preliminary examinations stage has expanded under Bensouda's leadership. Writing in 2015, she noted:

> As one of the three core activities of the office, stronger emphasis is now placed on the office's preliminary examinations activities. Through its preliminary examinations work, the office is committed to contributing to two overarching goals: the ending of impunity, by encouraging genuine national proceedings through its positive approach to complementarity, and the prevention of crimes.[422]

The prosecutor has likewise drawn a direct link between preliminary examinations and the catalytic potential of complementarity. In her words, the phase 'gives the states concerned the possibility of intervening to put an end to crimes before the Office of the Prosecutor initiates an investigation', enabling the latter 'to act as a catalyst for national proceedings'.[423]

Despite the threat that opening a formal investigation carries, there are potentially important 'positive' complementarity components to the preliminary examination stage as well. Indeed, according to the OTP, 'at all phases of its preliminary examination activities, consistent with its policy of positive complementarity, the office will seek to encourage where feasible genuine national investigations and prosecutions by the state(s) concerned and to cooperate with and provide assistance to such state(s) pursuant to Article 93(10) of the Statute'.[424] As Chapter 3 noted, however, the extent to which the OTP has affirmatively provided information to national authorities through use of the Article 93(10) regime is uncertain: there is no mention, for instance, of such assistance in any of the office's preliminary examination reports. Moreover, the provision of such information appears to itself be at odds with the OTP's declaration that it 'does not enjoy investigative powers' during the preliminary examination stage and 'cannot invoke the forms of cooperation specified in Part 9 of the Statute from states'.[425]

---

[422] Fatou Bensouda, 'Foreword', in Carsten Stahn (ed.), *The Law and Practice of the International Criminal Court*; see also 'Interview with Fatou Bensouda, ICC Chief Prosecutor', VRWG Bulletin, Issue 21 (Fall 2012), 4.

[423] Fatou Bensouda, 'Reflections from the International Criminal Court Prosecutor', *Case Western Reserve Journal of International Law* 45(1–2) (Fall 2012), 505–511, 508.

[424] OTP, 'Policy Paper on Preliminary Examinations', para. 94.

[425] Ibid., para. 85; see also Annual Report 2014, para. 11.

2 Preliminary Examinations in Practice: A Case Study of Kenya

Previous elections in Kenya had also seen outbreaks of violence, though not on the scale witnessed in 2007/2008. Gabrielle Lynch argues that while the crisis 'was unexpected', it was also 'compatible' with an increasingly ethnicized political landscape that had witnessed previous intercommunal attacks, as well as 'high levels of popular political skepticism, institutional decay, a culture of impunity, elite opportunism, and related strategies of action'.[426] At the time of the election, the two most prominent politicians amongst those who would later become ICC defendants – Kenyatta and Ruto – were members of rival political parties. Kenyatta had backed then president Mwai Kibaki of the Party of National Unity (PNU), who was running for re-election, while Ruto supported Raila Odinga of the Orange Democratic Movement (ODM). In the contested wake of the election, perceived PNU supporters (largely associated with the Kikuyu, Kenya's largest ethnic group) were attacked, while perceived ODM supporters, including members of the Kalenjin, Luo and Luhya communities, were victims of retaliatory violence.[427]

As a regional actor, the African Union (AU) engaged with the Kenyan state in the immediate aftermath of the election violence. The OTP's involvement in Kenya thus ran alongside the AU's engagement. Beginning in late January 2008, an AU Panel of Eminent African Personalities, overseen by former UN Secretary-General Kofi Annan, mediated a political settlement through the Kenyan National Dialogue and Reconciliation process. This led to the National Accord and Reconciliation Agreement ('National Accord'), signed between Kibaki and Odinga in February 2008. The National Accord set forth a four-part agenda to address the consequences of the violence, including the establishment of a power-sharing, coalition government between Kibaki and Odinga; the creation of a

[426] Gabrielle Lynch, *I Say to You: Ethnic Politics and the Kalenjin in Kenya* (Chicago: University of Chicago Press, 2011), 3.
[427] For a more detailed history of the historical antecedents of Kenya's election violence, see Makau Mutua, *Kenya's Quest for Democracy: Taming Leviathan* (Kampala: Fountain, 2009); Michela Wrong, *It's Our Turn to Eat: The Story of a Kenyan Whistleblower* (London: Fourth Estate, 2009); Gabrielle Lynch, *I Say to You*; Daniel Branch, *Kenya: Between Hope and Despair, 1963–2011* (New Haven, CT: Yale University Press, 2011). Like Lynch, Branch traces an escalation of government corruption over time that evolved in conjunction with an increasingly ethnicized political landscape, leading to the explosive violence of late 2007. For an account of that period, see Human Rights Watch, 'Ballots to Bullets: Organized Political Violence and Kenya's Crisis of Governance' (March 2008).

Commission of Inquiry on Post-Election Violence (Kenya) (CIPEV), also known as the Waki Commission; and a Truth, Justice and Reconciliation Commission (TJRC).[428]

The CIPEV's remit 'was to investigate the facts and circumstances surrounding the [post-election] violence, the conduct of state security agencies in their handling of it, and to make recommendations concerning these and other matters'.[429] The commission's mandate expired in October 2008, at which point it published its final report. Chief amongst its many recommendations was that a Special Tribunal for Kenya (STK) – established by an act of Parliament and operating outside of the existing judicial system – be set up to 'seek accountability against persons bearing the greatest responsibility for crimes, particularly crimes against humanity, relating to the 2007 General Elections in Kenya'.[430] Other recommendations further provided:

> 2. The special tribunal shall apply Kenyan law and also the International Crimes Bill, once this is enacted, and shall have Kenyan and international judges, as well as Kenyan and international staff to be appointed as provided hereunder.
>
> 3. In order to fully give effect to the establishment of the special tribunal, an agreement for its establishment shall be signed by representatives of the parties to the Agreement on National Accord and Reconciliation within 60 days of the presentation of the Report of the Commission of Inquiry into the post-election violence to the Panel of Eminent African Personalities, or the panel's representative. A statute (to be known as 'the Statute for the Special Tribunal') shall be enacted into law and come into force within a further 45 days after the signing of the agreement.[431]

---

[428] The National Accord and Reconciliation Act, 2008; Kenya National Dialogue and Reconciliation: Commission of Inquiry on Post-Election Violence, 4 March 2008; Kenya National Dialogue and Reconciliation: Truth, Justice and Reconciliation Commission, 4 March 2008. The TJRC Act provided that the commission's broad objective would be to 'seek and promote justice, national unity, reconciliation and peace, among the people of Kenya by inquiring in to the human rights violations in Kenya and recommending appropriate redress' (Preamble). Its temporal jurisdiction was enormous: 12 December 1963 to 28 February 2008 (see General Parameters). For more detailed examinations of the Kenyan TJRC, see Ronald C. Slye, *The Kenyan TJRC: An Outsider's View from the Inside* (Cambridge: Cambridge University Press, 2018) and Gabrielle Lynch, *Performances of Injustice: The Politics of Truth, Justice and Reconciliation in Kenya* (Cambridge: Cambridge University Press, 2018).

[429] Commission of Inquiry into Post-Election Violence (15 October 2008) ('CIPEV Report'), vii, at www.kenyalaw.org/Downloads/Reports/Commission_of_Inquiry_into_Post_Election_Violence.pdf.

[430] Ibid., 472.

[431] Ibid., 472–473.

Crucially, in an effort to ensure the implementation of these terms, the commission recommended referral of the post-election violence to the ICC – including a sealed envelope with 'a list containing names of … those suspected to bear the greatest responsibility' – in the event that the STK failed to materialize, or if 'having commenced operating, its purposes [were later] subverted'.[432] In short, it sought to leverage domestic criminal prosecutions through The Hague.

Complementarity's coercive dimension was thus the dominant logic behind the CIPEV's recommendation. If the STK was not established within the commission's specified time frame, and if the government proved unwilling or unable to investigate and prosecute, the report and its confidential findings would be turned over to the Office of the Prosecutor. In this regard, the commission's conditioned approach was itself a novelty. As Muthoni Wanyeki notes, 'This [approach] was … in contrast with the recommendations of previous commissions of inquiry [in Kenya], which had been only partially implemented, if at all, often preferring to focus on more straightforward legal, policy or institutional reforms rather than on more contentious and pressing matters of legal and political accountability'.[433] The ICC's shadow threatened to change that.

Special Tribunal for Kenya: January 2008–February 2009

According to submissions made by the OTP, the office's preliminary examination formally commenced '[once] the violence erupted in the context of national elections held on 27 December 2007' and remained in this posture for approximately two years, until at least the prosecutor's announcement in November 2009 that he would submit a request to the court for permission to open a full investigation. In the interim, the OTP undertook measures to cajole Kenyan authorities into action similar to those identified in its policy paper. Following the formal declaration that President Kibaki had been re-elected, Moreno-Ocampo issued a public statement on 5 February 2008, recalling that Kenya was both a state party to the Statute and that the office would 'carefully consider all information' related to alleged crimes within the court's jurisdiction.[434] From this time onward, communications channels

---

[432] Ibid., 473 (paragraph 5).

[433] L. Muthoni Wanyeki, 'The International Criminal Court's Cases in Kenya: Origin and Impact', Institute for Security Studies, Paper no. 237 (August 2012), 8, at www.issafrica.org/uploads/Paper237.pdf.

[434] 'OTP Statement in Relation to Events in Kenya', 5 February 2008.

existed between state-level actors in Kenya and the OTP. The prosecutor sought additional information, including a copy of the report on the post-election violence undertaken by the Kenya National Human Rights Commission (KNHRC, the state's national human rights commission), which it produced in August 2008.[435] OTP submissions also indicate that letters dated March 2008 sought additional information from the government, the Kenya Human Rights Commission (a prominent NGO) and the Waki Commission.[436]

The coercive dimension to the ICC's involvement in Kenya lent political urgency to the establishment of the STK. Indeed, while the proposed tribunal raised unique constitutional challenges, work on preparing a draft statute began promptly after the government (unanimously, and without amendment) adopted the Waki Commission's report on 16 December 2008. Martha Karua, Kenya's then minister for justice, national cohesion and constitutional affairs, took the lead in its drafting, with the support of the attorney general's office and the Law Reform Commission, the body responsible for amendments to Kenyan legislation.

Known as the 'Iron Lady' of Kenyan politics, Karua enjoyed significant influence, but her style – criticized by many in civil society as imperial and insufficiently consultative – led to criticisms of the bill for its perceived concessions to the executive branch, including the power of presidential pardon.[437] Nevertheless, notable features of the proposed tribunal included its primacy over local courts for the crimes under its jurisdiction (not only crimes against humanity, but also genocide, gross human rights violations and other crimes committed in relation to the 2007 elections); a significant effort to internationalize the court's judicial composition;

---

[435] The KNHRC report, 'On the Brink of the Precipice: A Human Rights Account of Kenya's Post-2007 Election Violence' (August 2008) was referenced in the OTP's Article 15 request and controversially, was relied on significantly by the office in bringing its charges against the six officials initially accused. See *Situation in the Republic of Kenya*, Request for authorization of an investigation pursuant to Article 15, ICC-01/09, PTC II (26 November 2009), paras. 29–31 ('Kenya Article 15 Request'); see further the discussion on OTP investigations later.

[436] Kenya Article 15 Request, para. 7.

[437] See Godfrey M. Musila, 'Options for Transitional Justice in Kenya: Autonomy and the Challenge of External Prescriptions', *International Journal of Transitional Justice* 3 (2009), 452 ('The few members of civil society who were contacted by the author suggested that it was too late for them to make any input, having been given less than two days to respond before the bill was presented to parliament'.).

and, borrowing heavily from the ICC Statute, attempts to incorporate the participation of victims within domestic proceedings.[438] Importantly, because such a tribunal would operate outside of the Kenyan High Court system, a constitutional two-thirds majority (rather than a simple majority) would be required to pass the legislation.

Significant pressure was subsequently placed on parliamentarians to approve a constitutional amendment establishing the STK. Both Kibaki and Odinga supported the legislation's passage in principle (though the degree of political leadership they provided is questionable), while opponents of the bill included then MP Ruto, who represented the district of Eldoret North.[439] The latter formed a bloc of parliamentarians who favoured the ICC in part because it was seen to be less of a threat: it would prosecute fewer suspects and take more time.[440] Thus, the failure of Karua's bill was largely the product of an 'unholy alliance' between those MPs who opposed it because they feared being implicated and those parliamentarians – primarily reform-minded backbenchers – who favoured accountability in principle, but lacked faith in the idea of a national judicial process, particularly one that would displace the ICC.[441]

Against this backdrop the February 2009 debate in the National Assembly on the STK was contentious, particularly as compared to the unanimous domestication of the Rome Statute (discussed further in the

---

[438] See The Special Tribunal for Kenya Bill, 2009, at www.kenyalaw.org/Downloads/Bills/2009/The_Special_Tribunal_for_Kenya_Statute_2009.pdf. The provisions on victim participation in the proposed bill are found in Article 50 ('Rights of Victims') and are nearly identical to Article 68(3) of the Rome Statute. Notably, victim participation is not a feature otherwise available in Kenya's judicial system.

[439] Several Kenyan politicians have since gone on record as critical of Kibaki and Odinga's leadership: MP Mutula Kilonzo stated that they were 'failing in leadership', and Karua later said they had provided 'little or no support' during the parliamentary debates. See Nichols, *The International Criminal Court and The End of Impunity in Kenya*, 105.

[440] This view was expressed by several interlocutors in Kenya. For a similar analysis, see Lydia Kemunto Bosire, 'Misconceptions II – Domestic Prosecutions and the International Criminal Court', in *African Arguments*, 18 September 2009, available at http://africanarguments.org/2009/09/18/misconceptions-ii-domestic-prosecutions-and-the-international-criminal-court/.

[441] See Wanyeki, 'The International Criminal Court's Cases in Kenya', 9–10; Stephen Brown and Chandra Lekha Sriram, 'The Big Fish Won't Fry Themselves: Criminal Accountability for Post-Election Violence in Kenya', *African Affairs* 111(43) (2012), 244–260; Materu, *The Post-Election Violence in Kenya*, 72–73.

following chapter), which had taken place only several months before.[442] At the outset, MP Gitobu Imanyara, a noted advocate for accountability, but one who had favoured 'The Hague option', argued that the CIPEV's confidential findings should already be turned over to the ICC, because the '45 days period within which the government had to comply with [its] recommendations' had lapsed.[443] While he was joined by several MPs in this view, other STK advocates, notably Mutula Kilonzo (later Karua's successor as justice minister), insisted on greater time for Parliament to act, noting that the commission's timeline should not 'tie the hands of this august house'.[444]

As the bill's sponsor, Karua presented the amendment as recognition that Kenya had 'not been able, up to now, to deal with the issues arising from the post election violence', but also as an opportunity for domestic ownership and agency.[445] In her words:

> Mr. Deputy Speaker, sir, this bill is coming about because we, as a nation, are accepting that there are inherent weaknesses in our national institutions. … [It] is time to take responsibility. We are the assembly as national leaders of this country, and that is why this is a National Assembly. It is our duty to take responsibility to ensure that we put an end to impunity, to ensure that election violence ends once and for all, and that we hold each other to account whenever such things arise.[446]

---

[442] Unlike the narrowly defeated STK bill, the parliamentary debate on the International Crimes Act records no opposition to its passage. The attorney general's proposal was supported by Karua as well as MP Danson Mungatana (an STK opponent), who '[took] the opportunity to thank the attorney general for, once again, rising to the occasion and bringing our country's laws in line with the international community, especially in criminal jurisprudence'. See second reading of International Crimes Bill in Kenya National Assembly Official Record (Hansard) (7 May 2008). The International Crimes Act (ICA) was tabled and passed in a matter of months; it came into effect on 1 January 2009.

[443] Reference herein is to Kenya National Assembly Official Record (Hansard), the Constitution of Kenya (Amendment) Bill, Second Reading (3 February 2009) ('STK Amendment Bill'), 27 (MP Gitobu Imanyara). The National Assembly is the lower house of the Parliament of Kenya, while the Senate is the upper house. Prior to the structural reforms laid out in the 2010 Constitution, the assembly served as the country's unicameral legislature; hence, the debate on the STK only took place there.

[444] Ibid., 30. Other MPs similarly saw the amendment as a matter of parliamentary supremacy. For instance, MP Peter Mwathi stated that he would vote against the amendment, 'so that the final decision to take those people to The Hague, or wherever it will be, will arise from the recommendations of the Waki Commission, not here'!, 49. On whether a debate on the constitutional amendment could proceed, Imanyara's procedural concerns over the lapsing of the Waki Report's 45-day deadline were overruled. The deputy speaker issued a 'considered ruling' that 'An external body [CIPEV] cannot dictate how Parliament conducts business'. Ibid., 35.

[445] Ibid., 36.

[446] Ibid.

Other MPs, however, cast doubt on both the gravity of the violence and the imminence of the ICC threat when voicing their opposition. In their words:

> If you look at the history of [conflicts in Sudan, Uganda, and the Democratic Republic of Congo] and the matters which have been taken before The Hague, it is not more than some people who have gone to the International Criminal Court because the threshold is so high for it to act.[447]

> I want to caution this house, that it is not a given; it is not guaranteed that if we do not act domestically, one Moreno-Ocampo, the chief prosecutor of the ICC will be on the next flight to Nairobi.[448]

> What happened in Kenya in 2007 was tragic and really tragic. But it is not sufficient to call for the intervention of the ICC.[449]

Even with the promise of international involvement, concerns about a domestic tribunal's ability to penetrate the higher ranks of the Kenyan political class motivated opposition to the STK amongst those (like Imanyara) who favoured an accountability process in principle. One parliamentarian, for instance, noted that while he 'strongly believed[ed] that the Waki Report [was] correct', he nevertheless objected to the recommendation that 'we should have the tribunal in our country'. In his view:

> Our interest is not in the proposals of the magistrates courts and the other issues. Our interest is in the leaders. Who are these people who caused pain to this country? Suppose the investigations point, God forbid, at his excellency the president, do you want to tell me that this country has the capacity to try him? Suppose the investigation points at the prime minister, do you want to convince the Republic of Kenya that we have the capacity to try him?[450]

He concluded, '[This] tribunal is being set up for the small people. This country has a history of punishing the small people when the big ones have committed the crimes'![451]

Despite the criticisms of the bill, the legislation that Karua proposed was the only one that would ever come close to receiving parliamentary assent.[452] In continued exercise of the ICC's oversight function, the

---

[447] Ibid., 31 (MP Orengo).
[448] Ibid., 35 (MP Namwamba).
[449] Ibid., 34 (MP Baiya).
[450] Ibid., 48 (MP Cyrus Khwa Shakhalaga Jirongo).
[451] Ibid.
[452] Musila, 'Options for Transitional Justice in Kenya', 452.

prosecutor publicly reaffirmed on the eve of Parliament's vote that the OTP was monitoring the situation in Kenya, but that proved insufficient to alter the votes. Ultimately, the STK amendment failed to command a constitutional majority: on 12 February 2009, it was defeated in a vote of 101 (in favour) to 93 (opposed).[453]

Subsequent Efforts: March–November 2009

Following the government's failure to establish the STK, more direct and frequent contact between the OTP and national-level actors took shape; however, the office's engagement was still largely conducted 'through press statements and media interviews, rather than through face-to-face meetings'.[454] The Kenyan government subsequently promised to reintroduce improved legislation, but a second attempt to do so was rejected in June 2009.[455] After two successive extensions lapsed, Annan forwarded the Waki envelope and evidence to the OTP in July 2009. Thereafter, the prosecutor met with a formal delegation from Kenya (including Kilonzo as the new minister of justice and constitutional affairs), which resulted in an agreement stating that the government would provide him, by the end of September, with a report on the current status of investigations and prosecutions. Furthermore, if no 'modalities for conducting national investigations and prosecutions' were put in place within a year's time, it was agreed that the government would refer the matter to the ICC in accordance with Article 14.[456]

Following Annan's hand over of the envelope and more frequent interactions with the OTP, the government made renewed efforts at establishing a domestic accountability process, but to no avail. Kilonzo, for

---

[453] While a majority of parliamentarians in fact voted in favour of the tribunal, passage of the bill required a two-thirds majority given that it required a constitutional amendment. See Francis Mureithi, 'How MPs Rejected the Proposed Special Tribunal for Kenya Bill', *The Star*, 12 March 2011. A full breakdown of the votes is recorded at Bill: Second Reading: The Constitution of Kenya (Amendment) Bill, in *Kenya National Assembly Official Record (Hansard)*, 12 February 2009, 30–34.

[454] Nichols, 80–81. See, e.g., 9 July 2009, OTP Press Release; 16 July 2009, OTP Press Release; 18 September 2009, OTP Press Release. See also Kenya Article 15 Request, paras. 13–14, 16, 18–20.

[455] This bill was introduced by Karua's successor, Justice Minister Mutula Kilonzo. It never reached Parliament as it was rejected at the cabinet level.

[456] Agreed minutes of meeting of 3 July 2009 between the ICC prosecutor and delegation of the Kenyan government (3 July 2009, The Hague).

instance, reintroduced an STK Bill that sought to ameliorate some of the criticisms of the first draft; however, Kibaki's cabinet was unable to come to a political agreement and eventually opted to abandon the idea of a hybrid tribunal. Ultimately, after a series of meetings, President Kibaki announced at a press conference that all suspects would be dealt with through regular national courts as well as the TJRC (even though the latter had no prosecutorial authority) and that the government would first focus its efforts on reforming the judiciary and the police, objectives that also became central features of Kenya's new 2010 Constitution.[457]

During this time, the OTP maintained a public profile. It held a round-table discussion in The Hague with Kenyan civil society representatives in September 2009 and, in October, Moreno-Ocampo requested another meeting with national authorities. A letter was also sent to the Kenyan authorities later that month, informing them that the office's preliminary examination was complete and reiterating that two options were available: either for an Article 14 referral by the government or an independent decision of the prosecutor to request judicial authorization to start an investigation. On 5 November 2009, the prosecutor met with Kibaki and Odinga in Nairobi and announced in a joint press conference his intention to request such authorization. Six months later, in a divided opinion of Pre-Trial Chamber II, it was granted.[458]

Catalytic Effect? The Kenyan Examination Reconsidered

The Waki Commission's report and its unique use of the ICC as an enforcement mechanism created great interest in and demand for accountability across Kenya, pushing the government closer than it had ever before come to setting up a domestic criminal process.[459] But while

---

[457] In November 2009, MP Gitobu Imanyara also sought to introduce a private members' bill, but it did not advance on formal grounds as parliamentary quorum was not met. Brown and Sriram note that 'a boycott by MPs, allegedly with support their party leaders, prevented the assembly from reaching quorum whenever the bill was due to be discussed'. Brown and Sriram, 'The Big Fish Won't Fry Themselves', 254. See further Kenya National Assembly Official Report, The Constitution of Kenya (Amendment) Bill, Second Reading (2 December 2009).

[458] Kenya Article 15 Decision; see, however, dissenting opinion of Judge Hans-Peter Kaul.

[459] Two commentators have also suggested that the preliminary examination 'raised international concern about sexual violence during the post-election violence, giving unprecedented exposure to these issues and, for the first time, allowing Kenyans to talk about being victims of sexual violence'. Christine Bjork and Juanita Goebertus, 'Complementarity in Action: The Role of Civil Society and the ICC in Rule of Law Strengthening in Kenya', *Yale Human Rights and Development Journal* 14 (2011), 218.

the current historical narrative may tend to overlook how close Kenya came to establishing a special tribunal in February 2009, the history and conduct of the OTP's preliminary examination illustrates several ways in which it failed to sufficiently appreciate or engage with the country's complex political and social contexts. These failings also left the office ill-prepared for the investigations that would follow.

First, the examination procedure did not succeed in producing its desired outcome, which was the establishment of a domestic tribunal (later referred to more obliquely as 'modalities') for the prosecution of election-related violence. The difficulty of such a task should not be over-looked: such a tribunal would have effectively functioned outside of the Kenyan 'regular' criminal justice system and would have, by design, been insulated from a judiciary that had long been criticized for its susceptibility to executive influence.[460]

The defeat of the STK Bill thus largely owed to a political calculus on the part of many parliamentarians who saw the prospect of such a tribunal, at the time, as a greater threat than the ICC itself.[461] Whereas the ICC, by its own admission, could only pursue a handful of perpetrators at the highest level, an STK could likely have pursued a significantly greater number of individuals; therefore, MPs 'who were implicated but who were not among the "big fish" had little to fear from the ICC'.[462] Indeed, they may have had much to gain if the court proved successful in removing senior political rivals from the domestic electoral arena. Proceedings in The Hague, it was thought, would undoubtedly last longer than the next Kenyan election cycle. As one MP noted during parliamentary debate, 'There are those who will come to this floor to debate this law with the determination to ensure that this law does not pass; with the determination that, that [this] tribunal will not be set up, because their political rivals will be added to The Hague.'[463]

---

[460] See, e.g., Makau Mutua, 'Justice Under Siege: The Rule of Law and Judicial Subservience in Kenya', *Human Rights Quarterly* 23 (2001), 96–118.

[461] For a more detailed discussion of these dynamics, see Wankeyi, 'The International Criminal Court's Cases in Kenya', 8–9.

[462] Brown and Sriram, 'The Big Fish Won't Fry Themselves', 253. For a similar analysis, see Yvonne Dutton and Tessa Alleblas, 'Unpacking the Deterrent Effect of the International Criminal Court: Lessons from Kenya', *St. John's Law Review* 91(1) (2017), 148–55.

[463] STK Amendment Bill, 33–34 (MP Namwamba). Indeed, Raila and Odinga – who had politically allied themselves in the 2007 election – were amongst those who took opposing views of the STK. Odinga supported the tribunal largely because he believed it would sideline political opponents, while Ruto opposed the idea. Interview with a Kenyan academic (Nairobi, 18 June 2011).

While the phrase 'Don't be vague, go to The Hague' emerged, then, as part of Kenya's political lexicon to ostensibly indicate a preference for the ICC's involvement, it also signalled that many political actors saw the court as a more limited threat. In short, although key factions of the Kenyan political elite feared the ICC, it was not feared enough.

The two-year period of the Kenyan examination also underscores the importance of timing, both in terms of duration, but in the light of the domestic political environments in which the OTP acts. In Kenya, the power of the examination procedure was arguably at its peak throughout 2008, buttressed as it was by the ongoing CIPEV investigation and the active role of Annan, who had yet to hand the commission's envelope over to The Hague. Yet the OTP only became more publicly active and engaged in the examination procedure following the STK Bill's defeat, by which point the court's coercive power (having already failed to ensure the setting up of a domestic mechanism) had diminished considerably. This dynamic continued and deepened over the course of 2009 such that, by the time Annan handed the commission's envelope to the OTP in July, it was clear that a domestic tribunal was a political impossibility.

Retrospectively, then, the wisdom of continuing to engage with a government whose proposals had become increasingly incoherent should be questioned. As Wanyeki noted in late 2009, 'The state has done just enough, the bare minimum, to maintain the masquerade that it intends to pursue criminal justice for the organised violence on both sides of the political divide as well as the state violence last year'.[464] In this instance, the length of the ICC's preliminary examination may have prolonged that masquerade.

Furthermore, it is important to ask how wisely the OTP made use of this two-year period of time, or how appropriately staffed the JCCD division was to ensure that it could undertake the kind of situational analysis that was needed at the time. The CIPEV report was released in October 2008 (ten months after the office's examination had allegedly begun); yet, prior to and during the period leading up to the February 2009 parliamentary vote, there is little evidence that the OTP undertook a significant field mission to Kenya, or that there was any serious attempt to engage with Kenyan victims and affected communities. Informal communications channels may have existed between state actors and the OTP, but, as noted, face-to-face meetings with government officials and members of civil society were relatively

---

[464] L. Muthoni Wanyeki, 'Kenya: We Remember, and Have Evidence', *The East African* (9 November 2009). Brown and Sriram likewise conclude that 'While performing sham compliance, the government dragged its feet and delayed and undermined the process as much as it could, without repudiating it', 258.

rare until much later in the examination. Moreno-Ocampo himself only made his first visit to Kenya in May 2010, while the first formal meeting between Kenyan civil society groups and the OTP took place not in Nairobi, but in The Hague, more than 18 months after the examination had begun.[465]

Given this, it is unsurprising to note (as other Kenyan scholars have) that almost no one in Kenya even knew that the ICC had opened a preliminary examination, much less what that meant.[466] As a report by Kenyans for Peace, Truth, and Justice (KPTJ, an influential coalition of NGOs that came together following the disputed presidential election) later noted, 'long before Uhuru [Kenyatta] became president it should have been obvious that the Kenyan government was always going to be ambivalent in its dealings with the ICC and that it would do everything it could to shield those of supporters indicted by the ICC'.[467] Indeed, it was partly the failure to independently identify and gather information that led the office to later rely so heavily on witness testimony in the Kenyan cases, with all of the attendant risks that entailed.[468]

Finally, a paradox appears to have lain at the heart of the Kenyan experiment. Whereas the Waki Commission sought to use the threat of the ICC's intervention as leverage for the establishment of a domestic process, many victims and advocates in Kenya, in fact, saw the court's involvement as a necessary condition of such a process. Kenyan civil society, in particular, while not a monolith, took an exceedingly dim view of the government's willingness to pursue accountability absent the assurance of external proceedings, one that political leaders could not control. It is precisely because of this distrust in a judicial system that was 'heavily compromised and "beholden to the executive"'[469] that the core features of the proposed tribunal – located outside of the domestic justice system,

[465] Anne Perrot, 'Kenyan Victims Consulted on Opening of Prosecutor's Investigation', in *Victims' Rights Working Group Bulletin*, Victims' Rights Working Group, Summer 2010, no. 16, p. 2 ('The prosecutor of the ICC made his first visit to Kenya in mid-May 2010 to carry out investigations and meet with the victims' communities'.).

[466] See, e.g., Evelyne Asaala, 'The Deterrence Effect of the International Criminal Court: A Kenyan Perspective', in Jennifer Schense and Linda Carter (eds.), *Two Steps Forward, One Step Back: The Deterrent Effect of International Criminal Tribunals* (International Nuremberg Principles Academy, 2016), p. 256.

[467] Kenyans for Peace with Truth and Justice, 'Impunity Restored? Lessons learned from the failure of the Kenyan cases at the International Criminal Court' (2016), 14–19.

[468] Ibid. One interlocutor remarked to me in June 2011 his disappointment with the ICC's witness protection program, predicting – accurately – that people were 'going to get [...] killed' as a result of 'incompetence' in the court's protection operations (Nairobi, 16 June 2011). See also Lucy Hannan, 'Witness protection in the Kenya cases: balancing secrecy with accountability' (KPTJ, December 2019) (on-file).

[469] Musila, 'Options for Transitional Justice in Kenya', 456.

with international judicial participation – were seen as non-negotiable and why the perceived compromises in Karua's legislation were viewed with suspicion (for instance, with respect to presidential immunity).

In short, trust in the Kenyan government and faith in its institutions were so low that most within the civil society sector were reluctant to support any domestic legal reform efforts until *after* the ICC intervened. In the words of two prominent Kenyan advocates:

> In tandem with the ICC's intervention, civil society groups [were] at the forefront of advocating for [a judicial mechanism], *though such advocacy had to take place after the commencement of the Kenyan cases.* Given the pervasive climate of impunity, many organisations feared that any domestic accountability processes might be hijacked to justify an admissibility challenge before the ICC.[470]

Similarly, in their study of the advocacy strategies of Kenyan NGOs during the ICC's preliminary examination, Christine Bjork and Juanita Goebertus conclude that 'in most cases, even the NGOs that actually had the power to impact national criminal justice system reform were inclined, instead, to encourage ICC intervention at the time that the preliminary examination was being conducted'.[471] This was because they 'feared that improvements of the criminal justice system or installment of transitional justice mechanisms would avert ICC intervention and create impunity for the main perpetrators'.[472] Given the pervasive distrust in Kenya's institutions, most supporters of accountability would thus not accept complementarity's catalytic potential without the engagement of the very institution the preliminary examination sought to avoid: the ICC itself.

The presumptions driving Kenya's preliminary examination again demonstrate the ways in which legalism animates the complementarity-as-catalyst vision. They reflect, in McEvoy's words, 'a capacity to disconnect from the real political and social world of transition through a process of "magical legalism"'.[473] Kenya's history of 'ever-changing political alliances', as Lynch

---

[470] Njonjo Mue and Judy Gitau, 'The Justice Vanguard: Kenyan Civil Society and the Pursuit of Accountability', in *Contested Justice: The Politics and Practice of International Criminal Court Interventions*, 216 (emphasis added).

[471] Bjork and Goebertus, 'Complementarity in Action', 218.

[472] Ibid., 223.

[473] McEvoy, 'Letting Go of Legalism', 25–26. For a similar conclusion, see Thomas Obel Hansen and Chandra Lekha Sriram, 'Fighting for Justice (and Survival): Kenyan Civil Society Accountability Strategies and Their Enemies', *International Journal of Transitional Justice* (2015). Hansen and Sriram quote several Kenyan activists as having 'now learned that approaches dominated by legal language and influenced by international norms may be flawed in facing a government that … can draw upon a range of political, historical and ethnic language in a divided society to build counter-narratives', 20–21.

had described them – and the prosecutor's failure to 'grasp the incestuous links, and the mendacity, of Kenya's political elite', as a KPTJ report aptly put it – illustrates the need to ensure that legal decisions are made with a deeply informed assessment of a situation's domestic and local politics.[474] Indeed, few foresaw that one perverse outcome of the ICC's attempted prosecutions would be to bring Kenyatta and Ruto, former political enemies, together in political victory. As Moreno-Ocampo later reflected, 'I never suspected [Kenyatta and Ruto] were so smart to create [that] ticket'.[475]

Preliminary Examinations Post-Kenya

As one of the early, extended preliminary examinations to both conclude and move into an investigation phase, the Kenyan experience stands as an instructive chapter in the OTP's history.[476] Indeed, the office's practice with respect to examinations has changed significantly since its early practice in the Kenyan context, as other commentators have noted.[477] These changes include not only a more transparent approach to examinations and a more deliberate, phased approach to the examination procedure, but also greater emphasis on complementarity's managerial dimensions.

For instance, whereas the Kenyan examination was characterized by a coercive approach – the threat of ICC intervention if a domestic tribunal was not established – the OTP's approach to Colombia in the later years of its examination suggests a different strategy. Rather than focusing on catalysing domestic criminal proceedings per se as it had in Kenya, the OTP instead drew on complementarity's cooperative, managerial features as a way to influence the scope and content of the December 2015 peace agreement. Rene Urueña suggests that the OTP's engagement in Colombia 'can be roughly divided into two

---

[474] See Lynch, 'Electing the "Alliance of the Accused"', 93–114; KPTJ, 'Impunity Restored?', 19. A 2018 independent review undertaken of the Kenyan situation – finally made partially public by the OTP in December 2019 – is similarly withering. See 'Executive Summary of the Report of the External Independent Experts' (2018).

[475] James Verini, 'The Prosecutor and the President', *The New York Times* (22 June 2016).

[476] Subsequent examinations of significant duration that have advanced to the investigations stage have since increased. These include Afghanistan (OTP sought authorization to open an investigation in November 2017; examination made public in 2007), Georgia (OTP authorized to open an investigation in January 2016; examination begun in August 2008) and Burundi (OTP authorized to open an investigation in October 2017; examination begun in April 2016).

[477] See Human Rights Watch, 'Pressure Point' (noting that 'OTP practice has changed significantly' since 2011).

distinct periods': a 2004–2007 period, which was largely dominated by the ICC as 'looming threat', and a 2008–2016 period, which was instead characterized by greater interaction between the ICC and Colombian institutions and civil society, as well as the prosecutor giving greater 'priority to gaining influence in domestic legal developments regarding the peace process'.[478]

OTP engagement was thus more nuanced than it had been in the Kenyan context, focused on influencing certain priorities – the exclusion of amnesties for war crimes or crimes against humanity, the unacceptability of wholly suspended sentences (as part of an alternative sentencing regime) – rather than on one particular outcome.[479] In this sense, Urueña concludes, 'the OTP was transformed by Colombia as much as Colombia was transformed by the OTP'.[480] Scholars have also noted the significant influence of another international court, the Inter-American Court of Human Rights, on the evolution of Colombia's negotiated peace. Indeed, Alexandra Huneeus has argued, that the ICC 'stepped back' from its earlier, 'maximalist interpretation of the Rome Statute by way of the Inter-American Court's jurisprudence'.[481]

Importantly, the OTP has also invested greater resources in the preliminary examination procedure, allowing for increased staff to monitor

---

[478] Urueña, 104.

[479] See Urueña, 120 (contending that the Ugandan experience, 'and Colombia's civil society insistence, may have nudged the OTP towards adopting a more flexible approach'); see also Kirsten Ainley, 'The Great Escape? The Role of the International Criminal Court in the Colombian Peace Process', Justice in Conflict (13 October 2016), at http://eprints.lse.ac.uk/68228/1/Ainley_The%20great%20escape.pdf. On the issue of alternative sentencing, for instance, Deputy ICC Prosecutor James Stewart gave a speech in Bogota in 2015 that set out parameters that the office suggested be used to assess the legitimacy of alternative or reduced sentences, including an assessment of the broader transitional justice context and an accused's engagement in other truth telling processes. See 'Transitional Justice in Colombia and the Role of the International Criminal Court' (13 May 2015), at www.iccnow.org/documents/DPs_Keynote_Speech_on_Transitional_Justice_in_Colombia_and_the_Role_of_the_ICC_English.pdf; see also Statement of ICC prosecutor, Fatou Bensouda, on the conclusion of the peace negotiations between the government of Colombia and the Revolutionary Armed Forces of Colombia – People's Army' (1 September 2016), at www.icc-cpi.int/Pages/item.aspx?name=160901-otp-stat-colombia ('I note, with satisfaction, that the final text of the peace agreement excludes amnesties and pardons for crimes against humanity under the Rome Statute'.).

[480] Urueña, 104.

[481] Alexandra Huneeus, 'Legitimacy and Jurisdictional Overlap: The ICC and the Inter-American Court in Colombia', in Nienke Grossman, Harlan Grant Cohen, Andreas Follesdal and Geir Ulfstein (eds.), Legitimacy and International Courts (Cambridge: Cambridge University Press, 2018), 139.

situations and more time spent in-country. In Colombia, for instance, the OTP has undertaken six trips to the country since 2013 (including a high-level mission led by Bensouda herself in 2017), as compared to three missions in the previous nine years from when it was first opened.[482] Similarly, in Guinea, Human Rights Watch has commended the office's impact there, noting that 'the frequency of visits by the OTP to the country helps to explain how, over a number of years during which [domestic] investigations were at times stalled, they nonetheless managed the situation in a manner that contributed to incremental progress'.[483] It would seem that this greater investment of staff resources has yielded dividends for the OTP in at least some of its examinations. They have still been criticized as too limited, however, even as the office has struggled annually to press for greater financial support from the Assembly of States Parties.

The OTP's evolving approach to preliminary examinations again underscores complementarity's dual dimensions. Whereas the Kenyan approach was distinguished by a threat-based approach, strategies in other contexts have responded to different political dynamics, reflecting a more contextually driven strategy that relies on complementarity's capacity to engage national governments in dialogue, or to magnify the influence of domestic actors. As Human Rights Watch noted in its 2018 report, 'the OTP's approach has and is likely to continue to differ from one situation to the next. In one situation, the OTP may prolong its deference to national authorities because it considers genuine proceedings may yet materialize, while in another situation, it may not afford national authorities an equivalent space'.[484] This balance, in turn, 'requires a deep appreciation of context'.[485] Such appreciation has perhaps been better exercised in other ICC situation countries, but, in Kenya, it was lacking.

3   Investigations and Complementarity

Investigations by the ICC have drawn increasing attention in the wake of several high-profile acquittals, as well as the collapse of the Kenyan cases. Judicial treatment of OTP investigatory practices has been withering

---

[482] By contrast, Moreno-Ocampo did not make his first trip to Colombia until October 2007, three years after the examination had formally opened. Subsequent missions followed in August 2008 and October 2009. See Urueña, 112; Human Rights Watch, 'Pressure Point', 165–166. On Bensouda's visit, see Coalition for the ICC, 'ICC Prosecutor in Colombia' (13 September 2017).
[483] Human Rights Watch, 'Pressure Point', 10.
[484] Ibid., 9.
[485] Ibid., 10.

in several cases; furthermore, as noted above, the relatively high rate of dismissal and acquittal portends poorly for the court if it is to maintain a credible posture as threat or source of pressure.[486] At the same time, investigations have the potential to capitalize upon complementarity's cooperative elements, as illustrated in the office's early endorsement of a partnership-based approach to national jurisdictions, including possible 'consensual divisions' of labour. In practice, however, the OTP has struggled to realize this vision.

The OTP's Early Approach to Investigations: Uganda, DRC and Kenya

While the Rome Statute is silent as to how evidence collection is to be carried out, the OTP adopted early on a policy of 'focused investigations'.[487] As articulated by the former head of the JCCD, 'The ICC prosecutor's policy [was] to carry out investigations in a few months, involving as few witnesses and incidents as possible'.[488] Related to this policy was the office's use of small teams of rotating investigators to carry out its investigations.[489] Bernard Lavigne, who oversaw the ICC's early investigations in the DRC, testified that his investigation teams never consisted of more than twelve people for the entire country, which he considered to be 'insufficient'.[490]

---

[486] In acquitting the ICC's second defendant, Mathieu Ngudjolo Chui, Trial Chamber II dedicated a portion of its judgment to criticizing the OTP's investigatory methods and the credibility of its witnesses. The Prosecutor v. Mathieu Ngudjolo, Judgment pursuant to Article 74 of the Statute, ICC-01/04-02/12, TC II, 18 December 2012, para. 516 ('Ngudjolo Judgment'). See also The Prosecutor v. Thomas Lubanga Dyilo, Judgment pursuant to Article 74 of the Statute, ICC-01/04-01/06-2842, TC I (14 March 2012), paras. 482–483; The Prosecutor v. Uhuru Muigai Kenyatta, Decision on defence application pursuant to Article 64(4) and related requests, ICC-01/09-02/11, TC V (26 April 2013), Concurring Opinion of Judge Christine Van den Wyngaert, paras. 1, 4–5. Similar concerns have been raised over sexual- and gender-based crimes, which the OTP, particularly under Bensouda's tenure, has identified as a priority, but remain amongst those most vulnerable to failing judicial scrutiny.
[487] See ICC-OTP, 'Report on Prosecutorial Strategy', 14 September 2006, 5, para. 2(b); 'Prosecutorial Strategy 2009–2012', para. 20.
[488] Katy Glassborow, 'ICC Investigative Strategy on Sexual Violence Crimes Under Fire', Institute for War & Peace Reporting (27 October 2008). Glassborow quotes Beatrice Le Fraper du Hellen, who headed the JCCD from 2006 to 2010.
[489] An early OTP policy paper noted that its 'operations are informed by three basic principles', one being that 'it functions with a variable number of investigation teams'. See OTP, 'Paper on some Policy Issues before the Office of the Prosecutor', 8.
[490] Lavigne Deposition, 16:11–16.

Similarly, in the case against former President Gbagbo, eight investigators reportedly worked on the ground 'in rotating teams of two'.[491] According to the OTP's proposed 2012 budget (the last year of Moreno-Ocampo's tenure), only 44 professional staff were requested for the 'investigations teams' section, to be dispersed amongst what was then six active situation countries.[492]

The pursuit of this early strategy meant that ICC investigators spent relatively little time in the field. Although Moreno-Ocampo indicated in 2004 remarks that some investigators would 'be based in headquarters and others will be deployed in the field', in practice all ICC investigators have been Hague-based and travel 'on mission'.[493] Moreover, they were only deployed in the field for limited periods of time, undertaking repeated, short-term trips. Indeed, according to testimony, investigators working in the DRC spent only an average of ten days (per mission) in the field, making it difficult for them to interview witnesses, much less develop the sort of long-term connections that a more sustained field presence would enable.[494] Speaking in 2005, Jane Odwong, a former Ugandan parliamentarian, also criticized the ICC's investigations for 'operating in a clandestine manner'. In her words, 'Nobody knows the issues of the ICC

[491] John James, 'Ivory Coast – Who's Next after Laurent Gbagbo?', *International Justice Tribune* (29 February 2012).
[492] Ibid. The report further notes that the number of professional staff employed in the investigations division 'has *decreased* since 2007, despite the increase in the number of situations in which the court is active'. Ibid., 30–31 (emphasis in original); see also ASP, 'Proposed Programme Budget for 2012 of the International Criminal Court', ICC-ASP/10/10 (21 July 2011), 47, at https://asp.icc-cpi.int/iccdocs/asp_docs/ASP10/ICC-ASP-10-10-ENG.pdf. These numbers were largely unchanged from previous years, including 2008–2010 when there were 4–5 situations under active investigation (DRC, Uganda, CAR, Darfur and later Kenya). As discussed further later, the allocation of additional resources has since led to a modest increase in investigation staffing: as of late 2017, the OTP's investigation section was comprised of sixty-five established posts. See ASP, 'Proposed Programme Budget for 2018 of the International Criminal Court', ICC-ASP/16/10 (11 September 2017), para. 353, at https://asp.icc-cpi.int/iccdocs/asp_docs/asp16/icc-asp-16-10-eng.pdf.
[493] 'Statement of the prosecutor Luis Moreno-Ocampo to Diplomatic Corps' (12 February 2004), 2, at www.iccnow.org/documents/OTPStatementDiploBriefing12Feb04.pdf.
[494] Lubanga Judgment, para. 165; Lavigne Deposition, 75:7–8. In the DRC, the OTP reported that, as of 2006, investigators had 'conducted more than 70 missions inside and outside the DRC'; the same report noted that the Ugandan team has conducted '[i]n just ten months … over 50 missions in the field'. See ICC-OTP, 'Report on the Activities Performed During the First Three Years (June 2003–June 2006)' (12 September 2006), 11, 15.

even within our communities, and the country'.[495] Consequently, a 2008 report by Human Rights Watch noted that:

> The opportunities for Hague-based investigators to interact and develop strong contacts with witnesses are limited in number and timeframe... [E]ven when key witnesses agree to a specified time to meet with investigators, circumstances may change, rendering them unavailable by the time that The Hague-based members of the investigative teams travel to the field.[496]

This small-team approach made the possibility of a permanent presence in the field impossible. As summarized by the trial chamber in Lubanga, 'because there were only a few investigators it was not possible to have someone in the field permanently', even though, according to Lavigne, 'This would have been the correct approach'.[497]

Pascal Kambale, formerly the DRC country director for the Open Society Initiative for Southern Africa, has also argued that the OTP's failure to bring charges against other, higher-ranking commanders in the DRC situation was 'a direct result of the ... strategy of conducting quick investigations with the lowest cost possible'.[498] In his view, the investigative teams assigned to Ituri 'were too undersized and too short-term to generate good analysis of the intricately entangled criminal activities' taking place in the region.[499] Kambale further recalled a meeting in December 2003, at which Moreno-Ocampo reportedly told a group of international NGOs that the investigative teams deployed to the field 'would be composed almost entirely of temporary staff'.[500] This plan was later reconsidered, but the 'cost-efficient' approach means that investigators were 'sent to the field for short periods of time'.[501] The OTP's minimal field presence in the Kivus region of eastern DRC – which was even more

[495] Jane Odwong (Kitgum), 23 March 2005. Similar criticisms were also conveyed by a former ICC investigator I interviewed who worked on the Ugandan situation (The Hague, July 2012). Indeed, I was surprised to learn that it was not until after the Kampala Review Conference in 2010 that members of the Ugandan Director of Public Prosecutions (DPP) came to even be aware of the ICC investigators acting in-country, and subsequently initiated contact with the Office of the Prosecutor. Interview with a senior DPP official (Kampala, December 2011).
[496] Human Rights Watch, 'Courting History: The Landmark International Criminal Court's First Years' (2008), 55.
[497] Lubanga Judgment, para. 166; Lavigne Deposition, 75:16–18.
[498] Pascal Kambale, 'The ICC and Lubanga: Missed Opportunities' (16 March 2012), at http://forums.ssrc.org/african-futures/2012/03/16/african-futures-icc-missed-opportunities/.
[499] Ibid.
[500] Ibid.
[501] Ibid. According to local NGOs and UN staff in Bunia, 'Investigators never spent more than a few days', n. 21.

limited than its presence in Ituri – led to similar results before ICC judges. In December 2011, a majority of Pre-Trial Chamber I declined to confirm any of the charges against Callixte Mbarushimana (a Rwandan national residing in France) for crimes committed by the Democratic Forces for the Liberation of Rwanda (FDLR) in the DRC.[502] In its judgment acquitting Ngudjolo Chui, Trial Chamber II also drew attention to the OTP's lack of field presence in assessing deficiencies in the evidence presented. While acknowledging the difficulty of conducting investigations in a 'region still plagued by high levels of insecurity', the chamber emphasized the importance of 'mak[ing] as many factual findings as possible, in particular forensic findings … in loci in quo'.[503]

The OTP's approach to investigations at the time was closely linked to resources and financing. Indeed, the number of small missions conducted in a relatively short period was extolled in a 2009 document as part of the 'court-wide efficiency drive'.[504] Yet the office's 'lean and flexible' approach was also criticized for its effectiveness and the strain it placed on court staff. In a private 2008 letter that Human Rights Watch sent to the OTP executive committee (later made public), the organization expressed concern with the high attrition rate of ICC investigators and noted that there were 'simply not enough of them to handle the rigorous demands for conducting investigations'.[505] In addition, few to any of the ICC's early investigators were nationals of those countries under investigation; indeed,

---

[502] See The Prosecutor v. Callixte Mbarushimana, Decision on the confirmation of charges, ICC-01/04-01/10-465-Red, PTC I (16 December 2011). The chamber, by majority, expressed 'concern' over the OTP's apparent attempt to 'keep the parameters of its case as broad and general as possible', pleading certain charges with insufficient specificity and 'in such vague terms', seemingly 'in order to allow it to incorporate new evidence relating to other factual allegations at a later date without following the procedure [governing amendments to the charges]', paras. 82, 110. In the case against FDLR commander Sylvestre Mudacumura, a separate pre-trial chamber denied the OTP's first request for an arrest warrant for a similar 'lack of specificity'. It later granted the warrant, but excluded all of the requested counts of crimes against humanity, while noting that the application bore 'some similarities' to the case brought against Mbarushimana. See The Prosecutor v. Sylvestre Mudacumura, Decision on the prosecutor's application under Article 58, ICC-01/04-01/12, PTC II, 13 July 2012, paras. 20, 22–29.

[503] Ngudjolo Judgment, paras. 115–117.

[504] 'Second Status Report on the Court's Investigations in to Efficiency Measures', ICC-ASP/8/30, 4 November 2009, para. 4. The report noted that the office's strategy 'of having a small, flexible office', as well as 'lean and flexible' investigation teams had 'enabled [it] to perform more investigations and prosecutions simultaneously, with the same number of staff'.

[505] Human Rights Watch, Letter to the Executive Committee of the Prosecutor (15 September 2008), at www.article42-3.org/Secret%20Human%20Rights%20Watch%20Letter.pdf.

only a limited number were African.[506] Kambale's notes from a 2004 meeting with OTP staff indicate that the choice not to seek out experienced national investigators was deliberate. Part of the 'short and focused' investigative strategy, as articulated by the then prosecutor, was 'the fact that it would minimize the need for having local people in the investigative teams, thus helping avoid situations where impartiality is questionable'.[507]

Unlike predecessor tribunals, the OTP also hired no country experts as either permanent or temporary staff.[508] In the DRC, it appears that there was only one Congolese national who served for a brief period of time, in a formal capacity, as a country expert and advisor to investigators.[509] A study conducted by the International Refugee Rights Initiative (IIRI), in consultation with the Congolese NGO Aprodivi, notes that '[T]he fact that court staff was ... dominated by internationals did little to diminish the sense that the court could have done more to understand the local context. ... Failure to ["verify the information that they got"], and to engage the "real community leaders", left the ICC "looking ridiculous a large percentage of the time"'.[510] Similar criticisms were raised in Kenya as well, prior to the cases collapsing. One filing from the victims' representative in the case against William Ruto and Joseph Sang, for instance, alleged that the OTP had not conducted a 'meaningful investigation into eyewitness experiences' and that the victims – who numbered nearly 300 at the time – had reportedly not been interviewed by the OTP, were not aware of anyone in their locality having been interviewed nor were they aware of the prosecutor having ever come to their localities to conduct on-site investigations.[511]

Finally, while country nationals have not formally been a part of OTP investigations teams, the office has nevertheless made extensive use of intermediaries. Intermediaries are not ICC employees as such, but may

---

[506] Interview with member of ICC Investigations Division (The Hague, July 2012).

[507] Kambale, 'Missed Opportunities', n.22.

[508] In contrast, both Louise Arbour and Carla del Ponte, former prosecutors of the International Criminal Tribunal for the Former Yugoslavia (ICTY), hired specialists to act as political advisors in dealing with governments and key figures within the former Yugoslavia. See Victor Peskin, *International Justice in Rwanda and the Balkans: Virtual Trials and the Struggle for State Cooperation* (Cambridge: Cambridge University Press, 2008).

[509] Interview with member of ICC Investigations Division (The Hague, July 2012).

[510] IRRI and *Association pour la promotion et la défense de la dignité des victimes* (Aprodivi-ASBL), 'Steps Towards Justice, Frustrated Hopes: Some Reflections on the Experience of the International Criminal Court in Ituri' (January 2012), 20.

[511] See *The Prosecutor v. William Samoei Ruto*, et al., Request by the victims' representatives for authorisation to make a further written submission on the views and concerns of the victims, ICC-01/09-01/11, PTC II, 9 November 2011, paras. 10–11. The victims' subsequent legal representative, Fergal Gaynor, filed a motion requesting judicial

assist the office (and other organs of the court) in a volunteer capacity, as well as being hired on a short-term, contract basis.[512] No definition of 'intermediary' is found in the Statute or the Rules of Procedure and Evidence; however, the court defines an intermediary as 'someone who comes between one person and another; who facilitates contact or provides a link between one of the organs or unit of the court or counsel on the one hand, and victims, witnesses, beneficiaries of reparations and/or affected communities more broadly on the other'.[513] In short, intermediaries are locally based actors who, '[b]ecause of their long-term presence', carry out important functions for the court.[514] As summarized by the trial chamber in Lubanga, they 'undertake tasks in the field that staff members cannot fulfil without creating suspicion; they know members of the community, and they have access to information and places that are otherwise unavailable to the prosecution'.[515]

Intermediaries were a feature of the *ad hoc* tribunals as well, although on a more limited basis. The ICC's engagement across multiple countries, combined with its increasingly constrained resources, means that they are a more permanent part of the court's practice. Indeed, reliance on intermediaries attracted particular attention in the wake of Lubanga's trial, where the chamber determined early on that their role, together with the manner in which they discharged their functions, had

review of the OTP's decision to suspend its investigation into President Kenyatta's role in the post-election violence. *Situation in the Republic of Kenya*, Victims' request for review of prosecution's decision to cease active investigation, ICC-01/09, PTC II (3 August 2015).

[512] Testimony from the Lubanga proceedings indicate that the term intermediary 'began to be used in the summer of 2004, but intermediaries only received contracts much later'. See Lubanga Judgment, para. 194. Furthermore, while travel expenses for intermediaries were generally reimbursed, 'the majority of the intermediaries were not paid and did not request payment', para. 198.

[513] See 'Guidelines Governing the Relations between the Court and Intermediaries – for the Organs and Units of the Court and Counsel working with intermediaries' (March 2014), at www.icc-cpi.int/iccdocs/lt/GRCI-Eng.pdf.

[514] Lubanga Judgment, para. 167. For a similar assessment of these actors in the context of the ICC's first situation in CAR, see Marlies Glasius, '"We Ourselves, We Are Part of the Functioning": The ICC, Victims, and Civil Society in the Central African Republic', *African Affairs* 108(430) (2009), 67 ('In the CAR, this relation [between local civil society and the ICC] is currently almost too close for comfort: the court relies on a small alliance of civil society groups for doing outreach, collecting evidence and finding victims and witnesses willing to testify'.).

[515] The Prosecutor *v.* Thomas Lubanga Dyilo, Redacted decision on intermediaries, ICC-01/04-01/06, TC I, 31 May 2010, para. 88.

become 'an issue of major importance'.[516] In its judgment, the chamber ultimately found that the 'essentially unsupervised actions of three of the principal [prosecution] intermediaries [could not] safely be relied upon', a determination that, in turn, led to the exclusion of the testimony of witnesses who claimed to have served as child soldiers in Lubanga's rebel army.[517] The court further found that 'There was no formal recruitment procedure for selecting intermediaries. An intermediary was simply someone who could perform this role; there was no process of candidacy or application and instead it was a matter of circumstance'.[518]

The uncertain relationship of intermediaries to the OTP (and to the court at large) underscores the crucial, but potentially destabilizing, role that they can play in investigations. On the one hand, as the trial chamber concluded, the OTP inappropriately 'delegated' its investigative responsibilities to intermediaries, relying on them, in some cases, to not only contact, but also propose potential witnesses. At the same time, the role of intermediaries was apparently 'limited, in the sense that [they] were excluded from the decision-making process'.[519] As it was explained to the court, intermediaries 'were not supposed to know the objectives of the investigation team', nor were they 'given any substantive information about the case' because it would have been 'too complicated to enable discussions with anyone who was not a member of the investigation division'.[520]

---

[516] Ibid., paras. 135–138; see also Christian De Vos, '"Someone Who Comes between One Person and Another": Lubanga, Local Cooperation and the Right to a Fair Trial', *Melbourne Journal of International Law* 12 (2011).

[517] Lubanga Judgment, para. 482.

[518] Lubanga Judgment, para. 195. The prosecutor also drew heavily on evidence gathered from confidential agreements with intermediaries in its cases against Katanga and Ngudjulo Chui, leading the Pre-Trial Chamber to similarly lament 'the reckless investigative techniques during the first two years of the investigation into DRC'. Prosecutor v. Katanga, Decision on Article 54(3)(e) documents identified as potentially exculpatory or otherwise material to the defence's preparation for the confirmation hearing, ICC-01/04-01/07, PTC I (20 June 2008), para. 123. Notably, in Kenya, the prosecutor later initiated a case against Walter Barasa, a Kenyan journalist and an OTP intermediary, under Article 70 for allegedly offering money to witnesses if they withdrew their testimony against the accused. While Barasa remains at large, similar, successful Article 70 proceedings were brought against Bemba and members of his defence team for witness tampering as well.

[519] Lubanga Judgment, para. 181.

[520] Ibid., para. 183.

It would appear that, as a matter of policy, intermediaries remained at the margins of the OTP's decision-making process.[521] Kambale, for instance, notes that local Congolese NGOs and activists, 'had more raw intelligence on the crimes than any other entity, [but] were deliberately sidelined and their invaluable expertise not fully integrated into the investigative process'.[522] Similarly, IIRI, which has worked extensively with intermediaries in the DRC, Uganda and Sudan, notes that in the context of the DRC, the prosecution did not know enough about who was giving it information and why. This 'lack of expertise … was viewed as reducing the capacity of the office [in The Hague] to navigate the complex local politics'. Simply put, 'They trusted anyone who called themselves civil society'.[523]

Shifts in Strategy: Investigations and the OTP's 'Basic Size'

The OTP's approach to investigations in Uganda, DRC and Kenya belies the lofty principles that animated much of the office's initial rhetoric on 'positive' complementarity. Driven on the one hand by the catalytic vision of an empty courthouse – wherein, in Moreno-Ocampo's words, 'the absence of trials [before the ICC]… would be a major success'[524] – the office is also faced with the more prosaic, pragmatic task of demonstrating that it can deliver on its mission: to competently and efficiently prosecute international crimes. As with the narrow approach of ICC judges to complementarity assessments, the OTP's early emphasis on 'focused' investigations was undertaken to the apparent detriment of building sustained relationships with national-level actors in its situation countries. In short, its ambitions to secure convictions in the name of the ICC sat awkwardly with complementarity as a principle of burden sharing and

---

[521] See, e.g., Elena Baylis, 'Outsourcing Investigations', *UCLA Journal of International Law and Foreign Affairs* 14 (2009), 121; Emily Haslam and Rod Edmunds, 'Managing a New "Partnership": "Professionalization", Intermediaries and the International Criminal Court', *Criminal Law Forum* 24 (2013), 49.

[522] Kambale, 'Missed Opportunities'.

[523] IRRI and Aprodivi-ASBL, 'Steps Towards Justice, Frustrated Hopes', 20. The Trial Chamber in Lubanga drew a similar conclusion, finding that 'There was no formal recruitment procedure for selecting intermediaries. An intermediary was simply someone who could perform this role; there was no process of candidacy or application and instead it was a matter of circumstance'.

[524] Luis Moreno-Ocampo, statement made at the ceremony for the solemn undertaking of the chief prosecutor of the International Criminal Court (16 June 2003), at www.iccnow.org/documents/MorenoOcampo16June03.pdf.

coordinated action. One notable exception (though in the context of a third state, not a territorial state) was the 2015 conviction by a German court of two Rwandan nationals: Ignace Murwanashyaka and Straton Musoni, the president and vice-president of the Democratic Forces for the Liberation of Rwanda, respectively.[525] Begun in 2011, these national prosecutions (for attacks on the civilian population of North and South Kivu) were the first held on the basis of universal jurisdiction under the German criminal code and were linked to the ICC's (unsuccessful) prosecution of Callixte Mbarushimana, who was also amongst the FDLR's leadership.[526]

Importantly, following the election of Prosecutor Bensouda, the office's strategic plans have explicitly moved away from a policy of 'focused investigations' to, in its words, 'prioritize quality over quantity'.[527] Rather, in a 'radical shift', the office now favours 'in-depth, open-ended investigations while maintaining focus', and is committed to ensuring that its 'cases at the confirmation hearings … are as trial-ready as possible'.[528] In line with

---

[525] See OTP Factsheet, 'Situation in the Democratic Republic of Congo: Callixte Mbarushimana' (11 October 2010), at www.icc-cpi.int/NR/rdonlyres/DEB862E4-1E38-4C6E-9197-2953EC6D7EC9/282525/FactsheetENG2.pdf ('These three arrests are a concrete result of close coordination between the OTP and states such as Germany, France, the DRC and Rwanda to bring to justice those most responsible for crimes committed by the FDLR. Moreover, the collaboration with the German authorities is a clear example of positive complementarity in action'.); Kai Ambos and Ignaz Stegmiller, 'Prosecuting International Crimes at the International Criminal Court: Is There a Coherent and Comprehensive Prosecution Strategy?', *Crime, Law and Social Change* 58(4) (2012), 429 (describing the close cooperation as a 'shining example for positive complementarity').

[526] The convictions for war crimes were later overturned on appeal; however, their convictions on the grounds of membership in a terrorist organization were sustained. See 'German court partially overturns war crimes verdict for Rwandan', *Reuters* (20 December 2018).

[527] ASP, 'Report of the Court on the Basic Size of the Office of the Prosecutor', ICC-ASP/14/21 (17 September 2015), paras. 4, 7, at https://asp.icc-cpi.int/iccdocs/asp_docs/aspl4/icc-asp-14-21-eng.pdf. See also OTP strategic plans from 2012 onwards, which, unlike, previous strategies, emphasized 'open-ended, in-depth investigations'. Notably, the 2019–2021 draft describes this 'radical shift' in strategy as 'showing positive outcomes' in cases that were the beneficiaries of the shift, and that, 'the office considers this approach to be more important than ever'. See OTP strategic plan 2019–2021, para. 14 (on-file).

[528] ICC, Office of the Prosecutor, strategic plan, June 2012–2015 (11 October 2013), paras. 4, 18, 23–24, 90, at www.icc-cpi.int/iccdocs/otp/OTP-Strategic-Plan-2013.pdf. Drawing on the lessons of the Kenyan experience and the criticisms of its DRC cases, the office also announced a departure from its previous policy of prosecuting only those 'most responsible' for crimes in favour of a strategy of 'gradually building upwards', wherein it 'first investigates and prosecutes a limited number of mid-and high-level perpetrators in order to ultimately have a reasonable prospect of conviction for the most responsible'. Ibid., para. 4(a).

this reorientation, Bensouda noted in her inaugural speech to the ASP that the OTP is also 'sending longer investigative missions with less frequent travel', and has endorsed the potential value of more open-ended preliminary examinations and investigations as a form of maintaining leverage on states.[529] The office's 2016–2018 and 2019–2021 strategic plans reiterate these objectives, while also adopting a strategic goal of developing, 'with partners, a coordinated investigative and prosecutorial strategy to close the impunity gap'.[530] In this regard, the office affirmed its 'willing[ness] to contribute, where appropriate and within its mandate and means, by sharing information and evidence in its possession that may be relevant to these interconnected areas of criminality'.[531]

Changes have also been made with respect to the treatment of intermediaries by ICC organs. Guidelines – described as an attempt to 'provide a framework with common standards and procedures in areas where it is possible to standardize the court's relationship with intermediaries' – were first circulated in 2010, and finally put into effect in 2014.[532] They address the existing legal and policy framework governing the court's relationship with intermediaries and seek to provide greater clarity as to the rights intermediaries may expect from the ICC, including their selection, payment of expenses (where appropriate) and, crucially, their protection when placed at risk. Notably, however, the guidelines have been a source of contention. While text for them was agreed upon in 2012, they were not formally promulgated for two more years, in part because of concerns about the 'cost effectiveness' of intermediaries. As Deirdre Clancy notes, 'While a fiscally sensitive ASP was clearly wary of institutionalising the intermediary role, reports by the court to the ASP

---

[529] Fatou Bensouda, Address to the Assembly of States Parties, Eleventh Session of the Assembly of States Parties (14 November 2012), para. 6.

[530] International Criminal Court, Office of the Prosecutor, strategic plan, 2016–2018, Strategic Goal 9 (6 July 2015). This goal is maintained in the 2019–2021 strategy as 'Strategic goal 6: to further strengthen the ability of the office and its partners to close the impunity gap'.

[531] Ibid., para. 102.

[532] See 'Guidelines Governing the Relations between the Court and Intermediaries – for the Organs and Units of the Court and Counsel working with intermediaries'. Notably, while many organizations (for instance, local NGOs) can also serve as intermediaries, the guidelines only govern the ICC's relationships with individuals. In addition to the guidelines, a 'Code of Conduct for Intermediaries' and a 'Model Contract for Intermediaries' have also been created.

at the same time indicated that use of intermediaries was "ultimately cost effective".[533] Intermediaries are thus vital to the court's success, even if they remain at the edges of the OTP's work.

Finally, unlike the 'cost efficiency' previously championed, Bensouda during her tenure has in fact sought greater financial support for the office's expanding workload (including the hiring of additional situation analysts and country-based experts) and to align a more robust prosecutorial docket with a 'reasonably stable basis for budgetary planning'.[534] Critical to this initiative was the OTP's 2015 proposal, in advance of its 2016–2018 strategy, to increase its capacity over the next three years to what it termed its 'basic size', a proposal that significantly increased the office's overall proposed budget. The 'basic size' proposal sought to ensure that the office attained 'a staffing size which is stable for the foreseeable future, but also one with sufficient depth to absorb new demands'.[535] Under the proposed terms, the OTP would be able to open one new situation each year with a maximum of six active investigations underway at any one time, across all situations.[536] While the office acknowledged that even this level of resources would be insufficient to meet its existing needs for investigations, it would be able to do so 'with a reasonable degree of prioritisation'.[537] The ASP, however, has thus far refused to provide

---

[533] Deirdre Clancy, '"They Told Us We Would Be Part of History": Reflections on the Civil Society Intermediary Experience in the Great Lakes Region', in *Contested Justice: The Politics and Practice of International Criminal Court Interventions*, 245. See further the 'Second Report on the Draft Guidelines' (30 October 2013), which states that 'while there are unavoidable costs for the court in implementing the draft Intermediaries Guidelines … the use of intermediaries is ultimately cost effective for the court. Intermediaries undertake work that would be extremely costly for the court to perform', para. 19.

[534] ASP, Basic Size of the OTP, para. 1.

[535] Ibid., para. 3; OTP strategic plan 2016–2018, paras. 9–10.

[536] ASP, Basic Size of the OTP, para. 5. While the OTP has yet to formally close an investigation, it distinguishes between what it considers 'active' and 'hibernated' investigations. Ibid., 33. See also Prosecutor Bensouda, 'Statement to the United Nations Security Council on the situation in Darfur, pursuant to UNSCR 1593 (2005)', 12 December 2014 (announcing OTP's decision to 'hibernate' its investigation in Sudan, in order to 'shift resources to other urgent cases, especially those in which trial is approaching'), at www.icc-cpi.int/iccdocs/otp/stmt-20threport-darfur.pdf.

[537] ASP, Basic Size of the OTP, para. 5 (noting that, under the proposal, the OTP would still 'not be in a position to immediately respond to all demands for its intervention'). This position has not been without criticism from NGOs. See, e.g., Comments of Human Rights Watch to OTP's Draft Policy Paper on Case Selection and Prioritisation (3 May 2016) (concluding that 'the OTP will be left far short of the resources it needs').

funding adequate to meet even the 'basic size', maintaining instead an annual nominal 'zero growth' approach.[538]

4   Bridging the Gap? Examinations and Investigations as 'Positive' Complementarity

The OTP post-2012 has sought to reconcile some of the contradictions inherent in its earlier approach to preliminary examinations and investigations. But the office's conviction and confirmation rate suggest that it has not sufficiently guarded the court's catalytic potential as a coercive threat. Furthermore, its early investigatory practices, in particular, sat uneasily with a commitment to responsible, cooperative, engagement with national-level actors.[539] This dimension of complementarity, extolled by scholars like Burke-White and ratified by the office itself, underscores the importance of cultivating meaningful relationships between The Hague and in-country actors. Such an orientation to the field in countries like Uganda and DRC – where the ICC was itself 'invited' in – could have offered important opportunities to build the sort of beneficent relationship imagined for the court and national jurisdictions, one in which the judicial intervention becomes a site for knowledge transfer and capacity building.[540] It would also have provided greater opportunity to understand the political, social and cultural contexts in which its examinations unfold. Unfortunately, this did not occur.

Like investigations, preliminary examinations are also an area where the potential of 'positive' complementarity could be realized. Examinations provide a potentially greater dialogic space between the court and national authorities, one that narrows substantially once the OTP moves from 'situation' to 'case'. Indeed, whereas investigations might necessarily initiate a more adversarial relationship with the state, nothing prohibits the OTP (provided the state in question consents) from locating staff on the territory of countries under preliminary examination. Seils has advocated

---

[538] Indeed, the OTP still remains well below the proposed 'basic size': from an optimal yearly budget of 60 million euros, its approved budget for 2017 was just under 45 million. See OTP strategic plan 2016–2018, para. 9 ('The basic size of the OTP would require a yearly budget of 60.6 million euros'.); ASP Proposed Programme Budget for 2018, para. 216.

[539] For a qualified defence of ICC investigations, see Alex Whiting, 'Dynamic Investigative Practice at the International Criminal Court', *Law & Contemporary Problems* 76(3–4) (2013), 163–189.

[540] OTP strategic plan 2016–2018, para. 57.

such an approach, noting that 'A longer presence on the ground should allow analysts to improve their understanding of the institutions that are of interest, both in terms of those providing information and those conducting national proceedings'.[541] The OTP's policy paper likewise notes that 'for the purpose of analysing the seriousness of the information' it receives, it 'may also undertake field missions to the territory concerned in order to consult with the competent national authorities, the affected communities and other relevant stakeholders, such as civil society organisations'.[542]

The Kenyan experience, where the failed prosecutions did great damage to the ICC's credibility, illustrates the important link between these stages. For instance, it would appear that the OTP did not use the extended preliminary examination period to conduct more thorough independent inquiries in Kenya or, as discussed above, to develop a meaningful presence within the country or amongst affected communities. (The prosecutor's Article 15 request makes no public mention of any in-country inquiries that the office undertook, relying instead on the CIPEV and KNHRC reports, as well as those of other UN and NGO offices.) Notably, the decision not to do so – in Kenya and elsewhere – appears to have been premised, at least initially, on a presumption that distancing the court from local contexts would better preserve its impartiality and efficiency, when it appears to have hobbled it instead.[543] By contrast, developing closer relationships with national-level interlocutors, particularly intermediaries, could better ensure that the office 'knows the lie of the land well enough to identify reliable and credible counterparts to begin the investigation'.[544] Indeed, although the OTP's missteps with respect to ill-intentioned intermediaries have dominated discussions about the topic, most intermediaries are committed advocates who have sought to help the ICC, often at great personal risk.

The office has since sought to chart a different course, proposing a baseline budget that, in theory, would reflect both the cooperative dimension

---

[541] Seils, 'Making Complementarity Work', 1000.

[542] OTP, 'Policy Paper on Preliminary Examinations', para. 85.

[543] Phil Clark makes a similar point, arguing based on his extensive ethnographic research in the DRC that 'the court has generally failed to foster meaningful relations with … ground-level institutions that are vital to its cause. … [T]he ICC has not always sought this collaboration and often perceived itself as the lead organisation to which all others are answerable'. Phil Clark, 'If Ocampo Indicts Bashir, Nothing May Happen' (13 July 2008). For a fuller treatment of this theme, see also Clark, *Distant Justice*.

[544] Seils, 'Making Complementarity Work', 1000; see also WCRO Report, 6.

of 'positive' complementarity and its coercive potential. Placing the question of resources squarely (and perennially) at the centre of discussions about the ICC's capacity, and advocating policies that would seek to mitigate the distance between The Hague and situation countries (including the introduction of 'situation-specific investigation assistants', as foreseen in the court's most recent proposed budget), thus mark some promising changes in the OTP's strategic direction.[545]

But challenges remain. In particular, on-going negotiations with ICC member states illustrate the tensions of realizing an institutional mandate built on the supportive, cooperative dimensions of 'positive' complementarity. This challenge was starkly acknowledged by the office itself in its 2016–2018 strategic plan, where it noted:

> The notion of positive complementarity during the preliminary examinations and investigations by the OTP is generating conflicting responses from stakeholders, with some indicating that strengthening national jurisdictions is the role of international cooperation programs while others expect the office to assume a more robust role in this regard. As regards positive complementarity, the office's position is that it will not act as a development agency towards situations under preliminary examination or under investigation but that it can contribute to complementarity through the normal execution of its mandate, including through (1) the sharing of its expertise in international criminal law, investigations or witness protection upon request, (2) the inclusion, where appropriate, of national investigators or prosecutors into its teams for the duration of an investigation, or (3) the participation in the coordination of national and ICC investigations.[546]

This enumeration of how the OTP would seek to realize complementarity's policy goals is itself a departure from the office's early practices. But even if such concrete steps are realized, they signal an ongoing tension between what is understood to be the court's 'normal' mandate and what

---

[545] The introduction of such 'situation specific' assistants – who would bring 'a deep knowledge of the situation country under investigation, including a better understanding of its socio-economic and cultural aspects' – was included in the court's proposed 2018 budget. See ASP Proposed Programme Budget for 2018, para. 341.

[546] International Criminal Court, Office of the Prosecutor, strategic plan, 2016–2018, para. 57. The strategic plan for 2019–2021 likewise notes 'diverging views in relation to the concept of positive complementarity', para. 49. Olympia Bekou describes a similar conflict, noting that 'Before the Review Conference, positive complementarity was understood as part of the ICC's role and its potential to enhance national systems; in Kampala, that understanding shifted, primarily because of the limitations in the capacity of the ICC to take on such a role'. See Bekou, 'The ICC and Capacity Building at the National Level', in Carsten Stahn (ed.), *The Law and Practice of the International Criminal Court*, 1252.

others regard as an exceptional function, i.e., the ICC as 'development agency'.[547] Amidst a growing austerity politics, then, complementarity remains a contested principle.

5 Conclusion

Reflecting on the evolution of the OTP's approach to preliminary examinations and investigations underscores the relationship between complementarity and institutional design. The degree to which the ICC's ability to function as a credible threat to national jurisdictions, or as a partner to them, depends on the office's capacity to inhabit these dual roles and to mediate amongst various national-level actors (state and non-state). Playing these various roles in turn requires sufficient political and financial resources to undertake them effectively. If one dimension of complementarity is its sword – the prosecutor's ability to wrest cases away from member states, or to initiate proceedings where there are none – then the ICC's record of convictions must itself be convincing. And if another dimension of complementarity is to catalyse domestic proceedings through engagement with national-level actors and politics, then it needs the staff (field-based and Hague-based) and political resources to do so competently. A court increasingly dominated by its committee on budget and finance chafes against this vision.[548]

Such reflection also illustrates the tensions that exist between an ambitious policy concept like 'positive' complementarity and the everyday practices of an international court financed by states. Indeed, notwithstanding the implementation of new strategic changes, the organizational constraints of the OTP – housed as it is within an international bureaucracy – are likely to continue to strain against the more capacious vision that 'positive' complementarity imagines. As Jens Meierhenrich argues in his history of the OTP's early institutional development, 'junctures set in motion path dependent dynamics that led to a routinization of certain behavioural practices, both virtuous and pathological'.[549] These

---

[547] See also Report of the Bureau on Stocktaking: Complementarity, ICC-ASP/8/Res.9 (25 March 2010), para. 4 ('[T]he court is not a development agency ... Activities aimed at strengthening national jurisdictions as set out in this paper should be carried forward by states themselves, together with international and regional organizations and civil society, exploring interfaces and synergies with the Rome Statute system'.).

[548] See, e.g., Sara Kendall, 'Commodifying Global Justice: Economies of Accountability at the International Criminal Court', *Journal of International Criminal Justice* 13(1) (2015).

[549] Meierhenrich, 'The Evolution of the Office of the Prosecutor at the International Criminal Court', 101. S.

practices, in turn, 'open or foreclose opportunities for shaping the prosecution of international crimes'. For instance, while the OTP's record of successful prosecutions to date, and the dissatisfaction amongst some affected communities with its performance, belie the desirability of the 'light touch' approach to the field that Moreno-Ocampo once championed, this approach has itself elided with larger constraints, including an increasingly limited appetite by member states to appropriately resource the court.[550] It is also unclear the extent to which these policy changes have taken shape in practice, given the paucity of successfully executed arrest warrants under Prosecutor Bensouda.

The policy changes taken by the office illustrate the dynamic properties of the complementarity principle: they suggest that, as with the more recent turn in the court's admissibility jurisprudence, the OTP is an evolving institution, one that may yet become more responsive to the unique domestic contexts in which it operates. Still, these unique contexts underscore the fact that the leverage (or support) the prosecutorial function may bring to bear is necessarily limited; it must approach each situation sui generis. Notwithstanding the OTP's evident missteps in Kenya, in retrospect it is unlikely that the threat of the court alone was sufficiently great for the STK to receive the domestic political support it needed. The failure of the Kenyan state to comply with this particular desired outcome has not meant, however, that the ICC's intervention there (and elsewhere) was without effect, as the following chapters illustrate.

---

[550] See, e.g., Janet H. Anderson, 'Ocampo's shadow still hangs over the ICC', *International Justice Tribune* (18 June 2018); Meierhenrich, 98 (concluding that 'the downstream effects of institutional development in the early stages of the OTP have substantially increased the costs of institutional adaptation in more recent years'). A more detailed recounting of the OTP's early turbulent institutional history and development, particularly the dysfunctions visited upon it under the tenure of Moreno-Ocampo, is offered by Morten Bergsmo, 'Institutional History, Behaviour and Development', in *Historical Origins of International Criminal Law: Volume 5*, 1–31.

PART II

The ICC in Uganda, Kenya and the Democratic Republic of Congo

5

Compliance and Performance

Implementation as Domestic Politics

The adoption of the Rome Statute inaugurated not only the ratification process that brought the International Criminal Court (ICC) into existence, but also a far-ranging effort to embed the Statute in the normative legal framework of states. As one legal scholar has ambitiously characterized it, the Statute was a 'quasi-legislative event that produced a criminal code for the world'.[551] Conceived and led by the same network of global civil society actors that had campaigned for the ICC's establishment, these campaigns for national implementation have been intimately linked to the idea of complementarity as a catalyst for compliance. The Coalition for the International Criminal Court (CICC) notes that 'For the principle of complementarity to become truly effective, following ratification, states must also implement all of the crimes under the Rome Statute into domestic legislation'.[552] Similarly, Amnesty International claims that a state that fails to enact national legislation risks 'being considered unable and unwilling genuinely to investigate and prosecute crimes within the court's jurisdiction'.[553]

As with the creation of domestic 'complementarity' courts (discussed in the following chapter), implementation reflects a broader interest in routing governance objectives through international criminal law

---

[551] Leila Nadya Sadat, *The International Criminal Court and the Transformation of International Law: Justice for the New Millennium* (Martinus Nijhoff, 2002), 263.

[552] Coalition for the International Criminal Court (CICC), at www.iccnow.org/?mod=ratimp.

[553] Amnesty International, 'The International Criminal Court: Checklist for Effective Implementation' (2000). A more recent report states, 'Under the Rome Statute system, and due to the principle of complementarity, state parties to the ICC are under a duty to enact domestic implementing legislation. This legislation should domesticate the Rome Statute crimes as well as provide for procedures of cooperating with the ICC'. Amnesty International, 'Malabo Protocol: Legal and Institutional Implications of the Merged and Expanded African Court' (2016), 29.

and an attendant investment in compliance with 'international stan-dards'.[554] This chapter explores the Rome Statute's implementation in Uganda, Kenya and the Democratic Republic of Congo (DRC) to makes two interrelated arguments. First, implementation has become an increasingly technocratic exercise in applying the Statute as a 'global script' with which states must comply.[555] Rome Statute 'model laws' have emerged and a variety of international NGOs, advisors and consultants – a transnational expert community of practice – offer counsel to states on how best to harmonize their domestic legal and constitutional orders with the purported requirements of the Statute.[556] This emphasis on com-pliance and harmonization has, in turn, furthered a strict interpretation of what complementarity purportedly requires.

Second, while the ICC's intervention in these countries acceler-ated advocacy campaigns for the passage of national implementation legislation, it was not the direct catalyst for implementation in either Kenya or Uganda. In Uganda, implementation did not take place until six years after the ICC's investigations; in Kenya, implementa-tion actually preceded the court's investigations. Rather, other events, geared predominantly towards international audiences, precipitated the Statute's implementation. In Uganda, the country's role as host of the 2010 Review Conference of the Rome Statute hastened a legislative process that had long stagnated, while, in Kenya, the desire to publicly demonstrate a departure from the election violence led parliamentar-ians to 'fast-track' implementation following the Waki Commission's recommendation. The union of these two factors – uniformity of application and the power of external constituencies – was largely

---

[554] For instance, the CICC states that 'implementation of the Rome Statute provides an opportunity to reinvigorate reforms of the criminal and procedure codes, which, in the long term, will strengthen rule of law, peace, and security globally'. See CICC, at www.iccnow.org/?mod=romeimplementation. For quantiative analysis supporting this claim, see Mark S. Berlin and Geoff Dancy, 'The Difference Law Makes: Domestic Atrocity Laws and Human Rights Prosecutions', *Law & Society Review* 51(3) (2017) (arguing that atrocity laws 'increase the speed with which new democracies pursue prosecutions, as well as the overall numbers of trials they initiate and complete').

[555] My use of the term 'global script' borrows from Carruthers and Halliday's use of the term as a 'formalized expression or codification of global norms'. See Bruce G. Carruthers and Terence C. Halliday, 'Negotiating Globalization: Global Scripts and Intermediation in the Construction of Asian Insolvency Regimes', *Law & Social Inquiry* 31(3) (2006), 535–536.

[556] Drumbl, *Atrocity, Punishment, and International Law*, 135.

responsible for driving the implementation process in both countries, but they glossed over lingering political fissures about the desirability of international criminal law as a framework for domestic
accountability.

By contrast, in the DRC, domestic politics long thwarted the efforts to
press for comprehensive implementing legislation, notwithstanding the
efforts of a dedicated minority. As in Uganda, implementing legislation in
the DRC did not pass until more than a decade after the ICC had begun
its investigations, suggesting that neither the perceived threat of prosecutions nor the desire to displace the court's jurisdiction were sufficient to
compel political action. And while the release of the United Nation's (UN)
2010 'mapping report' of crimes in the DRC lent a similar urgency (and
opportunity) for domestic political actors to be seen as 'doing something'
for a primarily international audience, this in itself was insufficient to persuade Congolese parliamentarians. As with the government's proposed
special chambers legislation, these domestic political actors continued to
regard transnational intervention, including efforts to pass Rome Statute
'compliant' legislation, with suspicion. It would not be until late 2015 when
the Congolese parliament finally, quietly adopted a package of laws implementing the Statute.

Returning to previous arguments that have animated why implementation of the Rome Statute should be understood as a duty of ICC member states, this chapter first focuses on how international NGOs and the
capacity building sector – communities of practice with a shared interest in embedding the ICC's normative framework – have drawn on these
arguments in their promotion of implementation guidelines and 'model
laws'. I suggest that these tools, while not without value, have contributed
to a view of implementation as an increasingly disciplinary exercise, one
that privileges conformity with the Rome Statute. Part two then turns to
the particular experiences of Uganda and Kenya to show how it was not
the ICC's intervention itself, but the mediated influence of external actors
and events that pushed the formal implementation process forward.
However, key political questions that were overlooked in this process soon
re-emerged, as the third section details. The fourth section considers the
experience of the DRC, noting some initial similarities with Kenya and
Uganda in the relationship between implementation and political action,
but also fundamental differences. Based on these histories, the chapter
concludes by focusing on three dimensions of implementation: as purity,
as politics and as a form of political theatre.

1   Implementation, Standardization and Compliance

The incorporation of treaty protections is one form that the legal protection of human rights may take at the domestic level. Implementation thus reinforces not only the primacy of states in international law, but also a general rule: states, in general, have far-going freedom as to the manner in which they give effect to their international obligations.[557] Notwithstanding this principle, Chapter 2 examined how complementarity became, over time, a site of influence for norm entrepreneurs to argue that member states are obliged to implement the Rome Statute's provisions in their domestic legal orders. This duty is rooted in a purposive reading of the Statute, particularly its preambular language, which recalls 'that it is the duty of every state to exercise its criminal jurisdiction over those responsible for international crimes'.[558] Yet the text of the Statute requires only that a country's domestic law facilitate cooperation with the ICC and that it criminalize offences against the 'administration of justice'.[559] There is no obligation as such to implement its substantive (or procedural) provisions.

The difference between 'ordinary' and international crimes has also been advanced as a basis for domestic implementation; however, as noted, while this distinction was critical to the criminal tribunals for Rwanda and the former Yugoslavia, the Rome Statute does not make such a distinction.[560]

---

[557] As Ward Ferdinandusse argues, however, the extent of this freedom can be, 'easily overestimate[d]', particularly in the context of international criminal law. See *Direct Application of International Criminal Law in National Courts* (Academisch Proefschrift, 2005), 148. Scholars have argued that the special character of international humanitarian law distinguishes it from other crimes, thus requiring greater fidelity to the manner of its implementation at the national level. Similar arguments point to the uniquely expressivist function of international criminal law as requiring its identical enunciation in national law.

[558] Para. 6, Rome Statute. As two NGOs noted, for instance, in an amicus curiae submission to the court in the case against the LRA, 'The use of ordinary offenses in lieu of international crimes itself fails to capture the gravity and aggravated nature of the international crimes'. The Prosecutor *v.* Joseph Kony, Vincent Otti, Okot Odhiambo, Dominic Ongwen, amicus curiae submitted by The Uganda Victims' Foundation and the Redress Trust, ICC-02/04-01/05, ICC Pre-Trial Chamber II (18 November 2008).

[559] Article 88. Further, as a matter of treaty interpretation, the preambular recital is not part of the Statute's operative text; rather, it 'recalls' a suggested pre-existing duty, not one arising from the treaty itself. While states may be obliged to investigate or prosecute crimes based on other rules of international law, the Statute itself does not so oblige. See Robinson, 'The Mysterious Mysteriousness of Complementarity', 94–95.

[560] Further, both of the ICTY and ICTR statutes explicitly allowed for the retrial of persons who had already been tried by a national court if 'the act for which he or she was tried was characterized by an ordinary crime'. See ICTR, The Prosecutor *v.* Michel Bagaragaza, Decision on Rule 11 *bis* Appeal, ICTR-05-86-AR11bis, Appeals Chamber, 30 August 2006.

States are permitted to prosecute international crimes as ordinary crimes, provided that their doing so is not designed to shield perpetrators from criminal responsibility. Indeed, as illustrated by the Statute's drafting history, states explicitly rejected a proposal that would have made a case admissible before the ICC where the national proceeding failed to consider the international character or grave nature of a crime.[561] Recalling the 'same conduct' test that has emerged in ICC jurisprudence (explored at greater length in Chapter 3), the Statute refers instead to the conduct of an accused, 'to make clear that a national prosecution of a crime – international or ordinary – did not prohibit ICC retrial for charges based on different conduct'.[562]

Such threat-based approaches to complementarity are central to the ICC-as-catalyst framing. More broadly, however, implementation discourse also reflects anxieties about fragmentation in international law.[563] As Carsten Stahn and Larissa van den Herik note, 'One of the inherent features of international criminal law is a desire for uniformity', which 'flows from the need for certainty, stability and predictability [that] is required in criminal proceedings'.[564] A related concept is that the Statute establishes a common juridical floor: it reflects the desire to maintain uniformity in law and procedure. Cattin, for instance, sees the Statute as posing a minimum standard for national criminal justice systems. In his words, 'States can do more, but shall do no less, than what the Rome Statute prescribes, so as to ensure that all crimes against humanity, war crimes and acts of genocide be duly incorporated in the relevant legal order and not left unpunished'.[565] If complementarity means that accountability will (and should) increasingly migrate from the ICC to national courts, then the idea of minimum,

---

[561] Article 20(3), Rome Statute. As Jo Stigen notes, the ordinary crime criterion, initially endorsed by the [ILC], 'was proposed but rejected [in the negotiations] as it met too much resistance'. Stigen, *The Relationship between the International Criminal Court and National Jurisdictions*, 335.

[562] Heller, 'A Sentence-Based Theory of Complementarity', 224.

[563] See Conclusions of the Work of the Study Group on the Fragmentation of International Law, 'Difficulties Arising from the Diversification and Expansion of International Law', UN Doc. A/61/10 (2006).

[564] Carsten Stahn and Larissa van dan Herik, '"Fragmentation", Diversification and "3D" Legal Pluralism: International Criminal Law and the Jack-in-the-Box?', in *The Diversification and Fragmentation of International Criminal Law*, 58 (citing Appeals Chamber, Prosecutor v. Aleksovski, Judgment, IT-95-14/1-A (24 March 2003), para. 101).

[565] Cattin, 'Approximation or Harmonisation as a Result of Implementation of the Rome Statute', 373.

or 'international', standards is attractive. To that end, 'the play between ... unity and diversity, is one of the discursive patterns used by the [legal] discipline to deploy criticism and propose reform projects'.[566]

Human rights NGOs have been perhaps the most influential contributors to popular understandings of what Rome Statute domestication requires.[567] As a report of the Southern Africa Litigation Centre notes, 'implementing legislation has been a key focus area of civil society', and 'CSOs have been instrumental in the drafting and adoption process [of implementing legislation]'.[568] There now exists an array of implementation materials prepared by such organizations. As early as 2000, Amnesty International created a 'checklist for effective implementation', while Human Rights Watch and the International Centre for Criminal Law Reform published similar manuals shortly thereafter.[569] Similarly, as part of its 'Global Advocacy Campaign for the International Criminal Court', the Coalition for the International Criminal Court (CICC) maintains a detailed chart of those states that have either enacted, or are in the process of enacting, 'Rome Statute crimes legislation' and/or 'cooperation legislation'.[570] The coalition includes a resource page with links to 'model' national implementation laws, as well as 'template statutes' endorsed by various regional organizations like the Commonwealth Secretariat.[571]

The Commonwealth's model law – of particular relevance to Kenya and Uganda – is a 58-page document with prepared language that closely tracks the text of the Rome Statute. While noting that 'there is no 'one-size-fits-all' solution to the complex process of domestic implementation', the law presents

[566] Anne Charlotte Martineau, 'The Rhetoric of Fragmentation: Fear and Faith in International Law', *Leiden Journal of International Law* 22(1) (2009), 2–3.
[567] The CICC is one international NGO that has made implementation a centrepiece of its work; however, others like Amnesty International, Avocats Sans Frontiers, the International Federation for Human Rights (FIDH), No Peace Without Justice, PGA and Human Rights Watch have all been similarly engaged.
[568] Southern Africa Litigation Centre, 'Positive Reinforcement: Advocating for International Criminal Justice in Africa', 45.
[569] AI Updated Checklist; Human Rights Watch, 'Making the International Criminal Court Work: A Handbook for Implementing the Rome Statute' (September 2001) ('HRW Handbook'); ICCLR, 'International Criminal Court: Checklist of Implementation Considerations and Examples Relating to the Rome Statute and the Rules of Procedure & Evidence' (April 2002).
[570] See CICC webpage.
[571] The secretariat describes itself as 'provid[ing] guidance on policy making, technical assistance and advisory services to commonwealth member countries'. For further information, see http://thecommonwealth.org/organisation/commonwealth-secretariat.

itself as 'model legislation (i.e., a textual basis to be modified and adapted to a given national system)'.[572] Interested states are invited to insert the name of their country at relevant points throughout the document, and to include select optional additional provisions, ranging from the appropriate penalties for crimes ('imprisonment for a term not exceeding 30 years or a term of life imprisonment when justified by the extreme gravity of the crime') to extending the law's coverage to violations of the Geneva Conventions.[573]

Various 'best practice' tools for implementation supplement such material. One such tool is the National Implementing Legislation Database (NILD). NILD seeks to provide users with 'access to a fully-searchable, relational database of national implementing legislation'.[574] Part of the ICC's Legal Tools project,[575] NILD further allows states that have adopted legislation to 'monitor the impact of their legislation on other states and undertake necessary amendments if the content of the Rome Statute changes, or if improvements are deemed necessary'.[576] One publication highlights not only NILD, but other legal tools projects as well – e.g., Case Matrix, a Means of Proof Digest – as examples of access to legal information. It notes that such access 'should be provided in line with this new paradigm shift towards positive complementarity that focuses on strengthening domestic capacity and empowering national actors'.[577]

These tools accompany the literature of NGOs, which, consistent with the framing of complementarity as a catalyst for compliance, endorses a maximalist approach to implementation. According to Amnesty's

---

[572] Commonwealth Secretariat, 'Cover Note: International Criminal Court (ICC) Statute and Implementation of the Geneva Conventions', SOLM(11)10, May 2011, para. 3(a).

[573] Ibid., Annex B, Model Law to Implement the Rome Statute of the International Criminal Court. See, e.g., Part II ('International crimes and offences against the administration of justice').

[574] National Implementing Legislation Database of the International Criminal Court Statute ('NILD Database'), www.nottingham.ac.uk/hrlc/documents/projectsummaries/pdfs/projectnild.pdf. NILD is managed by the legal academic Olympia Bekou, who has contributed an extensive literature on complementarity and implementation. See, e.g., Olympia Bekou and Sangeeta Shah, 'Realising the Potential of the International Criminal Court: The African Experience', *Human Rights Law Review* 6(3) (2006), 499–544; Olympia Bekou, 'Crimes at Crossroads: Incorporating International Crimes at the National Level', *Journal of International Criminal Justice* 10(3) (2012), 677–691.

[575] See 'ICC Legal Tools', www.legal-tools.org/en/go-to-database/.

[576] NILD Database.

[577] Morten Bergsmo (ed.), *Active Complementarity: Legal Information Transfer* (Torkel Opsahl Academic EPublisher, 2011), vi; see also Morten Bergsmo, Olympia Bekou and Annika Jones, 'Complementarity After Kampala: Capacity Building and the ICC's Legal Tools', *Goettingen Journal of International Law* 2(2) (2010).

implementation checklist, 'principles of criminal responsibility in national legislation should be at least as strict as ... the Rome Statute'.[578] This includes, for instance, that 'all crimes of accessory criminal responsibility such as aiding, abetting, and direct and public incitement as contained in Article 25 [of the Statute] should be punishable under national law'.[579] Conformity with the Statute has also been presented as encompassing far-reaching procedural requirements. Human Rights Watch notes that whether states guarantee the 'highest international standards for fair trials at the national level' will 'be important in the determination of the admissibility of a case by the ICC'.[580] Such standards would include not only programs of victim and witness protection, but even procedural regimes unique to the Rome Statute, such as a trust fund for victims or provisions for victim participation. A related issue is punishment: effective implementation, it is strongly suggested, would be inconsistent with the death penalty.[581]

Thus, even where commentators and NGOs acknowledge that the Rome Statute contains no positive obligations to implement its substantive (or procedural) law provisions, complementarity is framed in their literature in a manner that nevertheless compels it. As a technique of governance, then, the approach is disciplinary and coercive: failure to abide by the purported requirements of the Rome Statute opens states up to the risk that the ICC will intervene. This view has been furthered by much academic commentary on implementation, which overwhelmingly focuses on fidelity to the Rome Statute's text.[582] Just as the coercive pull of complementarity could catalyse national proceedings, it might

---

[578] AI Updated Checklist, 17.

[579] Ibid.

[580] HRW Handbook, 19.

[581] In Amnesty's words, 'it would be inappropriate for national courts to impose a more severe penalty for a crime under international law than the one chosen by the international community itself'. AI Updated Checklist.

[582] As an example, see the articles gathered in the 'Symposium on National Implementation of the ICC Statute', which appeared in two parts in the *Journal of International Criminal Justice*, 2(1), March 2004 and 5(2), May 2007. In the second instalment, editor Luisa Vierucci notes that 'states tend to stick to the definition of the crimes as contained in the ICC Statute' and that this 'seems ... to be a response to the states' inherent concern to avoid the risk of possibly adverse decisions on complementarity by the ICC'. Luisa Vierucci, 'National Implementation of the ICC Statute (Part II): Foreword', *Journal of International Criminal Justice* 5(2) (2007), 419–420. For a critique of Rome Statute implementation from a gender perspective, see Bonita Meyersfeld, 'Implementing the Rome Statute in Africa: Potential and Problems of the Prosecution of Gender Crimes in Africa in Accordance with the Rome Statute', in Kai Ambos and Ottilia A. Maunganidze (eds.), *Power and Prosecution: Challenges and Opportunities for International Criminal Justice in Sub-Saharan Africa* (Göttingen Studies in Criminal Law and Justice, 2012).

also 'induce national courts … to conform to a variety of modalities that mimic those found in international criminal law regarding sanction (i.e., no death penalty) and procedure (i.e., a fair trial)'.[583] The proliferation of 'model laws' abets this process. Indeed, as described below, the Kenyan and Ugandan ICC laws are themselves largely identical, insofar as they are both drawn from the Commonwealth Secretariat's model legislation.

2   Implementation in Practice: Uganda and Kenya

Like many treaties that Uganda has signed, but not domesticated, Nouwen argues that the government ratified the Rome Statute in June 2002 because it was 'internationally fashionable and improved the [government's] image in the eyes of European donors'.[584] The adoption of implementing legislation at the time appeared 'bleak', however, as it was not seen as a priority for either the executive or the legislature. Nevertheless, as a result of the attention increasingly paid to the government's conflict with the Lord's Resistance Army (LRA), and following President Museveni's referral of the situation to the ICC in 2003, international human rights organizations and their national-level partners began to prioritize implementation of the Statute.

After receiving authorization to prepare a draft implementation bill, Uganda's Ministry of Justice and Constitutional Affairs assembled a first draft in 2004. It used Canada and New Zealand's ICC legislation as an example, and the Commonwealth Secretariat reportedly provided 'technical support' and 'drafting assistance'.[585] Groups like Parliamentarians for Global Action (PGA) also 'conducted seminars and workshops on the Rome Statute for MPs, and facilitated relevant contacts for them with others, including the European Union, the ICC, and local civil society'.[586] Notably, the rationale for the legislation was intended less as a potential basis for challenging the admissibility of any future ICC cases, but rather to 'provide a legal framework for the ICC intervention'[587] and to 'smooth the progress of court proceedings'.[588]

---

[583] Drumbl, *Atrocity, Punishment, and International Law*, 139.

[584] Nouwen, *Complementarity in the Line of Fire*, 194.

[585] International Criminal Court Bill, XCVII(26) *Uganda Gazette*, 28 May 2004; e-mail communication from Ministry of Justice, Uganda (on-file).

[586] *Putting Complementarity into Practice: Domestic Justice for International Crimes in DRC, Uganda, and Kenya* (Open Society Foundations, 2011), 61–62. See also remarks of Mr Wacha in The Eighth Parliament of Uganda, Third Reading, The International Criminal Court Bill, 2006, 10 March 2010, 10950 ('ICC Bill Third Reading').

[587] Barney Afako, 'Country Study V: Uganda', in *Unable or Unwilling? Case Studies on Domestic Implementation of the ICC Statute in Selected Africa Countries*, 93.

[588] Ibid., 196.

Yet political developments on the ground soon stalled any desire to press for the ICC bill's passage. After ICC arrest warrants for the LRA's leaders were unsealed in mid-2005, the legislation was seen, much like the court itself, as a hindrance to the advancement of peace negotiations. As explained in a letter by the Uganda Coalition for the International Criminal Court (UCICC) for its 'Domestication Campaign 2008', the bill had 'been proposed and has lapsed in Parliament before because too many legislators feared that adopting these laws means that the ICC would take jurisdiction away from Uganda and potentially interrupt the peace process'.[589] Preparations for multi-party elections in 2006, along with 'backlogs in Parliament',[590] further delayed consideration of the bill, and it ultimately lapsed.

A substantially similar version of the bill was reintroduced in late 2006.[591] The executive, however, 'prioritised commercial laws for debate' and commentators have noted that Parliament was instructed to 'go slow' with the legislation because its passage was still 'thought to send the wrong message in relation to the ongoing Juba talks'.[592] As the then Deputy Attorney General Freddie Ruhindi testified during parliamentary debate over what would become the 2010 Act:

> [T]he long time taken on deliberating on this matter was not by accident. Interestingly, we are not even recalling that the first one was a 2004 bill, which lapsed with the Seventh Parliament. Then we came out with the Seventh Parliament. Then we came out with the 2006 bill and at one point, you may recall that we were in very serious negotiations with the Kony group and everyone of us was actually quite reluctant to disturb that process by coming on the floor of the House and at the end of the day derailing the process. But as we speak, that has gone bad and there is nothing to stop us from going ahead with the enactment of this law in full swing.[593]

---

[589] UCICC, Domestic Campaign 2008, 10 July 2008 (letter on-file).

[590] Afako, 'Country Study V: Uganda', 94.

[591] International Criminal Court Bill, XCVIX(67), *Uganda Gazette*, 17 November 2006.

[592] Nouwen, *Complementarity in the Line of Fire*, 197. Ugandan jurist Afako also describes the 'prospects of Uganda implementing a suitable national scheme in the next two years ... as "low" (on a scale of "unlikely – low – fair – good – highly likely")'. See Afako 'Country Study V: Uganda'.

[593] The Eighth Parliament of Uganda, Second Reading, The International Criminal Court Bill, 2004, 10 March 2010, 10941 (Mr F. Ruhindi) ('ICC Bill Second Reading'). Notably, although the title of the second reading is 'The International Criminal Court Bill, 2004', the MPs clarified that 'the committee chairman [was] reading a report entitled, "The International Criminal Court Bill 2006"'. Ibid., 10932 (remarks of Mr Kawuma).

Thus, whereas there were a variety of competing and superior interests during the previous six years that implementation legislation was pending, by 2010 this calculus had shifted. Peace negotiations were no longer a confounding variable, while the imminent arrival of delegates from around the world to Kampala for the first-ever 'Review Conference of the Rome Statute' provided the necessary political push for adoption.[594]

Uganda: The ICC's Host State

The significance of Uganda hosting the 2010 Rome Statute Review Conference is evident from public documents. During the bill's second reading, Ruhindi noted that 'on the sidelines of the substantive debate on this bill, Uganda is privileged ... [to] be hosting the first ever Review Conference'.[595] In its annual report, the Justice Law and Order Sector (JLOS) – a government mechanism operating a 'sector-wide approach' to donor-driven judicial reform – stated that 'one of the conditions that was set by the ICC to allow [Uganda] to host the conference was domestication of the Rome Statute'.[596] Mirjam Blaak, Uganda's ambassador to The Hague, confirms this view. In her words, 'It was important to have the bill signed before the review conference took place. They wouldn't have cancelled the review conference if it hadn't been, but it was an understanding that we would'.[597]

In the end, the act as passed in 2010 was nearly identical to the version that was put forward almost six years before.[598] Substantively, the ICC Act proscribes war crimes, genocide and crimes against humanity in a manner identical to the Rome Statute; the latter's definitions were incorporated by reference into the act, as were the modes of

---

[594] Nouwen, *Complementarity in the Line of Fire*, 198; see also Christopher Mbazira, 'Prosecuting International Crimes Committed by the Lord's Resistance Army in Uganda', in Chacha Murungu and Japhet Biegon (eds.), *Prosecuting International Crimes in Africa* (Pretoria University Law Press, 2011). Mbazira argues, 'It appears that the hasty passing of the overdue bill was catalyzed by Uganda's hosting of the ICC Review Conference from 31 May to 1 June 2010', 215.

[595] ICC Bill Second Reading, 10931.

[596] 'JLOS Annual Performance Report 2009/2010' (September 2010), 65.

[597] Bill Oketch, 'Uganda Set for First War Crime Trial', *Institute for War & Peace Reporting*, 14 July 2010; interview with Ambassador Mirjam Blaak (The Hague, 25 May 2011).

[598] See, e.g., ICC Bill Third Reading, 10950 (remarks of Mr Wacha) Mr Wacha notes that 'the two bills: the 2004 Bill and this particular bill were not any different, they were the same'.

responsibility and general principles of criminal law.[599] The act also granted the Ugandan High Court first-instance jurisdiction to hear cases of war crimes, crimes against humanity and genocide.[600] Those amendments that were made focused on minor procedural issues.[601] This mirror imaging belied the concerns of some parliamentarians, however, who in an otherwise non-contentious debate, raised questions about the scope of the Rome Statute's protection and whether Uganda was entitled to amend it. Geoffrey Ekanya, an MP from Tororo County, asked:

> I want to find out from the attorney-general and the committee chairperson, what harm would it cause to expand the definition of the bill as regards the crimes against humanity, to include plunder. As we speak now, the international community has been facilitating some countries to plunder natural resources in Africa and I think this should be part of the crimes against humanity. I am talking about DRC, for example; I am talking about the conflicts we had in other parts of Africa. The guns come from the West to facilitate conflicts; to plunder Africa and then they take the minerals; but the bill does not talk about those who facilitate plundering because this is what leads to conflict and finally crimes against humanity. So, would it be wrong for us to expand the definition of crimes against humanity to include the agents who facilitate plunder?[602]

Ekanya also expressed concern that 'certain provisions within the Rome Statute', particularly those concerning presidential immunity, were 'not in consonance' with Ugandan law, and urged that these questions be 'taken care of so that we and innocent people are not used as guinea pigs'.[603] Other MPs raised similar concerns: John Kawanga agreed that

---

[599] International Criminal Court Act, 2010, *Uganda Gazette* no. 39, Vol. 103, 25 June 2010, sections 7–9; 19.

[600] The legislation makes no reference to the specialized division that has become the International Crimes Division (ICD), even though that division was established by administrative decree in 2008, two years before the ICC Act became law (see further Chapter 5).

[601] For instance, the act states that consent for prosecution under the ICA must come from the Department of Public Prosecutions, rather than the attorney general. Further, jurisdiction vests with the Ugandan High Court, not Magistrates' Courts. See Report of the Sessional Committee on Legal and Parliamentary Affairs on the International Criminal Court Bill, 2006 ('Sessional Committee Report'), March 2010, 4–5.

[602] ICC Bill, Second Reading, 10935.

[603] Ibid., 10936.

'at another stage we shall have to deal with commercial crime, corruption and things of the kind', while Alice Alaso asked what passage of the law would 'mean with our amnesty law', whether it would 'put the final nail on the peace process', and 'the place of traditional justice vis-à-vis the ICC Bill'.[604]

The interventions of these MPs raised questions about the place of the ICC Act within Uganda's broader transitional justice architecture, as well as the state's ability to tailor the Statute to suit its particular national context. In reply to Ekanya's concerns, MP Stephen Tashobya, who chaired the Committee on Legal and Parliamentary Affairs, replied (incorrectly) that 'you may not actually go beyond what [the Rome Statute] says and, therefore, you have to confine yourself' to its text.[605] Furthermore, as Ms Alaso's comments indicate, the bill as passed offered no provisions on alternative criminal justice proceedings, nor did it address the role of Uganda's Amnesty Committee, which had been issuing amnesties to former combatants, including those from the LRA, for the past 10 years.[606] Indeed, whereas the 2004 version of the ICC Bill included a proposed amendment by MP Jacob Oulanyah that would have recognized 'alternative criminal justice proceedings' in addition to 'formal' criminal proceedings,[607] no such proposals were later considered or debated.

Similarly, whereas previous versions of the bill had provided for application of the death penalty, the 2010 Act provided that the maximum applicable penalty would be life imprisonment.[608] Although the Ugandan Penal Code (UPC) still recognized the death penalty as a permissible form of punishment, according to the parliamentary committee that reviewed the 2010 Bill, such 'inconsistency' between the UPC and the Rome Statute required

---

[604] Ibid., 10938-30 (remarks of Messrs Kawanga and Kyanjo); see also 10934 (remarks of Ms Alaso).

[605] Ibid., 10936. MP Tashobya added, 'But as to whether we can amend the Rome Statute, I do not know. You are intending to expand and that will be an amendment of the Rome Statute'.

[606] See Amnesty Commission, 'The Amnesty Act: An Act of Forgiveness', 15–24 ('The Amnesty Commission').

[607] Jacob Oulanyah, 'Proposed new Part to ICC Bill; Part X – Alternate Proceedings', 12 December 2004 (proposed amendments on-file). Oulanyah's proposal suggested a possible truth commission model, not unlike that adopted in South Africa. The 'alternative proceedings' would, for instance, 'provide a system of individual accountability', including 'public and open hearings', 'participation of victims and affected persons', 'full disclosure of all relevant facts', a 'written determination of the case' and 'sanctions'.

[608] International NGOs that had pushed the implementation bill saw the exclusion of capital punishment as the result of their 'input and advocacy'. E-mail communication, 15 March 2010.

amending the maximum penalty available for 'extremely grave crimes'.[609] By 2010, then, an increasingly Hague-centric framework for punishment had taken hold.[610]

Hastened by a perceived need to pass the legislation prior to the start of the ICC Review Conference, a similar mindset informed the influential network of Ugandan justice sector donors. Stephen Oola notes, for example, that an initial agreement to present the ICC Bill to Parliament in 2009 together with a proposed National Reconciliation Bill – in order to generate a 'comprehensive national discussion on Uganda's justice needs' – was scuttled when donor governments made it clear that they wanted the ICC Bill fast-tracked.[611] As a result, Oola argues that the ICC Act was rushed through Parliament with little consultation and 'without much-needed acknowledgment of the domestic legal reality, given the existence of the Amnesty Act'.[612] This lack of acknowledgement would return to haunt accountability discussions in Uganda once the 2010 Review Conference had passed.

---

[609] Report of the Sessional Committee, 4–5.

[610] Uganda's ICC Act did not incorporate provisions for victim participation similar to those of the Rome Statute, even though many NGOs had lobbied to include participatory rights in Ugandan proceedings. A special session of the Legal and Parliamentary Affairs Committee of the Ugandan Parliament was held in July 2009, co-sponsored by the PGA and attended by ICC Judge Daniel Nsereko, which included proposals to amend the proposed legislation with specific provisions on victims' participation, protection and reparations. These were themselves extracted from a similar ICC domestication law passed in Uruguay in 2006, referred to by the PGA as an 'exemplary incorporation of the rights of victims of Rome Statute crimes into a national system'. See Note from PGA to the Legal and Parliamentary Affairs Committee, Parliament of Uganda and other Concerned Legislators and Members of PGA in the Parliament of Uganda (on-file).

[611] See Stephen Oola, 'In the Shadow of Kwoyelo's Trial: The ICC and Complementarity in Uganda', in *Contested Justice: The Politics and Practice of International Criminal Court Interventions*, 165–166. The bill proposed, in part, the establishment of a National Truth and Reconciliation Commission to 'facilitate the process of reconciliation within the country and to investigate the circumstances under which the gross violations and abuses of human rights were committed, including their motives, perpetrators and victims and to disclose the truth with respect to the violations in order to prevent a repeat of the violation or abuses in future'. National Reconciliation Bill, draft of 10 June 2011 (on-file). The bill was later reproduced in the Refugee Law Project's exhaustive audit of Uganda's history of conflict, *Compendium of Conflicts in Uganda: Findings of the National Reconciliation and Transitional Justice Audit* (Refugee Law Project, 2014) (on-file).

[612] Oola, 'In the Shadow of Kwoyelo's Trial', 166.

Kenya: 'Becoming a Global Village'

As in Uganda, international pressure was a key dynamic that drove the passage of Kenya's domestic implementing legislation. Following the election of President Kibaki in 2002, the government ratified (as an executive act) the Rome Statute in 2005. Little is known about the administration's intentions in choosing to do so other than that, in the wake of an ostensibly reformist political moment, ratification of the Statute was seen as a positive step by the new administration. One prominent Kenyan activist described the ratification as 'one of those things you do to look good',[613] while Yvonne Dutton's analysis suggests that Kenya's classification as a democracy in the post-Kibaki era played a role in the government's decision to join the court.[614] International NGOs also seized on the moment. The CICC, for instance, chose Kenya as a target country on which to focus its efforts, noting that ratification would send an 'important signal to other African states who have yet to ratify about Africa's growing commitment to international justice and the rule of law'.[615]

At the time, Kenya did not have any laws in place that would have enabled it to prosecute international crimes as such. Neither the Kenyan Penal Code (KPC) nor the Armed Forces Act, which governs the Kenyan military, contained any such provisions, nor had a Kenyan court ever dealt with international crimes.[616] Following ratification, then, the Kenyan National Commission on Human Rights began drafting a bill that sought to implement provisions of the Statute domestically. At the time, however, the country was also undergoing a constitutional review process, with a referendum set for November 2005. As a result, the draft International

---

[613] Interview with Kenyan NGO director (Nairobi, 30 November 2012).

[614] See Yvonne Dutton, *Rules, Politics, and the International Criminal Court: Committing to the Court* (Routledge, 2013). The analysis of Simmons and Danner also suggests that 'ICC ratification is associated with tentative steps toward peacemaking'. See Beth A. Simmons and Allison Danner, 'Credible Commitments and the International Criminal Court', *International Organization* 64(2) (2010), 253.

[615] CICC, 'Global Coalition Calls on Kenya to Ratify International Criminal Court' (11 January 2005).

[616] Antonina Okuta, 'National Legislation for Prosecution of International Crimes in Kenya', *Journal of International Criminal Justice* 7 (2009), 1063. The one exception was Kenya's Geneva Conventions Act, which, like Uganda, incorporated into Kenyan law the 'grave breaches' provisions of the Geneva Conventions. This act would not have been applicable for Kenya's post-2007 election violence, however, as that did not occur in the context of an international conflict.

Crimes Bill was temporarily shelved. It went through an initial reading
in Parliament in June 2006, but, before it could proceed further, the 2007
elections had arrived.

In the wake of the electoral violence, a process that might have otherwise proceeded in a quiet, internal manner was quickly internationalized.
Following its hearings, a key recommendation of the Waki Commission
was that implementation of the Rome Statute be 'fast-tracked for enactment by Parliament to facilitate investigation and prosecution of crimes
against humanity'.[617] Likewise, as Antonina Okuta notes, the commission's recommendation that a special local tribunal be created to try the
alleged perpetrators brought 'into sharp focus the country's national legislation as well as its capacity to handle the investigation and prosecution
of international crimes'.[618] Thus, even before the ICC came to be involved
in Kenya's post-conflict landscape, Rome Statute implementation was
underway.

As in Uganda, the Commonwealth Secretariat played an influential
role in the drafting process. At the bill's second reading in May 2008,
Kenya's then Attorney General Amos Wako stated that the government
had been 'well guided' by the United Nations and the Commonwealth
Secretariat, which had 'developed model legislation to guide the countries'.[619] He continued:

> Mr. Speaker, Sir, we talk about the world being a global village. It is,
> indeed, becoming a global village, whether it is from the perspective of
> communications; that is telephones, mobile phones, television and so on,
> but for institutions such as the national state and so on. Also, from the
> point of view of issues relating to law and order, there can be no state
> as such which does not have a criminal justice system. Therefore, to the
> extent that the international community is developing an international
> criminal justice system, we are indeed and truly becoming a global
> village.[620]

Reflecting the perception that states are legally bound to implement
the Statute, Wako added in his remarks that '[B]y the mere fact we have

[617] Commission of Inquiry on Post-Election Violence (Kenya) (CIPEV) Report, 476. See also
Karuti Kanyinga, 'Hobbling Along to Pay-Offs: The Kenya Grand Coalition Government'
(April 2009) (on-file). Kanyinga argues that 'fast tracking' was part of a broader political
dispensation post-2008, in which longstanding debates about constitutional reform that
has been 'paralyzed … for over 10 years' were 'fast tracked during the crisis', 9.
[618] Okuta, 'National Legislation for Prosecution of International Crimes in Kenya', 1065.
[619] Kenya National Assembly Official Record (Hansard), The International Crimes Bill,
Second Reading, 7 May 2008, 907 ('ICA Second Reading').
[620] Ibid., 906.

ratified this Rome Treaty, we are, as a state, under an obligation to domesticate the treaty, so that it has a force of law in Kenya'.[621]

Unlike the narrowly defeated Special Tribunal for Kenya (STK) Bill the following year, the 2008 parliamentary debate on the International Crimes Act (ICA) records no opposition to its passage. The attorney general's proposal was supported by Martha Karua (architect of the failed STK Bill and then minister for justice, national cohesion and constitutional affairs), as well as MP Danson Mungatana (an STK opponent), who '[took] the opportunity to thank the attorney-general for, once again, rising to the occasion and bringing our country's laws in line with the international community, especially in criminal jurisprudence'.[622] MP Farah Maalim, a leading figure in the Orange Democratic Movement and himself a member of PGA, made the most extensive remarks on the bill, supporting its passage, but expressing scepticism about the limitations of international criminal law. In particular, Maalim endorsed the 'need to redefine … the definition of the UN of what genocide is', calling for it to encompass 'cultural' and 'economic' genocide.[623] In his words:

> It is easier for the West to arm, facilitate and finance the warlords, while they take away the timber from the Congo forest. All these raw materials end up in the West. The money [that] is stolen from the continent often ends up in Switzerland, American and European banks… Economic genocide should have been included in the Statute more than anything else. The permanent impoverishment of the black man, the slavery and the colonization that we suffered is still what keeps us where we are. There has been no compensation and responsibility for what happened. The context of the Statute tells us how little the black continent participated in the formulation of this Statute.[624]

Maalim further lamented the absence of Kiswahili 'as one of the languages of the ICC'. He opined: 'I have seen that they have included Russian, Spanish, Arabic, English and Chinese. There are more speakers of Kiswahili than Russian. Our own governments, and the continental body, would have been done a lot of pride if we also had Kiswahili as one of the languages in the ICC'.[625]

---

[621] Ibid., 907.
[622] Ibid., 913.
[623] Ibid., 917.
[624] Ibid., 918. In response to MP Maalim, the attorney general replied: 'Sir, a lot was spoken about economic genocide. This bill is not concerned with what one may call "economic genocide". Important as it is, it is only concerned with criminal genocide', 927.
[625] Ibid., 917.

Despite MP Maalim's remarks, the International Crimes Act (ICA), as a model for the Ugandan legislation that followed, imports directly almost all provisions of the Rome Statute. It refers entirely to the Statute's definition of international crimes (none of which were previously provided for in the KPC),[626] while provisions on command responsibility, statutes of limitation and superior orders are likewise directly imported.[627] Similar to Uganda, the Act provides that the maximum penalty is life imprisonment, even though the ordinary penal code maintained the death penalty for crimes such as murder, armed robbery and treason.[628]

The ICA was tabled and passed with remarkable speed, coming into effect as of 1 January 2009. Standing in support, MP Ekwee Ethuro took note of the bill's rapid passage:

> I am aware of many of the international protocols and statutes that have been consented to by the government, that have not seen the floor of this House. That is not the proper way to do it. I want to believe the business of knee-jack reaction— Maybe the greatest motivation of the International Crimes Bill to even see the walls of this House, is a consideration of what we have gone through in terms of the Waki Report. ... All the protocols and any other international protocols that the government of Kenya has committed itself to should be domesticated.[629]

---

[626] The International Crimes Act, 2008 ('ICA 2008'), Art. 6(4). One significant difference between Kenya's ICA and the Rome Statute is its provisions on immunity. Rather than incorporate Article 27 of the Rome Statute, which makes official capacity irrelevant to immunity, the ICA's Section 27 only provides that the official capacity of a person shall not be used as a reason to refuse a request for the surrender of that person to the ICC. Thus, while there is no immunity for purposes of transfer or surrender to the court, the president's constitutional grant of immunity would prevail for the purpose of domestic prosecutions in Kenya under the ICA. A similar immunity exception was also debated in the Ugandan context; however, the provision there was ultimately defeated, again owing largely to the vigorous efforts of civil society. See M. Ndifuna, J. Apio and A. Smith, 'The Role of States Parties in Building the ICC's Local Impact: Findings from Delegates' Visits to Uganda' (2011), which notes that the ICC Bill 'faced delays throughout 2009–10, reportedly in part due to efforts ... to provide immunity for heads of state', 11 (on-file).

[627] ICA 2008, Art. 7(1)(f), (g), (k).

[628] Ibid., Art. 7(5)(b). The Supreme Court of Kenya has since held that the mandatory death penalty is 'out of sync' with the 2010 Constitution, as well as 'harsh, unjust and unfair'. See Francis Karioko Muruatetu and Another v. Republic of Kenya, Supreme Court of Kenya, Pet. Nos. 15 & 16 (2015) (judgment delivered 14 December 2017).

[629] ICA Third Reading, 4084. MP Githae (later appointed as Kenyan ambassador to the United States) likewise took the occasion to state, '[N]ow that the attorney-general is in the mood of domesticating international agreements, we have so many of them that we have not domesticated in this country, which Kenya has ratified. I would like to ask him to bring them to this House so that we can domesticate them'. Ibid.

Reflecting the exceptional nature of the legislation, the ICA remains one of very few international treaties to be domesticated into Kenya's national law.

3   Surfacing Political Discomforts: Post-Implementation Politics

Uganda: The End of Amnesty?

In Uganda, Parliament's rushed support for the ICC Act's passage – seen at the time as a necessary and symbolic pre-condition for hosting the 2010 Review Conference – soon gave way to a deeper set of political concerns over the future of the Amnesty Act and, by extension, to the dominance of the complementarity framework. This was not surprising. Uganda had passed the Amnesty Act in January 2000, within a year of its first signing the Rome Statute, but 'without considering any possible inconsistency in obligations'.[630] Subsequently amended in 2002 and 2006, the act provided amnesty for anyone who had engaged in armed rebellion against the government since the '26th day of January 1986' and who agreed to renounce and abandon such rebellion. The conditions for amnesty were broadly conceived, with the declaration that 'amnesty means a pardon, forgiveness, exemption or discharge from criminal prosecution or any other form of punishment by the state'.[631]

Furthermore, while some MPs had raised questions about the Amnesty Act's future in the light of the ICC Act, at the time Attorney General Ruhindi had assured them that, 'International criminal justice does not throw away our own initiatives to try some of these renegades'. He correctly noted that 'you can actually have amnesty internally or domestically under the complementarity principle'.[632] Nevertheless, the possibility of conflict was apparent. What might happen, for instance, if an amnesty applicant became a target for domestic prosecution under Ugandan law?

This precise question confronted Parliament only one month after the ICC Act's passage, when the executive sought a 'carve out' declaration for the eligibility of four individuals to receive amnesty: Thomas

---

[630] Nouwen, *Complementarity in the Line of Fire*, 206.

[631] See Amnesty Commission, 'The Amnesty Act: An Act of Forgiveness' (August 2009), 26 (on-file).

[632] ICC Bill Second Reading, 10942; see also McEvoy and Mallinder, 'Amnesties in Transition', 420 ('[B]oth international and domestic law accept a role for prosecutions *and* amnesties in transitional justice settings'.).

Kwoyelo and three of the ICC's named suspects. The Minister of State for Internal Affairs purportedly sought the exemption because these individuals 'have been engaged and continue to engage in acts that are contrary to international standards and are rebellious and injurious to the citizens of this country and the neighbouring states'.[633] At this point (and as discussed further in the following chapters), Ugandan authorities had already seized Kwoyelo, and he had already applied for amnesty under the existing law. This led one MP who opposed the government's motion to note that it was in a 'catch-22' situation:

> The minister is telling us that the fourth person [Kwoyelo] is already in the hands of the security agencies; they do not know what to do with him. Actually, they just want us to pass this request so that they can have this person prosecuted, because they can't grant him amnesty; they can't release him, and they can't take him to court while the peace process is going on. Why should we operate like that?[634]

Another MP from northern Uganda raised similar objections, expressing confusion as to the criterion used in selecting Kwoyelo for prosecution.[635] She added:

> Now, I want to know the effects of the declaration beyond the indictment. Suppose tomorrow, Kony comes out and says, 'I want to sign for amnesty and I will stop all this suffering for the people of Sudan, DRC and for the people of Central African Republic'. What will be the political decision of Uganda, DRC and Sudan for the sake of their people, what will be the effect of this? Is this decision written in stone, or can it be undone?[636]

In the end, the ministry withdrew its motion; however, the failed attempt soon inaugurated a more concerted effort to cease the issuing of amnesties entirely. Indeed, although amnesty remained strongly supported by Ugandans in the north and amongst their political representatives, its continuance increasingly conflicted with Uganda's carefully crafted image as a 'complementarity state', one of the few that now had both a dedicated domestic war crimes division and domesticated ICC legislation.

---

[633] Request for Parliament to Approve the Declaration of Named Individuals as Persons Not Eligible for Amnesty, 13 April 2010 (on-file); remarks of Mr M. Kasaija, 785.

[634] Ibid., 787 (remarks of E. Lukwago). Notably, Hon. Lukwago (now mayor of Kampala) had also served as a member of the Committee of Legal and Parliamentary Affairs that considered the ICC Bill before it went to the floor of Parliament. See Sessional Committee Report.

[635] Ibid., 788 (remarks of B. Amongi).

[636] Ibid.

The growing tide against amnesty was partly reflected in the attitude of Uganda's JLOS.[637] While JLOS was meant to act as a 'neutral' justice coordinator, from 2010 onwards it progressively undertook a more aggressive effort to discontinue the act, arguing that it was incompatible with Uganda's obligations under international law.[638] Organizations like Amnesty International took a similar approach. Following the Ugandan Constitutional Court's first decision halting the Kwoyelo trial in September 2011 (on the grounds that he was entitled to amnesty), it issued a statement calling the decision a 'setback' for accountability and urged the Ugandan government to 'revoke any amnesty applicable to crimes under international law'.[639]

A more urgent crisis thus presented itself in mid-2012 when the Ministry of the Interior chose not to renew Part II of the Amnesty Act, which was the provision that empowered the commission to grant amnesties.[640] The provision's lapsing – largely understood as a response to the Constitutional Court's ruling – was met with intense opposition.[641] Stephen Oola notes that it 'angered many victims and leaders from the conflict affected sub-regions in northern Uganda', so much that local leaders and domestic civil society groups petitioned the Speaker of Parliament, condemning the 'illegal and unconstitutional manner' in which the amnesty provision had been removed.[642] Ultimately, the matter

---

[637] See JLOS, 'Annual Performance Report 2009/2010' (September 2010), 9.

[638] See, e.g., The Amnesty Law (2000) Issues Paper, Review by the Transitional Justice Working Group, JLOS (April 2012). To date, more than 27,000 former combatants have received amnesty under the act, approximately half of whom were former LRA members.

[639] Amnesty International Public Statement, 'Court's decision a setback for accountability for crimes committed in northern Uganda conflict', AFR 59/015/2011 (23 September 2011).

[640] Statutory Instruments 2012 no. 34, The Amnesty Act (Declaration of Lapse of the Operation of Part II) Instrument, 2012 (23 May 2012, issued by MP Hilary Onek, minister of internal affairs) (on-file).

[641] As discussed further in Chapter 7, the Constitutional Court's decision was later overturned by the Ugandan Supreme Court in April 2015.

[642] Oola notes that, in addition to the suspicious manner of the lapsing, it was procedurally improper: Under the Amnesty Act, the decision to renew or lapse any part of the law is at the discretion of the minister of the interior. Here, the chief justice and attorney general both were alleged to have improperly intervened in the process. For further accounts of this episode, see Oola, 'In the Shadow of Kwoyelo's Trial', 168; Anna Macdonald, "'Somehow This Whole Process Became So Artificial': Exploring the Transitional Justice Implementation Gap in Uganda', *International Journal of Transitional Justice* 13(2) (2019), 241–243.

was referred to the Parliamentary Committee on Defence and Internal Affairs, which proceeded to undertake extensive consultations with key stakeholders.

In its final, 45-page report, published in August 2013, the committee concluded that the lapsing of Part II of the act was 'premature and out of step with the sentiments of affected communities, and recommended that it be "restore[d] in its entirety"'.[643] Far more than the debate over the ICC Act, the committee's report surfaces the complexity of Uganda's post-conflict landscape. It reviews, for instance, the arguments in favour of amnesty – the fact that 'the vast majority of rebels were forcibly abducted, many at a very tender age'; the concern that there is 'now no legal protection for returnees from prosecution' – and assesses the executive branch's contention that the granting of amnesty 'was inconsistent with the Rome Statute of the International Criminal Court (1998) (domesticated in Uganda in 2010)'.[644] It notes that JLOS and the UCICC played a leading role in advancing this argument, along with 'diverse external pressure from some of Uganda's development partners as well as agencies of the United Nations and other international commentators who have policy objections to the amnesty'.[645] In the committee's view, these external actors 'appear to have exerted a disproportional influence on the executive's approach to the amnesty issue, by promoting their own policy preferences'.[646]

The committee's conclusions also dispel a number of the misconceptions about complementarity's purported obligations. It notes, for instance, that there 'is in fact no provision of [the Rome Statute] which outlaws amnesties, neither does the Statute impose any express obligations upon states to prosecute relevant crimes'.[647] It further notes the common view encountered by committee members that the Statute 'imposes upon states parties a general obligation to establish international crimes courts and to introduce criminal legislation in order to prosecute ICC crimes nationally'.[648] In perhaps its strongest passage, the report concludes:

---

[643] Report of the Committee on Defence and Internal Affairs on the Petition on the Lapsing of Part II of The Amnesty Act ('Committee Report – Amnesty Lapse'), August 2013, para. 13.1.
[644] Ibid., para. 9.8.
[645] Ibid., paras. 9.4, 9.6.
[646] Ibid., para. 9.38.
[647] Ibid., para. 9.18.
[648] Ibid., para. 9.21.

There is … a broader political issue at stake here, which relates not only to Uganda, but generally to the African continent: it concerns the extent to which African values and priorities inform the content of international law. There is a greater need for African states to be more assertive in ensuring that their values are reflected in the development of international law.[649]

Following the committee's conclusions, the Ugandan government reinstated the Amnesty Act in its entirety. In 2015, the provision lapsed, but was again reinstated the following year; in May 2019 it was further extended for another two years (although now, following a 2015 Supreme Court ruling, amnesties are excluded for war crimes and crimes against humanity).[650]

Kenya: A Return to the Political

The politically contested nature of amnesty in Uganda, and the relative detachment of that debate from the ICC Act's passage, resonates in the Kenyan context as well. There, the swift approval of the ICA was soon followed by political stalemate on the attendant institutional question of whether or not to establish, as the Waki Commission had also stipulated, a special tribunal for Kenya that would be empowered to retroactively judge alleged perpetrators of the election violence. As previously noted, the defeat of the STK was largely the product of an 'unholy alliance' between politicians who feared that genuine, independent domestic proceedings would never be possible through Kenyan courts and those who saw such a tribunal, at the time, as a greater threat than the ICC itself.

Unlike the ICA, which saw minimal debate as to the incorporation of its substantial obligations into Kenya's legal framework, the STK Bill was deeply contested. Parliamentarians rejected the overt directives of the executive to vote in favour of the STK, raising questions about its comportment with the Kenyan Constitution as well as the risk of creating

---

[649] Ibid., para. 9.39.
[650] E-mail communication with Amnesty Commission legal officer (12 July 2019). For instance, the commission granted two amnesty certificates to former LRA rebels, Bosco Kilama and Simon Peter Ochora, in early 2017. See Peter Labeja, 'Uganda Amnesty Commission Issues Postdated Certificates' (Uganda Radio Network, 26 April 2017), at https://ugandaradionetwork.com/story/uganda-amnesty-commission-issues-postdated-certificates; Pierre Hazan, 'Uganda's Amnesty Law and the Peace/Justice Dilemma' (24 July 2017), at http://pierrehazan.com/en/2017/07/ugandas-amnesty-law-and-the-peacejustice-dilemma/. Recent plans have suggested that the act would be renamed the Transitional Justice Act; however, this has not yet taken place.

a parallel structure to the country's broader legal system. Repeated attempts by the Kenyan Parliament to withdraw from the Rome Statute and to repeal the ICA also reflect the deeply contested nature of the ICC's intervention.[651] At the time of the court's summons, domestic legislation was, in fact, tabled seeking to repeal the ICA. Although the government took no action on the bill, only one parliamentarian (former Justice Minister Karua) opposed the motion.[652] Furthermore, in contrast to the 'global village' invoked by Attorney General Wako three years before, at a special session of the Senate in December 2013 (and following a similar debate by the National Assembly that September), senators spoke of cooperation with the ICC as 'singing the tune of the whites'; of 'playing politics with the boundaries of this country and the flag and the national anthem of our nation'; and of an 'unsupervised prosecutor who can … arrest people who he thinks do not suck up to international neocolonial ideology'.[653]

This discourse has increasingly cast civil society as shadowy hands conspiring against the Kenyan state and people – 'evil society' in the words of Kenyatta's 2013 presidential campaign.[654] Furthermore, according to the Senate Majority Leader:

> What has happened … is that a few people especially from the Non-Government Organisations (NGOs) world decided to convert the misery and the tragedy that befell our country into a money-minting business where a few citizens have converted themselves into running rings and

---

[651] See, e.g., Nicholas Kulish, 'Legislators in Kenya Vote to Quit Global Court', *International Herald Tribune*, 5 (6 September 2013).

[652] See Peter Opiyo, 'Isaac Ruto: Kenya Should Pull Out of ICC', *Standard Digital* (15 December 2010); Thomas Obel Hansen, 'Transitional Justice in Kenya? An Assessment of the Accountability Process in Light of Domestic Politics and Security Concerns', *California Western International Law Journal*, 42(1) (2011).

[653] Parliament of Kenya, Convening of Special Sitting of The Senate to Debate Motion on Withdrawal of Kenya from the Rome Statute, Official Record (Hansard) ('Senate Debate'), 10 September 2013; comments at 46 (Senator Keter) and 14,16 (Senator (Prof.) Kindiki). Unlike previous legislative debates on the ICC Act and the establishment of the STK, the various Rome Statute withdrawal motions have been debated in both the Senate and the National Assembly, following the introduction of a bicameral legislature in March 2013.

[654] John Githongo, 'Whither Civil Society?', *The Star* (6 April 2013). See also Mattia Cacciatori, 'When Kings Are Criminals: Lessons from ICC Prosecutions of African Presidents', *International Journal of Transitional Justice* 12(3) (2018) (arguing that ICC prosecutions of sitting heads of state in Kenya and Sudan have been the cause of governmental retaliation against NGOs).

organisations in the name of victims' support. These are people who have been responsible and have been used by foreigners to cook up the stories and bring up the kind of friction that is now being witnessed before the [ICC]. As I said, we should be all ashamed as Kenyans.[655]

The Senate ultimately passed a motion expressing its intention to bring forward a bill that would compel the government to withdraw from the ICC. As with broader threats of withdrawal by the African Union, however, this motion appears to have been largely symbolic: to date, no bill has been formally tabled.

4 Democratic Republic of Congo: Resistance and Contestation

By many accounts, the DRC was the 60th state to ratify the Rome Statute; its ratification formally brought the ICC into existence. While it is unclear how significant this symbolic threshold was in influencing President Kabila's decision to ratify the Statute in 2002, the symbolism has itself been summoned by many advocates in their long-running efforts to urge the Congolese Parliament to pass implementing legislation. For example, Olivier Kambala notes that 'it was the [DRC's] 60th ratification that triggered the Statute's entry into force – and made the human rights community applaud the birth of something impossible to envision fifty year earlier'.[656] Unlike Kenya and Uganda, however, international crimes were crimes under Congolese law since well before the ICC's establishment, much less its intervention in the DRC.

---

[655] Senate Debate, 22. See also Parliamentary Debates, National Assembly Official Report (Hansard), 15 October 2014, in which one MP suggests that the Open Society Initiative in East Africa is a 'terrorist organisation', and that NGOs such as the Africa Centre for Open Governance, Kenyans for Peace Truth and Justice and the Kenya Human Rights Commission 'bear the greatest responsibility for the post-election violence'. In his words, 'The forest might be different at different times but the monkeys are always the same' (remarks of Hon. Moses Kuria).

[656] Olivier Kambala wa Kambala, 'International Criminal Court in Africa: "alea jacta est"', Oxford Transitional Justice Research Working Paper Series (12 July 2010). Several interlocutors expressed similar sentiments to the effect that the 'ICC exists thanks to the DRC; it brought the court into existence'. It should be noted that other commentators have suggested the '60th ratification' narrative is somewhat of a myth, given that a number of other states also submitted their ratifications at around the same time (March–April 2002) as the DRC did. One Congolese jurist even questioned whether the DRC's ratification was genuinely deposited.

Congolese criminal law is mainly written in the 1940 penal codes and can be split in two parts: the ordinary civilian penal code (*code penal congolais*) and the military criminal code. Genocide, war crimes and crimes against humanity were first codified in the latter in 1972, although the Congolese Parliament enacted new criminal (*code pénal militaire*) and judicial codes (*code judiciaire militaire*) for the military in 2002, shortly after the DRC's ratification of the Rome Statute.[657] While the revised military criminal code (MCC) defined the criminal offences to be tried before DRC military courts (including, but not limited to international crimes), the judicial code determined the applicable criminal procedure. Thus, under Congolese law, Rome Statute crimes committed during any period prior to 2003 would fall under the 1972 Code, while crimes committed post-2003 would fall under the 2002 codes or, as some domestic courts have since determined, the Rome Statute. The country's 1940 penal code (applied by civilian courts), however, did not include international crimes until its amendment in 2015.

The preamble to the revised MCC acknowledges that the DRC had ratified the Statute, even if the definitions of crimes under Congolese law depart from it in certain respects.[658] Indeed, not unlike the 'mirroring' effect observed in Uganda and Kenya's domestic ICC legislation, most of the limited commentary on the revised MCC has been drawn to its deficiencies as compared to the Rome Statute. Scholars have noted, for instance, that the 2002 MCC failed to criminalize the conscription of minor children into the armed forces; that it 'seemingly merges the current normative understandings of crimes against humanity and war crimes'; that 'the domestic law of crimes against humanity in the DRC is not as clearly defined as the current norms of international law' and 'for restricting sexual violence merely to crimes against humanity while the Rome Statute also includes sexual violence

---

[657] A compendium of the DRC's criminal laws was published in 2010 with the support of USAID as 'Code pénal congolais: décret du 30 janvier 1940 tel que modifie jusqu'au 31 décembre 2009 et ses dispositions complémentaires' (on-file). The 2002 criminal code is loi no. 024/2002 du 18 novembre 2002 portant code pénal militaire ('2002 code pénal militaire/MCC'); the judicial code is loi no. 023/2002 du 18 novembre 2002 portant code judiciaire Militaire, at www.leganet.cd/Legislation/Droit%20Judiciaire/ Loi.023.2002.18.11.2002.pdf.

[658] See Règlement du 10 septembre 2010 relatif aux éléments de crime, para. 1 (in 'code pénal congolais').

as war crimes'.[659] These shortcomings, it has been suggested, 'resulted from the fact that the MCC was not well drafted and hastily adopted by an unelected legislative body during an on-going armed conflict'.[660] At the same time, however, the MCC also offered more expansive definitions than the Rome Statute. Political groups, for instance, were a protected class under the MCC's definition of genocide, while the 'destruction of natural heritage' and 'universal culture' were included as crimes against humanity.[661]

DRC Implementation Law of 2010–2011

Draft implementation legislation for the DRC – intended to transpose the Rome Statute's definitions into the *code pénal ordinaire* – existed for many years, but did not receive serious attention until 2010, following the publication of a long-awaited 'mapping' report on crimes committed between 1993 and 2003 in the DRC by the UN Office of the High Commissioner for Human Rights.[662] Cooperation legislation with the ICC had been drafted as early as 2002 and later revised in 2003 after consultation with various stakeholders, including civil society.[663] A later version of

[659] See, e.g., Antonietta Trapani, 'Bringing National Courts in Line with International Norms: A Comparative Look at the Court of Bosnia and Herzegovina and the Military Court of the Democratic Republic of Congo', *Israel Law Review* 46(2) (July 2013), 239–240; Labuda, 'Applying and "Misapplying" the Rome Statute', in *Contested Justice: The Politics and Practice of International Criminal Court Interventions*, 420–421; UN Mapping Report, paras. 820–825; Balingene Kahombo, 'The Principle of Complementarity in Practice: A Survey of Congolese Legislation Implementing the Rome Statute', in H. J. van der Merwe and Gerhard Kemp (eds.), *International Criminal Justice in Africa, 2016* (Strathmore University Press and Konrad Adenauer Stiftung, 2017), 208. Several of the MCC's perceived deficiencies were remedied by the adoption in July 2006 of a special law on sexual violence, which criminalized acts of rape and sexual exploitation at the national level and provided for their prosecution as international or ordinary crimes. See loi no. 06/018 du 20 juillet 2006 modifiant et complétant le décret du 30 janvier 1940 portant code pénale congolais (on-file).
[660] Kahombo, 'The Principle of Complementarity in Practice', 208.
[661] See 2002 code pénal militaire, Arts. 164, 169(9), 169(10).
[662] See 'Report of the Mapping Exercise documenting the most serious violations of human rights and international humanitarian law committed within the territory of the Democratic Republic of the Congo between March 1993 and June 2003' (August 2010) ('UN Mapping Report').
[663] Earlier versions of this legislation (from 2001 and 2002) are appendixed in Godfrey Musila, 'Between Rhetoric and Action: The Politics, Processes and Practice of the ICC's Work in the DRC', Institute for Security Studies Monograph 164 (July 2009); see Appendices III and IV.

a government-led *projet de loi* was also published in 2005, following 'a number of expert meetings supported by Human Rights First, Human Rights Watch, the CICC and the African Association for the Defence of Human Rights, a Congolese non-governmental organization'.[664]

Despite these numerous campaigns, this legislation was never put on the parliamentary agenda. Godfrey Musila suggests that this may be attributed to the law 'not [being] considered a priority in view of other issues that … occupied the government and legislators' time', as well as 'perceptions among some people that the ICC's work… is a project of the executive, directed at destroying its political enemies'.[665] (The 2008 arrest and transfer of Bemba, Kabila's main political rival, to The Hague did little to allay such perceptions.) Furthermore, the 2004 signing of a comprehensive Agreement on Judicial Cooperation between the government and the Office of the Prosecutor – similar to cooperation agreements signed with the OTP in Kenya and Uganda – may have obviated the need for more comprehensive legislation.[666]

Discussion of domestic implementation thus remained stalled in the DRC until the release of the UN's report.[667] Notably, again reflecting a duty-based understanding of complementarity, the UN's report stated that 'by ratifying the Rome Statute, the DRC subscribed to the *obligation to adapt* its domestic legislation to the law enshrined in the Statute'.[668] Several months after the report's release, proposed implementation legislation (*proposition de loi de mise en oeuvre*) finally emerged on the National Assembly's agenda. Two MPs, the Honourable Mutumbe Mbuya and Professor Nyabirungu mwene Songa, a well-known Congolese intellectual and human rights activist,[669] had first introduced such legislation in March 2008, but no action had yet been taken on it.[670]

---

[664] Ibid.

[665] Ibid., 16, 17.

[666] Judicial Cooperation Agreement between the Democratic Republic of Congo and the Office of the Prosecutor of the International Criminal Court (reproduced as Appendix 2 in Musila, 'Between rhetoric and action', 81–90).

[667] UN Mapping Report (August 2010).

[668] Ibid., para. 1022 (emphasis added).

[669] Nyabirungu has been an important figure in Congo's legal and political landscape and has been the focal point for a number of international organizations engaged in domestic complementarity efforts. He and mwene Songa both are also members of Parliamentarians for Global Action. Interview with ICTJ staff (Kinshasa, 21 June 2011); interview with PGA consultant (Kinshasa, 27 June 2011).

[670] See ICTJ, 'The Democratic Republic of Congo Must Adopt the Rome Statute Implementation Law' (April 2010) ('Two Congolese members of parliament introduced a draft bill before the National Assembly, Congo's lower house, in March 2008'.).

Patryk Labuda, who closely followed the 2010 legislative process for the *proposition*, notes that the bill had four main objectives: (1) to incorporate the Rome Statute's classification of international crimes into domestic criminal law (the bill 'copied most of' the Statute's definition of crimes); (2) to transfer jurisdiction over international crimes to civilian courts, not military tribunals; (3) to provide for a greater number of fair trial guarantees, 'especially relating to defendant rights, victim participation and witness protection'; and (4) to establish a 'coherent framework regulating collaboration between the ICC's field units and domestic Congolese judicial and governmental authorities'.[671] In addition to these practical objectives, compliance and complementarity were again rhetorically marshalled in support of the legislation's passage. A briefing note prepared by the ICTJ states that '[y]ears have lapsed' since the DRC ratified the Rome Statute, 'but the DRC government has yet to meet its legal obligation to incorporate the statute into national law'.[672] Further, adopting such legislation 'is essential to ensure complementarity between domestic Congolese courts and the ICC' and to 'strengthen the country's legal system'.[673]

Despite having languished for two and a half years, 'heated' and 'stormy' debates on the draft bill were held within the assembly in November 2010 whereupon, under Congolese parliamentary procedure, it was declared admissible (recevable) and transferred to the National Assembly's Political, Administrative and Judicial Committee (PAJ) Committee for further consideration.[674] In spite of its advancement, the debates on the law – as with the competing Special Chambers/Court legislation (discussed in Chapter 6) – underscored the opposition expressed by many MPs, reflecting a critical discourse akin

---

[671] Labuda, 'Applying and "Misapplying" the Rome Statute', 414.

[672] ICTJ, 'The Democratic Republic of Congo Must Adopt the Rome Statute Implementation Law'. The ICTJ also states that it, Avocats sans Frontières (ASF) and the Konrad Adenauer Foundation convened in 2008 'and issued a memorandum of suggested amendments to the draft bill to maximize conformity with the Rome Statute'. Ibid.

[673] Ibid.

[674] The debates were characterized as such privately by several interlocutors, but also in the following press releases: CICC Press Release, 'Global Justice Coalition welcomes advances in the criminal law reform in the Democratic Republic of Congo', 9 November 2010; CN-CPI Press Release, 'The DRC Coalition for the ICC welcomes the admission of the law proposal on the implementation of the Rome Statute', 5 November 2010.

to the post-implementation discomforts that emerged in Kenya and Uganda. The involvement of outside actors in advocating for the bill's passage was both seen and described as a form of neocolonialism and a threat to national sovereignty.[675] Again, a particular point of contention was punishment: the DRC legislation, at least in its earlier iteration, prohibited the application of the death penalty. By contrast, under the MCC, Congolese military courts retain discretion to impose the death penalty for crimes against humanity, genocide as well as certain war crimes.[676] Most Congolese MPs found this provision unacceptable, and it became a central point of contention during the assembly's debate.[677]

Such opposition has largely been presented as a distraction to the substantive issues raised by the bill. As elsewhere, however, many proponents of the ICC's normative framework did see implementation of the Statute as an opportunity to push for broader human rights agendas, including, notably, abolition of the death penalty. Indeed, a *proposition de loi* to that effect was introduced at the same time as the Rome Statute implementation bill, which, though unsuccessful, was supported by a prominent Congolese NGO on the grounds that it was 'a valuable opportunity for the DRC to conform with international instruments it had ratified, notably the Rome Statute of the ICC'.[678] Another NGO circulated an advocacy

---

[675] See Pascale Kambale, 'Mix and Match: Is a Hybrid Court the best way for Congo to Prosecute International Crimes?', *Openspace* (February 2012).

[676] See 2002 code pénal militaire, Arts, 65, 164, 167, 169, 171, 172.

[677] See, e.g., PGA Press Release, 'La loi de mise en œuvre du statut de Rome déclare recevable par l'Assemblée Nationale de la République Démocratique du Congo', 4 novembre 2010. The release notes that the 'intense' debate lasted more than 2½ hours with a total of 15 interventions, which 'attracted criticism' for not retaining the death penalty as a form of punishment (author's translation).

[678] See Ligue pour la paix et les droits de l'homme, communique de presse no. 006/CN/ LIPADHO/2010, 'La majorité des députes s'opposent à l'abolition de peine capital', 18 novembre 2010 (author's translation). MP André Mbata, a former parliamentarian (2006–2011), presented the abolition bill; it was rejected in November 2010. On the fate of this bill and its imbrication with debates over Rome Statute legislation, see Lievin Ngondji Ongombe, 'RDC: la peine de mort, l'adoption de la loi de mise en oeuvre du statut du Rome', in *Power and Prosecution: Challenges and Opportunities for International Criminal Justice in Sub-Saharan Africa*, 67–105.

paper during the time of the debate urging passage of the implementation law, in part, because:

> The definitions of international crimes are different in the Rome Statute and the Congolese military judicial code. Moreover, the sentences are not the same in both systems (death penalty and no sentence for war crimes in the DRC).[679]

Similarly, a 2009 concept paper by the PGA for an 'international parliamentary conference on justice and peace' includes the following:

> It is time for the DRC to undertake this historic step to implement the Rome Statute of the ICC and equip itself with a strong arsenal of laws against impunity, and this legislation could also represent a definitive step towards abolishing the death penalty, even if the Rome Statute itself leaves to each state party the sovereign decision to legislate on penalties for international crimes that are adjudicated before domestic courts.[680]

Punishment was thus an integral part of the implementation debate in the DRC. As with insisting on 'international standards', advocates and norm entrepreneurs saw in implementation an opportunity to route broader political objectives through the principle of complementarity.

Even with the draft implementation law advancing to the PAJ, the legislation remained a relatively low political priority. A special subcommittee of the PAJ was not convened to review and revise the bill until June 2011, eight months after it had been declared recevable.[681] By

---

[679] Le Club des Amis du Droit du Congo, 'The Repression of International Crimes by Congolese Jurisdictions' (December 2010) (on-file). See also UN Mapping Report, para. 63 (noting, in reference to a proposed hybrid mechanism that 'Such a mechanism should also … not include the death penalty among its sentences, in compliance with international principles').

[680] Parliamentarians for Global Action, 'International Parliamentary Conference on Justice and Peace in the Democratic Republic of Congo, the Great Lakes Region and Central Africa' (10–12 December 2009), at www.pgaction.org/pdf/pre/Kin%20TOR%20EN.pdf, p. 3. As noted in the terms of reference, this event was co-organized with, inter alia, the ICTJ, ASF, the Konrad Adenauer Foundation and the DRC's National Coalition for the International Criminal Court.

[681] République Démocratique du Congo, Assemblée Nationale, Commission Politique, Administrative et Judiciaire, 'Proposition de loi modifiant et complétant le code pénal, le code de procédure pénale, le code judiciaire militaire et le code pénal militaire en vue de la mise en œuvre du Statut de Rome de la cour pénale internationale' (Juin 2011) (on-file). At the bottom of this document, March 2008 – the original date on which the legislation was introduced by Mutumbe Mbuya and mwene Songa – appears to be crossed out and replaced with June 2011.

this point, however, the executive was vigorously advancing a separate *projet de loi* focused on the establishment of special chambers. Unlike Kenya and Uganda, however, where legislative actors assented to hastily presented legislation, Congolese MPs objected to the executive's efforts to railroad its special chambers bill. This led to a further political divide between the legislative and executive branch: Parliament refused to endorse the government's *projet de loi*, while the government largely ignored the parliamentary *proposition de loi*.[682] Indeed, although the government used an exceptional procedure to present a revised version of its bill to the Senate in August 2011, the implementation bill of MPs Mbuya and mwene Songa was not included as part of that legislative package.

DRC Implementation Law of 2015

Amidst the failure to pass implementing legislation in 2010–2011, the monist tradition of the Congolese legal order has instead become an avenue through which military court judges have been able to apply certain provisions of the Rome Statute directly in the course of domestic criminal proceedings. This phenomenon has led to a number of notable decisions, including several wherein DRC military courts have declined to impose punishments prohibited in the Rome Statute, notably the death penalty. While such opinions have not been without controversy, it would appear that the success of NGO-led efforts to engage with the Congolese military justice system may well have delayed subsequent efforts at domestic implementation of the Rome Statute. Congolese jurist Balingene Kahombo notes, for instance, that the 'approach to the direct application of treaties [in DRC] has been so successful that the debate over the adoption of new national legislation implementing the Rome Statute remained side-lined for several years'.[683] In effect, jurisprudential creativity outpaced the legislative calendar.

---

[682] See Human Rights Watch, 'Letter to DRC Minister of Justice on the Draft Legislation Establishing Specialised Mixed Chambers in the Congolese Justice System' (22 December 2010) ('Substantively, the two bills are intricately linked. It would be very unfortunate if the adoption of the bill for specialized mixed chambers had the effect of undercutting the adoption of the ICC implementing legislation'.).

[683] Kahombo, 'The Principle of Complementarity in Practice', 210.

By 2015, however, the situation had changed. First, in 2013, a new organic law was adopted that granted parallel jurisdiction over international crimes from the DRC's military justice system to ordinary (civilian) courts of appeal.[684] With this victory, long advocated for by civil society, the need for legislation that would apply to both civilian courts and military tribunals – a so-called *droit commun* – was more acutely needed. Because the Congolese MCC could not, in principle, be applied to civilians, courts of appeal needed substantive national legislation that they could apply.[685] There was also a growing desire to, as Kahombo argues, 'put an end to the controversy surrounding the kind of penalties that could be imposed by domestic courts in respect of core international crimes'.[686] To that end, MP Boniface Balamage (a member of the PGA) submitted a new *proposition de loi* for Rome Statute implementation, which was again transferred to the National Assembly's PAJ Committee and subsequently endorsed in December 2013.[687]

Second, rather than a campaign led (or perceived to be led) by international actors, national stakeholders strategically framed subsequent efforts at implementation as part of a broader effort to strengthen the Congolese justice system. To that end, government-led meetings were organized in late April/early May 2015 by the Ministry of Justice and the judicial service council (*Conseil Supérieur de la Magistrature*) to 'evaluate the functioning of the judicial system in Congo and the reforms that have already begun and to formulate recommendations about priority reforms and actions that should now be implemented'.[688] Bringing together staff from the military and civilian judicial systems, as well as representatives of the DRC's parliament, bar associations, universities and national and international civil society, these *Etats Généraux* were the first such meetings since 1996 to evaluate justice sector reform in the

---

[684] Loi organique no. 13/011-B du 11 avril 2013 portant organisation, fonctionnement et compétences des juridictions de l'ordre judiciaire (on-file).

[685] Stefaan Smis, Derk Inman and Pacifique Muhindo, 'Impunity in the DRC: One Step Forward, Two Steps Back?' Jurist (12 February 2015) ('With the lack of recognition of international crimes under national law, the principle of legality prevented the courts of appeals from hearing these cases'.).

[686] Kahombo, 'The Principle of Complementarity in Practice', 213.

[687] E-mail correspondence with Roger Mvita, OSISA-DRC (13 December 2017).

[688] See Human Rights Watch, 'Etats Généraux of the Justice System in the Democratic Republic of Congo: Recommendations on the Fight Against Impunity for Grave International Crimes' (27 April 2015).

DRC. Taking as its focus a need to strengthen the DRC's existing judicial apparatus, a critical recommendation that emerged was the adoption of national implementation legislation.

Following these meetings, the National Assembly passed, in early June 2015, the PAJ-endorsed bill, whereupon it was sent to the Senate for approval.[689] Seeking to build on this momentum, a coalition of Congolese civil society organizations met over the course of June to develop recommendations to improve the bill, which were then developed and submitted for Senate approval.[690] In contrast to the acrimonious debates of 2011, these observations were subsequently harmonized with the adopted text and passed in late 2015. Notably, national human rights organizations (rather than international) took a more prominent role in this process, helping to allay earlier concerns that efforts to alter the DRC legal framework were being pushed from the outside. Indeed, the comparative lack of international scrutiny in 2015 – coupled with the fact that, by this time, the ICC itself was increasingly disengaged from the DRC – was likely critical to the bill's passage.

On 15 December 2015, President Kabila signed the Parliament-backed bill into law; formal incorporation followed in February 2016. In effect, his signature brought three different laws into existence, meant as they were to not only harmonize national law with the Rome Statute, but to also fill existing gaps in the domestic penal code.[691] Noting amongst its reasons for passage the fact that the DRC has a 'double obligation' (*la double obligation*) to both cooperate with the ICC and to 'harmonize its criminal law with the provisions of the [Rome] Statute', the first law (Law no. 15/022) amended and supplemented the ordinary criminal code (of 1940) by inserting into its provisions identical definitions of genocide, war crimes and crimes against humanity as the Rome Statute,

---

[689] Labuda, 'Whither the Fight against Impunity in the Democratic Republic of Congo?'
[690] E-mail correspondence with Roger Mvita, OSISA-DRC (13 December 2017).
[691] Journal Officiel de la Republique Démocratique du Congo, Cabinet du Président de la Republique, 57e année/no. spéciale (Kinshasa, 29 février 2016), Loi no. 15/022 du 31 décembre modifiant et complétant le décret du 30 janvier 1940 portant code pénal ('Law no. 15/022'); loi no. 15/023 du 31 décembre 2015 modifiant la loi no. 024-2022 du 18 novembre 2002 portant code pénal militaire ('Law no. 15/023'); loi no. 15/024 du 31 décembre 2015 modifiant et complétant le décret du 6 aout 1959 portant code de procédure pénale ('Law no. 15/024') (on-file). To that end, Kahombo has noted that the legislation's 'mixture of provisions' in this respect has 'been a source of some confusion'. Kahombo, 'The Principle of Complementarity in Practice', 215.

as well as integrating verbatim the Statute's provisions on individual criminal liability, including its provisions on principal and accessory liability.[692] Capital punishment is also a notable, expanded feature of law 15/022: unlike the proposed legislation of 2011, it provides that all Rome Statute crimes (genocide, crimes against humanity, war crimes) are punishable by death.[693] The law also makes no distinction between perpetrators and accomplices as to sentencing, effectively expanding the scope of punishment to accomplice liability.[694]

The second law (Law no. 15/023) amends and supplements the 2002 military criminal code, making the ordinary criminal code, as amended by law 15/022, applicable before military courts. It further repeals the MCC's previous provision granting military courts exclusive jurisdiction over international crimes.[695] Most significantly, together with law 15/022, it amends the Congolese national law on superior responsibility, which, under the 2002 MCC, had previously allowed only for the prosecution of a commander if his subordinates were also prosecuted (and then only as an accomplice or co-perpetrator).[696] Now, both military and civilian superiors can be prosecuted as direct perpetrators. A third law (law 15/024) provides the legal framework for DRC authorities' cooperation with the ICC (notwithstanding the existing MOU that the government had signed with the OTP), including providing immunities to ICC staff and clarifying institutional liaisons to The Hague.[697] The law further affirms that the ICC is a subsidiary court to the DRC's domestic jurisdiction, but, notably, specifies that the government retains the right to 'self-refer' situations to the court, as it did

---

[692] Law no. 15/022, Arts. 221–223.

[693] Ibid., Titre XI, Art. 221 ('Le crime de génocide est puni de mort'); Art. 222 ('Le crime contre l'humanité est puni de mort'); Art. 223 ('Le crime de guerre est puni de mort').

[694] Ibid., Art. 2 modifiant Art. 21 quater de code pénal ('Par dérogation aux dispositions de l'alinéa précèdent, les complices des crimes vises au titre IX relative aux crimes contre la paix et la sécurité de l'humanité seront punis de la peine prévue par la loi a l'égard des autres de ces crimes'.).

[695] Law no. 15/023, Art. 1 modifiant MCC ('Sous réserve de la présente loi, les dispositions du livre premier et du titre IX du livre II du décret du 30 janvier 1940 portant code pénal sont applicables devant les juridictions militaires'.); Art. 2.

[696] Law no. 15/023 , Art. 1 modifying 2002 MCC (incorporating Rome Statute Art. 28 (a)); Law no. 15/022, Arts. 21 bis, ter and Art. 22 bis (incorporating Rome Statute articles 25 and 28(b)).

[697] Law no. 15/024.

in 2004.[698] Finally, a fourth law, not passed until March 2017, sought to harmonize conflicts arising out of dual civilian/military jurisdiction where there may be co-perpetration between civilians and military officers. It provides that civilian courts have general jurisdiction over international crimes, provided 'one of the co-perpetrators or accomplices' does not fall under military court jurisdiction.[699]

While passage of the DRC's implementation legislation was both long-awaited and welcomed by many in civil society, the extent to which the law will, in fact, be applied in practice remains unclear.[700] Commentators have criticized lacunae and lingering ambiguities created by the legislative text.[701] Indeed, in its amendments to both the MCC and the civilian criminal code, the 2015 legislation constitutes a regression in certain respects, narrowing as it does the MCC's previous inclusion of political groups as a protected class (by copying the Rome Statute's identical provisions), while otherwise broadening the scope of the death penalty's application. As a practical matter, then, it remains unclear whether DRC domestic courts will, in fact, choose to apply the 2015 legislation or whether they will continue the previous practice of applying the Statute directly.

5 Implementation Reconsidered: Purity, Politics and 'Performance'

The histories recounted herein suggest three tentative fault lines around implementation of the Rome Statute and its relationship to complementarity. First, rather than a catalyst for domestication of the Statute, the

---

[698] Ibid., Article 21 octies ('La cour pénale internationale n'intervient qu'à titre subsidiaire'); Article 21-10 ('En application de l'article 14 du Statut de Rome, le Président de la République peut, sur décision délibérée en Conseil des ministres, déférer a la cour pénale international une situation dans laquelle un ou plusieurs crimes relevant de la cour paraissent avoir été commis et demander au procureur de la cour pénale international d'enquêter sur cette situation en vue de déterminer si une ou plusieurs personnes identifiées doivent être inculpées de ces crimes'.).

[699] Loi organique no. 17/003 du 10 mars 2017 modifiant et complétant la loi no. 023-2002 du 18 novembre portant code judiciaire militaire, available at www.leganet.cd/Legislation/Droit%20Judiciaire/Loi.17.003.10.03.2017.html.

[700] See, e.g., Comite exécutif de ligue pour la paix, les droits de l'homme et la justice, communique de presse no. 04/CP/CE/05/2017 (30 April 2017) (on-file).

[701] See, e.g., Pacifique Muhindo Magadju, 'Législation congolaise de mise en œuvre du Statut de Rome: un pas en avant, un pas en arrière', in HJ van der Merwe and Gerhard Kemp (eds.), International Criminal Justice in Africa, 2016, 167–199; Kahombo, 'The Principle of Complementarity in Practice', 215–236.

ICC's arrival brought with it an array of transnational non-state actors who summoned complementarity (and the 'shadow' of the court) to pursue broader reform projects. ICC intervention was thus not itself a catalyst for domestic implementation of the Rome Statute in Uganda, Kenya or the DRC; rather, other events either intervened in, or preceded, the court's involvement. The passage of Uganda's ICC Act did not come until eight years after the court had started its work (at a time when any threat of further investigation seemed sufficiently remote); in the DRC, formal implementation for military and civilian jurisdictions alike took more than a decade, even as certain domestic judges had already begun directly applying the Rome Statute in national proceedings. By contrast, implementation of the ICA in Kenya should be understood primarily as a consequence of the Waki Commission's recommendations. Even if the spectre of the ICC may have animated the commission's work, Kenyan MPs did not see domestic legislation as an inoculative measure against the threat of court intervention. Rather, it was a politically low cost means to demonstrate legislative compliance with the commission's recommendations.

Thus, rather than a causal factor unto itself, the ICC's involvement in each of these countries – either prior to the initiation of formal investigations or in their wake – should instead be understood as an enabling environment in which broader anti-impunity advocacy could flourish. Implementation of the Rome Statute was at the centre of many of these efforts. In Uganda, for instance, it is now clear that the country's role as host state for the 2010 ICC Review Conference, part of an orchestrated performance for the international community, pushed forward long-standing draft legislation that advocates had pressed for, but which had otherwise languished. In this sense, the conference itself was the catalyst for the ICC Act. Its passage also dovetailed with a new chapter in the relationship between Uganda and the principle of complementarity. Whereas complementarity – understood as jurisdictional rivalry with the ICC – was once the dominant logic for the creation of a specialized court in Uganda to address conflict-related violence, by 2010 the principle had a new meaning: Uganda's law and institutions would complement The Hague, not compete with it. The next chapter examines this phenomenon in greater detail.

The desire to be seen as a compliant, cooperative state in the eyes of international actors likewise motivated Kenyan politicians, at least in the early phase of the post-election violence. At that stage, in 2008, the imminence of ICC intervention still appeared remote – indeed, it was the remoteness that led many MPs to reject the special tribunal bill – but passage of the ICA was seen as a politically strategic move. As a standalone recommendation of the Waki Commission, it was an opportunity to signal a break with the past, even as the act's own retrospective applicability to those events appeared doubtful. The ICA may have been, in the words of the director of a leading Kenyan NGO, the country's 'never again' moment, but, unlike the STK bill, the political price it threatened to extract was low.

In the DRC, the closest the country came to passage of implementing legislation prior to 2015 was in 2011, in the wake not of the ICC's initiation of its investigations, but rather as a result of the release of the UN's 2010 Mapping Report and amidst renewed calls for the establishment of a hybrid tribunal. Here, in fact, it was the growing realization that the ICC alone was an inadequate international response to impunity in the DRC that propelled the report's recommendation even if, at the same time, the court's ongoing work helped provide a legal rationale for the Rome Statute's implementation. But the opposition of many Congolese parliamentarians to much of the proposed legislation that followed the UN's report reflected a deeper resistance on the part of national political actors to international intervention. Indeed, Congolese parliamentarians raised many of the same concerns about implementation of the Statute – the risk of exceptionalism, the threat to constitutionalism, an encroachment on sovereignty – that Kenyan and Ugandan politicians would later come to raise, after their countries' implementation legislation had already passed.

These trajectories suggest that implementation of ICC crimes was often less a domestic preoccupation, than it was a performative act for predominantly international audiences. In both Kenya and Uganda, passage of domestic Rome Statute legislation was hailed for its swift passage with large majorities, demonstrating the entrenchment of global norms domestically and vindicating the ICC's catalytic potential. In Uganda, however, implementation of the Statute had long stagnated and was only accelerated later in order to 'perform' complementarity for external actors, well after the threat of the ICC had passed; similarly, in the Kenyan context, implementation was perceived as an easy political gesture that could signal the country's return to the 'global village' in the wake of enormous international scrutiny.[702] Much like the international

---

[702] For further analysis of the Kenyan response to post-election violence as a 'performance of transition', see Lynch, *Performances of Injustice*, 12 (arguing 'for greater recognition to be given to the extent to which transitional justice's constrained capacities are contingent upon persuasive performances').

criminal trial itself, then, implementation served a symbolic function, even as the post-implementation domestic politics of both countries remained deeply contested.[703]

Second, while often presented as a seemingly technical exercise, implementation is fundamentally a political process. As the following chapters illustrate further, domestic responses to ICC engagement did not follow the linear process that legalism imagines, wherein the implementation of a normative legal framework precedes institutional change. Indeed, in each country, prosecutions proceeded either in the absence of, or, in spite of, the passage of formal legislation: in the DRC, certain judges applied the Rome Statute directly (if selectively); in Kenya, the few, early trials that did move forward were prosecuted as ordinary crimes; and in Uganda, the lone trial of Thomas Kwoyelo has been pursued under the domestic penal code and customary international law, not the ICC Act.[704] Furthermore, in each country, the passage of implementing legislation was delayed not due to a lack of effort on the part of international justice advocates, but because it was not a sufficient political priority (indeed, in some cases, it was at odds with other political priorities). But when implementation aligned with domestic political interests – when it became important enough to external constituencies and carried little perceived political cost – the process moved forward.

Still, important distinctions remain. In Kenya and Uganda, the politics that enabled implementation were one of wanting to be seen, even if briefly, as compliant states: implementation was evidence of putting complementarity 'into practice' and a means of signalling to external constituencies the governments' purported commitment to accountability.

At the time those countries' acts were passed, these priorities briefly outweighed other domestic concerns. In Uganda, what passage of the ICC Act might mean for the continued practice of granting amnesties was glossed over, even if they quickly returned to the political fore. Similarly,

---

[703] On the symbolic function of the criminal trial, see Martti Koskenniemi, 'Between Impunity and Show Trials', in J. A. Frowein and R. Wolfrum (eds.), *Max Planck Yearbook of United Nations Law, Volume 6* (The Hague, the Netherlands: Kluwer Law International, 2002), 1–35.

[704] Balingene Kahombo makes a similar point in the context of the DRC. In his view, 'the problems of the Congolese legal system are not due to incongruities of Congolese positive law with international standards', notwithstanding their 'numerous flaws'; rather, justice is 'suffocated by political power'. See Kahombo, 'Comment – the Congolese Legal System and the Fight against Impunity for the Most Serious International Crimes', in *Inducing Compliance with International Human Rights Law*, 259.

Kenya's charged domestic politics were largely absent from the 2008 parliamentary debate on the ICA's passage, yet the unexpected swiftness of the ICC's intervention there radically altered the political landscape. This, in turn, led to repeated threats to nullify the domestic legislation, withdraw from the ICC and (successfully) derail its proceedings.

By contrast, complementarity's coercive power was largely absent in the DRC, in favour of what was intended to be from the outset a more cooperative arrangement. However, here, too, political considerations were the primary drivers of domestic action. With presidential elections on the horizon in 2011, the need to be seen as 'doing something' led Kabila's administration to push for action in the form of a special chambers bill, even as it ignored a complementary Rome Statute implementation bill. Indeed, rather than pass legislation to pursue cases the ICC might otherwise covet, the government waited until most of those cases were already taken. It was not until 2015 – after the passage of legislation granting civilian courts concurrent jurisdiction over international crimes, and after international NGOs took more of a backseat to advocacy than they had in 2010/2011 – that domestic implementation legislation finally passed. At the same time, while political mistrust in international judicial intervention may have delayed the passage of comprehensive implementing legislation, it also appeared to encourage a more syncretic approach in the longer run. Indeed, political contestation within the DRC was itself a catalyst that allowed other implementation strategies to take root, including the direct application of the Rome Statute by Congolese military judges, effectively bypassing parliamentary assent.[705]

Finally, it is clear from the trajectory of these debates that, in most cases, domestic NGO coalitions were stimulated and supported by larger, international organizations who saw Rome Statute implementation not only as a way to facilitate cooperation with the ICC or enable domestic prosecutions, but also as a step in broader criminal justice reform. Abolition of the

[705] See Jacques B. Mbokani, *Congolese Jurisprudence under International Criminal Law: An Analysis of Congolese Military Court Decisions Applying the Rome Statute – A Review by Open Society Initiative for South Africa (OSISA) OSISA-DRC* (Open Society Foundations, 2016), 377 (praising the 'extraordinary dynamism of Congolese military judges', who 'unquestionably deserve a great deal of credit for having been able to free themselves from the sluggishness of Congolese lawmakers in passing a suitable law for dealing with the crimes under the Rome Statute'). This text was previously published in French as *La jurisprudence Congolaise en matière de crimes de droit international: Une analyze des decisions des juridictions militaires Congolaises en application du Statut de Rome* (Open Society Foundations); it is accessible at www.africanminds.co.za/wp-content/uploads/2017/07/9781928331421OSISADRCtextfrench.pdf.

death penalty is perhaps the clearest illustration of such reform efforts. The normative stake of many of these actors, however, has largely been to preserve the Rome Statute in its technically correct or 'pure' form, transplanting its complex substantive and unique procedural provisions into national legal frameworks. One sees in this process a certain decoupling from the politics of the Statute's enactment and the text of the legislation itself. The proliferation of 'model laws' and legal tools – most of which copy the Statute in both content and form – can be understood as a means towards this end.

A focus on the 'ceremonial conformity' of Uganda's ICC Act and Kenya's ICA with the Rome Statute can thus be understood as a desire to gain or maintain international legitimacy, but it also reflects the power and influence of private, non-state actors to mediate the relationship between the international and national spheres.[706] The symmetry of both the ICC Act and ICA with the Rome Statute's substantive and procedural provisions also underscores the influence of these actors in the social construction of a new norm of complementarity, one that, as outlined in Chapter 2, became increasingly unshackled from its legal constraints as an admissibility principle in the service of a broader governance goal: compliance. This goal may be normatively desirable; however, it also risks supplanting democratic deliberation with what Drumbl has called 'a treaty-centered international administrative bureaucracy', contributing to a 'whittling down of democratic input in important aspects of national lawmaking' and a 'homogenizing effect on the kind of sanction visited upon atrocity perpetrators'.[707] The presentation of implementation as an international duty rather than a choice (or even a priority) amongst domestic political actors has arguably contributed to such homogenization.

And yet 'distortions' in implementation are an issue of pluralism; they are an inevitable product of importing new principles into an established legal system.[708] In her work on the 'translation' of international

---

[706] Marion Fourcade and Joachim J. Savelsberg, 'Global Processes, National Institutions, Local Bricolage: Shaping Law in an Era of Globalization', *Law & Social Inquiry* 31(3) (2006), 516. For a trenchant critique of a similar power dynamic in the context of post-Soviet countries, see Mertus, 'From Legal Transplants to Transformative Justice', 1377–1384.

[707] Drumbl, *Atrocity, Punishment, and International Law*, 70, 135. For a similar critique in the context of constitutional drafting, see Sara Kendall, '"Constitutional Technicity": Displacing Politics through Expert Knowledge', *Law, Culture and the Humanities* 11(3) (2015).

[708] On the relationship between 'legal transplantation' and ICL, see Cassandra Steer, 'Legal Transplants or Legal Patchworking? The Creation of International Criminal Law as a Pluralistic Body of Law', in Elies van Sliedregt and Sergey Vasiliev (eds.), *Pluralism in International Criminal Law* (Oxford: Oxford University Press, 2014).

law into local justice, the anthropologist Sally Engle Merry contends that the efficacy of human rights depends on their 'need to be translated into local terms and situated within local contexts of power and meaning'. In other words, they need 'to be remade in the vernacular'.[709] Merry helpfully defines translation as 'the process of adjusting the rhetoric and structures of … programs or interventions to local circumstances', but she notes that the process can also yield replication: rather than a merger of global frames with local forms (hybridization), they are appropriated wholesale.[710]

Analogized to the implementation efforts detailed herein, there is little evidence of such vernacular 'remaking' in Kenya or Uganda, and increasingly less in DRC post-2015. In the former countries, the Statute's core substantive and procedural provisions were copied, based almost entirely on 'model' ICC legislation that had been prepared for export. Rather than an opportunity to tailor domestic legislation to reflect more localized concerns and desires – to encompass, for instance, suggestions that it incorporate the crime of pillage or corporate liability or to accommodate other transitional justice measures – implementation was instead an exercise in mimicry. Similarly, whereas the 2002 MCC and earlier domestic court decisions in DRC reflected greater hybridity – with divergent definitions of Rome Statute crimes and uneven incorporation of its procedural provisions – the 2015 legislation hewed closer to the ICC's statutory text, consequently narrowing the protective scope of previous domestic legislation (e.g., excluding political groups as a protected class). Parallel efforts to persuade domestic DRC judges to apply the Rome Statute directly in criminal proceedings, including its prohibition on capital punishment, ran alongside these legislative efforts.

This mimicry is not accidental. As noted, much of the academic literature and related advocacy materials have deliberately presented complementarity as requiring uniformity with the Rome Statute, while the

---

[709] Sally Engle Merry, *Human Rights and Gender Violence: Translating International Law into Local Justice* (Chicago: University of Chicago Press, 2006), 1. For a similar argument in the context of rule-of-law promotion, see Zimmerman, *Global Norms with a Local Face*. Kamari Clarke takes Merry's attention to 'vernacularization' further, suggesting 'certain relations are governed by a *politics of incommensurability*', which 'cannot be explained in terms of particular forms of norm internalization or straightforward attempts to supplant vernacular forms, nor can they be understood as simply vernacularization'. See *Fictions of Justice*, 32.

[710] Ibid., 135. In a similar vein, Drumbl notes that 'Pressures emanating from dominant international norms [can] narrow the diversity of national and local accountability modalities'. Drumbl, *Atrocity, Punishment, and International Law*, 121.

ICC itself has adopted the language of the 'mirror' in weighing admissibility determinations. NGO implementation materials and other capacity-building programs have been similarly designed. Indeed, even though international law certainly permits amendments in the form of broader protection at the national level, few (if any) of these materials encourage them. Moreover, the focus on identical implementation at national level raises troubling questions about the African continent's equal and consensual participation in the creation of this body of law, a question that several domestic lawmakers in Kenya and Uganda also raised.

6   Conclusion

Implementation narratives often present the process as a linear progress march towards global compliance – as something above the state, rather than a part of it. Model laws and toolkits facilitate this legalist vision; however, as this chapter has suggested, such questions of technique overwhelmingly privilege uniformity with the Rome Statute, often stifling deeper political debates within the state itself. In Uganda, subsequent efforts to abandon the country's long-standing amnesty program were met with strong opposition, signalling significant discomfort amongst some with the domestic legislation's retributive framework. Similarly, in Kenya, the initiation of ICC investigations in 2009 fractured the apparent unanimity of political elites over the desirability of the domestic legislation that had been ratified only one year prior, even as it united former political rivals Kenyatta and Ruto.

Furthermore, despite the passage of Rome Statute legislation in all three countries, implementation appears to have had little influence on the actual conduct of national investigations and prosecutions. Of the handful of cases related to the ICC's investigation that have been prosecuted domestically in Kenya, they have been for ordinary crimes. Similarly, in the DRC, judges have drawn interpretive guidance from the Rome Statute in the adjudication of international crimes since well before the passage of the country's 2015 ICC legislation, while, to date, that legislation has not been the source of law for prosecutions before Congolese courts. As yet, it is unclear whether it will be.

Finally, the outsized role of external actors and constituencies in these processes (most of who regard deviation from the Statute with suspicion) also raises questions about who the agents of implementation are, as well as the content and form of the domestic legislation that is enacted. Efforts to progressively narrow discussions about alternative forms of justice from the Ugandan ICC Act, the DRC's 2002 code or the mistaken belief that a domestic Rome Statute could not incorporate economic crimes in Kenya, suggest a view of implementation driven less by domestic political interests than in mimicking the Statute as a 'global script'. The following chapter explores this phenomenon in greater detail, from the perspective of the creation of domestic courts.

6

Competing, Complementing, Copying

Domestic Courts and Complementarity

This chapter examines the emergence of specialized domestic courts or chambers for international crimes as one of the most frequently cited effects catalysed by International Criminal Court (ICC) interventions. If a fundamental 'rule' of the complementarity-as-catalyst framework is that national-level actors investigate and prosecute international crimes themselves, ensuring domestic venues for their prosecution is a key preoccupation for state and non-state actors alike. The attendant focus of much complementarity discourse has thus been on the establishment of institutions at the national level that are capable of accommodating such prosecutions. As Human Rights Watch has put it, 'The ICC's authority to act only where national authorities are unable or unwilling ... encourages the development of credible and independent judicial systems within national jurisdictions'.[711]

Similarities and differences mark the domestic judicial arrangements of Uganda, Kenya and the Democratic Republic of Congo (DRC) in response to the ICC's intervention in each country. In Uganda, the establishment of a special division within the High Court in which to adjudicate Rome Statute crimes, now called the International Crimes Division, was the key domestic institution whose creation was catalysed by the threat of the court's engagement. In Kenya, efforts to create a special tribunal for the country's post-election violence represented a high-water mark in the establishment of a domestic accountability process in lieu of ICC proceedings. As the previous chapter illustrated, the failure to establish the Special Tribunal for Kenya (STK) suggests the limits of the court's catalytic potential; however, following this failure, subsequent discussions later contemplated the establishment of an International Crimes Division (ICD) akin to Uganda's within Kenya's High Court system.

In both cases, these divisions have been created or proposed to satisfy perceived obligations under the ICC's complementarity regime, although

---

[711] Human Rights Watch, 'Establishing a Special Tribunal for Kenya and the Role of the International Criminal Court: Questions and Answers' (25 March 2009), 3.

there has been only one attempted domestic prosecution to date before the Ugandan ICD related to the Lord's Resistance Army (LRA) conflict. By contrast, in the DRC, domestic military courts have undertaken a far greater (if still limited) number of prosecutions following failed efforts in 2010/11, and again in 2014, to create special chambers for the prosecution of international crimes. Significantly, however, the DRC's courts were not created in response to the ICC's involvement in the country; rather, they have had longstanding jurisdiction over international crimes. A more recent turn to domestic prosecutions through the use of so-called 'mobile' courts in the eastern DRC region represents a novel invocation of complementarity (explored further in Chapter 7); however, most of these efforts have been undertaken by international donors and NGO actors, who have deliberately sought to characterize the courts as an extension of and 'complementary' to the ICC's work.

This chapter first offers a descriptive account of the various domestic judicial institutions outlined above, tracing the history of their establishment (or attempted establishment) vis-à-vis the ICC's interventions in each of the countries. It also considers the shifting ways and competing purposes in which complementarity has been invoked as the basis for the existence of these courts. Here, again, the central premise is that the ICC's role as catalyst rests on the polysemy of complementarity. In certain cases, the threat of the court's jurisdiction has been used to prompt the setting up (or attempted setting up) of domestic legal bodies. In this sense, the ICC's catalytic potential has been largely coercive. By contrast, recent descriptions of these bodies depict them more literally as institutional extensions of the ICC: rather than displacing the court, they are meant to complement, and even 'complete', its work. A related depiction has been of complementarity as a cooperative venture, wherein a managerial, division-of-labour approach between The Hague and national institutions is meant to facilitate the pursuit of accountability at the domestic level.

But while the establishment of national courts specialized in the adjudication of serious crimes is typically presented as a normative good, their depiction by ICC advocates as part of complementarity 'in practice' has been largely directed towards an international audience of donors, norm entrepreneurs and other states. To that end, in its second half, the chapter focuses more closely on the manner in which these courts have evolved at the national level, the donor economies that surround them and some of the institutional tensions that are produced through these arrangements. In doing so, complementarity's dualities come again to the fore: its impulse towards conformity (between the design of specialized domestic courts and the ICC) and towards competition (between the exceptionalism of specialized courts and their relationship to a country's ordinary justice system). Borrowing a concept from evolutionary biology, I suggest the concept of a 'justice meme' as one way in which domestic conformity with ICC structures and practices – typically, but vaguely shorthanded as 'international standards' – has been transmitted as part of the compliance-centred understanding of complementarity.

1   Uganda

Complementarity as Coercion: The ICC and Juba

Uganda was the first country in which the ICC intervened and also the first to set up a specialized judicial forum for the prosecution of Rome Statute crimes. Established in 2008 as the War Crimes Division (WCD; later rebranded the International Crimes Division), the forum is a specialized division of the Ugandan High Court with jurisdiction to try war crimes, genocide and crimes against humanity, as well as other serious transnational crimes, including human trafficking, piracy and terrorism. Although it has yet to convict any individuals related to the LRA conflict, the court to date has received a great deal of attention. As Nouwen notes, it is '[p]ossibly the most visible effect indirectly catalysed by complementarity in Uganda', one that 'has become the focus of donors' transitional-justice interest'.[712]

Although the establishment of the WCD has often been depicted as a product of the ICC's investigations, the history of its establishment is more accurately traced to the Juba peace talks that sought to bring a negotiated settlement to the government's long running conflict with the LRA.[713] The Ugandan government formally announced the referral of the 'situation concerning the Lord's Resistance Army' in January 2004.[714] At the time, as many commentators have noted, the ICC referral suited the interests of both the ICC and Uganda. For the Museveni government, it was an opportunity to 'rally international assistance for the arrest of the government's military opponents', as well as a savvy 'international

---

[712] Nouwen, *Complementarity in the Line of Fire*, 179.
[713] See, e.g., Wes Rist, 'Why Uganda's New War Crimes Court Is a Victory for the ICC', JURIST (29 May 2008), at http://jurist.org/forum/2008/05/why-ugandas-new-war-crimes-court-is.php (arguing that 'the ICC has been the key player in using the threat of international criminal responsibility to create a judicial body that can address the same issues of war crimes and crimes against humanity at the domestic rather than international level').
[714] OTP Press Release, 'President of Uganda Refers Situation Concerning the Lord's Resistance Army (LRA) to the ICC', 29 January 2004.

relations campaign'.[715] Furthermore, it was a low-risk approach given the unlikelihood that the Office of the Prosecutor (OTP), despite having recharacterized the referral as concerning the situation in northern Uganda (rather than the LRA alone), would pursue investigations against Ugandan military officials (UPDF). Meanwhile, for the ICC, the 'voluntary referral of a compelling case by a state party represented both an early expression of confidence in the nascent institution's mandate and a welcome opportunity to demonstrate its viability'.[716] This view was endorsed by Pre-Trial Chamber II, which accepted the government's contention that the ICC was the 'most appropriate and effective forum' for investigating those bearing the greatest responsibility in the conflict, and its assertion that it was 'unable' to arrest the LRA leadership.[717]

For these reasons, cooperation between the ICC and Uganda was the dominant logic in the early phase of the court's intervention. This logic began to change, however, in mid-2006 when, for the first time, the Ugandan government and the LRA entered into an internationally mediated peace negotiation. Although previous attempts at a negotiated settlement had proven unsuccessful, the Juba peace talks benefited from a changed political calculus on both sides: the Ugandan government was under increasing pressure to ameliorate the humanitarian situation in the north (and appeared no closer to apprehending Kony following the ICC referral), while the LRA had lost the support of the government of Sudan, its primary benefactor.[718] The talks were thus seen as a credible attempt to find a peaceful solution to the conflict.[719] After signing a cessation of

---

[715] Nouwen and Werner, 'Doing Justice to the Political', 949. The government's previous attempts at defeating the LRA had chiefly been through unsuccessful military campaigns and a policy of forced displacement, resulting in a growing humanitarian crisis that was weakening the government's (faltering) international standing. These campaigns included Operation North (Operation Simsim) in 1991, Operation Iron Fist in 2002 and Operation Iron Fist in 2004. While President Museveni had always favoured a military approach, he had on occasion allowed peace initiatives, such as the one undertaken by Betty Bigombe, then Ugandan minister for the pacification of the north, in 1994. For a detailed history, see Branch, *Displacing Human Rights*.

[716] Payam Akhavan, 'The Lord's Resistance Army Case: Uganda's Submission of the First State Referral to the International Criminal Court', *American Journal of International Law* 99(2) (2005), 404. See also Clark, 'Chasing Cases', 1198–1202.

[717] *Situation in Uganda*, Warrant of Arrest for Joseph Kony, ICC-02/04-01/05-53, PTC II, 8 July 2005 (as amended on 27 September 2005), para. 37 (citing government letter from Uganda's Solicitor General).

[718] See International Crisis Group, 'Northern Uganda: Seizing the Opportunity for Peace', Report no. 124 (2007).

[719] Refugee Law Project, 'Ambiguous Impacts: The Effects of the International Criminal Court Investigations in Northern Uganda', Working Paper no. 22 (October 2012), 7.

hostilities agreement in August 2006,[720] four additional agreements were concluded over the course of the next 18 months.[721]

In the shadow of these negotiations stood the ICC's arrest warrants for Kony and four other senior LRA members, which had been unsealed in October 2005.[722] Despite the progress being made in Juba, one of the key points of contention was the question of accountability, as the LRA had demanded from the outset that the ICC's warrants be withdrawn. It was in response to this point of contention – a desire to displace the ICC in order to secure Kony's support for a negotiated peace – that the court, by reference to the principle of complementarity, catalysed the creation of what would become the WCD. As Nouwen notes, 'The closest thing the [government of Uganda] could offer the LRA was to conduct domestic proceedings'.[723] In this way, it would be either for the government or the ICC suspects to successfully challenge admissibility under the Rome Statute.

The 'Agreement on Accountability and Reconciliation (A&R) between the Government of Uganda and the Lord's Resistance Army', signed in June 2007, laid the legal framework for these arrangements.[724] This was followed by the signing of an annexure in February 2008, which set out a framework for the A&R Agreement's implementation.[725] The agreement states at the outset that its purpose is to 'promote national legal arrangements ... for ensuring justice and reconciliation with respect to the conflict'.[726] Point 6.1 further reads:

> Formal courts provided for under the constitution shall exercise jurisdiction over individuals who are alleged to bear particular responsibility for the most serious crimes, especially crimes amounting to international crimes, during the course of the conflict.[727]

---

[720] Agreement on Cessation of Hostilities between the Government of the Republic of Uganda and Lord's Resistance Army Movement (Agenda Item no. 1), 26 August 2006.

[721] Other agreements focused on comprehensive solutions; the disarmament, demobilization and reintegration of LRA forces; and on a permanent cease-fire. See Comprehensive Solutions Agreement (Agenda Item no. 2), 2 May 2007; Permanent Ceasefire Agreement (Agenda Item no. 4), 23 February 2008; Agreement on Disarmament, Demobilization and Reintegration of the LRA Forces (Agenda Item no. 5), 29 February 2008. All documents available at www.beyondjuba.org/BJP1/peace_agreements.php.

[722] The other warrants of arrest were for Vincent Otti, Raska Lukwiya (deceased), Okot Odhiambo and Dominic Ongwen.

[723] Nouwen, *Complementarity in the Line of Fire*, 133.

[724] Accountability and Reconciliation Agreement (Agenda Item no. 3), 29 June 2007 ('A&R Agreement').

[725] Annexure to the Agreement on Accountability and Reconciliation, 19 February 2008 ('Annexure'), at   www.iccnow.org/documents/Annexure_to_agreement_on_ Accountability_signed_today.pdf.

[726] A&R Agreement. Clause. 2.1.

[727] Ibid., Clause 6.1.

Notably, the language of the A&R Agreement did not restrict itself to formal criminal justice mechanisms alone: it also acknowledged 'reconciliation proceedings', while the annexure provided for a national truth-telling process, reparations and a role for traditional justice mechanisms.[728]

Although the A&R Agreement does not invoke the principle of complementarity by name, the annexure does. In it, the parties recalled 'their commitment to preventing impunity and promoting redress in accordance with the constitution and international obligations and recalling, in this connection, *the requirements* of the Rome Statute of the [ICC] and in particular the principle of complementarity'.[729] The annexure further provided for the establishment of a 'special division of the High Court of Uganda ... to try individuals who are alleged to have committed serious crimes during the conflict', as well as 'a unit for carrying out investigations and prosecutions in support of trials and other formal proceedings'.[730] In the end, however, the Final Peace Agreement (FPA) – a collection of the agreements reached over the course of the negotiations – was never signed. Kony, unconvinced that the A&R Agreement would indeed keep the ICC at bay, ignored the government's ultimatum that the FPA be signed by the end of November 2008. Shortly thereafter, the Ugandan military renewed its offensive against the LRA, which continues to operate today outside of the country, largely in remote eastern regions of the DRC.[731]

Uganda's International Crimes Division

Despite not being signed, the Ugandan government expressed its intention to unilaterally implement the FPA agreement to the extent that it could. Amongst the agreement's provisions, implementation of the special division has advanced the furthest. Indeed, while the ICD is already operational, the other transitional justice measures foreseen under the A&R Agreement have developed only haltingly.[732] Indeed, writing in 2015, Stephen Oola noted that Uganda's formal transitional justice policy,

---

[728] For instance, Clause 3.1 of the agreement states: 'Where a person has already been subjected to proceedings [...] or has been subjected to accountability *or reconciliation proceedings* for any conduct in the course of the conflict, that person shall not be subjected to any other proceedings with respect to that conduct' (emphasis added).

[729] Annexure, Fifth Recital (emphasis added).

[730] Ibid., Clauses 7 and 10.

[731] On joint military operations between the Uganda People's Defence Force (UPDF) and the United States Africa Command (AFRICOM), see Branch, 216–239.

[732] Interview with Uganda Law Reform Commission (Kampala, 13 December 2011).

overseen by a Justice Law and Order Sector (JLOS) National Transitional Justice Working Group, 'has dragged on for eight years and, despite being now on its sixth draft, has yet to be finalized, let alone operationalized'.[733] Its ultimate fate remains unclear. Donor interest, likewise, has dwindled, with strategies 'shifting away from dealing with the past to focusing on the present'.[734]

The court, however, was formally established as the WCD in July 2008 pursuant to an administrative notice issued by then Chief Justice James Ogoola, who ordered it staffed with judges and a registrar. This notice – an act of administrative fiat – effectively served as the statutory basis for the court. In 2011, by a similar act of fiat, the WCD was rebranded the ICD, with practice directions that expanded the division's jurisdiction to include other transnational offences including piracy, human trafficking and terrorism, as well as Uganda's 2010 International Criminal Court Act, the 1964 Geneva Conventions Act and the Penal Code Act.[735] Its current docket has largely encompassed terrorism-related cases, notably the Kampala bombings of 2010.[736] As discussed further in the next chapter, only one case related to the LRA conflict has actually come before the division to date: that of former LRA commander (and former child soldier) Thomas Kwoyelo.

---

[733] Stephen Oola, 'Will LRA Victims Get Justice?', *Saturday Monitor* (11 August 2015). In 2013, the JLOS Working Group had reportedly circulated a draft 'National Transitional Justice Policy', which was then finalized five years later. See JLOS, National Transitional Justice Policy (March 2018) (on-file). The policy foresees, inter alia, the passage of a Transitional Justice Act and the expansion of Uganda's Amnesty Commission to address reparations, traditional justice mechanisms and reconciliation. Ibid., 31. For a similar conclusion, see Macdonald, 'Somehow This Whole Process Became So Artificial', 236 (noting that 'observers express concern that the draft policy will continue to gather dust, or will be bounced around because it is not in the executive's interest to push forward').

[734] Tania Bernath, 'Off the Agenda as Uganda Moves toward Development', in Paige Arthur and Christalla Yakinthou (eds.), *Transitional Justice, International Assistance, and Civil Society: Missed Connections* (Cambridge: Cambridge University Press, 2018), 114–143. For a similar assessment of donor dynamics following the post-election crisis in Kenya, see Stephen Brown and Rosalind Raddatz, 'Dire Consequences or Empty Threats? Western Pressure for Peace, Justice and Democracy in Kenya', *Journal of Eastern African Studies* 8(1) (2014), 43–62.

[735] The High Court (International Crimes Division) Practice Directions 2011 – Legal Notices Supplement to the Uganda Gazette no. 38 Volume CIV (31 May 2011) (on-file).

[736] See, e.g., JLOS Annual Performance Report 2014/15 (September 2015), 69; Kasande Sarah Kihika and Meritxell Regué, 'Pursuing Accountability for Serious Crimes in Uganda's Courts: Reflections on the Thomas Kwoyelo Case', ICTJ (January 2015), 3 (noting that with its expanded jurisdiction, the 'ICD now has nine cases, most of which involve human trafficking and terrorism').

Notably, while the 2011 practice directions provided that the ICD would apply the same rules of procedure and evidence applicable to criminal trials in Uganda, it left an opening for more specialized procedures as well. Subsequently, special rules of procedure and evidence were adopted in August 2016, following extensive consultations with an array of international NGOs and advisors.[737] These procedures mimic a number of ICC procedures, including, inter alia, the introduction of pre-trial proceedings and the establishment of a confirmation of charges phase, a victim participation regime and general provisions on protective measures.

Structurally, the ICD sits as a panel minimally comprised of three judges, although the total division consists of five judges. Uganda's principal judge appoints them, in consultation with the High Court Chief Justice. One of the ICD judges serves as head of the division, and is responsible for its administration, in cooperation with the registrar.[738] Initially, judges rotated out of the division since it is 'common for judges, registrars, prosecutors, and investigators in Uganda to be frequently rotated on and off work relating to specific divisions'.[739] The ICD is headquartered in Kampala although it is mobile in the sense that the judges can travel. Proceedings related to the Kwoyelo trial have to date taken place both at the Gulu High Court in northern Uganda, as well as the division's seat in Kampala. Decisions of the ICD can be appealed to Uganda's Constitutional Court and, in the final instance, to the Supreme Court.[740]

The ICD receives technical assistance through JLOS, which, in 2008, established a high level Transitional Justice Working Group to 'give

---

[737] Statutory Instruments 2016 no. 40, The Judicature (High Court) (International Crimes Division) Rules, 2016 – Supplement to the Uganda Gazette no. 42, Volume CIX (15 June 2016) (on-file).

[738] Interview with ICD judge (Kampala, 13 December 2011). Attached to the ICD are a series of relevant units. A unit of Uganda's Directorate of Public Prosecutions oversees the ICD's prosecutorial function, although the prosecutors appointed to that unit may also be responsible for crimes not heard by the ICD. A similar unit resides within the Criminal Investigations Department and is responsible for investigating crimes that may be tried before the division.

[739] Human Rights Watch, 'Justice for Serious Crimes before National Courts: Uganda's International Crimes Division' (2012), 19.

[740] JLOS, 'Frequently Asked Questions on the International Crimes Divisions of the High Court of Uganda', 5, at www.judicature.go.ug/files/downloads/ICD_FAQs.pdf.

effect to the provisions of the Juba Peace Agreement'.[741] JLOS oversees the budgetary allocation of the ICD, a substantial portion of which, as discussed further below, relies on international donor support. As of late 2017, about ten prosecutors had been assigned to handle cases before the ICD, five of whom act on 'special duty' to prosecute the Kwoyelo case.[742]

From Competing to Complementing

The creation of Uganda's ICD initially placed the ICC and the Ugandan government in an antagonistic relationship. As the ICD has developed, however, its origins as an outcome of the A&R Agreement have evolved away from a competition-based model of complementarity – a way to displace the ICC – towards a more harmonious, cooperative vision of the principle. The ICD's website states that 'While originally meant to be part of a comprehensive peace agreement with the LRA, the International Crimes Division has come to be viewed as a court of 'complementarity' with respect to the International Criminal Court, thus fulfilling the principle of complementarity stipulated in the preamble and Article 1 of the Rome Statute'.[743]

A 2010 publication of the Uganda Law Society likewise notes that 'the War Crimes Division of the High Court of Uganda has been set up as a complementary institution to the ICC', while the Ugandan Victims Foundation's legal advisor has suggested that a 'running and well equipped WCD of Uganda has the potential of becoming a regional criminal tribunal which may complement well the work of the ICC'.[744] And in the words of one judicial spokesperson, '[T]his court now complements the [International Criminal Court]. We now have the

---

[741] "'The Dust Has Not Yet Settled": Victims' Views on the Right to Remedy and Reparation – A Report from the Greater North of Uganda', United National Human Rights Office of the High Commissioners (Kampala, 2011), 59. The Transitional Justice Working Group is comprised of five thematic sub-committees including: (1) war crimes prosecutions; (2) truth and reconciliation; (3) traditional justice; (4) sustainable funding; and (5) integrated systems.

[742] For further details on the ICD's staffing, framework and financing, see *Options for Justice: A Handbook for Designing Accountability Mechanisms for Grave Crimes* (Open Society Foundations, 2018), 278–291, at www.opensocietyfoundations.org/sites/default/files/options-for-justice-20180918.pdf.

[743] International Crimes Division, available at www.judicature.go.ug.

[744] 'Does the High Court of Uganda Have a Wider Jurisdiction than the ICC?', *Lawyers' Voice* (July–September 2010), 5; Joseph A. Manoba, 'First Trial before the War Crimes Division of the High Court in Uganda', VRWG Bulletin, Issue 17 (Winter 2010), 6.

equivalent of Geneva or The Hague in Africa'.[745] Burden-sharing, at least rhetorically, thus appears to now define complementarity in Uganda, wherein the ICD and ICC are positioned as partners in a cooperative, joint enterprise.

This shift is striking as compared to the Ugandan government's response to a 2008 request by the ICC Pre-Trial Chamber for information on the implication of the division's establishment, where it averred that 'those individuals who were indicted by the [ICC] will have to be brought before the special division of the High Court for trial'.[746] The ICC never opined on this admissibility question given its prematurity; however, the government later indicated that – notwithstanding the substantial investment of resources that have been made into the ICD – it would not seek to challenge the admissibility of any of the ICC's outstanding cases.[747] Indeed, speaking at a 2012 conference, Uganda's state minister for justice and deputy attorney general, Freddie Ruhindi, indicated that while he was confident the Ugandan courts could try the LRA leader, Kony, if apprehended, would nevertheless be sent to the ICC for trial.[748] The January 2015 arrest and transfer of LRA commander Dominic Ongwen to The Hague confirmed Ruhindi's statement. Questions about Uganda's primary duty to investigate and prosecute Rome Statute crimes thus became, as Nouwen notes, 'increasingly detached from the possibility of actually using the right in order to challenge admissibility'.[749]

---

[745] Nouwen, *Complementarity in the Line of Fire*, 181 (quoting Cyprian Musoke, 'Uganda: Nation Ready to Try Col. Gaddafi', *New Vision*, 11 June 2011).

[746] See Letter from Jane F. B. Kiggundu, solicitor general, reply to request for information from the Republic of Uganda on the status of execution of the warrants of arrest, ICC-02/04-01/05-285-Anx2, government of Uganda (27 March 2008); see also Uganda Admissibility Decision. The letter further clarified that the government referred the situation to the ICC 'because the leadership of the Lord's Resistance Army was beyond the borders of Uganda and the international community was not being helpful', not because of 'the competence of its courts to handle cases connected with the situation',

[747] See Florence Ogola, 'Uganda Victims Question ICC's Balance', Institute for War & Peace Reporting (14 June 2010). A similar assessment was made in the course of my interview with a senior DPP official (Kampala, December 2011).

[748] See Mark Kersten, 'Outsourcing Justice to the ICC – What Should Be Done?' (31 October 2012), at http://justiceinconflict.org/2012/10/31/outsourcing-justice-to-the-icc-what-should-be-done/. A senior ICD prosecutor indicated the same to me in an interview (Kampala, December 2011).

[749] Nouwen, *Complementarity in the Line of Fire*, 237.

2 Kenya

Special Tribunal for Kenya

As the previous chapter detailed, a key recommendation of the Commission of Inquiry on Post-Election Violence (CIPEV) was that a special tribunal be established to 'seek accountability against persons bearing the greatest responsibility for crimes, particularly crimes against humanity'.[750] Much like the A&R Agreements in Uganda, then, complementarity's coercive dimension was also the dominant logic behind CIPEV's recommendation. If a special tribunal was not established within a specified time frame, and if the government proved unwilling or unable to investigate and prosecute, the ICC might intervene. Ultimately, the 'unholy alliance' amongst those MPs who supported a domestic accountability process, but had substantive objections to the bill put forward by then Minister for Justice Karua – and those who considered the threat of ICC intervention less than that of a domestic process – doomed the tribunal's prospects.

Notably, many supporters of the STK option framed the proposal for the court in opposition to the ICC and as an opportunity for the country to exercise its sovereign power over the administration of criminal responsibility.[751] MP James Orengo, who seconded the bill, explicitly cast the STK in this light:

> I am happy that in Kenya, we have not allowed a foreign institution, or power, to either establish a court through some instrument, for example through the UN Security Council, or through some arrangement, regional or otherwise; we are doing it through this sovereign Parliament, which has the authority to establish the tribunal. To that effect, we were saying in the beginning that we cannot allow ourselves to be guided, or managed by other institutions of government which are not part of the instruments of power in Kenya as a whole.[752]

At the same time, the expression of sovereignty also resonated with those parliamentarians who opposed the special tribunal. One MP argued that the STK was itself a concession to foreign interference, characterizing it as a 'house we want to build with foreign materials'.[753]

---

[750] CIPEV Report, 472–473.
[751] See Kenya National Assembly Official Record (Hansard), The Constitution of Kenya (Amendment) Bill, Second Reading, 3 February 2009 ('STK Amendment Bill'), 36 (Minister Karua).
[752] Ibid., 38. MP Kilonzo invoked a similar call to sovereignty, noting, 'I want as a country, to respect our sovereignty by acknowledging that we are signatories to the International Criminal Court Charter. ... Let the citizens of other failed states go to the Hague', 46.
[753] Ibid., 43 (MP Danson Mungatana).

From Special Tribunal to International Division

The defeat of the STK – and the subsequent admissibility challenge that the Kenyan government filed before the ICC in early 2011 – helped lay the seeds for subsequent discussions around the establishment of an ICD in Kenya. Muthoni Wanyeki, a Kenyan human rights advocate, notes that the possibility of establishing a special division of the High Court was initially floated 'half-heartedly' by the subsequent minister for justice, Mutula Kilonzo, as an alternative to a private members' bill for a special tribunal that had been put forward in the wake of the STK's defeat.[754] This proposal was 'vigorously opposed', however, by the governance, human rights and legal sectors of civil society groups who argued that the investigative and prosecutorial arms of the judiciary were too compromised to be credible.[755]

Discussions around an ICD did not seriously re-emerge until the appointment of Willy Mutunga as chief justice and president of the Supreme Court. A dedicated human rights advocate, Mutunga's reformist credentials in Kenyan politics were well-known: his appointment was widely seen as a victory for the Kenyan left and, at the time, a promising step in the country's new constitutional dispensation.[756] (By contrast, the appointment of Keriako Tobiko as director of public prosecutions was considered a major defeat.[757]) In this capacity, Mutunga chaired the Judicial Services Commission (Kenya) (JSC), whose mandate encompasses the appointment of judges and advising on 'improving the efficiency of the administration of justice'.[758] In May 2012, at Mutunga's request, the JSC appointed a working committee to 'look into modalities of establishing an international crimes division in the High Court, to hear and make determination on the pending post-election violence cases and deal with other international and transnational crimes'.[759]

---

[754] Wanyeki, 'The International Criminal Court's Cases in Kenya', 9–10.
[755] Interview with Kenyan NGO director (Nairobi, 3 December 2012).
[756] Mutuma Ruteere, 'Dr. Willy Mutunga: Why They Fear Him', *The Nairobi Law Monthly* 2(6) (June 2011), 31–39.
[757] Interview with Kenyan human rights advocate (Nairobi, 16 June 2011).
[758] 'Judicial Service Commission – The Judiciary', at www.judiciary.go.ke/portal/the-judicial-service-commission.html.
[759] The Judicial Service Commission, 'Report of the Committee of the Judicial Service Commission on the Establishment of an International Crimes Division in The High Court of Kenya' (30 October 2012), 32 ('JSC Report') (on-file).

Chaired by the Reverend Samuel Kobia, the JSC's working committee published an extensive report in October 2012 setting forth six recommendations, the first of which called upon 'the chief justice to establish the International Crimes Division as a division of the High Court, to prosecute the pending post-election violence cases, international and transnational crimes'.[760] As with the Ugandan ICD, the legal framework for such a division would be rooted in the unlimited original jurisdiction of the High Court, while appeals would lie with the Kenyan Court of Appeal, and in the final instance, the Supreme Court. The division's proposed subject matter jurisdiction would include Rome Statute crimes (domesticated under Kenya's International Crimes Act 2008), but could be expanded to include transnational crimes as well: money laundering, cyber-laundering, human trafficking, terrorism and piracy. Other recommendations included the establishment of an independent prosecution unit with the Director of Public Prosecutions (DPP) 'to deal exclusively with international crimes', fully funding the country's existing (but underfunded) Witness Protection Agency, and setting up a 'special fund to help victims'.[761]

The commission's recommendation that an ICD be formed for 'international-scale crimes' – including, but not limited to the post-election violence – was partially endorsed in a May 2013 report of Kenyans for Peace with Truth and Justice (KTPJ). Although the coalition expressed a firm preference for a special tribunal option, it acknowledged that '[g]iven the lack of political will..., the special division option is more feasible, if not the only viable option in the near future'.[762] The report recommended that 'the overall structure of the accountability model take the form of a special division of the High Court', although it went further than the JSC's report, advocating as well for the establishment of a special prosecutor for the post-election violence cases and for the participation of international staff.[763] None of these recommendations ever received serious consideration.

Despite the focus of the JSC's report on the post-election violence and the prosecution of international crimes in particular, it was chiefly

---

[760] Ibid., 146. Section 8(2) of the International Crimes Act no. 16 of 2008 grants Kenya's High Court jurisdiction to conduct trials over persons responsible for international crimes committed locally or abroad by a Kenyan or committed in any place against a Kenyan as of January 2009. See Chapter 5 for further discussion.

[761] Ibid., 149.

[762] KPTJ, 'Securing Justice: Establishing a domestic mechanism for the 2007/8 post-election violence in Kenya' (May 2013), 49.

[763] Ibid., 51–53.

Mutunga's influence that led to the proposed expansion of the ICD's jurisdiction to include other transnational crimes (similar to Uganda, subsequent proposals came to refer to the IOCD, i.e., the International and Organised Crimes Division of the Kenyan High Court).[764] This proposal was of particular concern to civil society advocates who feared that the court may be more active as a forum for adjudicating transnational crimes, rather than post-election violence cases. Illustrative of that concern, an earlier proposal by the JSC to appoint a special prosecutor for the sole purpose of investigating post-election violence crimes within the ICD was opposed by the DPP, who argued that such powers were constitutionally vested in his office.[765] As a result, many advocates were sceptical of the proposed division, seeing it as yet another attempt to obstruct ICC proceedings in The Hague through the 'appearance' of complementarity. In KPTJ's words, 'the proposed ICD could end up being a white elephant, with no cases to prosecute'.[766]

Shifts in Complementarity

Whereas the threat of ICC intervention was clearly a catalyst for the attempted special tribunal in Kenya, the predominant driver behind the push for an ICD was then Chief Justice Mutunga (Mutunga took early retirement from his post in 2015). Following the STK's defeat, domestic leadership on the issue of accountability for election violence migrated almost totally to Kenya's judicial branch, particularly following the 2013 election

---

[764] The JSC report notes that 'The chief justice … prevailed on the committee to, during its conceptualization and design of the architecture of this court, devise mechanisms of vesting on the court [an] expansive mandate to deal with other international crimes and transnational crimes other than having jurisdiction only limited to international crimes as proscribed in Kenya's International Crimes Act, 2008', 31.

[765] Report of Second Stakeholder's Conference on the Proposed International Crimes Division (on-file). A compromise was later reached, wherein a special unit focused exclusively on post-election violence cases would be established within the DPP.

[766] KPTJ, 'A Real Option for Justice? The International Crimes Division of the High Court of Kenya', 9. It should be noted that an international crimes division within Kenya's DPP has since been established, although little is known about it. The formation of such a division was part of the injunctive relief requested by petitioners in domestic litigation that was subsequently filed alleging state failure to adequately investigate and prosecute post-election violence (see discussion in Chapter 7). A senior prosecutor in Kenya's DPP testified in March 2017 that there was an international crimes division now active in the office. See Tom Maliti, 'Senior Prosecutor Tells Kenyan Court About Challenges of Taking SGBV Cases to Trial', International Justice Monitor (31 March 2017).

of Kenyatta and Ruto.[767] The establishment of an ICD also promised to be more feasible than any attempt to revisit the failed special tribunal proposal, as that would have required a political impossibility: parliamentary assent.

Notwithstanding repeated efforts by various international organizations to 'train' Kenyan prosecutors and judges in 'best practices' to support the proposed division, the division ultimately proved to be a failed project.[768] In 2014, many civil society actors boycotted a February consultation convened by the government on the grounds that the process was not genuine, while statements attributed to DPP Tobiko at the same meeting suggested that his office did 'not believe the ICD is appropriate or necessary to prosecute post-election crimes'.[769] Undoubtedly, the collapse of the Kenyan cases in the ICC removed any remaining incentive that the government may have had to demonstrate that it was pursuing domestic accountability. At the same time, and not unlike Uganda, broader transitional justice efforts in Kenya have largely withered in the shadow of the collapsed ICD talks.[770]

---

[767] See JSC Report, 32, 40 ('The JSC now finds itself in the position of having to play a gigantic and momentous historic role of putting in place mechanisms to deal with and eliminate the culture of impunity that has for years been deeply ingrained in the socio-political fabric of the Kenyan society'.).

[768] For an extensive accounting by a leading non-profit organization involved in these efforts, see the Wayamo Foundation's final report, 'Complementarity in Practice: Capacity Building for the Establishment of the International and Organised Crimes Division (IOCD) of the Kenyan High Court' (December 2015) (on-file). Another reason for the Kenyan ICD's failure may also owe to a lack of support from international donors, whose previous strong support for accountability began to yield to political pressure following the election of Kenyatta and Ruto in 2013. See Patrick Mutahi and Mutuma Ruteere, 'Where is the Money? Donor Funding for Conflict and Violence Prevention in Eastern Africa', Institute of Development Studies, Evidence Report no. 217 (January 2017), 16 ('The Jubilee Government has … never quite mended relations with most of the country's donors and has at times refused to approve requests for development aid or to have joint programmes, especially those touching on governance. Indeed, donors note these frosty relations in their strategic plans, saying they are a point of concern and can affect their activities in Kenya'.).

[769] Amnesty International, 'Crying for Justice: Victims' Perspectives on Justice for the Post-Election Violence in Kenya' (July 2014), 26. According to the same report, 'as of June 2014, no concrete steps had been taken towards establishing the ICD', 25–26. Additionally, in December 2013, President Kenyatta temporarily suspended six JSC members after the National Assembly requested an investigation into allegations of misconduct and misappropriation of funds. Although a subsequent High Court ruling reinstated the six members pending the outcome of their legal challenge against the investigation, the allegations further stalled the JSC's efforts. See Mathews Ndanyi, 'Setbacks for Kenya's Special Court', *Institute for War & Peace Reporting* (23 December 2013), at http://iwpr.net/report-news/setback-kenyas-special-court.

[770] See Lynch, *Performances of Injustice*; Kimberly Lanegran, 'The Kenyan Truth, Justice and Reconciliation Commission: The Importance of Commissioners and Their Appointment Process', *Transitional Justice Review* 1(3) (2015), 42.

Still, the discourse in support of the ICD's establishment was notable given its shift away from a threat-based model of complementarity to one that instead painted the proposed ICD as an extension of the ICC's work, rather than an alternative to it. The JSC report endorsed, for example, the burden-sharing model of complementarity: the ICD would have tried 'middle and lower perpetrators of crimes against humanity as related to the post-election violence period', while the ICC would have dealt with those 'who bear the highest responsibility for crimes against humanity that were perpetrated against citizens'.[771] The Nairobi-based NGO Kituo cha Sheria similarly wrote that 'The ICD should be seen as complementary to the International Criminal Court that only holds those who bear the greatest responsibility to account'.[772] Prior to the collapse of the ICC's cases, the court's outreach coordinator in Kenya had also suggested an ICD would complement the ICC's work. In her words, 'It is not a question of comparing the ICD and the ICC. It is a question of the complementing role the two institutions can play to bring about justice to victims. It is our hope that the ICD will meet international standards'.[773]

3   Democratic Republic of Congo

Complementarity as Cooperation:
Understanding the DRC's ICC Referral

Like the A&R Agreement in Juba and the National Accords in Kenya, the Sun City Accords – the 2002 peace agreement that brought a nominal end to the DRC's long-running conflict – also foresaw the creation of accountability mechanisms for atrocity crimes. In December 2002, participants in the Inter-Congolese Dialogue (I-CD), meeting in Sun City, South Africa reached a Global and Inclusive Accord (*Accord Global et Inclusif*), which included recommendations regarding the establishment of a truth and reconciliation commission and an international special tribunal for war crimes in the DRC.[774] Subsequently, in September 2003,

---

[771] JSC Report, 98.
[772] Aimee Ongeso, 'An International Crimes Division in Kenya's High Court: Meaningful Justice or a White Elephant?', VRWG Bulletin, Issue 22 (Spring 2013), 3.
[773] Nzau Musau, 'ICC Welcomes International Crimes Court in Kenya', *The Star*, 7 February 2014 (quoting Maria Mabinty Kamara).
[774] The Commission on Peace and Reconciliation – one of the five commissions established under the I-CD – had been tasked with 'recommending measures to ensuring lasting peace within the national borders and security in the region'. The commission's recommendations were adopted by all I-CD delegates. See P. Bouvier and F. Bomboko, *Le Dialogue intercongolais, anatomie d'une négociation à la lisière du chaos*, Cahiers africains No 63–64 (Paris: L'Harmattan, 2004), 177–178.

the transitional government approved a decision to refer the situation in the DRC to the ICC and to request the creation by the United Nations (UN) Security Council of an international special tribunal to deal with crimes that fell outside the court's jurisdiction.[775] With respect to other mechanisms, little is known about the DRC's truth commission other than that its mandate ended in controversy in 2007, having opened no enquiries during its tenure and awarded no reparations.[776] One commentator has noted that the 'presence of belligerents' in the TRC and the 'lack of public engagement' in its creation, 'fundamentally undermined it from the start'.[777]

In 2004, President Kabila formally referred the situation to the ICC, initiating an engagement that has produced the greatest amount of prosecutorial and judicial activity for the court to date.[778] Yet whereas complementarity had an important coercive dimension in Kenya and, later, Uganda, this was not the case in the DRC. Indeed, from the outset, both the OTP and the Congolese government envisaged the ICC's intervention as a burden sharing arrangement between international and domestic jurisdictions. As Pascal Kambale has argued, the court's intervention in the DRC was premised on a 'clear division of labour whereby the ICC would prosecute a handful of individuals among those bearing the greatest responsibility, while the Congolese justice system, with the support of the international community, would take on other cases'.[779] For Kabila, the referral also held strategic interest: an invitation to the ICC symbolically signalled his administration's commitment to accountability, even as the court's post-2002 jurisdiction likely posed a greater threat to his political opponents than to Kabila himself.[780]

---

[775] Ibid.

[776] Little has been written about the DRC's truth commission although its performance was deeply criticized in the UN's Mapping Report's of 2010. See UN Mapping Report, paras. 1063–1072.

[777] Laura Davis, 'Power Shared and Justice Shelved: The Democratic Republic of Congo', *The International Journal of Human Rights* 17(2) (2013), 302.

[778] Letter of Referral from President Joseph Kabila to Prosecutor of the ICC (Kinshasa, 3 March 2004), ICC-01/04-01/06-32-US-Exp-AnxA1 12-03-2006 1/1UM (letter reproduced as Appendix I in Musila, 'Between Rhetoric and Action', 79–80).

[779] Pascal Kambale, 'A Story of Missed Opportunities: The Role of the International Criminal Court in the Democratic Republic of Congo', in *Contested Justice: The Politics and Practice of International Criminal Court Interventions*, 177.

[780] Phil Clark, 'Law, Politics and Pragmatism: The ICC and Case Selection in the Democratic Republic of Congo and Uganda', in *Courting Conflict?* 37–45.

The elements of such an arrangement were later outlined in a letter that the OTP sent to Kabila, soliciting his referral of the situation in the DRC in September 2003:

> Since the International Criminal Court will not be in a position to try all the individuals who may have committed crimes under its jurisdiction in Ituri, a consensual division of labour could be an effective approach. We could prosecute some of those individuals who bear the greatest responsibility for the crimes committed, while national authorities, with the assistance of the international community, implement appropriate mechanisms to deal with others. This would send a strong sign of the commitment of the Democratic Republic of the Congo to bring to justice those responsible for these crimes. In return, the international community may take a more resolved stance in the reconstruction of the national judiciary and in the re-establishment of the rule of law in the Democratic Republic of the Congo.[781]

The letter echoed then prosecutor Moreno-Ocampo's speech to the Assembly of States Parties earlier that month, where he noted that the court and the DRC 'may agree that a consensual division of labour could be an effective approach'. He added:

> The office could cooperate with the national authorities by prosecuting the leaders who bear most responsibility for the crimes. National authorities with the assistance of the international community could implement appropriate mechanisms to deal with other individuals responsible.[782]

[781] 'Letter from Prosecutor Luis Moreno-Ocampo to H. E. Joseph Kabila, president of the Democratic Republic of Congo', 25 September 2003 (quoted in Kambale, 'The ICC and Lubanga: Missed Opportunities'). Kambale notes that former Minister of Justice Ngele Masudi articulated this vision as well. In opening remarks at a meeting on the ICC in October 2002, Masudi 'indicated that the government's strategy to address war crimes was based on the principle of complementarity, by which he meant that the DRC would leave to the ICC the task of prosecuting those in the top leadership of armed groups who bore the greatest responsibility for crimes under the ICC jurisdiction, whereas the Congolese justice system would deal with the lower ranking perpetrators and the less complex crimes'. Ibid. See also Clark, 'Chasing Cases', 1188 ('the prosecutor and other OTP personnel engaged in lengthy discussions with the president's office in Kinshasa, outlining the domestic political benefits of ICC investigations into serious crimes'); Burke-White, 'Complementarity in Practice', 570–572 (quoting successor Minister of Justice Kisimba-Ngoy as also advocating a division of labour).

[782] Second Assembly of States Parties to the Rome Statute of the International Criminal Court Report of the prosecutor of the ICC, Mr Luis Moreno-Ocampo, 8 September 2003, at www.icc-cpi.int/NR/rdonlyres/C073586C-7D46-4CBE-B901-0672908E8639/143656/LMO_20030908_En.pdf.

The OTP's announcement of the formal opening of investigations in June 2004 – in which Moreno-Ocampo stated that his office would target only those 'people that bore the highest responsibility' – reinforced the intention to pursue a joint approach.[783] As a catalyst for accountability, then, complementarity in the DRC was envisioned less as a coercive arrangement than a cooperative one. Other benefits were also seen to accrue from this relationship, including the promise of state cooperation and a 'positive' role for the court in helping to build the state's own capacity and will to undertake prosecutions.

Unfortunately, this vision of the OTP's role largely failed to materialize: little of the skills or knowledge transfer that was envisioned took place. Colonel Toussaint Muntazini Mukimapa, who served as the focal point for cooperation between the ICC and the DRC's military justice system (until his appointment as chief prosecutor of the Special Criminal Court for the Central African Republic) has subsequently characterized the court's approach as 'a one-way street', with information flowing to The Hague, but not in reverse.[784] Similarly, as noted in Chapter 3, the OTP took a strong line against cooperation in the Katanga litigation, stating that 'the ICC was not created to be an international investigative bureau with resources to support national authorities'.[785] Finally, over time, it became clear that the individuals for whom the court had issued warrants were far from those who bore the highest responsibility.[786] Amidst pressure to begin bringing cases, the promise of a division-of-labour between the court and the DRC proved difficult to implement in practice.

---

[783] OTP Press Release, 'The Office of the Prosecutor of the International Criminal Court opens its first investigation', ICC-OTP-20040623-59, 23 June 2004.

[784] Interview with Colonel Muntazini (Kinshasa, 27 June 2011). The colonel noted in particular that one request for information had been made (in writing) to the OTP, but, after an initial exchange, it was not followed up on. Colonel Muntazini later wrote of his experience, stating that 'The DRC … cannot unfortunately help but express its frustration at having so little benefit from the ICC's consideration, when it could reasonably expect a better fate'. See 'A Close-Up Look at the Fight against Impunity in the DRC' (18 April 2016), at www.ictj.org/news/icc-drc-complementarity.

[785] OTP Response to Katanga Admissibility Challenge, paras. 100–101.

[786] See, e.g., Clark, 'Chasing Cases', who argues that 'Lubanga is at best a middle-ranking perpetrator, with more senior regional actors responsible for the crimes committed', 1191. Indeed, the Pre-Trial Chamber appeared to raise similar concerns when, following Lubanga's confirmation hearing, it stated that the OTP's charges failed to recognize the international nature of the conflict in eastern DRC, given the involvement of Rwanda and Uganda in arming opposition groups. See The Prosecutor v. Thomas Lubanga Dyilo, Decision sur la Confirmation des Charges, ICC-01/04-01/06-806, PTC I, 5 February 2007.

Turning Away from the ICC: Special Chambers
for the DRC (2010–2011)

The attempted creation of a special tribunal for the DRC for crimes committed dating back to 1993 reached a political turning point in late 2010, six years after the ICC began its investigations. As with the attempted passage of ICC implementation legislation that same year, the political momentum for a special tribunal owed largely to the August 2010 publication of the UN's long-awaited 'mapping' report on crimes committed in DRC between 1993 and 2003. Amongst its many recommendations, the report explicitly endorsed the creation of a 'mixed judicial mechanism – made up of national and international personnel – [as] the most appropriate way to provide justice for the victims of serious violations'.[787] More generally, as previously noted, the report also lent renewed interest and impetus for the establishment of a domestic accountability mechanism and prompted increasing pressure from international actors. The United States, in particular, put significant political weight behind the idea, building upon the momentum of a visit by former Secretary of State Hillary Clinton to the eastern Congo in 2009.[788] In contrast, reception by the OTP and other EU actors was more muted, including concerns that the proposal would be potentially 'duplicative' of other rule-of-law building efforts supported by the latter in eastern DRC.[789]

In November 2010, the Ministry of Justice circulated a government-sponsored bill (*projet de loi*) for the creation of so-called special chambers (*chambres specialises*).[790] The chief architect of the *projet de loi* was

---

[787] See UN Mapping Report, paras. 61–63.

[788] See the history of the initiative recounted in Luzolo Bambi Lessa and Ba Meya Nicolas Abel Bayona, *Manuel de Procedure Penale* (Presses Universitaires du Congo, 2011), 746–751, 758–761. Interviews in the DRC confirmed that US support for the mechanism was the most aggressive, in spite of persistent concerns about harmonization of the proposed *projet de loi* with Rome Statute implementing legislation. I also observed frequent reference to the proposal as 'putting complementarity into practice' by other officials from the State Department's Office of Global Criminal Justice.

[789] In interviews, several interlocutors conveyed concern about the speed with which the proposal for a special chambers seemed to be moving and about elements of its design (June 2011, Kinshasa). Although the ICC did not officially comment, OTP representatives apparently expressed scepticism about the proposal at an April 2011 seminar in Goma.

[790] In the DRC, a *projet de loi* is a government supported draft law endorsed in most cases by the ministry of justice. A *proposition de loi* is, by contrast, brought before Parliament by one or more parliamentarians, usually without government support (and occasionally with its explicit disapproval). The special chambers legislation was a *projet de loi*, while the Rome State implementation legislation (discussed in Chapter 6) was a *proposition de loi*.

the DRC's then minister of justice, Luzolo Bambi Lessa, although it was heavily influenced by the input of a number of international organizations. Though 'clearly unfinished' when it was first circulated, the ministry signalled unusual openness to external actors, convening a multi-sector conference of international and national NGOs to discuss improvements shortly after the bill was circulated.[791] The initial draft prepared by the government made clear that the chambers were intended to function within the existing court system, although it contemplated the possibility of appointing foreign judges and other international staff; hence, the proposal for 'mixed' chambers. Following extensive input from international and Congolese human rights NGOs, a three-member drafting committee that was appointed to collate the proposals of the stakeholders submitted a report that recommended the establishment of such a mechanism.[792] This proposal was later endorsed in the final version of the bill drafted by the Congolese Law Reform Commission, which submitted it to the National Assembly in April 2011.[793]

While non-state actors and donor states invoked complementarity in a literal sense in support of the special chambers proposal, government documents did not use the term. Rather, the Ministry of Justice's rationale for the proposal as presented to the National Assembly (*exposé des motifs*) was a litany of the ICC's failings and an indictment of the international community.[794] Of the latter, the ministry's note recalled the I-CD's support for a UN Security Council-sponsored tribunal to deal with crimes that fell outside of the ICC's jurisdiction. It states that Kabila had 'pleaded' for the creation of such a tribunal, but that his 'request was ignored by the United Nations and the international community', leaving the DRC government to

---

[791] Interview with EU Police Mission for the DRC (EUPOL) (Kinshasa, 23 June 2011).

[792] Ibid.

[793] Patryk Labuda, 'The Democratic Republic of Congo's Failure to Address Impunity for International Crimes: A View from Inside the Legislative Process 2010–2011', International Justice Monitor (8 November 2011) at www.ijmonitor.org/2011/11/the-democratic-republic-of-congos-failure-to-address-impunity-for-international-crimes-a-view-from-inside-the-legislative-process-2010-2011/. The DRC Parliament is bicameral: the National Assembly is the lower house and was established by the 2006 Constitution; the Senate is the upper house.

[794] 'Projet de loi relative aux chambres spécialisées pour la répression des violations graves du droit international humanitaire: organisation, fonctionnement, droit applicable, compétence et procédure' (11 April 2011) ('Projet de loi') (on-file).

'give up' on the proposal for reasons of 'feasibility, resources and finances, notably in the absence of support for the international community'.[795] Having observed the international community's 'reticence' for the creation of international criminal tribunals, and in light of their 'mitigated results', the proposal further stated that the responsibility to prosecute grave crimes thus 'returns to Congolese jurisdictions, through the establishment of specialized chambers within [those] jurisdictions'.[796] The publication of the UN's mapping report is specifically referenced as indicating a new, 'positive international dynamic, which the DRC intends to support for the repression of international crimes'.[797]

The government's characterization of the ICC was more scathing. The ministry's proposal stated that the court's engagement in the DRC could not produce 'the desired results', and that the cases it pursued 'do not realize the magnitude of the [impunity] deficit'.[798] To that end, a separate document prepared for donor states in June 2011 presented the *projet de loi* as a necessary alternative to the ICC, which, despite 'nine years of coop-eration with the DRC, has only realized three or four prosecutions, while the violence continues'.[799] The document further criticized the ICC for entertaining the asylum petitions of three Congolese nationals who were transferred to The Hague to serve as defence witnesses in the Lubanga and Katanga/Ngudjolo Chui trials.[800] In doing so, 'the court encroached on the jurisdiction of the DRC in its role as state party despite its exemplary cooperation with the ICC'. The government also noted that the proposed

---

[795] Ibid., 1 (author's translation). This history is contested by some, but supported by a num-ber of sources. See, e.g., Nyabirungu mwene Songa, *Droit international pénal: Crimes contre la paix et la sécurité de l'humanité* (Editions Droit et Société: Kinshasa, 2013), 142 (stating that the DRC government had demanded the creation of an international criminal tribunal for crimes committed on its territory since 1996, and that the Belgian government had, in 2002, supported this request (citing Eric David, 'La pratique du pou-voir exécutif et le contrôle des chambres législatives en matière de droit international (1999–2003)', in *Revue belge de droit international* (2005), 49).).

[796] Ibid.

[797] Ibid., 2.

[798] Ibid., 1. The note concludes: 'The ICC cannot, and is not intended, to judge all of these crimes; other mechanisms must be put in place'.

[799] Comite mixte de justice, 'Compte rendu de la réunion politique du comite mixte de jus-tice', 28 June 2011, 3 ('CMJ note') (on-file). Like JLOS, the Comite mixte de justice was established in an effort to coordinate government and international donor priorities and management. Interview with CMJ official (Kinshasa, 28 June 2011).

[800] On the applications of these three witnesses and the ensuing proceedings, see Jennifer Easterday, 'Asylum Applicants Must Be Returned to the DRC, Trial Chamber Orders', *International Justice Monitor* (8 December 2011), at www.ijmonitor.org/2011/12/asylum-applicant-must-be-returned-to-the-drc-trial-chamber-orders/.

hybrid court would 'be a good accompaniment to the [forthcoming] electoral process', in order to 'prevent disturbances' that could arise as a result of certain, unnamed 'political ambitions'.[801]

Notwithstanding the executive branch's support for a national approach to accountability and its criticisms of the ICC, most parliamentarians were deeply wary of the *projet de loi*. In addition to the political implications, they were unsettled by the swiftness with which the proposed legislation was being pushed, as well as the outsized role of external actors in amending it.[802] Moreover, important questions about the structure of the chamber, its scope of jurisdiction and the applicable law – including its proposed relationship to Rome State implementation legislation, which, as previously noted, was being considered at the same time through a separate bill – had yet to be resolved. Indeed, although the *projet* was being increasingly presented as a rival to the implementation legislation that had been proposed, it was clear that both bills complemented each other.[803] Amidst these continued concerns, substantive debate was tabled until the last day of the assembly's spring session.

In the face of these criticisms and in a desire to push the legislation through, Kabila's government adopted a series of extraordinary measures. It first opted to have Minister Luzolo present a different authorization law (*loi de habilitation*) directly to the Senate, effectively bypassing the Assembly.[804] This law asked the Senate to grant the executive exceptional powers to legislate in a number of areas of 'heightened importance', of which the proposed court was part, in advance of the presidential elections later in the year. This effort failed, but the Ministry of Justice made a

[801] The government also presented the non-execution of ICC arrest warrants in explicitly political terms, noting Uganda's failure to arrest LRA members (the failure of which has 'harmed the credibility of Congolese political governance') and the non-arrest of Bosco Ntaganda ('not because of the Congolese government but because the international community decided in 2006 that he could not be pursued') in the face of its own 'exemplary' cooperation. Ibid.

[802] Interview with PGA consultant (Kinshasa, 27 June 2011).

[803] See, e.g., Human Rights Watch, 'DR Congo: Commentary on Draft Legislation to Establish Specialized Chambers for Prosecution of International Crimes' (11 March 2011). HRW notes that 'the draft legislation creating the specialized chambers refers to the implementing legislation a number of times, as if it had already been passed, which is obviously not the case. These passages must be amended to avoid any possibility of legal gaps or inconsistency'. Chapter 5 discusses the proposed implementation legislation in further detail.

[804] See Labuda, 'The Democratic Republic of Congo's Failure to Address Impunity for International Crimes'.

renewed effort by putting the legislation on the agenda of a special summer session of Parliament.[805] A moderately revised version of the bill – rather than special chambers, the proposal now called for a stand-alone 'special court' – was presented in August 2011.

The Senate rejected the proposed *court spécialisée* in strong terms, characterizing it as an intrusion by the international community in the DRC's internal affairs.[806] Notwithstanding this opposition, the president of the Senate, Leone Kengo wa Dondo, forced the bill through to the Senate's Political, Administrative and Judicial (PAJ) Committee (DRC).[807] The senators there rebelled as well, objecting to the attempted circumvention of established parliamentary procedure. In strong words, the committee rejected the bill outright, recommending that any such legislation should be merged with the Rome Statute implementing legislation.[808] (That bill, whose deadline for parliamentary approval had since lapsed, was absent from this agenda.) Committee members also voiced serious concerns about the potentially unsettling impact that the bill would have on the Congolese judiciary, raising questions about the compensation of foreign judges, the treatment of Congolese magistrates alongside international counterparts and the orientation of resources and attention around a select number of crimes as compared to the welfare of the legal system as a whole.[809]

The exceptional powers invoked by the executive in its attempt to force legislative assent of the Special Court Bill underscores the degree to which Kabila's government saw its establishment as a necessary concession to international demands for accountability, particularly with presidential elections looming. Concerns articulated by a number of national actors and NGOs that the legislation needed further refinement were largely ignored, however, and the legislation was generally seen as a rushed effort driven by outside actors. In Kambale's words, 'a number

---

[805] Ibid.

[806] Press Release FIDH/ASADHO/GL/LE, 'RDC: Les sénateurs torpillent le projet de loi dur la court spécialisée mixte', 23 August 2011 (on-file).

[807] See Labuda, 'The Democratic Republic of Congo's Failure to Address Impunity for International Crimes' (quoting Kengo wa Dondo as saying that 'If you don't approve it now, the UN will force you to do so anyway').

[808] République Démocratique do Congo Senat, commission politique, administrative et juridique, session extraordinaire d'aout 2011, 'Rapport relatif a l'examen du projet de loi portant création, organisation et fonctionnement de la court spécialisée chargée de la répression des crimes de génocide, crimes de guerre et des crimes contre l'humanité' (August 2011) ('Rapport relatif au projet de loi') (on-file).

[809] Ibid. (author's translation).

of senators felt that the campaign amounted to an international conspiracy against Congolese sovereignty'.[810] The failure to connect the Special Chambers Bill with Rome Statute implementing legislation was also a concern, making it appear 'as if the government was acting precipitously and only because the international community was demanding action'.[811]

After the failure of the government's *projet de loi*, discussions about a specialized court abated until late 2013/early 2014, when a similar proposal re-emerged. Unlike the special court presented in August 2011, the 2014 proposal again proposed the setting up of special chambers within the DRC's existing courts. This proposal followed the abolition in 2013 of exclusive jurisdiction over international crimes by Congolese military courts to include the civilian justice system and proposed creating three special chambers of the first degree: within the appeals courts of Goma (North Kivu province), Lubumbashi (Katanga province) and Mbandaka (Equateur province). A Special Chamber of Appeal would have resided within the Supreme Court of Justice in Kinshasa, and the courts would have again included international staff to work alongside Congolese officials. Despite a less intrusive approach by many international NGOs to this proposal, concerns over sovereignty and *la pérennisation* were still critical sites of contestation, as 'MPs [remained] increasingly wary of any suggestion of external influence in the management of Congolese internal affairs, including in [the] justice sector'.[812] Nick Elebe ma Elebe, director of the Open Society Initiative for Southern Africa's DRC office, has likewise noted that the bill's fate again suffered from poor handling by the Ministry of Justice with Congolese MPs, including members of the government's own party.[813] In May 2014, the National Assembly rejected the special chambers bill for a second time.

---

[810] Kambale, 'Mix and Match'. 65. For helpful analysis of this period, see Nick Elebe ma Elebe, 'Why DRC Lawmakers Again Rejected Special Chambers to Prosecute International Crimes' (23 May 2014), at www.ijmonitor.org/2014/05/drc-a-bill-on-special-chambers-rejected-for-the-second-time/.

[811] Ibid., 66.

[812] Elebe; see also Kahombo, 'The Principle of Complementarity in Practice'. 209 ('This time, the main reason given was that the country did not need a new judicial jurisdiction but rather the reinforcement of the existing judicial apparatus'.).

[813] See Elebe ('The government's tardy responses to MP's queries, and mishandling of the bill while it was still in committee, may have antagonized MPs, many of whom demonstrated a desire to … not be taken for granted'.).

Military/Mobile Courts in the DRC: Complementing the ICC?

In the absence of a special tribunal or mixed court, military courts remain the principal forum for the domestic adjudication of ICC crimes. Military courts have a long history in the DRC, dating back to the founding of the Congolese colonial state.[814] The 1972 military code criminalized genocide, war crimes and crimes against humanity and, as noted, in 2002, the government ordered an overhaul of the legal framework for its military court system; however, there is no record of trials prior to 2005.

The system has undergone numerous transformations since that time, however, including the first introduction of a code of military justice in 1972. That code, as the Congolese academic Marcel Wetsh'okonda Koso has noted, 'organized the military courts for the first time into a complete judicial system, distinct from that of ordinary courts'.[815] Military justice has since become increasingly normalized in the post-1972 period. Efforts to reform the system – recognizing, for instance, its independence from the prosecutor's office – were attempted in the early 1990s with the onset of a democratic opening in Congolese society, but were largely ignored following Mobutu's fall from power.[816] Indeed, in 1997, the new regime of then President Laurent Kabila established a single court, the *Court d'Ordre Militaire* (COM), 'which reduced the independence of magistrates and wrecked the organization, procedures and jurisdiction of the military justice system'.[817] During this time, the courts' jurisdiction was progressively extended to encompass, in certain cases, civilians as well.

Growing criticism of the COM's abuses helped augur further change in 2002, when the Inter-Congolese Dialogue adopted a resolution on reform of the system. This led, in turn, to the adoption of the new *code de justice militaire* and the revised military criminal code, which incorporated, in large part, the Rome Statute's crimes. In practice, then, military courts

---

[814] AfriMAP and Open Society Initiative for Southern Africa, 'The Democratic Republic of Congo: Military Justice and Human Rights – An Urgent Need to Complete Reforms' (OSISA, 2010), 17.

[815] Ibid., 18.

[816] The *Conférence nationale souveraine* (Sovereign National Conference) that took place from 1991 to 1992 focused on the military justice system in particular, and made several recommendations for reform, including abolishing the 'double supervision of military courts by both the defence and justice ministries', as well as ensuring the independence of military magistrates from the high command. Ibid., 19; see also Deibert, 39–40.

[817] Ibid.

have remained the exclusive arbiters of international crimes domestically, even amidst deep criticism about their lack of independence from the executive and other fair trial concerns. It is particularly noteworthy that, since 2002, the system has 'extended its material and personal jurisdiction to a degree unprecedented in its history', including over civilians.[818] The 2015 passage of ICC implementing legislation was meant, in part, to curtail this trend.

Mobile military courts have also received increasing attention as a rule-of-law intervention amongst international donors (in the DRC and other Francophone Africa states), leading some commentators to wrongly suggest that they are a recent innovation. Known as *chambres foraines* or *audiences foraines*, Congolese law specifically has provided for their operation since 1979, and were designed to be used by the central government to administer justice in its remote interior.[819] Wetsh'okonda Koso further notes that because the jurisdiction of the basic military courts (*tribunaux militaires de garnison*) is set at district level, accessing them is often difficult: they are typically situated far from the places where offences are committed. Thus, 'practically all the trials for international crimes recorded up to this point have been arranged as a result of hearings in the mobile courts'.[820]

The mobile courts have to date operated predominantly in the eastern part of the DRC, where intense fighting has continued despite the 2002 power-sharing agreement. The first mobile court program with international support was implemented in 2004 by *Avocats sans Frontières*. In its annual report, ASF described its work as providing support to 'move the courts of three provinces, during short periods of time, from the main cities where they were based to local towns under their jurisdiction', in order to 'bring justice closer to the population'.[821] Other programs include those run or financially supported by the American Bar Association's Rule of Law Initiative (ABA-ROLI), TRIAL International, Open Society

---

[818] 'The Democratic Republic of Congo', 17. Jurisdiction over civilians was justified, for instance, by broad, vaguely defined clauses that include civilians accused of ordinary crimes committed merely with 'weapons of war'. See Amnesty International, 'The Time for Justice Is Now: New Strategy Needed in the Democratic Republic of Congo: Summary', AFR 62/007/2011 (August 2011).

[819] Article 67 of the Code d'organisation et de compétence judiciaire. An interlocutor active in one mobile court program noted that provisions for such courts exist in other African Francophone countries as well. Interview with ABA-ROLI staff member (Washington, DC, 12 February 2014).

[820] 'The Democratic Republic of Congo', 33.

[821] ASF, 'Rapport Annuel 2014'. at www.asf.be/fr/blog/publications/annual-report-asf-2014/.

Foundations, as well as international and regional organizations including the UN Development Program and the European Union's Program for the Restoration of Justice in Eastern Congo (REJUSCO).[822]

Operating principally in the North and South Kivu regions of the country, two ABA-ROLI attorneys write that the courts 'are deployed to remote locations to enable access to justice for victims unable to travel to courts in town and cities'.[823] They add:

> Everything about the courts is temporary: the court is housed in a community centre or town hall, with magistrates, a registrar, a bailiff, defence attorneys and lawyers brought in from the closest towns and cities. Mobile courts remain in a given location for a period of between one and two months, hearing as many cases as possible. While the mobile courts are primarily established to hear cases relating to sexual violence, they do deal with other matters affecting the community.[824]

Informational material by donor organizations further describes the need for a 'specialized approach' to the endemic sexual violence in the DRC region. However, while the courts' specialization in gender issues is what 'distinguishes' them, they also have 'discretion to hear other cases', such as murder and torture.[825]

---

[822] See Uganda People's Defence Force (UNDP), 'Evaluation of UNDP's Support to Mobile Courts in Sierra Leone, Democratic Republic of the Congo, and Somalia' (May 2014), at www.undp.org/content/undp/en/home/librarypage/crisis-prevention-and-recovery/evaluation-of-undp-s-support-to-mobile-courts-in-drc--sierra-leo.html ('UNDP has been supporting mobile courts in eastern DRC (North Kivu, South Kivu Provinces and Ituri District) since 2010'.). In a published paper, the ABA notes that its program initially began in January 2008 and was funded by the United States Department of State's Bureau of Human Rights, Democracy and Labor. Tessa Khan and Jim Wormington, 'Mobile Courts in the DRC: Lessons from Development for International Criminal Justice', Oxford Transitional Justice Research Working Paper Series, 19. 18, n.93. United States Agency for International Development (USAID) is no longer the primary grant maker: ABA-ROLI now sub-partners (or has partnered) with a number of other organizations, including the Open Society Foundations (for a program begun in South Kivu in late 2009), as well as USAID, the Norwegian Ministry for Foreign Affairs and The Netherlands. These programs focus on the provinces of Maniema and North and South Kivu. Ibid., n.84. For an overview of various donors engaged in mobile courts, see *Putting Complementarity into Practice*, 55–56; Passy Mubalama and Simon Jennings, 'Roving Courts in Eastern Congo', *Institute for War & Peace Reporting* (13 February 2013).

[823] Khan and Wormington, 19.

[824] Ibid.

[825] 'Mobile Gender Justice Court', Women's UN Report Network. In informational material, OSF similarly writes that 'The court, which is staffed entirely by Congolese and functions within the Congolese judicial system, also has flexibility – it has the discretion to hear other serious crimes, including murder and theft'. See 'Justice in DRC: Mobile Courts Combat Rape and Impunity in Eastern Congo'.

Like the depictions of international divisions in Uganda and Kenya, a cooperative vision for complementarity emerges in descriptions of the relationship between the ICC and the DRC's mobile courts program. The courts are typically depicted as completing and 'complementing' the work of the ICC (the court's logo of the enwreathed scales of justice even adorns many of the courtrooms' makeshift walls). As an example of this descriptive tendency, two commentators note that 'The mobile courts complement the work of the International Criminal Court, ICC, in The Hague … In parallel with its own investigation, the ICC has a policy of encouraging local judicial systems to develop their ability to try cases of this kind'.[826] Elsewhere, Mark Ellis writes that the courts were created to 'prosecute persons who committed crimes under the ICC's jurisdiction', while Khan and Wormington describe the mobile courts as operating 'alongside' the [ICC's] efforts.[827] A Human Rights Watch report describes them as follows:

> Since the beginning of the ICC's investigation in Congo in 2004, Congolese authorities and international partners have sought to encourage 'complementarity' between the ICC and the national justice system. The 'complementarity' principle, defined in the preamble and Article 17 of the Rome Statute of the ICC, means that national judicial systems retain primary responsibility to investigate and prosecute war crimes, crimes against humanity, and genocide, and that the ICC will only step in as a court of last resort – in essence, to 'complement' judicial efforts when national courts are unable or unwilling to act.[828]

A burden-sharing relationship between the ICC and the mobile courts has also been depicted, with the former 'going after the highest level accused often out of reach of domestic jurisdictions – and the local courts,

---

[826] See Mubalama and Jennings, 'Roving Courts in Eastern Congo',
[827] Ellis, *Sovereignty and Justice*, 247 ('In 2010, the [DRC] created mobile courts in the eastern part of the country to prosecute persons who committed crimes under the ICC's jurisdiction, particularly crimes involving sexual violence'); Khan and Wormington, 18. For a similar description, see Michael Maya, 'Mobile Courts in the Democratic Republic of Congo: Complementarity in Action?' in Juan Carlos Botero, Ronald Janse, Sam Muller and Christine Pratt (eds.), *Innovations in Rule of Law: A Compilation of Concise Essays* (HiiL and The World Justice Project, 2012), 33–36.
[828] Human Rights Watch, 'Justice on Trial: Lessons from the Minova Rape Case in the Democratic Republic of Congo' (2015), 72. See also Open Society Justice Initiative, 'Fact Sheet: DRC Mobile Gender Courts', at www.opensocietyfoundations.org/sites/default/files/mobile-court-20110725.pdf (stating that the mobile courts were 'designed … to support the concept of "complementarity" … and hence to complement the work of the International Criminal Court in The Hague, which is tasked with prosecuting high level suspects otherwise outside the capacity of the domestic court system').

including mobile courts, going after lower level suspects'.[829] As elsewhere, however, there is no coordination or cooperation between the two.[830]

4   Between Competition and Conformity

The attempted transformation of domestic judiciaries for the prosecution of atrocity crimes highlights the shifting, protean nature of complementarity. As the histories of Uganda and Kenya suggest, an initially threat-based relationship with the principle – spurred by the potential of ICC intervention – catalysed efforts to establish credible bodies that could potentially displace the court's jurisdiction. Over time, however, complementarity has become a more harmonious principle, offering a way to narrate the ICC's influence on domestic jurisdictions even where the court is itself absent. By contrast, in the DRC, a complementary relationship between the ICC and domestic courts was the declared vision from the outset, even as that promise gave way to a more acrimonious, competitive relationship with Kinshasa in the years following the court's intervention.

Many criminal justice and human rights advocates welcome the development of specialized domestic fora, seeing their establishment as a step towards accountability, as well as an opportunity to invest in the successful functioning of the broader national legal system.[831] Yet tensions also beset these arrangements. In particular, the attention paid to initiatives like the ICD or the mobile courts – both of which are typically presented as extensions of the ICC's work, or even as legacies of its intervention – reflect a preference by some actors to focus on the court's purported 'demonstration effects', rather than on the equal development

---

[829] Kelly Askin, 'Fizi Mobile Court: Rape Verdicts'. A publication by the Southern African Litigation Centre is also representative: the DRC mobile courts are highlighted as a case study of 'Complementarity in Action: The Mobile Gender Courts', in *Positive Reinforcement: Advocating for International Criminal Justice in Africa* (May 2013), 79–83.

[830] Interview with Congolese magistrate at High Military Court (Kinshasa, 28 June 2011); interview with ABA-ROLI staff member (Washington, DC, 12 February 2014).

[831] See, e.g., Jane Stromseth, 'Justice on the Ground: Can International Criminal Courts Strengthen Domestic Rule of Law in Post-Conflict Societies', *Hague Journal on the Rule of Law* 1(1) (2009), 87–97; Victor Peskin and Eric Stover, 'A hopeful future for Kenya', *Los Angeles Times* (7 June 2010) ('A fair and effective [domestic] tribunal will open the way to an independent judiciary, which is a cornerstone of the proposed constitution'); Ottilia Anna Maunganidze, 'Uganda's International Crimes Division: A Step in the Right Direction', in Beitel van der Merwe (ed.), *International Criminal Justice in Africa: Challenges and Opportunities* (Konrad Adenauer Stiftung, 2014).

of national judicial institutions overall.[832] The following sections explore complementarity's impulse towards this competition with domestic criminal justice systems and towards conformity with ICC norms and standards.

Complementarity as Competition: Exceptional Justice

Exceptionalism – treating or giving something the status of being unique or special – has both positive and negative connotations in the context of criminal justice. Understood as the former, seeking criminal accountability for mass violence has typically required exceptional responses by the international community. Notable examples include the establishment of international *ad hoc* and/or hybrid tribunals, the participation of non-national staff as judges and/or investigators (either alone or in partnership with national staff), as well as the creation of 'high risk courts' or even the exercise of military jurisdiction.[833] Exceptionalism may also be justified as an antidote: the failures of the 'ordinary' criminal justice system necessitate the establishment of independent structures or, indeed, supra-national jurisdiction. As articulated by Wilfred Nderitu, former chair of the Kenyan Section of the International Commission of Jurists (ICJ-Kenya), in his testimony before the Waki Commission:

> We find that depending on who is heading a particular unit within the security agencies – then just by looking at him or by knowing what his name is in 90% of the cases you will be able to know what kind of decision he would make with regard to which particular community or you will be able to know whether he will turn a blind eye to something that is happening. So the issue of getting people who are not unduly affected by the politics behind the violence coming to help us, I think that … is very important.[834]

[832] On 'demonstration effect', see Jane Stromseth, David Wippman and Rosa Brooks, *Can Might Make Rights? Building the Rule of Law After Military Interventions* (Cambridge: Cambridge University Press, 2006), 259–261. For a thorough exploration of tensions between/amongst 'transitional justice' practitioners and rule-of-law/development actors, see Padraig McAuliffe, *Transitional Justice and Rule of Law Reconstruction: A Contentious Relationship* (Routledge, 2013). Bringing development and rule-of-law actors together in support of 'implementing the complementarity principle' has been a topic of increasing focus in recent years, see, e.g., 'Greentree Principles' of 2010.

[833] The creation of special jurisdictions is nevertheless understood to require the satisfaction of certain conditions under international law, in order to ensure equal and impartial proceedings. See, e.g., UN Human Rights Committee, General Observation no. 32, 'Article 14: right to equality before courts and tribunals and to a fair trial', CCPR/C/GC/32, 23 August 2007.

[834] Record of Evidence Taken Before the Commission of Inquiry into Post-Election Violence (CIPEV), 24 July 2008 (verbatim recording) (on-file). The historian Daniel Branch makes a similar point about the ICC's intervention: 'The only way that Kenyans could expect to check the abuses of power of those in high office and find justice was through external intervention'. Branch, *Kenya: Between Hope and Despair*, 288.

Nderitu's testimony illustrates the need for erecting mechanisms that function outside the normal structures of state. The creation of specialized institutions, personnel and regulations can help inoculate transitional justice measures from the corrosive influence of a compromised justice sector, but, more ambitiously, they also hold the potential to positively influence the development of the rule of law domestically.[835] Indeed, it was on this basis that the UN's 'mapping' report recommended that a special mechanism in the DRC should also contribute to strengthening and rehabilitating the national justice system.[836]

Yet in each of the country contexts described, the institutional forms that have emerged (or been proposed) in the wake of the ICC's intervention raise concern about what the Congolese interlocutors described in the prologue as *la pérennité*: the structure, resourcing and functioning of these forms relative to the well-being of the broader domestic criminal justice system. As articulated by Kenyan MP Danson Mugatana in his opposition to the proposed STK:

> We are going to have another court for the ordinary *mwananchi* who was sent to go and actualize the ideas of these bigger crime suspects ... entrenching a system where we have a special procedure for those who are going to be eminent people or suspects and a different procedure for the ordinary.[837]

As institutions that are rooted, to varying degrees, within the domestic structures of the state, the ICDs of Kenya and Uganda, the proposed special chambers in the DRC and the mobile military courts reflect broader tensions over the role of external actors in their design, as well as the priorities of donor benefactors versus those of domestic actors.

Democratic Republic of Congo

The failed creation of the special chambers/court in the DRC illustrates perhaps most directly the tension between the need for specialized jurisdiction and the concern for *la pérennité* of the broader justice system. The reasons enumerated by the Senate in its August 2011 rejection of the ministry's bill illustrate the divergent views held by international and domestic actors over the benefit of such a mechanism. As noted, committee members voiced serious concerns about the potentially

---

[835] For a fuller discussion of this debate, see Stromseth, Wippman and Brooks, *Can Might Make Rights?*

[836] UN Mapping Report, paras. 1038, 1044, 1055. Notably, the DRC's *projet de loi* also noted the ability of a 'hybrid composition' to 'reinforce the independence integrity and capacity of Congolese magistrates'.

[837] STK Amendment Bill, MP Danson Mungatana.

unsettling impact that a special court would have on the Congolese judiciary and the risk that it would 'lead to a duplication of jurisdictions'.[838] The incorporation of international staff also appears to have been one of the main reasons for the Senate's rejection of the bill. In the committee's words:

> The integration of foreign judges in this national jurisdiction, under the pretext of ensuring the effectiveness and independence of the judiciary, would appear to be an admission of powerlessness on the part of the government, which itself has the duty to strengthen the capacities of Congolese judges and would be an insult to them.[839]

The committee also noted that 'the adoption of a special status for the judges of this [special] court is likely to create discrimination between them on the one hand and the other judges in other jurisdictions, on the other'.[840] Opponents of the proposed STK raised similar concerns during parliamentary debates.[841]

In some respects, concerns about the special court's potentially distorting impact have been realized in the functioning of the DRC's mobile courts, where international donors exert considerable influence. Here, exceptionalism extends in particular to the predominant focus on sexual violence crimes. Séverine Autesserre, a political scientist who has conducted extensive fieldwork in the DRC, argues that sexual abuse against women and girls is one of several narratives that have 'dominated the discourse on the Congo and oriented the interventions strategies ... of some of the most powerful states and organizations', such

---

[838] Rapport relatif au projet de loi ('la création d'une cour spécialisée avec les mêmes compétences entrainerait un dédoublement de juridictions, avec risqué de litispendance') (author's translation).

[839] Ibid. ('l'intégration des magistrats étrangers au sein de cette juridiction nationale, sous prétexte d'assurer l'efficacité et l'indépendance de la justice, apparaitrait comme un aveu d'impuissance de la part du gouvernement charge de renforcer les capacités des magistrats congolais et serait une injure pour ces derniers') (author's translation).

[840] Ibid. ('l'adoption d'un statut special en faveur des magistrats de cette cour est de nature a créer une discrimination entre eux, d'une part et entre ceux-ci et les magistrats de autres juridictions, d'autre part') (author's translation).

[841] MP Danson Mungatana, for instance, spoke out against the 2009 Bill in similar terms:

> First and foremost, if you look at this tribunal, it is a huge monolith that is going to set up a parallel legal system in this country. If you look at the bill that has been circulated, we are going to have several offices created. There is going to be the office of the public prosecutor, office of the defender, office of the registrar, a trial chamber, special prosecution court and an appeals chamber. This is a very big parallel structure to the legal system of Kenya that already exists (STK Amendment Bill, 40).

that other forms of violence are increasingly overlooked.[842] She further notes that 'according to donors and aid workers, sexual violence is such a buzzword that many foreign and Congolese organizations insert references to it in all kinds of project proposals to increase their chances of obtaining funding'.[843] A 2012 study of the DRC mobile courts by two Dutch academics similarly warns of the deleterious effects that such a singular focus can have.[844] As it argues, 'NGOs pay for lawyers on the side of victims, while suspects are usually left with unpaid, and hence unmotivated, public defenders. This enhances the possibility for suspects to be convicted regardless of the evidence that is presented'.[845] Other jurists have raised similar due process concerns.[846]

National-level actors have also noted the displacing effects of the mobile courts in the competition for limited resources. One Congolese jurist noted that 'ordinary' justice institutions are effectively stalled when the mobile courts are in session, as they draw personnel 'from the closest towns and cities' away from those institutions for the duration of the time that the court is sitting.[847] Another publication refers explicitly to the courts as 'palliative', noting their high cost and the fact that they depend almost entirely on the logistical assistance provided by MONUSCO, the UN's mission to the DRC.[848] Finally, of their (relative) high cost, several interlocutors expressed unease about the distortions such interventions

---

[842] Séverine Autesserre, 'Dangerous Tales: Dominant Narratives on the Congo and Their Unintended Consequences'. *African Affairs* (2012), 13. Autesserre argues further that these dominant narratives have 'diverted attention from much more needed policy actions, such as the resolution of grassroots antagonisms, the fight against corruption, and the reform of the state administration', 11. For a similar argument in the context of the need for 'local peacebuilding'. see also Séverine Autesserre, *The Trouble with the Congo: Local Violence and the Failure of International Peacebuilding* (Cambridge: Cambridge University Press, 2010).

[843] Ibid.

[844] Nynke Douma and Dorothea Hilhorst, 'Fond de commerce? Sexual violence assistance in the Democratic Republic of Congo', Disaster Studies, Occasional Paper no. 2 (Wageningen University, 2012), 11 ('Although mobile courts should see all kinds of cases, they are almost uniquely organized around sexual violence cases and, linked with the predominant perception that sexual violence is caused by armed perpetrators, they are mostly targeting military justice'.) (on-file).

[845] Ibid. The authors further note that 'legal personnel receive compensation (*primes*) during mobile hearings from the NGOs'.

[846] See, e.g., Mbokani, *Congolese Jurisprudence under International Criminal Law*, 292–324; see Avocats Sans Frontieres, 'The Application of the Rome Statute of the International Criminal Court by the Courts of the Democratic Republic of Congo' (2009), 100–112.

[847] Interview with Congolese jurist (Kinshasa, 21 June 2011).

[848] AfriMAP and OSISA, 'The Democratic Republic of Congo: Military Justice and Human Rights', 34–35.

can visit on the local economy, where the per diem offered for three days travel often well exceeds the compensation that a public court official would otherwise receive.[849] A 2009 needs assessment of the DRC's justice system similarly noted that 'since more international actors get involved in mobile courts initiatives, magistrates have started to demand additional pay before agreeing to participate'.[850] While the *chambres foraines* are thus part of the Congolese system, the resources necessary to activate them may well come at the price of other rule of law building efforts.

Uganda

The permanence of a structure like Uganda's ICD was, in part, a response to concerns that the benefits of transitional justice mechanisms would not accrue to domestic justice systems. As Human Rights Watch describes it, 'As a division of Uganda's High Court, the ICD is a fully integrated part of Uganda's domestic system, operating according to standard judicial procedure and practice'.[851] Yet even such specialized divisions can produce tensions between and amongst other justice sector actors. In Uganda, for instance, the perception amongst several of my interlocutors that the ICD was a 'prized' division, attracting not only the interest of international NGOs, advocates and academics, but also donor money, has contributed to a sense that it enjoys a special status within the High Court structure.

---

[849] Interview with MONUSCO official (Kinshasa, 23 June 2011). A UNDP assessment of its support to mobile court programs concluded that 'Seventy percent of the [$25,000] budget was for the per diems of mobile court staff'. UNDP, 'Evaluation of UNDP's Support to Mobile Courts in Sierra Leone, Democratic Republic of Congo, and Somalia' (May 2014), 9; see also *Putting Complementarity into Practice*, 56 ('Judges who are usually reluctant to accept remote postings have eagerly participated in mobile courts for the per diem payments').

[850] 'Rebuilding courts and trust: An assessment of the needs of the justice system in the Democratic Republic of Congo', An International Legal Assistance Consortium and International Bar Association Human Rights Institute Report (August 2009), 27. The report concludes that having mobile courts 'run by the government, under specific and consistent guidelines, would contribute to solving the problem'. Similar tensions are described in a 2004 report of Human Rights Watch, concerning a joint effort, known as REJUSCO, spearheaded by the DRC government and the European Commission to restore the criminal justice system in Bunia, Ituri. The report noted that judges and investigate judges' monthly stipend was 'worse than meaningless' as it did 'not even cover 30% of … monthly needs'. It recommended that all parties involved 'should reaffirm the principle that the burden of paying the salaries of judicial personnel should be borne by the government'. Human Rights Watch Briefing Paper, 'Making Justice Work: Restoration of the Legal System in Ituri, DRC' (1 September 2004), 10.

[851] Human Rights Watch, 'Justice for Serious Crimes before National Courts' (January 2012), 18.

What this status confers ranges from the level of the seemingly mundane to the potentially constitutional.[852] Several Ugandan jurists, for instance, pointed to the fact that ICD judges were receiving a paid legal assistant (something Ugandan judges do not traditionally use) as a form of patronage. Donors were in fact asked to consider supplemental funding for legal assistants for ICD judges in 2011, although this request was not funded (at the time).[853] Judicial 'training' has been another site of institutional tension, as ICD judges have received extensive training on a variety of topics in international law.[854] The Institute for Security Studies, a think tank based in South Africa, notes that, since March 2011, it has 'provided the ICD with intensive training workshops on international criminal justice, counterterrorism and mechanisms for international cooperation. The judges and the registrar of the ICD have also benefited from exchange programmes or study tours to the ICC and the International Criminal Tribunal for Rwanda'.[855] Given the resources invested in such trainings, concern has been expressed that the rotation of judges off of the ICD, an otherwise common practice within the High Court system, will now cause 'a loss of developed knowledge and expertise in a specialized legal area'.[856]

---

[852] For instance, the JSC proposal that would have vested jurisdiction for piracy and other transnational crimes with the Kenya's ICD would likely have face a constitutional challenge at some point (or required a change in legislation), as currently such cases are handled at the magistrate's court level. Second interview with Kenyan NGO director (Nairobi, 3 December 2012). Similar constitutional issues are raised with special tribunals as well, as was the case in both Kenya and the DRC.

[853] In its recommendations to donors, Human Rights Watch included that they 'consider prioritizing funding of legal assistants to support ICD judges'. See 'Justice for Serious Crimes before National Courts', 27. It appears that ICD judges now do work with legal assistants who are recruited on a contract basis (information provided by ICD Registrar, 9 August 2017).

[854] See, e.g., *Putting Complementarity into Practice*, 72 (noting that ICD judges 'have requested extensive additional trainings, including in plea-bargaining, as well as ongoing trainings that address other particular challenges').

[855] Max du Plessis, Antoinette Low and Ottilia Maunganidze, 'African efforts to close the impunity gap: Lessons for complementarity from national and regional actions', ISS Paper no. 241 (November 2012), 17, at www.issafrica.org/uploads/Paper241.pdf. Other trainings – by the Public International Law and Policy Group, International Criminal Law Services, the Institute for International Criminal Investigations and the International Center for Transitional Justice – have likewise been offered to investigators and prosecutors.

[856] Human Rights Watch, 'Justice for Serious Crimes Before National Courts', 20.

Funding is again intimately intertwined with these tensions. JLOS is ostensibly meant to serve as the Ugandan government's coordinating body for justice issues, but the interest in its transitional justice mandate, for which a working group was established in 2008, has attracted particular attention. Stephen Oola notes that JLOS 'received significant donor money' in support of expediting the ICD's first trial of Thomas Kwoyelo and, 'with it, pressure to abandon its earlier roadmap towards a more comprehensive transitional justice process'.[857] Another assessment concludes that 'for such a small court with a small caseload, [the ICD] consumed an outsized share of available time, resources, and funding'.[858] By contrast, a 2018 report of the Uganda Law Society concluded that although the ICD was 'set up to ratify and replicate the International Criminal Court model', it has 'faced major constraints (inadequate financing, manpower and technical support)'.[859] In this telling, relative to its ambitious, expanding mandate, the ICD's funding has been less than adequate, leading another commentator to compare it directly to The Hague. She writes, 'There are also high expectations from the victims, who make comparisons between themselves and victims participating in the [ICC] trial against Dominic Ongwen. However, the ICC has a well-established mechanism for victims and more funding, as opposed to the ICD'.[860]

[857] Oola, 'In the Shadow of Kwoyelo's Trial', 165. To Oola's point, the sector secured over UGX 400m (apx. $115,000 USD) to initiate the Kwoyelo trial alone. See JLOS, 'Annual Performance Report 2010/2011', 72. Nouwen likewise concludes that the establishment of a division specialized in ICC crimes was another iteration of Uganda's expensive patronage system. *Complementarity in the Line of Fire*, 182 ('International donor money for such special bodies guarantees income outside the ordinary national budget', while domestic patronage networks are rewarded by 'secondment to a body that promises training with sitting allowances, access to international networks and travel abroad as fringe benefits'.). The repeated recommendation of international organizations that the ICD is 'under-staffed and under-resourced' arguably adds to the patronage potential of such bodies.
[858] *Options for Justice*, 290. As such, 'the challenge to both domestic and international professionals in Uganda remains in ensuring that the resources allocated to the ICD have a broader effect on the overall judiciary, when possible'.
[859] Uganda Law Society, 'The International Crimes Division of the High Court of Uganda: Towards Greater Effectiveness' (2018), x, at www.uls.or.ug/site/assets/files/1355/the_international_crimes_of_the_high_court_of_ugandatowards_greater_effectiveness.pdf.
[860] Brenda Nanyuja, 'The Thomas Kwoyelo Case at the ICD: Issues of Victim Participation', International Justice Monitor (13 March 2017), at www.ijmonitor.org/2017/03/the-thomas-kwoyelo-case-at-the-icd-issues-of-victim-participation/.

Complementarity as Copying: The 'Justice Meme'

The creation of specialized judicial divisions invests them with an exceptional, if contested, status in the domestic legal sphere. But, as I have argued, they also demonstrate a striking uniformity with the institutional form of justice that the ICC represents, promoting in Mark Drumbl's words, 'the iconic status of the courtroom and the jailhouse as the best practice to promote justice in the aftermath of grave mass violence'.[861] As with domestic implementation legislation, where the Rome Statute functioned (in Kenya and Uganda, in particular) as a 'global script', the procedure and practice of the ICC as an institution have likewise been taken up as part of what complementarity compels.

The court itself has abetted this process through a line of admissibility jurisprudence that privileges the 'mirroring effect' of its procedures at the national level. But, as Chapter 2 highlighted, the role of transnational communities of practice in constructing a new understanding of complementarity as compliance-focused has been even more pivotal. Academics and other norm entrepreneurs have encouraged this development, seeing it as salutary, an elevation of domestic criminal justice through greater adherence to 'international standards' and, by extension, towards a more unified legal order. Ellis, for instance, posits that the 'importance of stressing *international standards of justice* is paramount', while George Fletcher argues that 'the long range-value of the ICC is that it will teach countries of the world how to do justice as they seek to apply repressive measures in the name of social protection'.[862]

Fletcher's vision of 'how to do justice' has been effectively transmitted to influential actors in both Uganda and Kenya. In 2010, Principal Judge Ogoola, the first presiding judge of the Ugandan ICD, wrote:

> The court's standards and procedures – including a trial bench of three judges, prosecution, investigation, and defence office, and in-house translation service – all mirror those of the modern international criminal courts such as the Hague, Arusha, Bosnia, Yugoslavia, Sierra Leone,

---

[861] Drumbl, *Atrocity, Punishment, and International Law*, 198.

[862] Ellis, *Sovereignty and Justice*, 8–10 (emphasis in original); George Fletcher and Jens David Ohlin, 'Reclaiming Fundamental Principles of Criminal Law in the Darfur Case', *Journal of International Criminal Justice* 3 (2005), 540; see also European Commission, 'Toolkit for Bridging the Gap between International [and] National Justice: Joint Staff Working Document on Advancing the Principle of Complementarity', SWD(2013) (1 January 2013), 11 ('Is the existing normative framework [constitution, penal code, procedural code...] in line with international standards on justice?').

etc. In the legislation, we have sought to go even further by, for instance, providing the opportunity for an International Criminal Court observer at the hearings of cases by the [Ugandan War Crimes Chamber] – let alone the use of international experts to assist the court's proceedings.[863]

Ugandan Justice Akiki Kiiza, who later presided over the division, has likewise stated that 'war crimes trials held in the country will function in a similar fashion to those in The Hague, with three judges officiating each case'.[864] (Whereas single judges typically preside over judicial matters in Uganda, the ICD employs a three-judge bench, in keeping with ICC practice.) These messages have been furthered by key NGOs. The Uganda Victims Foundation, for instance, has stated that 'Given the special international nature of the crimes coming before the WCD, a structure similar to the ICC should be upheld and adhered to'.[865] The introduction of specialized rules of procedure for the division in 2016 implemented a number of such structures modeled on the ICC.

The proposals for Kenya's ICD mirrored the 'best practice' discourse simultaneously circulating in Uganda. Justices Ogoola and Kiiza's remarks are nearly identical to those of Reverend Samuel Kobia, who, speaking at the annual Assembly of States Parties in November 2013, said that Kenya's proposed ICD would be established 'modelled on standards of the ICC – the same standards… with the same rules, with the same practice and with the same procedures'.[866] To that end, the sub-committee proposed that the ICD sit 'in panels of three judges with one extra judge in case one of the judges cannot sit'.[867] The JSC's report on the Kenyan division further concludes that:

> Special rules of procedure and evidence should be formulated to provide the procedure on the prosecution of crimes in this division. This is so because, this division will be dealing with criminal matters with significant international character and needs to be modelled in accordance with international standards of the International Criminal Court and tribunals.[868]

---

[863] Justice James Ogoola, 'Lawfare: Where Justice Meets Peace', *Case Western Reserve Journal of International Law* 43 (2010), 184. Justice Ogoola references the work here of the Public International Law & Policy Group.

[864] Ogola, 'Uganda Victims Question ICC's Balance'.

[865] Uganda Victims Foundation, 'Statement on the International Crimes Bill of 2009' (4 November 2009).

[866] Simon Jennings and Thomas Bwire, 'Kenyan Chief Justice Announces Special Court', *Institute for War & Peace Reporting* (10 December 2012); Nzau Msua, 'Kenya: Mutunga to Establish ICC Model Court', *The Star* (26 February 2013).

[867] JSC Report, 144.

[868] Ibid., 96. Because of the nature of crimes to be tried, the report recommends that 'before the court commences its trials, all measures should be put in place to ensure that the court room has modern ICT facilities e.g. cameras, videos etc.', 145.

Kenya's nascent Witness Protection Agency, which became for some time a critical focus of 'positive' complementarity-related efforts, has described its mission – to be 'the leading Witness Protection Agency in the World' – in similarly ambitious, best-practice oriented terms.[869]

As noted, procedural provisions are also considered part of 'proper' adjudication. The ICC's victim participation regime, for instance, has been frequently invoked as a necessary corollary of criminal proceedings in Kenya and Uganda, even though such participation is largely foreign to their common-law systems.[870] Advocacy by several leading victims' rights NGOs played a key role in ensuring that the ICD's special rules of procedures enshrine participatory rights for victims broader than in other criminal proceedings before ordinary Ugandan courts.[871] The division has since ruled that victims in the Kwoyelo proceeding enjoy participation rights akin to those available before the ICC, substantially expanding the scope of the right beyond participation at sentencing, as is otherwise the general practice.[872] One commentary piece further notes the importance of getting victim participation 'right' in the Kwoyelo case by relying on a 'thorough analysis of past ICC decisions'.[873] ICC-modelled practice has similarly animated debates around victim participation in the DRC's mobile courts as well.[874]

---

[869] The Witness Protection Agency, Republic of Kenya Service Charter (brochure on-file).

[870] See, e.g., Uganda Victims Foundation (UVF), 'Statement on the International Crimes Bill of 2009' ('Whilst it is recognized that the Ugandan legal system does not normally provide for victims to participate in criminal proceedings (other than as witnesses) or to be legally represented, the UVF is of the firm belief that the special nature of the crimes coming before the WCD merits significantly greater involvement of victims in the process'.); Prosecutor v. Joseph Kony et al., Observations on behalf of victims pursuant to Article 19(1) of the Rome Statute with 55 public annexes and 45 redacted annexes, ICC-02/04-01/05-349, Office of Public Counsel for Victims, 18 November 2008.

[871] See, e.g., REDRESS, 'Ugandan International Crimes Division Rules 2016: Analysis on Victim Participation Framework, Final Version' (August 2016).

[872] See Lino Owor Ogora, 'Landmark Ruling on Victim Participation in the Case of Thomas Kwoyelo', International Justice Monitor (4 October 2016), at www.ijmonitor.org/2016/10/landmark-ruling-on-victim-participation-in-the-case-of-thomas-kwoyelo/.

[873] Lino Owor Ogora and Beini Ye, 'To Participate or Not? Getting Victim Participation Right in the Kwoyelo Case', International Justice Monitor (18 October 2016), at www.ijmonitor.org/2016/10/to-participate-or-not-getting-victim-participation-right-in-the-kwoyelo-case/. It is worth noting that ICC jurisprudence itself with respect to victim participation is far from uniform; different trial chambers have not been consistent in their treatment of the issue.

[874] See, e.g., Derek Inman, Stefaan Smis and Pacifique Muhindo Magadju, 'International Crimes, National Trials and the Role of Victims Rights: Locating the Problems and Possibilities of Victim Participation in the Democratic Republic of Congo', in T. O. Hansen (ed.), Victims and Post-Conflict Justice Mechanisms in Africa (Law Africa, 2017); Derek Inman and Pacifique Muhindo Magadju, 'Prosecuting International Crimes in the Democratic Republic of Congo: Using Victim Participation as a Tool to Enhance

Punishment, as the previous chapter illustrated, has been another area of ICC mirroring, where a false understanding that the Rome Statute requires domestic prohibition of the death penalty further demarcates international crime adjudication from the broader criminal justice system. For instance, the Kenyan JSC report calls upon the government to 'give an undertaking through a memorandum of understanding to the International Community and the ICC that any person charged, prosecuted and convicted for committing an international crime shall not be sentenced to death', even as Kenya retained the death penalty for other criminal offences.[875] A similar disparity is evident in Uganda, which, despite a de facto ban on the death penalty, retains criminal punishment for certain ordinary crimes.[876]

The suggestion that the Rome Statue's text, together with ICC case law and practice, should be copied wholesale, coupled with the message that 'international standards' and 'best practices' must be met, draws upon a compliance-oriented understanding of complementarity. But to what should the mimicry of such standards and practices be attributed? Writing in another context, the evolutionary biologist Richard Dawkins first introduced the concept of a 'meme' as a cultural replicator and 'unit of imitation' not unlike the gene itself that spreads virally by mutating, replicating and being selected. He wrote:

> Examples of memes are tunes, ideas, catch-phrases, clothes fashions, ways or making pots or building arches. Just as genes propagate themselves in the gene pool by leaping from body to body via sperms or eggs, so memes propagate themselves in the meme pool by leaping from brain to brain via a process, which, in the broad sense, can be called imitation. If a scientist hears, or reads about, a good idea, he passes it on to his colleagues and students. He mentions it in his articles and lectures. If the idea catches on, it can be said to propagate itself, spreading from brain to brain.[877]

the Rule of Law and to Tackle Impunity', *African Human Rights Law Journal* 18 (2018), 293–318. For a critique of this view, see Joseph Kazadi Mpiana, *La Position du droit international dans l'ordre juridique congolais et l'application de ses normes* (Publibook, 2013).

[875] JSC Report, 150.

[876] On the 'growing paradox' of excluding the death penalty for international crimes before international jurisdictions while national jurisdictions maintain it, see Boctor, 'The Abolition of the Death Penalty in Rwanda'.

[877] Dawkins, *The Selfish Gene*, 249. Finnemore and Hollis make a similar point in their process-centred analysis of norm construction, offering that socialization – defined as 'processes by which newcomers become incorporated into organized patterns of social interaction' – can initially take the form of mimicry. Such mimicry may be instrumental – wherein a state conforms its behaviour to that of another it perceives as successful – but also affective, 'such as "to be part of this group and respected by its members, I should emulate their behaviour"'. Norm promoters, in turn, can harness this desire in order for states to 'accept their preferred norms'. See 'Constructing Norms for Global Cybersecurity'. 451–452.

Dawkins elaborated on this theory to emphasize the 'fecundity' of a meme – 'its ability to provide a superficially plausible answer to deep and troubling questions about existence' – as essential to its 'survival value' and its successful replication.[878]

The popular view of complementarity-as-symmetry with Rome Statute standards and ICC practice recalls the mimetic process described above. Indeed, as traced out more fully in Chapter 2, the early understanding of complementarity as a legal test to allocate priority of jurisdiction was deliberately constructed to encompass a more expansive understanding of the concept, i.e., as a catalyst for domestic accountability, one that resonated with audiences well beyond the ICL community as such. That transformation of complementarity, which expanded its meaning and purpose, was the passing on of a more persuasive 'idea meme' in altered form.[879] Norm entrepreneurs engineered this expansive reading of complementarity to potentially realize a more ambitious set of governance goals, drawing upon the 'international standards' announced in Rome and baptizing them as minimum standards to which states must adhere.

This 'justice meme', in turn, has spread through a densely connected web of state and private actors who mediate it through practice on the ground. Indeed, what Dawkins called the 'survival value' of the meme to norm entrepreneurs and advocates – its allure as a way to magnify and fortify not a technical admissibility principle, but rather a 'Rome Statute system' – helps explain the speed and spread of its replication.[880] Complementarity was thus a blueprint for accountability, with the ICC at the top. Even if none of the ICC's own rules on punishment or procedural innovations like victim participation were themselves required of domestic proceedings, they have often been propagated as if they are. As part of that process, duty-based readings of the Rome Statute and the ICC's own rules of procedure and evidence were developed, repeated and passed down, travelling from academic conferences to philanthropic strategies, from diplomatic hallways to in-country embassies, from negotiating tables in The Hague to courtrooms and NGO offices in Kampala, Nairobi and Kinshasa.

---

[878] Dawkins, *The Selfish Gene*, 251–253.

[879] Ibid., 251, 254. Dawkins acknowledged that memes are not always 'high-fidelity replicators', as 'meme transmission is subject to continuous mutation, and also to blending'; rather, he emphasized the 'essential basis of the ['idea-meme'] which is held in common by all brains that understand the theory'. For further exploration of Dawkins' themes, see also Susan Blackmore, *The Meme Machine* (Oxford: Oxford University Press, 2000).

[880] Ibid., 250–252.

And yet, mimetic conformity with 'international standards' can also stymie domestic proceedings, rather than catalyse them. As Elena Baylis notes, 'the common approach has been to hold constant as an irreducible, unnegotiable value our commitment to trials that meet international due process standards and to … hold trials on the international level insofar as possible and to discourage and criticize national trials that do not meet international standards'.[881] Uganda's ICD illustrates this tendency. Whereas a 2011 needs assessment of the division concluded that 'the JLOS institutions are closer to being ready for war-crimes proceedings than some within those institutions believe',[882] a July 2012 speech by the ICD's registrar highlighted its ongoing deficiencies. In his words:

> Positive complementarity presupposes that national institution[s] like the ICD in Uganda should have the necessary and vital tools to effectively and efficiently handle investigations and prosecutions of international crimes under the Statute. Many countries, Uganda inclusive, have problems in fulfilling these obligations. This, therefore, calls for the ICC and other international organisations, as well as governments of the other state parties to facilitate the young national institution to cope with the expected standards.[883]

These same 'expected standards' have, in turn, been used to justify the long-running (and troubling) trial against Thomas Kwoyelo, discussed further in the next chapter. As ASF's country director in Uganda has written:

> The case is the first ever to be tried under the ICD Rules of Procedure and Evidence, a special set of rules that aims to bring the ICD up to the standards of international courts. As a party to the Rome Statute, the ICD answers to the principle of complementarity – it has to be capable of dealing with cases of genocide, war crimes, and crimes against humanity with the same standards as the ICC. These international requirements have created unprecedented situations for the ICD, and as a result, the case is moving slowly.[884]

---

[881] Baylis, 'Reassessing the Role of International Criminal Law', 8. For a similar conclusion in the context of Uganda, see Phil Clark, '"All These Outsiders Shouted Louder than Us": Civil Society Engagement with Transitional Justice in Uganda', Working Paper SiT/WP/03/15, 13.

[882] 'Final Report and Recommendations of Needs-Assessment Mission Experts', 4 March 2011 (on-file).

[883] Remarks by His Worship Asiimwe Tadeo, 'Effecting Complementarity: Challenges and Opportunities: A Case Study of the International Crimes Division of Uganda', paper presented at regional forum on international and transitional justice organized by ASF-Uganda Mission and the Ugandan Coalition for the ICC (20 July 2012).

[884] Romain Ravet, 'Thomas Kwoyelo in Uganda: Victims' Participation Brings Hope and Challenges', International Justice Monitor (17 October 2018), at www.ijmonitor.org/2018/10/thomas-kwoyelo-in-uganda-victims-participation-brings-hope-and-challenges/.

Thus, the 'justice meme' is, on one level, a reflection of private actors' successful expansion of complementarity from legal rule to policy innovation. On another, however, it reflects a troubling elevation of institutional form over function. In the words of one observer who visited Uganda's ICD in 2014, '[A] clerk lamented the lack of cases but proudly explained the premises were "designed to look like the ICC"'.[885] The following chapter explores how such questions of form and function have concretely played out in particular domestic proceedings to date.

5 Conclusion

To varying degrees, complementarity animates and sustains the creation (or proposed creation) of specialized institutions, personnel and regulations for the domestic prosecution of ICC crimes. Whether as admissibility rule or normative ordering principle, state and non-state actors alike have summoned the adaptive nature of complementarity as the basis for transforming and reforming domestic judicial systems, as well as their relationship to the ICC. Whereas complementarity was once a principle that Uganda sought to invoke to keep the court at bay, the ICD now frequently appears as the ICC's institutional partner: Thomas Kwoyelo tried in Uganda, Dominic Ongwen tried in The Hague. Non-state actors in the DRC have invoked complementarity in a similar manner, even though the (limited) domestic proceedings there are not connected in any material way to, nor the direct result of, the ICC's undertakings. Indeed, the opposite took place: an initial promise of cooperation between the ICC and the government gave way to greater contestation between The Hague and Kinshasa.

At the same time, the creation of specialized regimes or units for the prosecution of international crimes has arguably contributed to an ongoing bifurcation within these systems, often rigidly dividing international and national justice in a way that disadvantages the 'ordinary' criminal justice system in a competition for patronage and resources in already resource-limited settings. Instead, attention has been redirected to the creation of domestic courts, the focus of which has overwhelmingly

---

[885] Macdonald, 'Somehow This Whole Process Became So Artificial', 243.

measured compliance with complementarity through mimetic conformity with ICC practices and procedures. This 'justice meme' may be
compelling as a way to entice international donor support, but, as this
chapter has demonstrated, the pressures of accommodating a unique set
of crimes within a domestic judicial structure oscillate between a mutu-
ally reinforcing rhetoric of exceptionalism (special crimes requiring special treatment) and mimicry (to ICC rules and procedures).

7

Catalysing Opportunity

Complementarity and Domestic Proceedings

The previous two chapters traced the normative and institutional effects that have flowed from the International Criminal Court's (ICC) interventions in Uganda, Kenya and the Democratic Republic of Congo (DRC), even if the court itself was only occasionally the catalyst for these developments. This chapter moves further through this legal framework to canvass what actual criminal domestic proceedings have taken place in each of the three countries and queries the extent to which the ICC's engagement was itself a catalyst for these proceedings. In so doing, the role of the court as a mediating, rather than a causal, agent comes again to the fore. Specifically, in each country, state and non-state actors alike seized upon ICC intervention as an enabling condition for the realization of various accountability-related agendas, ranging from the funding of mobile military courts in the DRC, to strategic impact litigation in Kenya, to the high-profile prosecution of a former Lord's Resistance Army (LRA) rebel before Uganda's International Crimes Division (ICD). As with the evolution of specialized judicial units or the passage of Rome Statute legislation, the chapter illustrates that the ICC's involvement unfolded alongside a series of other developments and interventions that collectively facilitated these actors' efforts. Rather than catalysing domestic proceedings as such, the court's engagement made possible a series of opportunities upon which the advocacy of other, predominantly non-state, actors turned.

The chapter proceeds in three parts. It first considers in greater detail the turn to military court prosecutions in the DRC, and the substantial efforts by international NGOs and donors to provide operational and financial support to these initiatives as an example of 'complementarity in practice'. It highlights several of the more significant convictions that have resulted from these proceedings, which have typically been framed both as an extension of the ICC's trials and a necessary complement to them.

238

The second section considers the limited efforts that were undertaken to prosecute post-election violence in Kenya as 'ordinary crimes', while also charting the efforts by international and domestic human rights advocates to use civil litigation and even the possibility of private prosecution as part of an ongoing effort to press for accountability from the state, even as the ICC's own cases collapsed. Indeed, these domestic proceedings have come to represent one of the last potential avenues for legal redress in Kenya. Finally, through a case study of the trial of Thomas Kwoyelo – the only proceeding related to the LRA conflict to come before the Ugandan ICD thus far – the chapter considers how the domestic invocation of complementarity can spur accountability, but also accommodate to state power, leading to other abusive practices in the name of 'combatting impunity'.

1   Democratic Republic of Congo: Mobile Courts in the ICC's Shadow

Military courts have thus far been the near exclusive adjudicators of international crimes in the DRC, although since 2013 Congolese civilian courts, in theory, now have jurisdiction as well.[886] Although it is difficult to ascertain how many trials have been conducted – no official records are kept, nor are decisions published in casebooks – the DRC appears to have been the site of the greatest number of domestic criminal proceedings for Rome Statute/atrocity crimes.[887] A study published by Avocats sans Frontières (ASF) in 2009 identified 13 atrocity-related trials held by military courts between 2004 and early 2009, concerning a total of 188 defendants belonging either to the DRC's regular army or to non-state armed groups.[888] Wetsh'oknda Koso's 2010 study suggests

---

[886] The civil justice system was formally given jurisdiction over international crimes in 2013; however, only one case has been opened in that time; thus, de facto, jurisdiction of ICC crimes in the DRC remains with military courts. The case is nonetheless an interesting one: in 2016, a civilian court in the DRC issued a conviction for genocide against members of the Luba, a Bantu ethnic group, and Twa, a Pygmy people that populate the Great Lakes region on charges of inter-ethnic violence in the country's southeast region. See 'Congo charges 34 with genocide in inter-ethnic fighting', Reuters (14 August 2015).

[887] See, e.g., Mbokani, *Congolese Jurisprudence under International Criminal Law*, 4–5; Jean-Michel Kumbu, 'National Courts: The Situation in the Democratic Republic of Congo', in *Inducing Compliance with International Human Rights Law*, 217–246.

[888] See Avocats Sans Frontieres, 'The Application of the Rome Statute of the International Criminal Court by the Courts of the Democratic Republic of Congo' (2009), 100–112.

a similar figure,[889] while a comprehensive study published in 2016 by the Open Society Initiative for South Africa reviewed 29 military court decisions between 2004 and 2015 that it classified as having applied the Rome Statute.[890] Finally, a 2015 study by the International Center for Transitional Justice concluded that judicial authorities had opened 39 cases between 2009 and 2014 related to crimes that had occurred in the eastern provinces and districts (7 in Ituri, 210 in North Kivu, 22 in South Kivu) since 2002.[891] Notably, however, no Congolese military court has considered any atrocity-related case prior to 2002, i.e., the entry into force of the Rome Statute. While nothing prevents the courts from considering pre-2002 crimes, their post-2002 focus is consistent with the prioritization of the ICC's legislative framework.

Military courts also possess a subject matter jurisdiction greater than international crimes. Indeed, only a fraction of mobile court sessions in the DRC have dealt with international crimes as such, while a far greater number have prosecuted serious, if legally 'ordinary', crimes post-2002.[892] One article notes, for instance, that since 2011, 'military courts have tried some 8,000 cases of sexual violence committed by soldiers'.[893] A formal assessment done in 2012 of the courts managed by the American

---

[889] Marcel Wetsh'okonda Koso, 'La contribution de la justice militaire reformée a la lute contre l'impunité en République démocratique du Congo dix ans après: essai de bilan et perspectives d'avenir' (on-file).

[890] See Mbokani, *Congolese Jurisprudence under International Criminal Law*, 4–5; see also Human Rights Watch, 'Justice on Trial', 72 (concluding that 'the total can be estimated at about 30 over the past decade'). For a helpful enumeration of the methodological challenges in identifying judicial decisions in the DRC, see Elena Baylis, 'Reassessing the Role of International Criminal Law: Rebuilding National Courts through Transnational Networks', *Boston College Law Review* 50(1) (2009), 30, fn. 95.

[891] International Center for Transitional Justice, 'The Accountability Landscape in Eastern DRC: Analysis of the National Legislative and Judicial Response to International Crimes' (2009–2014) (July 2015), 20.

[892] Significantly, many of these 'ordinary' crimes may well constitute international crimes if certain contextual elements were established; however, as commentators have noted, decisions issued by mobile courts have generally failed to engage in such analysis or have done so inadequately. Chuck Sudetic (then a senior writer for the Open Society Foundations) offers an interesting description of a mobile court session, and the range of cases it adjudicated, when he travelled to the DRC in 2011. See 'Congo Justice: The Defendants Arrive' (13 April 2011), at www.opensocietyfoundations.org/voices/congo-justice-defendants-arrive.

[893] Louise Jones, 'The Rape Trial of Colonel 106: A Test for Congo's Military Justice', *International Justice Tribune* (10 September 2014); Stephanie van den Berg, 'Praise for Historic Congo Rape Conviction', *International Justice Tribune* (11 December 2014).

Bar Association's Rule of Law Initiative likewise concluded that 'it is these violent crimes – by intimates and civilians – that predominate today'.[894] An added dimension of the mobile courts is thus their connection to broader discussions around ensuring access to justice, as certain development and rule-of-law literature has illustrated.[895]

Support for Military Court Proceedings

Most domestic proceedings, as outlined in the previous chapter, have been conducted by 'mobile courts' (*chambres foraines*), wherein the courts themselves travel to remote territories in the DRC.[896] Supported, crucially, by the UN's MONUSCO (United Nations Organization Stabilization Mission in the DR Congo) mission, as well as international donors and NGOs, together with DRC-based partners, these sessions range in length from a matter of days to, less frequently, a week or two. MONUSCO and other partners typically provide financial and logistical support to enable the travel from the provincial capital of local judges, prosecutors, victims and defence lawyers.[897] Other UN actors in-country have also assisted the courts as well, including MONUSCO's Joint Investigative Teams and Prosecution Support Cells. The former, led by the UN's Joint Human Rights Office, includes human rights officers who work jointly with national DRC investigators on specific missions, facilitating access to evidence and crime scenes. The support cells have been operative since 2011 under MONUSCO's Rule of Law Section. While not framed as 'positive' complementarity per se, the cells similarly seek to provide case-specific 'tangible technical and logistical support' to Congolese military and civilian justice authorities by pairing them with international counterparts.[898]

---

[894] Open Society Initiative for Southern Africa, 'Helping to combat impunity for sexual crimes in DRC: An evaluation of the mobile gender justice courts' (2012), 28.

[895] See, e.g., United Nations Development Programme (UNDP) Discussion Paper, 'Complementarity and Transitional Justice: Synthesis of Key Emerging Issues for Development – New Opportunities arising from the Principle of Complementarity and Support for National Capacities to Investigate and Prosecute Serious Crimes of International Concern' (16 November 2012).

[896] While mobile courts can also sit as civilian tribunals, they have been convened almost exclusively as military proceedings. Interview with Marcel Wetsh'okonda Koso (Kinshasa, 21 June 2011).

[897] See International Center for Transitional Justice's (ICTJ) 'The Accountability Landscape in Eastern DRC', for an overview of financial arrangements as shared between the UN, international partners and the Congolese state, 25–26, 30–33.

[898] See MONUSCO, 'Military Justice' at https://monusco.unmissions.org/en/military-justice.

Mobile courts have achieved some notable convictions and, as noted in Chapter 5, they have also either applied provisions of the Rome Statute directly (if selectively), or used certain statutory provisions as an interpretive tool.[899] The first such decision appears to be the Ankoro case, which was rendered in 2004, and concerned the murder of 60 people and the destruction of hundreds of homes.[900] It led to nine convictions of Congolese army troops, a decision that was, at the time, unprecedented. A spate of similar decisions followed in 2005 and 2006, as international donor projects came increasingly to support the courts as a new rule-of-law intervention, setting aside initial concerns (though often not publicly disclosing) that they were, in fact, part of the DRC's much-criticized military justice system.[901] Amongst the international NGOs, Avocats sans Frontières and TRIAL International have worked most closely with the DRC's military justice system, conducting extensive trainings for judges and prosecutors of the military tribunals on the ICC and the Rome Statute.

One of the most prominent such cases to date was the conviction of Lieutenant Eliwo Ngoy and his co-defendants for crimes against humanity, for mass rapes committed in the town of Songo Mboyo in 2003. Sitting in Mbandaka, the capital of Équateur province, the court chose, in a novel development, to apply the Rome Statute directly in convicting the defendants, rather than under Congolese national law.[902] Notably, many

[899] See, e.g., Mbokani, *Congolese Jurisprudence under International Criminal Law*, 196 (arguing that 'there is a very strong tendency in Congolese case law to intertwine definitions of crimes under the Rome Statute and forms of liability defined by ordinary criminal law'). See also ICTJ, 'The Accountability Landscape in Eastern DRC', 8 ('Military courts, however, have not set aside domestic law provisions altogether. Instead, they have made use of a variety of sources to inform their decisions: the domestic military penal code, the Rome Statute and the jurisprudence of international tribunals'.).

[900] For the full Ankoro judgment, see ASF, 'The Application of the Rome Statute of the International Criminal Court by the Courts of the Democratic Republic of Congo'; further analysis in Mbokani, *Congolese Jurisprudence under International Criminal Law*, 34–38.

[901] One MONUSCO interlocutor noted that there was early resistance within the mission to engagement with the DRC's troubled military justice system, but this resistance waned as it became increasingly clear that there were few alternatives. See, e.g., Avocats Sans Frontières, 'Promoting Complementarity [sic] in the Democratic Republic of Congo' (document prepared for the 2010 Rome Statute Review Conference); see also 'Recueil de décisions de justice et de notes de plaidoiries en matière de crimes internationaux' (on-file). TRIAL International maintains an ongoing website of its work in the DRC at https://trialinternational.org/countries-post/democratic-republic-of-the-congo/.

[902] For the full *Songo Mboyo* judgment, see ASF, 'The Application of the Rome Statute of the International Criminal Court by the Courts of the Democratic Republic of Congo'; further analysis in Mbokani, *Congolese Jurisprudence under International Criminal Law*, 41–51.

of these same magistrates had also been 'trained' by ASF and other NGOs on international criminal law and the Rome Statute. These interventions were partly prompted by definitions in the DRC military code that did not comport with the Rome Statute and by the failure on the part of Congolese lawmakers to remedy these conflicts through domestic implementation. Thus, in *Songo Mboyo*, one sees the articulation of a more expansive definition of rape, including its extension to men.[903] Similarly, in other trials, DRC judges have applied the Statute's modes of liability (including article 28 of the Rome Statute on command responsibility, not a doctrine then provided for under Congolese law) and the ICC's rules of procedure and evidence to victim participation and testimony.[904]

Such progressive interpretations have been inconsistent, however, leading to a patchwork of jurisprudence and ongoing fair trial concerns. Indeed, mobile courts proceedings have been criticized almost as often as they have been applauded.[905] A 2014 judgment of a military court sitting in Goma, North Kivu, for instance, applied the Rome Statute in the convictions of 26 (out of 39) members of the Congolese armed forces for acts of looting and pillaging committed in the town of Minova in November 2012,

---

[903] See TMG de Mbandaka, *Songo Mboyo* (12 April 2006); see also TMG de Ituri, *Blaise Bongi* (24 March 2006), wherein judges held that the DRC's internal legislation failed to criminalize war crimes and left them without sanction; the judges concluded: 'in this situation, a remedy to these loopholes must be found by invoking the Rome Statute.' In other successful cases, DRC judges have applied the Congolese military code instead. In February 2011 (as featured on this book's cover), Colonel Kibibi Mutware was sentenced, along with ten of his commanding soldiers, to lengthy jail terms for their involvement in a mass rape (as a crime against humanity) in the town of Fizi, in South Kivu province, on New Year's Day in 2011. Kibibi was the first commanding officer in the DRC to be so convicted. See C. M. de Bukavu, *Daniel Kibibi et consorts* (21 February 2011).

[904] For example, in *Songo Mboyo* and another notable case, *Mutins de Mbandaka*, application of the Statute's rules 'allowed rape victims to testify beyond what it normally permitted in Congolese law, and helped secure convictions against the accused'. Patryk Labuda, 'The ICC in the Democratic Republic of Congo: A Decade of Partnership and Antagonism', in *Africa and the ICC: Perceptions of Justice*, 284–285.

[905] For more positive assessments of the courts, see 'Helping to combat impunity for sexual crimes in DRC: An evaluation of the mobile gender justice courts' (OSISA, 2012). at https://issuu.com/osisa/docs/open_learning-drc-web; for more critical views, see Heike Krieger, 'Where states fail, non-state actors rise? Inducing compliance with international humanitarian law in areas of limited statehood', in *Inducing Compliance with International Human Rights Law*, 504–550. NGO reports have been highly critical of various aspects of court proceedings and have made numerous recommendations for reform, but are generally uniform in acknowledging their need in an otherwise grim accountability landscape.

following their expulsion from Goma by M23 rebel groups.[906] While wide-spread rape and sexual assault were perpetrated upon local civilians as well, the court handed down only two rape convictions against senior offi-cers, disappointing many who had participated and supported the trial.[907] Elsewhere, a 2016 judgment for an armed attack on the village of Mutarule, in South Kivu province, concluded that while the massacre was itself a crime against humanity – with victims entitled to state compensation – none of the three defendants (including two commanders of the DRC's armed forces, known as FARDC) were convicted for that crime.[908]

Further, although some observers of the courts have noted that the mobile court proceedings meet fair trial standards, significant concerns remain about the independence of the Congolese military justice system. As a report of the Open Society Initiative for Southern Africa notes:

> [The] mobile court hearings are ... sometimes not held in conditions that allow military judges to issue rulings in a faithful and conscientious way, and with complete freedom. This is the case when these hearings draw a significant crowd, and there is public pressure for the accused to be sentenced. Judges are then very strongly tempted to make decisions that will satisfy public opinion.[909]

While donor pressure and the expectation that domestic criminal proceedings would yield convictions explain some of these concerns, several commentators have also notably framed their misgivings as a lack of compliance with complementarity. One notes, for instance, that 'the use of mobile courts was not contemplated under the Rome Statute', and suggests that the 'use of military penal code and mobile courts in the domestic prosecutions in the DRC makes the prosecutions fall short of complementarity-based prosecution'.[910]

---

[906] Milli Lake, 'After Minova: Can War Crimes Trials Overcome Violence in the DRC?' (8 May 2014), at http://africanarguments.org/2014/05/08/after-minova-can-war-crimes-trials-overcome-violence-in-the-drc-by-millie-lake/.

[907] See ASF, 'Congo: unsatisfactory verdict for crimes committed in Minova' (7 May 2014); UN News 'UN human rights office 'disappointed' by ruling in DR Congo mass rape trial' (6 May 2014).

[908] See TRIAL International, 'Judicial Reparations for the Mutarule Massacre' (23 February 2017). TRIAL had described the 2016 proceedings as especially tense, when one of the accused FARDC commanders was found dead midway through trial.

[909] 'The Democratic Republic of Congo', 34–35.

[910] Imoedemhe, *The Complementarity Regime of the International Criminal Court*, 99–100 (noting that 'because the prosecutions do not capture the conduct criminalized in the Rome Statute nor do they follow due process as recognised by international law').

Despite these concerns, mobile courts are likely to remain the most promising venue for domestic criminal proceedings in the DRC in the near future, with complementarity the operating principle that sustains them. Indeed, one of the most significant judgments to date was rendered in December 2017, when a court from Goma, set up in the village of Kavumu, convicted 11 Congolese military members of murder and rape as crimes against humanity. The court found that the accused constituted an armed group controlled by provincial lawmaker Frederic Batumike and, under Batumike's control, had carried out the rapes of 40 young girls.[911] The decision marked the first time that a sitting parliamentarian was found guilty of international crimes (Batumike was later sentenced to life imprisonment).[912] Reflecting on the successful judgment, two of TRIAL's legal advisors noted that it 'demonstrate[es] the full potential of the complementarity system enshrined in the Rome Statute of the ICC'.[913]

NGOs and Domestic Accountability in DRC

What accounts for the relative success of these proceedings in the DRC, which, while not materially connected to the ICC's intervention, have unfolded in the shadow of the court's continued judicial activity? Milli Lake, a political scientist, has advanced the argument that the opportunity structures enabled by state fragility, particularly acute in eastern Congo, 'have enabled both domestic and international NGOs and human rights practitioners to exert considerable influence over judicial processes at multiple levels of governance, most notably at the level of local courts'.[914] She contends that this lack of capacity has meant that NGOs, rather than the state itself, have effectively commandeered the administration of justice. As a result, state fragility has 'facilitated, rather than obstructed,

[911] TRIAL International, 'Kavumu Trial: High Military Courts Confirms All Condemnations' (26 July 2018).
[912] In July 2018, the High Military Court affirmed all convictions. Notably, however, it did not recognize the DRC itself as civilly liable under principle of state responsibility for its failure to protect.
[913] Daniele Perisi and Elsa Taquet, 'The Kavumu Trial: Complementarity in Action in the Democratic Republic of Congo', International Justice Monitor (5 February 2018), at www.ijmonitor.org/2018/02/the-kavumu-trial-complementarity-in-action-in-the-democratic-republic-of-congo/.
[914] Milli Lake, Strong NGOs and Weak States (Cambridge: Cambridge University Press, 2018), 7.

aspects of human rights advocacy, particularly legal attention to gender violence'.[915] The institutional presence of the ICC – and the positive obligations that the complementarity principle is understood to carry – have further enabled this dynamic.

Lake's argument lends support to the contention that ICC interventions appear to have had a more profound effect in catalysing opportunity for the agendas and priorities of non-state actors, than of state officials as such.[916] In the context of a fragile state like the DRC, these private actors have provided the necessary material, financial and technical support to enable complex justice interventions like the mobile courts project that, in turn, have spawned a measure of domestic judicial activity. Moreover, unlike the ICC, for whom the executive branch remains its principal interlocutor, non-state actors have advanced their agendas through a plurality of actors – DRC judges, court administrators, prosecutors, lawyers, penitentiary systems, hospitals – and at multiple levels of government (sub-state, provincial, district).[917] These interventions also encompass an array of actors well beyond the justice sector, drawing in officials from the development and rule-of-law sectors, who see the challenge of accountability less as (or not merely as) a function of complementing the ICC or realizing the Rome Statute's legal obligations, but as a more fundamental question of ensuring access to justice.

Rather than the cooperative vision of complementarity that Moreno-Ocampo first promised between the ICC and DRC, then, that relationship has instead characterized the interactions between certain state actors and civil society. Indeed, in more remote regions of the DRC, NGOs have assumed some of the basic functions of governance. In eastern Congo,

---

[915] Ibid., 12; see also Milli Lake, 'Organizing Hypocrisy: Providing Legal Accountability for Human Rights Violations in Areas of Limited Statehood', *International Studies Quarterly* 58(3) (2014), 515–526.

[916] Nouwen reaches a similar conclusion in the context of Uganda; see *Complementarity in the Line of Fire*, 236 ('[T]he ICC's involvement triggered the attention of and created space for, organisations with normative agendas. The questions that the ICC's involvement raised created an opportunity for local organisations to push for transitional justice in Uganda'.).

[917] Lake, 'Organizing Hypocrisy', 522 ('[B]ecause the state has historically had only very limited reach over its provinces, in reality the courts function with little input from Kinshasa'.). See also Ezequiel González Ocantos, 'Persuade Them or Oust Them: Crafting Judicial Change and Transitional Justice in Argentina', *Comparative Politics* (July 2014) (noting that 'deep transformations inside judicial branches are required' to 'observe sea changes in patterns of jurisprudential outcomes', and pointing to the success of Peruvian NGOs in 'training and re-socializing judges and prosecutors' to overcome anti-transitional justice measures).

in particular, this 'de facto assumption of power … has created opportunities through which nonstate actors can enter and influence judicial
processes by engaging in tasks normally reserved for representatives of
the sovereign government'.[918] These tasks range from paying per diems to
public officials (that can, in many cases, exceed their own state salaries),
to coordinating trials, to providing necessary psychosocial support and
protection to victims and/or witnesses.

Viewed from this perspective, a certain accommodation between state
interests and the objectives of private actors comes into focus. Lake herself has argued that the apparent success of a number of these domestic
trials in the DRC belies a more complex reality, wherein military elites
have often acted to preserve the 'outward appearance of cooperation' with
accountability efforts, while doing so in ways that serve to consolidate
(or at least not materially threaten) their hold on power vis-à-vis other
factions.[919] Similarly, Nouwen concludes that, in Uganda, the 'catalysing effect [of complementarity] was strongest when branches of government co-opted, on the basis of their cost-benefit analysis, the agendas of
the norm entrepreneurs'.[920] Indeed, this co-optation goes some length to
explaining why Uganda referred the LRA situation to the ICC in the first
place, as well as the government's continued embrace of the ICD notwithstanding the larger failure of the Juba peace accords.

ICC intervention in a fragile state like the DRC may thus enable opportunity structures that advance the cause of domestic accountability, but
these mediated arrangements introduce new ambiguities and concerns.
For instance, the effective 'sponsoring' of mobile courts by non-state
actors, presumably eager to see the impact of their own investments,
raises questions about the influence of donor interests on the fairness of
the criminal process. At a broader level, they also illustrate the ambivalent, dynamic relationship between Congolese civil society organizations
and their larger, international NGO counterparts, as well as the nature
of NGO 'partnerships' with the DRC government writ large.[921] In calling

---

[918] Lake, *Strong NGOs and Weak States*, 10.
[919] See Milli Lake, 'Building the Rule of War: Postconflict Institutions and the Micro-
Dynamics of Conflict in Eastern DR Congo', *International Organization* 71(2) (2017),
281–315.
[920] Nouwen, *Complementarity in the Line of Fire*, 236.
[921] See, e.g., William Fisher, 'Doing Good? The Politics and Anti-Politics of NGO Practices',
Annual Review of Anthropology 26 (1997), 439–464 (criticizing idealized depictions of
NGOs as 'disinterested apolitical participants in a field of otherwise implicated players'
and calling for a more chastened assessment that recognizes both the problems and the
potential of NGOs).

for Congolese civil society to be more actively involved in these cases, one commentator working in the DRC noted how, '[c]urrent judicial dynamics involve several international partners whose support and pressure often determine which cases go to trial and which do not'.[922] Reflecting on these vexed relationships in the context of the mobile courts, another Congolese interlocutor wryly observed that the number of international NGO-run trainings and capacity-building seminars for Congolese judges made them appear, at times, *comme les bonnes élèves des ONG* ('like good students of the NGOs').[923]

Thus, while these civil society efforts are admirable, they also present their own complications. Indeed, the private management of a state's justice sector through the logic of complementarity underscores a larger trend towards private involvement in basic development and service provision. In so doing, '[D]onors [have] bypassed states with low capacity for governance, giving money to NGOs when they believed doing so would enable their support to achieve their intended outcomes'.[924] This relationship is reciprocal as well; it shapes the practices of NGOs in turn. As Lake argues, 'The structure of NGO funding has meant that activities with quantifiable outcomes – such as the numbers of cases reported to the police, judgments delivered and processed, police or lawyers trained, or convictions reached – have been prioritized over activities that may lead to more incremental change'.[925] This blurring of governance boundaries underscores the critical and persistent concerns many DRC advocates articulated about *la pérennité* as well – their desire 'for sustainability beyond the temporal mandates of the current actors', as the DRC government's former focal point for the ICC put it.[926] What will happen, they ask, when the court finally goes?

---

[922] Myriam Raymond-Jetté, 'Small gains on large crimes in DR Congo', Peace Insight (1 7 July 2015), at www.peaceinsight.org/blog/2015/07/small-gains-large-crimes-dr-congo/.

[923] Interview with Congolese academic (Brussels, 8 September 2017). Indeed, a persistent concern articulated by interlocutors about the mobile courts program was the predominant influence international funders and implementers appeared to have over their national/local counterparts. For further analysis of how 'extraconstitutional' considerations have favoured the 'superiority' of the Rome Statute over the military penal code, see Joseph Kazadi Mpiana, *La position du droit international dans l'ordre juridique congolais et l'application de ses norms*, 492–493 (finding 'unconvincing' the importation of such provisions as the Rome Statute's prohibition on capital punishment or victim participation).

[924] Jennifer N. Brass, *Allies or Adversaries: NGOs and the State in Africa* (Cambridge: Cambridge University Press, 2017), 8–9.

[925] Lake, *Strong NGOs and Weak States*, 224; see also Autesserre, *The Trouble with the Congo*.

[926] Colonel Muntazini, 'A Close-Up Look at the Fight against Impunity in the DRC'.

2 Kenya: A Turn to Impact Litigation

Notwithstanding the failure of the ICC's Kenyan cases, claims that there have been no domestic proceedings related to the post-election violence are not entirely accurate. They have been exceedingly limited, however, relative to the scale of the violence, and the actual number of prosecutions varies widely depending on the source. Unsurprisingly, a series of reports issued by the government over the course of 2009–2012 contain conflicting information. The first report, prepared for the attorney general in early 2009 (prior to the onset of the ICC's investigation), indicated that 676 accused had been identified for prosecution, with cases pending in the Western, Rift Valley, Nyanza and Coast provinces.[927]

The data in that report, however, conflict with figures compiled in the government's subsequent 2011 report (after summonses for the 'Ocampo Six' had been announced), which concluded that cases involving sexual and gender-based violence had been erroneously excluded from the 2009 figures.[928] According to the 2011 submission, Kenyan courts had registered 45 convictions related to sexual- and gender-based crimes committed during the post-election violence, as well as another 94 convictions for other crimes.[929] A third report commissioned in 2012 by a subsequent 'task force' paints yet another picture: it reviewed slightly more than 6,000 cases from across the country and, as of August 2012, reported that only 24 suspects had been convicted for election-related violence.[930] In a sobering assessment (issued after the Appeals Chamber had affirmed the admissibility of the Kenyan cases), the task force also concluded that most alleged perpetrators from 2007 would never be prosecuted, due to alleged

---

[927] See 'A Report to the Hon. Attorney General by the Team on the Review of Post-Election Violence Related Cases in Western, Nyanza, Central, Rift Valley, Eastern, Coast and Nairobi Provinces' (February 2009) (on-file). The report noted that only 69 cases against approximately 170 accuses would likely proceed to trial, due to lack of evidence or inadequate investigations; further, another 3,627 cases were reportedly still pending investigation. Ibid., 33–34.

[928] 'Progress Report to the Attorney General by the team on the update of Post-Election Violence Related cases in Western, Nyanza, Central, Rift-Valley, Eastern, Coast and Nairobi Provinces' (2011) (on-file).

[929] Ibid., 70. Notably, however, a number of cases cited in the report concerned unrelated conduct or crimes that preceded the 2007 violence. See also Human Rights Watch, 'Turning Pebbles', 25–27.

[930] See Interim Report of the Task Force on Post-Election Violence (27 August 2012) (on-file). The data it released further indicated that only 15 people had been identified for the crime of murder. The report further stated that 889 people had been identified as having committed 'general offenses', while nearly 2,500 suspects were yet to be identified.

lack of evidence and the difficulty of pursuing investigations so many years later.[931] Finally, in February 2014, at another workshop organized to discuss the proposed establishment of an ICD, the Director of Public Prosecutions stated that there would be no cases capable of prosecution.[932]

In her commanding study of the ICC's intervention in Kenya, Antonina Okuta contends that the principal source of contradiction amongst the government's various reports is that no link was made with the context in which the post-election crimes were committed.[933] Through field visits undertaken to various courts around the country between May and August 2012, she concludes that none of the stations 'could, with precision, provide the number of persons prosecuted over the 2007 post-election violence cases'.[934] As she notes:

> One seeking this information had to peruse all the criminal files opened from March 2018. Even then, unless a conviction ensued and the [j]udgement indicated that the case emanated from the 2007 post-election violence, there was no manner of knowing which cases were linked to the violence. Instructively, Kenya 2007 post-election violence did not result in a substantial or complete break-down of structures, yet the data was hard to come by.

Another compounding factor was that the limited proceedings that did take place were not for international crimes, but ordinary ones.[935] Furthermore, where these cases did proceed to court, there were numerous acquittals.[936] Based on her research, Okuta concludes that only a

---

[931] Ibid. The report also noted that some of the areas with the highest casualties in Kenya had recorded no convictions at all, including no convictions for police officers despite an estimated 962 cases of police shootings that resulted in hundreds of deaths. Ibid., 25.

[932] See *Daily Nation* (6 February 2014).

[933] Antonina Okuta, Accountability for International Crimes at the Domestic Level: Case Studies of Kenya, Uganda, and Cote d'Ivoire (University of Amsterdam, PhD Dissertation) (29 March 2016) (on-file).

[934] Ibid., 123.

[935] Recorded convictions were for such offences as taking part in a riot, burglary, 'publishing a false rumor', creating disturbance, stock theft, possession of offensive weapons, stealing and other misdemeanours. For a similar assessment, see Evelyne Owiye Asaala, 'Prosecuting Crimes Related to the 2007 Post-Election Violence in Kenyan Courts: Issues and Challenges', in H. J. van der Merwe and Gerhard Kemp (eds.), *International Criminal Justice in Africa: Issues, Challenges and Prospects* (Strathmore University Press, 2016), 32–33.

[936] Two cases that captured national attention due to their gravity resulted in acquittals. These acquittals were principally the result of poor police investigations and/or tampered evidence. See, e.g., Republic of Kenya v. Stephen Kiprotich Leting and 3 Others, High Court of Kenya (Nakuru), Criminal Case no. 34 (judgment delivered 30 April 2009) (acquittals for four people charged with arson in relation to the burning of a church in Kiambaa, which led to the deaths of 25–35 women and children); Republic of Kenya v. Edward Kirui, High Court of Kenya (Nairobi), Criminal Case no. 9 (judgment delivered

handful of people were convicted for the crime of murder arising out of the 2007 violence (two of which commenced prior to the onset of the ICC's investigation), while a handful more were convicted for robbery.[937] A Human Rights Watch report from 2011 reached a similar conclusion, finding that, out of 76 cases that did reach the courts, 'not one demonstrates any attempt to investigate those responsible for organizing and directing the violence'.[938]

Thus, while there appears to have been a handful of domestic criminal proceedings as a result of Kenya's post-election violence, it cannot be said with certainty how many took place. Furthermore, the limited accountability that did result was due to cases that were instituted immediately after the 2007 violence and prosecuted as ordinary crimes, with no contextual analysis of the elements for crimes against humanity.[939] Once the Kenyan government's admissibility challenge failed, it abandoned the accountability roadmap that had underpinned its challenge entirely.

Post-2010: A New Constitution for Kenya

While most attention outside of Kenya in the post-election period was focused on the ICC, one outcome that has arguably had an even greater impact on the pursuit of domestic accountability were changes enshrined in the new Kenyan Constitution of 2010, which replaced the post-independence constitution of 1963. Domestic pressure for constitutional amendment in Kenya had been building steadily throughout the 1990s and calls for a comprehensive review intensified with the election of former President Kibaki in 2002. One outcome of this period, as Chapter 5 noted, was ratification of the Rome Statute; another was a process of official and civil

---

21 June 2010) (acquittal for a police officer accused of murdering two unarmed protestors). Despite video evidence of the shooting, the court found that the gun produced as evidence in evidence was different from that alleged to have been used by the officer. For further analysis of these cases, see Asaala, 'Prosecuting Crimes Related to the 2007 Post-Election Violence in Kenyan Courts', 36–39.

[937] Okuta, 125–126. Significantly, in several of these cases, defendants were sentenced to death for their crime; in one, the sentence was upheld on appeal (see Republic of Kenya v. James Mbugua Ndung'u and Raymond Munene Kamau, Criminal Appeal nos. 418 & 419 of 2008 [judgment delivered 2 July 2013]). As noted in the previous chapter, had these accused been prosecuted under Kenya's International Crimes Act (Kenya 2008) (ICA) (for more serious crimes), the death penalty would not have been an available sentence.

[938] See Human Rights Watch, 'Turning Pebbles', 29–42.

[939] Asaala, 'Prosecuting Crimes Related to the 2007 Post-Election Violence in Kenyan Courts', 32 ('[T]here has been no instance when local courts conceptualized the notion of crimes against humanity'.).

society consultation over a new constitution. When the promise augured by Kibaki's first term faded, however, negotiations on a new text stalled. It was not until the intervention of the African Union's Panel of Eminent African Personalities, overseen by Annan, that these discussions resumed.

As with the swift passage of Kenya's ICC Act, the new constitution came into effect quickly. An initial draft was released to the public in November 2009; Parliament unanimously approved it on 1 April 2010.[940] The new constitution introduced a number of significant legislative changes, including the creation of an upper house (Senate) where county governments would have more representation and more limited presidential powers. Judicial reform was another significant achievement and formed the basis, notably, for much of the government's unsuccessful ICC admissibility challenge. These included more dispersed judicial authority, a revised system for appointing judges (affording greater autonomy from the executive) and a more rigorous vetting process.[941] Of even greater importance, arguably, were reforms to Kenya's criminal justice system, with the task of exercising the state's powers of prosecution entrusted to an independent Director of Public Prosecutions, rather than the attorney general.[942]

Another significant change introduced by the constitution was the place of international law in the country's domestic legal order. Previously, Kenya was a dualist state: international treaties were not binding until they were implemented domestically, which was in part the legal logic for passage of the 2009 International Crimes Act (Kenya 2008) (ICA). The 2010 Constitution, however, adopts a more monist approach, providing that '[a]ny treaty or convention ratified by Kenya shall form part of the law of Kenya under this constitution'.[943] Moreover, while not explicitly granting a right of private prosecution, Article 157(6)(b) provides that the Director of Public Prosecutions

---

[940] The new constitution was subsequently put to a referendum in August 2010 and approved by a large majority of Kenyan voters.

[941] For a detailed analysis of these and other reforms, and the political battles waged to achieve them, see James Thuo Gathii, *The Contested Empowerment of Kenya's Judiciary, 2010–2015: A Historical Institutional Analysis* (Sheria Publishing House, 2016).

[942] Kenya Constitution, Article 157. As noted in Chapter 6, while the creation of an independent DPP was seen in principle as a promising step in the country's new constitutional dispensation, the appointment of Keirako Tobiko as its head was seen as a major defeat amongst many reformists.

[943] Article 2(5) ('The general rules of international law shall form part of the law of Kenya'.); Section 2(6) ('Any treaty or convention ratified by Kenya shall form part of the law of Kenya under this Constitution.').

(DPP) has the power to 'take over and continue any criminal proceedings commenced in any court (other than a court martial) that have been instituted or undertaken by another person or authority, with the permission of the person or authority'.[944] The 2013 act establishing the office of the DPP is more direct: it states that any person may initiate a private prosecution.[945]

The establishment of a fortified private prosecution right, taken together with the introduction of monism, subsequently became the basis for a series of legal actions filed by civil society organizations (and their international partners) in Kenya after the ICC's cases were declared admissible. While these cases would not be construed as 'proceedings' under complementarity's compliance framework – they are not criminal in nature, nor were they initiated by the state – they lend further credence to the mediated effects of ICC engagement on domestic accountability. Such litigation includes a case filed in the High Court addressing police shootings that took place between December 2007 and March 2008. Initiated against, inter alia, the DPP, the attorney general and former police commissioner (Mohammed Hussein Ali, whose charges had not been confirmed by the ICC) in early 2013 by fifteen individuals and four Kenyan NGOs, the complaint alleged a failure to prevent the violence following the 2007 elections (including

---

[944] If taken over, the DPP can opt to continue with the proceeding or terminate it; however, the litigant can also decline the DPP's offer and proceed in their private capacity. A qualified right to private prosecution existed under the previous constitution, but it was far more limited because the attorney general was empowered to take over proceedings as he/she wished, and the permission of the private prosecutor was not necessary. Further, 'The experience was that the AG would take over and terminate such proceedings'. See Munyao Sila, *Modern Law of Criminal Procedure in Kenya* (Partridge: South Africa, 2014), 114–115. Private prosecutions still require magistrate permission to proceed; a complaint cannot proceed if the court denies leave to do so. The following factors are considered by Kenyan courts in deciding whether to grant permission: (1) the DPP or other prosecuting body has failed to commence a prosecution; (2) the complaint concerns a cognizable legal offence; and (3) the complainant(s) must have locus standi, i.e., have suffered personal injury or damage. For a more detailed discussion, see J. D. Mujuzi, 'Private Prosecutions in Kenya', *African Journal of Legal Studies* 11(1) (2018).

A person permitted to proceed may prosecute pro se or through an advocate, and the DPP must be notified within 30 days of instituting a private proceeding. See Sila, 110 (citing *Floriculture International Limited and Others*, High Court Misc. Civil Application no. 114 (1997); Amwona & Others *v.* KBL, High Court Misc. Application no. 19 (2004)).

[945] See The Office of the Director of Public Prosecutions Act, Section 28(1) ('Notwithstanding any provision under this act or any other written law, any person may institute private prosecution'.).

the failure to train and instruct the police properly), as well as failures to investigate and prosecute.[946]

Another case, concerning sexual- and gender-based violence, was also filed against the attorney general in 2013 and has advanced the farthest to date.[947] The lawyers in that instance have likewise challenged the failure to adequately investigate post-election violence, to respond to sexual violence allegations with due diligence and to provide full reparations. The petition asked the court to find that the post-election violence rose to the level of crimes against humanity, as a result of which the government was obligated to investigate and prosecute (where evidence permitted). Notably, the case allegations have been described as shoring up geographical omissions in the ICC's early cases, noting, for instance, that the Office of the Prosecutor (OTP)'s charges were in relation to two locations (in and around the town of Naivasha and Nakuru), 'whereas sexual violence crimes were committed in numerous locations during the post-election violence'.[948] More recently, following years of conducting its own private investigation, a prominent Kenyan NGO filed a complaint to Kenya's Independent Police Oversight Authority (a complaint body also created by the 2010 Constitution), urging it to launch a formal investigation into crimes against humanity, including rape, committed by Kenyan security forces.[949]

Although not aimed at the perpetrators of the 2007–2008 political violence, provisions of the 2010 Constitution have also helped Kenya become a venue for enforcement litigation of other ICC arrest warrants. For instance, an application filed by the Kenyan Section of the International Commission of Jurists led to a November 2011 decision by a Kenyan

---

[946] The petition rooted its legal claims in the Kenyan Constitution, read in conjunction with international treaties, including the Rome Statute, the International Covenant on Civil and Political Rights and the African Charter on Human and Peoples' Rights. The petitioners seek public acknowledgement of the state's failure, apology, compensation and prosecution of those responsible and the establishment of an international team within the DPP to ensure credible and independent investigations. For further description of the petition's legal claims, see Open Society Justice Initiative, 'Fact Sheet: Police Shootings in Kenya' (February 2013), at www.opensocietyfoundations.org/fact-sheets/fact-sheet-police-shootings-kenya.

[947] See Coalition on Violence Against Women and Others v. the Attorney-General of Kenya and Others. Petitioners in this case included the Coalition on Violence Against Women, the Independent Medico-Legal Unit, Physicians for Human Rights and ICJ-Kenya.

[948] For further description of the petition's legal claims, see Open Society Justice Initiative, Briefing Paper, 'SGBV Victims Seek Justice for Post-Election Violence' (February 2013), at www.opensocietyfoundations.org/briefing-papers/briefing-survivors-sexual-attacks-kenya-seek-justice-post-election-violence.

[949] See https://twitter.com/PILPG/status/1068622120375201794.

High Court ordering the government to abide by the ICC's arrest warrant against Sudanese President Omar al-Bashir. The government had previously failed to arrest Bashir during his 2010 visit (ironically, on the occasion of the inauguration of the new constitution); to that end, ICJ-Kenya petitioned the High Court to pronounce upon the government's duty to execute the arrest warrant. The court found that the government was obliged to arrest Bashir under both the 2008 ICA and the Rome Statute, the latter of which now formed part of Kenyan law by virtue of the new constitution. A former attorney with ICJ-Kenya who helped file the case suggests that in addition to 'breathing life' into the new constitution, the decision also helped 'widen the space' for the progressive application and implementation of Kenya's human rights obligations.[950]

Accountability through Advocacy: Catalysing Civil Society

Not unlike the opportunities that the ICC's intervention in the DRC enabled for non-state actors, the court's involvement in Kenya unfolded during an exceptionally robust, transitional period for Kenyan human rights advocates where they sought accountability abroad from the ICC, while also turning to new opportunities domestically.[951] These new domestic opportunities assumed even greater importance as the ICC's cases faltered and as the government began to wage a more deliberate, vicious campaign to subvert the court's work. The failure to establish an ICD – much less one that would have jurisdiction over post-election violence – has further foreclosed prospects for domestic criminal accountability for the foreseeable future.

Given the other significant developments that unfolded in the post-2007 period in Kenya, the ICC's influence should not be overstated. As Lionel Nichols argues, 'Although these reforms occurred at the same time that the OTP was actively involved in Kenya, it must be recognized that the reforms were part of a wider reform agenda that not only pre-dated the commencement of the OTP's strategy of positive complementarity, but also the creation of the ICC itself'.[952] Still, the dovetailing of the onset of the court's investigation with the passage of Kenya's new constitutional dispensation

---

[950] Telephone interview with ICJ-Kenya attorney (June 2012). See further *From Rights to Remedies: Structures and Strategies for Implementing International Human Rights Decisions* (Open Society Foundations, 2013), 86–88.

[951] See Nichols, 223 (describing the period following Kenya's post-election violence marked 'the most sustained period of legal reforms in the country's history').

[952] Ibid., 223, 225 (concluding that 'the ICC appears to have provided Kenya's NGOs with increased leverage and legitimacy').

is important to consider as inter-related events that, together, provided new opportunities and framing strategies with which human rights advocates have sought to advance prospects for accountability domestically. While complementarity was often the rationale for pursuing these opportunities, it was not the ICC's involvement as such that was a causal factor; rather, the court's presence contributed to a normative environment that helped these advocacy efforts to flourish, even amidst growing pushback by the Kenyatta government. As put by Geoff Dancy and Florencia Montal, this 'beneficial intermediate side-effect' of the ICC's engagement was an 'unintended' consequence of positive complementarity.[953]

The use of strategic civil litigation by Kenyan advocates and, potentially, the exercise of a new private prosecution right also underscores, again, the importance of understanding complementarity from a process-based perspective, rather than as a matter of compliance with a particular outcome, i.e., criminal convictions. As principle 28 of the Nairobi Principles on Accountability (a set of principles developed by stakeholders engaged in accountability for the Kenyan post-election violence) states:

> Beyond a narrow understanding of complementarity, civil society organisations are encouraged to utilise alternative legal avenues to promote different forms of accountability, including [the] use of strategic litigation, which can be instrumental in promoting state responsibility and a level of redress for victims.[954]

Further, a focus on convictions alone places 'undue emphasis on determinative structures and fail to account for the processes behind the struggles for justice', whereas a process-based approach admits the critical role that private actors play in promoting accountability efforts and emphasizes their interaction with a range of available institutions and

[953] Dancy and Montal, 'Unintended Positive Complementarity', 715–717. Dancy and Montal argue that the ICC does not produce such local activism, but allows what they term 'reformer coalitions' to engage in 'gap-filling litigation', 700–701. While it is not clear if their definition of such litigation would include the sort of private civil litigation efforts described here in Kenya (although both authors refer to it as an example of the phenomenon they describe), it would encompass prosecutions for 'ordinary' crimes and human rights violations, 701, 703 ('Importantly, this study focuses on trials of *all* state agents for abuses to physical integrity—not just those trials that target high-level officials or rebel leaders for international atrocity crimes—as the outcome variable of interest'.).

[954] Principle 28, The Nairobi Principles on Accountability (on-file). The principles are a joint initiative between Kenyans for Peace with Truth and Justice (KPTJ) and Ulster University's Transitional Justice Institute and were developed over the course of 2017–2018 to 'set standards and create guidance for future accountability processes addressing international crimes'.

processes.[955] Sikkink, Michel and Dancy have argued, for instance, that it was the greater participation rights accorded to victims in domestic criminal procedures that contributed to much of the 'justice cascade' observed in Europe and Latin America, generating 'prosecutorial momentum' that was able to consolidate over time and eventually pushing state actors to action.[956] Time will tell if a similar process can yet take root in Kenya.

3 *Uganda v. Thomas Kwoyelo*: Complementarity and State Power

Commentators have previously drawn attention to the fact that the 'self-referrals' in both Uganda and the DRC were themselves concessions to state power. Resting on an implicit understanding that the referring government would not be a focus of the court's investigations, the ICC was instead seen as a tool to be used against political or military opponents.[957] While the OTP's choice of cases in these situations would appear to vindicate this criticism, less remarked upon has been the way in which the exercise of complementarity has likewise served to shore up existing domestic power structures. Uganda's case against Thomas Kwoyelo – presently the only LRA conflict-related criminal proceeding to be pursued in the ICD – is perhaps the most dramatic illustration of this phenomenon.

---

[955] Geoff Dancy and Verónica Michel, 'Human Rights Enforcement From Below: Private Actors and Prosecutorial Momentum in Latin American and Europe', *International Studies Quarterly* (2015), 14–15; see also Dancy and Montal, 'Unintended Positive Complementarity', 703 (advocating a 'process-based theory', wherein 'during ICC investigation, momentum builds for domestic initiatives by judicial reformers to hold state agents accountable for human rights crimes').

[956] See Dancy and Michel, 'Human Rights Enforcement From Below' (concluding, based on statistical evaluation, that 'victims' litigation efforts, not their state leaders or their cultures, largely created the human rights change that occurred in Latin America and Europe'); Verónica Michel and Kathryn Sikkink, 'Human Rights Prosecutions and the Participation Rights of Victims in Latin America', *Law & Society Review* 47(4) (2013) (arguing that 'strong participation rights like private prosecution … provide the legal framework that allows societal actors to push for accountability from below'), 873–907, 903. Michel expands on this research in the context of Chile, Guatemala and Mexico to argue that victims' rights to private prosecution can positively influence state accountability. See *Prosecutorial Accountability and Victims' Rights in Latin America* (Cambridge: Cambridge University Press, 2018).

[957] See, e.g., Clark, *Distant Justice*; Branch, *Displacing Human Rights*; Schabas, 'Complementarity in Practice'.

Procedural History

Kwoyelo, a former LRA fighter and child soldier who himself had been abducted by Kony's forces when he was 13, became the first war crimes suspect to face trial before Uganda's ICD.[958] Captured in March 2009, he was charged under the Geneva Conventions Act as well as Uganda's Penal Code Act. The government alleged that he 'committed his offences in the context of an international armed conflict that existed in Northern Uganda, Southern Sudan and North Eastern Democratic Republic of Congo between the LRA (with the support of and under the control of the government of Sudan), fighting against the government of the Republic of Uganda as by law established, between 1987 and 2008'.[959]

Kwoyelo was initially charged in June 2009, but applied for amnesty under Uganda's Amnesty Act in January 2010.[960] As the act prescribed, the Amnesty Commission sent Kwoyelo's application to the DPP for certification that he was not charged with offences unrelated to the LRA activity (a condition of receiving amnesty); however, in this instance, the DPP failed to respond to the commission's request.[961] Whereas thousands of other combatants like Kwoyelo had received amnesty, the DPP's refusal on this occasion to certify his application suggests that the ICD's establishment, coupled with the swift passage in 2010 of long delayed Rome Statute implementing legislation and the forthcoming ICC Review Conference (for which Uganda was the host state), signalled a decision to make him an 'example' of Uganda's commitment to complementarity.[962]

Kwoyelo's legal team raised several challenges in the first instance before the ICD, including whether the armed conflict between the

---

[958] Kwoyelo was captured in March 2009 in Ukwa, a northeastern part of the DRC during a joint military operation and as part of 'Operation Lightning Thunder', which was launched in December 2008, following the failed Juba peace process. See Anna Macdonald and Holly Porter, 'The Trial of Thomas Kwoyelo: Opportunity or Spectre? Reflections from the Ground on the First LRA Prosecution', *Africa: Journal of the International African Institute* 86(4) (2016), 698–722.

[959] Director of Public Prosecutions, International Crimes Division of the High Court of Uganda at Kampala, HCT-00-ICD-Case no. 02/10, Amended indictment, 5 July 2011, para. 1.

[960] Interview with Amnesty Commission official (Kampala, 13 December 2011).

[961] Ibid. My interlocutor indicated that the DPP typically certified within one month of the commission sending the file, which it had done in March 2010. The department did not respond, however, instead filing its initial indictment against Kwoyelo in August of that year. See also, 'The Amnesty Act: An Act of Forgiveness', 12 ('The Role of the DPP').

[962] See, e.g., Samuel Egadu Okiror, 'Ugandan Supreme Court Ruling Fuels Debate over Double Standards in War Crimes Prosecution', *International Justice Tribune* (21 April 2015).

LRA and the government was international in the sense of the Geneva Conventions, as well as his alleged torture during the time that he was held in pre-trial detention.[963] The most central question, however, was whether Kwoyelo was entitled to amnesty and whether the commission under the Ugandan Constitution had accorded him equal treatment.[964] Faced with these constitutional questions, the ICD referred the matter to the Constitutional Court in July 2011. In a turnabout from its previous position, the government responded that Kwoyelo was not entitled to amnesty because the Amnesty Act, which had been in existence for the previous ten years, was unconstitutional as it compelled Uganda to violate its 'international legal obligation to punish grave breaches of the Geneva Conventions on war crimes'.[965]

In November 2011, the Constitutional Court halted Kwoyelo's trial. In a unanimous decision, it dismissed the attorney general's arguments and upheld the act's constitutionality; further, it found that Kwoyelo had been unequally treated.[966] The court also rejected the argument that Uganda's Rome Statute obligations implied a duty not to grant amnesties, finding that it had 'not come across any uniform international standards or practices which prohibit states from granting amnesties'.[967] Upon remanding the case to the ICD, the Amnesty Commission sought renewed certification from the DPP to issue Kwoyelo's amnesty, which it again refused to issue.[968] Instead, the attorney general appealed to the Ugandan Supreme

---

[963] As discussed further below, while the DPP had first characterized the LRA-Uganda conflict as 'international' in character, it later reversed this position in an amended indictment filed in 2017.

[964] Uganda *v.* Thomas Kwoyelo alias Latoni, Constitutional Reference no. 36 of 2011, Reference to the Constitutional Court (25 July 2011).

[965] Uganda *v.* Thomas Kwoyelo alias Latoni, Constitutional Reference no. 36 of 2011, Attorney General's legal arguments (16 August 2011). Despite this pleading, the Ugandan government is not, in fact, charging Kwoyelo under the convention's grave breaches regime.

[966] Uganda *v.* Thomas Kwoyelo alias Latoni, Constitutional Court of Uganda, Petition no. 036/11, 22 September 2011 ('Kwoyelo Constitutional Court Decision'), 3–4.

[967] Ibid., 24. The court did not address another argument put forward by the government: that the Amnesty Act violates Uganda's international treaty obligations under the Rome Statute.

[968] Interview with Amnesty Commission official (Kampala, 13 December 2011). My interlocutor shared a copy of the DPP's reply to the commission (dated 17 November 2011), which stated that 'The grave breaches of the Geneva Conventions for which the accused is charged with constitute international crimes for which amnesty cannot be granted'. (Notably, Kwoyelo was not charged under the Geneva Conventions, but rather the Geneva Conventions Act of 1964, which, like the Penal Code Act, would appear to fall within the Amnesty Act's ambit.)

Court (a higher appellate court), challenging the Constitutional Court's decision. The Supreme Court had no quorum at the time, however, thus adding additional delay to the proceedings.

Subsequent, successful attempts by Kwoyelo to apply for bail (as an interim remedy) and for a writ of mandamus (to compel his release) in the light of the Constitutional Court's decision were likewise ignored by the DPP.[969] Instead, the attorney general sought to stay the successive orders of these lower courts by appealing to the Supreme Court, which convened, without quorum, a special one-hour sitting and thereupon granted the government's motion.[970] The appeal against the Constitutional Court's decision was not heard on the merits until April 2014.

In April 2015, Uganda's Supreme Court unanimously overturned the Constitutional Court decision on the grounds that any crimes committed against innocent civilians or communities (including crimes under Article 8(2)(e) of the Rome Statute) cannot be categorized as 'crimes committed in furtherance of the war or rebellion'; thus, Kwoyelo was not entitled to amnesty.[971] Finding it immaterial that other applicants in similar circumstances as Kwoyelo had been granted amnesty, the court opined that each case must be decided on its own merits.[972] More controversially, it also ruled that the DPP's decisions as to whether or not to certify future amnesty requests were not entitled to judicial review, effectively granting the government complete discretion in such determinations.[973] Furthermore, because the DPP could declare certain individuals

[969] Thomas Kwoyelo alias Latoni v. Attorney General, High Court (civil division), HCT-00-CV-MC-0162-2011, 25 January 2012 (Hon. Zehurikize) (on-file). The DPP issued a press release explaining its contempt, stating, 'This office maintains the position that under the principles of international law, no amnesty can be granted to persons accused of committing war crimes under the Geneva Convention. The war crimes he is charged with include killings and infliction of grave injuries'. See Edward Anyoli, 'DPP rejects Kwoyelo amnesty', New Vision (5 February 2012).

[970] See Oola, 'In the Shadow of Kwoyelo's Trial'.

[971] The Republic of Uganda in the Supreme Court of Uganda at Kampala, Constitutional Appeal no. 1 of 2012, Uganda v. Thomas Kwoyelo (8 April 2015) 41–42. Notably, Chief Justice B. M. Katureebe, who had previously served as Uganda's attorney general at the time that the Amnesty Act was first passed, authored the lead judgment. No objections were raised to this apparent conflict of interest.

[972] Ibid., 53 ('[I]t is not, and cannot be, unequal treatment under the law simply because one person has been charged with specific crimes and someone else has not been charged, unless there is evidence that the committed the same or similar crimes'.).

[973] Ibid., 56 ('The DPP did not have to give any reasons or explanations as to why he did not certify the respondent for amnesty'.); see also Sharon Nakandha, 'Supreme Court of Uganda Rules on the Application of the Amnesty Act' (16 April 2015), at www.ijmonitor.org/2015/04/supreme-court-of-uganda-rules-on-the-application-of-the-amnesty-act/.

ineligible for a grant of amnesty, the court reasoned that the law itself did not grant a 'blanket' amnesty; it was thus consistent with Uganda's international law obligations.[974]

Kwoyelo returned to the IDC yet again in early 2016, but it was not until two years later – following lengthy pre-trial hearings introduced under its new, special rules of procedure – that the division confirmed further amended charges against Kwoyelo and committed him to trial.[975] During this time, the DPP filed another amended indictment that raised the charges against him from 12 to 93, but significantly, dropped earlier 'grave breaches' charges that had been brought under Uganda's Geneva Conventions Act. This 'radically transformed third amended indictment' reversed the DPP's earlier characterization of the LRA conflict as international in character (a determination that ran noticeably counter to the ICC's determination of the same relevant period in the Ongwen case) and instead pled the existence of a non-international armed conflict.[976] Thus, Kwoyelo now stands charged under Common Article 3 of the Geneva Conventions and the Penal Code Act alone.[977] No charges have been brought under Uganda's ICC Act.

---

[974] Ibid., 63.

[975] See, e.g., International Justice Monitor, 'Kwoyelo's Trial Drags on in Ugandan Court as Defense Counsel Labels the Charges "Fatally and Incurably Defective"' (27 March 2017); 'Ugandan Court Fails to Hold Confirmation of Charges Hearing in Kwoyelo Case' (24 July 2017); 'Ten Years Later, Ugandan Court Finally Confirms 93 Charges Against Thomas Kwoyelo' (4 September 2018). After confirming charges in August 2018, the division also granted the defense's request for relief from the state's failure to implement previous court orders, including translation of the charge sheet, facilitation of interpretation and adequate financing of the defense teams' costs.

[976] See Paul Bradfield, 'Reshaping Amnesty in Uganda: The Case of Thomas Kwoyelo', *Journal of International Criminal Justice* 15 (2017), 848; The Prosecutor *v.* Dominic Ongwen, Decision on the confirmation of charges against Dominic Ongwen, ICC-02/04-01/15/422, PTC II, 23 March 2016, paras. 61, 71.

[977] Because Ugandan law does not criminalize violations of Common Article 3 (the 1964 Act extends only to the conventions' 'grave breaches' regime), the DPP now pleads its charges simply as 'violations of customary international law', with the remaining counts charged alternatively as ordinary crimes under the Penal Code Act. Realizing the legally untenable position it was in by having charged violations of the grave breaches regime in the apparent absence of an international armed conflict, the DPP received help from the University of California-Berkeley's International Human Rights Law Clinic in reformulating its argument. See Kim Thuy Seelinger, 'Uganda's Case of Thomas Kwoyelo: Customary International Law on Trial', *California Law Review Online* 8 (April 2017), 39 ('Interpreting the Ugandan Constitution as allowing direct application of law in pursuit of accountability for international crimes would … diminish the risk of challenges vis-à-vis the ICC with respect to crimes committed after 2002'.).

As these proceedings plod on, Kwoyelo has remained in pre-trial detention. Indeed, facing limited domestic avenues for further relief, he petitioned the African Commission on Human and Peoples' Rights in October 2012, challenging his continuing detention as arbitrary under the African Charter on Human and Peoples' Rights and that he had been mistreated in detention, as well as other due process violations.[978] In February 2018, the commission determined that, contrary to the Supreme Court's ruling, Kwoyelo's denial of amnesty did violate his equal protection rights under the African Charter (Article 3), that he should have qualified for amnesty and that his differential treatment was 'without reasonable justification or explanation'.[979] Furthermore, the commission found a procedural due process violation with respect to the Ugandan Supreme Court, holding that it failed to give 'proper reason or justification' for its decision to stay the Constitutional Court's orders and for its 'unjustified delay in the hearing of [Kwoyelo's] appeal ... caused by the lack of quorum'.[980] The commission ordered that compensation be paid to Kwoyelo as a remedy for the violations, but ordered no equitable relief (for instance, that his trial be halted or that Uganda be compelled to issue him an amnesty certificate).[981]

Hijacked Justice?

The complicated procedural maze that has defined the Thomas Kwoyelo trial points to a dark side of complementarity, particularly when criminal punishment is pursued by a state eager to be seen as making good on the 'investments' of donor bodies and 'compliant' with the norms and procedures of an international court. As a member of Kwoyelo's legal

---

[978] Bill Oketch, 'Rights Body to Assist Kwoyelo', *Daily Monitor* (2 January 2013).

[979] African Commission on Human and Peoples Rights, Communication no. 431/12 – Thomas Kwoyelo v. Uganda, 23 Extra-Ordinary Session (12–22 February 2018), paras. 181, 186–187, 195. Remarkably, the commission appears to not acknowledge the 2015 Supreme Court decision, but confines its analysis to the failure to release Kwoyelo following the 2011 decision of the Constitutional Court.

[980] Ibid., para. 245 (finding a violation of the right to fair trial under Article 7(1)(a) of the African Charter), para. 265 (finding a partial violation of Article 7(1)(d)).

[981] Ibid., para. 295. Interestingly, in an apparent effort to distinguish its assessment of Kwoyelo's due process violations from the larger question of amnesty, the commission included a section at the end of its opinion entitled 'obiter dictum', in which it states that 'blanket or unconditional amnesties that prevent investigations ... are not consistent with provisions of the African Charter'. Ibid., paras. 283–293. In a subsequent petition, the High Court denied Kwoyelo's bail application in March 2019.

defence team starkly explained, 'There is so much international pressure for [Uganda] to deal with the LRA'.[982] In response to such pressure, many of the same 'international standards' to which domestic systems must ostensibly comply have been violated. Amidst compelling legal claims that he was, in fact, subject to unequal application of the law and enduring a protracted, politically driven prosecution, Kwoyelo has now spent ten years in detention, in defiance of repeated orders by Uganda's own courts that he be released. While government contempt of the domestic judiciary is not new in Uganda, here complementarity has been its handmaiden.[983]

The disciplinary dimensions of complementarity can also be seen in the reaction of domestic justice actors to the Constitutional Court's decision that Kwoyelo be released, as when JLOS (incorrectly) insisted that the 'principle would require those responsible for serious human rights violations to be excluded from the amnesty process, and instead, be investigated by the national courts'.[984] In its words, 'The Amnesty Act presents challenges to Uganda's ability to *comply* with the principle of complementarity'. In a 'special report' issued following the decision, JLOS likewise stated that Uganda's ratification of the Rome Statute represented an 'international commitment to seek justice and accountability' and that its domestication 'reinforces Uganda's good reputation in ratification and domestication of international laws and its duty to apply the law'.[985] A 2016 release by the ICTJ sounded a similar note, stating that 'Kwoyelo's trial will attract significant scrutiny of its compliance with international standards, jurisprudence, and innovative practices it develops'.[986]

---

[982] Alexis Okeowo, 'Thomas Kwoyelo's Troubling Trial', *The New Yorker* (21 July 2012).

[983] See, e.g., Mari Tripp, *Museveni's Uganda*, 86–91; Kasaija Phillip Apuuli, 'The ICC's Possible Deferral of the LRA Case to Uganda', *Journal of International Criminal Justice* 6 (2008), 808. Mari Tripp recounts a notorious scene from November 2005, when opposition leader Kizza Besigye was arrested (on charges of treason and rape) and brought to the High Court to be released on bail, only be to surrounded by members of the Black Mamba Squad, a paramilitary unit, in the courtroom and arrested extralegally; Apuuli notes similar acts were repeated in March 2007.

[984] 'Community Dialogue on the Future of the Amnesty Act' (March 2012). JLOS convened the 'dialogue' in conjunction with UN Women and the UN Office of the High Commissioner with 'a view to understanding community views on the current operation and future of the [Amnesty] Act'. See also JLOS, 'The Amnesty Law (2000) Issues Paper, Review by the Transitional Justice Working Group (April 2012).

[985] JLOS, 'Justice at Cross Roads? A Special Report on the Thomas Kwoyelo Trial', 4.

[986] ICTJ, 'Kwoyelo and Ongwen Trials Show Progress in Fight against Impunity' (25 July 2016), at www.ictj.org/news/kwoyelo-ongwen-icc-uganda.

Kwoyelo's trial thus presents vexing questions about the ways in which complementarity may be used in the interests of state power. Here, Jelena Subotić's work on what she calls 'hijacked justice' is instructive. Subotić argues that the rise in popularity of transitional justice institutions (including courts) and their increasing ubiquity can lead 'states [to] use these mechanisms to achieve goals quite different from those envisaged by international justice institutions and activists'.[987] In Kwoyelo's case, and as the Supreme Court's decision suggests, the goal appears to be making him the public example of Uganda's evolution from an earlier period wherein amnesty largely held sway as state policy to an increasingly retributive model. This model, however, does not appear to portend a broader shift towards criminal accountability for atrocity-related conflicts. To date, there have been no other attempted prosecutions in the ICD (indeed, amnesty certificates have still been issued post-2015), nor have any Uganda People's Defence Force (UPDF) soldiers been pursued for violations in the conduct of the government's campaign against the LRA. Instead, Kwoyelo has become the symbolic figure upon which the ICD's existence as a forum for ICC-related prosecution must be vindicated.[988]

Similar concerns animated the Kenyan ICD, which many critics had long contended amounted to little more than 'sham compliance' on the part of the state. Writing in the *Daily Nation*, Betty Waithherero, a Kenyan commentator, argued that

> A lot of time, money and effort has ... been put into what looks like just smoke and mirrors; a political stillborn whose intention was to create the appearance of complementarity while utilizing dubious methods to create [it].[989]

Such 'domestic misuse of transitional justice norms', Subotić concludes, can lead to 'policy outcomes far removed from international transitional justice expectations'.[990] Thus, while one political goal of ICC interventions may be criminal prosecutions for Rome Statute crimes, that goal is only one of many to which domestic political elites may aspire. Others may range from side-lining political opponents (as in the DRC), to realigning domestic political interests (as in Kenya), to attracting material benefits from donor states (as in Uganda).

---

[987] Subotić, *Hijacked Justice*, 6.

[988] For a similar conclusion, see MacDonald 'Somehow This Whole Process Became So Artificial', 240.

[989] Betty Waithherero, 'Can the International Crimes Division prosecute Kenya's PEV cases?', *The Nation* (8 February 2014).

[990] Subotic, 6.

The fact that ICC interventions may be 'hijacked' for political ends should not itself be surprising. Indeed, just as domestic political elites might seek political gain from the ICC's engagement, domestic civil society actors have also harnessed the court for broader human rights agendas, as previous chapters have illustrated. But the relationship between supporting criminal accountability and the biases and inequities of a state's criminal justice system (of which pre-trial detention is amongst the most prominent) is one with which human rights advocates must reckon.[991] Amongst the many voices that have insisted on complementarity's due process requirements and adherence to 'international standards', little has been said about the Kwoyelo trial or his treatment to date.

4   Conclusion

This chapter has examined which domestic proceedings have taken root in the wake of the ICC's engagement in the DRC, Kenya and Uganda and how they have unfolded. While the ICC itself has not been the catalyst for the (limited) criminal proceedings that have followed in the wake of its involvement, its interventions have served to catalyse other private actors to incorporate anti-impunity efforts into their own program objectives. The mobile court projects in the DRC are a notable example of this phenomenon, even as the courts themselves depend on the financial support and operational assistance of NGOs and donor bodies. While materially unconnected to the ICC, the court has nonetheless helped frame the mobile court proceedings as 'complementary' to, and an extension of, its trials in The Hague. To a similar (though lesser) degree, the ICC's involvement in Kenya also allowed domestic justice advocates to frame their own litigation strategies around complementarity's duty to investigate and prosecute.

However, just as the ICC's involvement in the DRC should not occlude the efforts of other actors engaged in domestic accountability work (e.g., MONUSCO, international NGOs, development agencies), its role in Kenya should not overshadow more fundamental changes to the country's post-2010 legal order, which provided a range of more robust

---

[991] See, e.g., Open Society Justice Initiative, 'Presumption of Guilt: The Global Overuse of Pretrial Detention' (2014). See also Karen Engle, 'A Genealogy of the Criminal Turn in Human Rights', in *Anti-Impunity and the Human Rights Agenda*, 48 ('The alignment of human rights advocates with the carceral state cannot help but affect the extent to which the human rights movement is able to mount a serious criticism of mass and brutal incarceration and the biases we see in nearly every penal system in the world'.).

participation rights that are currently being tested domestically by a transnational community of lawyers and activists who have sought to fill the void left by the ICC's collapsed cases.

Finally, in Uganda, the Kwoyelo proceeding highlights the vexed relationship between state power and complementarity, demonstrating how 'compliance' with the latter can also facilitate abusive state practices. Although Kwoyelo cannot invoke complementarity as a legal matter given that he is not an ICC defendant, the domestic narrative of his trial has been built on the principle that the ICD 'complements' the court's work in The Hague. As a progress narrative, Kwoyelo's prosecution also indexes an apparent shift in Ugandan policy away from amnesty to accountability; it offers a picture of complementarity 'in practice' to an international audience keen to see a return on its 'investment'. As these evolving histories again suggest, the logic of complementarity shifts depending on the political priorities and goals of those who seek to invoke it.

8

Conclusions and Recommendations

[I]n the prospect of an international criminal court lies the promise of universal justice. That is the simple and soaring hope of this vision. We are close to its realization. We will do our part to see it through till the end. We ask you ... to do your utmost in our struggle to ensure that no ruler, no state, no junta, and no army anywhere can abuse human rights with impunity. Only then will the innocents of distant wars and conflicts know that they, too, may sleep under the cover of justice; that they, too, have rights and that those who violate those rights will be punished.

Kofi Annan (1997)[992]

The idea that all international problems will dissolve with the establishment of an international court with compulsory jurisdiction is an invitation to political indolence. It allows one to make no alterations in domestic political action and thought, to change no attitudes, to try no new approaches and yet appear to be working for peace.

Judith Shklar (1964)[993]

The International Criminal Court (ICC) has always needed to be more than the sum of its parts. By design, it was meant to be a court with potentially global remit, with jurisdiction over a collective category of crimes that have shaped the modern international justice movement.[994] The court is both the progeny of its celebrated predecessors – Nuremberg, Yugoslavia, Rwanda – under whose legacies it labours, and the culmination of Annan's utopian vision that all might 'sleep under the cover of justice'. But the ICC is not those courts: it is meant to be one (criminal) court for the world, built through painstaking negotiation and compromise. It is tasked with an extraordinary purpose, but saddled with the

[992] Kofi Annan, 'Advocating for an International Criminal Court', *Fordham International Law Journal* 21(2) (1997), 366.
[993] Shklar, 134.
[994] See, e.g., Philippe Sands, *East West Street: On the Origins of 'Genocide' and 'Crimes Against Humanity'* (Knopf, 2016); Mark Lewis, *The Birth of the New Justice: The Internationalization of Crime and Punishment, 1919–1950* (Oxford, 2014).

challenges all too common of international institutions – budget fights, internal power struggles and battles for political control. The damaging breakdown of a string of its cases (in Kenya and beyond) adds greatly to these challenges.

Still, amidst these sobering realities, the 'idea' of the ICC as an engine for domestic accountability endures. It continues to inspire human rights advocates – from Burundi to Venezuela, from Myanmar to Georgia – who toil either in the midst of conflict or in its shadow. In the promise of international criminal judgment they see not only hope for a measure of justice, but also for law's emancipation from politics.

The increasingly charged political space in which the ICC finds itself – its enduring promise, its increasing peril – is captured in the duelling views of Annan and Shklar above. The certitude of Annan's remarks is rooted in the vision of a progressive, cosmopolitan legal order of which the ICC is both agent and apex; by contrast, Shklar warns against seeking such certitude in the dream of a rules-based order, or its institutions.[995] Together, these competing visions also inform a number of the themes that this book has sought to trace in its examination of whether and how ICC interventions in Uganda, Kenya and the Democratic Republic of Congo (DRC) have catalysed domestic accountability efforts.

1   Reassessing Complementarity as a Catalyst

The evolution of what complementarity means and how it is now understood as part of a 'Rome Statute system' invites reflection. As I have argued, a critical assemblage of non-state actors, who presciently understood what the ICC's institutional limits would be and who sought early on to magnify the court's normative impact, deliberately engineered this evolution. As Charli Carpenter argues, 'new normative ideas do not float freely in global networks. It matters very much who is promoting them'.[996] In the ICC's case, these promoters evolved into an influential cross-section of NGO

---

[995] For a thoughtful reflection on Shklar and the ICC, see Samuel Moyn, 'Judith Shklar versus the International Criminal Court', *Humanity* (Winter 2013), 473–500. These polarities also recall Martti Koskenniemi's insights into the dynamics of the international legal field: the ICC and its body of law oscillates between deference to the power of states and openness to more cosmopolitan visions. See Martti Koskenniemi, *From Apology to Utopia: The Structure of International Legal Argument* (Cambridge: Cambridge University Press, 2006).

[996] Charli Carpenter, *'Lost' Causes: Agenda Vetting in Global Issue Networks and the Shaping of Human Security* (Cornell: Cornell University Press, 2014), 2–3.

advocates, legal academics, past and present court personnel and allied diplomats who together comprised a dynamic 'community of practice' that seeded and nourished this enlarged vision for complementarity.

Such a project is at once progressive and disciplinary: it insists that, in order to realize Annan's vision, states must follow certain rules. Complementarity, in turn, has become more than a question of admissibility, but the juridical logic through which these rules are articulated. As Chapter 2 argued, it has evolved from a principle that was originally protective of sovereignty to one that seeks to magnify the ICC's influence. In Mégret's words, 'Complementarity has become part of the way in which international criminal lawyers project a sense of the "international criminal law acquis", a sort of global package of norms that have to be developed by states that become part of the ICC club'.[997] Two principal conceptions animate this global package. One is the ICC as a tool for cooperation and burden-sharing (a 'gentle incentivizer'), and the other is as an instrument of coercion.[998] Both interpretations, however, position the court as a catalyst: the threat of ICC intervention prompts states to undertake their own accountability efforts, while the promise of assistance and cooperation encourages them to do so.

A central feature of this new norm has been the commonly held understanding that complementarity imposes explicit duties on states, thus linking the ICC-as-catalyst frame to the dominant discourse of compliance in international law. This duty-based conception of complementarity – with its attendant domestic obligations of implementation, investigation and prosecution – has come to dominate the popular understanding of the principle. Other shibboleths similarly endure, from the characterization of the court as one of 'last resort', to the truncated definition of complementarity that commonly treats 'unwilling/unable' as if it were the entirety of the Article 17 test. The reflection and advancement of these heuristic techniques in a broad array of literature, and the interpretations they subsequently command, demonstrates how, in Robinson's words, 'collective belief can influence our understanding not only of history but also of text'.[999]

---

[997] Mégret, 'Implementation and the Uses of Complementarity', 362.

[998] On the idea of international law as a civilizing agent, see Marti Koskenniemi, *The Gentle Civilizer of Nations: The Rise and Fall of International Law 1870–1960* (Cambridge: Cambridge University Press, 2002).

[999] Robinson, 'The Controversy over Territorial State Referrals and Reflections on ICL Discourse', 380.

This transformation has yielded something of a paradox: although complementarity was initially a mechanism to catalyse state actors in the pursuit of criminal accountability, its effects on non-state actors have been more profound. Indeed, while the evolution in complementarity's meaning was perhaps inevitable given the ICC's institutional limitations, its speed and spread owes largely to the critical role that private actors and organizations have played in the process. As part of a highly networked, transnational community of practice, these norm entrepreneurs have not only taken the most active role in shaping and transforming the normative content of complementarity, but they have also increasingly reoriented their own advocacy agendas towards the ICC. In this sense, as Emily Haslam has elsewhere argued, civil society organizations are both object and subject of the court's 'catalytic effect'. They seek to expand complementarity's normative influence, while having themselves been transformed by it.[1000]

In so doing, the domestic forms and possibilities for post-conflict justice are frequently compliance-oriented, with attention predominantly paid to criminal prosecutions and punishment as the principal measure of the ICC's effectiveness. The perceived duty to legislate, investigate and prosecute ICC crimes has similarly placed the Rome Statute at the textual heart of accountability discussions, with less attention paid to other forms of criminal conduct. Thus, while complementarity might have initially encouraged some of the plural approaches more commonly associated with transitional justice, a de facto form of ICC primacy has instead taken root. The court's early admissibility jurisprudence has contributed to this phenomenon. Indeed, as Chapter 3 demonstrated, the court has followed a relatively strict approach in its admissibility decisions, suggesting that a state's domestic proceedings must largely mirror court proceedings in order to successfully retain (or assert) control over them. The application of this test has been even stricter when brought by an accused under Article 19(2)(a). Meanwhile, the court's jurisprudence on 'positive' complementarity remains thin and underdeveloped.

These insights further illustrate that, in all aspects of the ICC's work, law and politics are inseparable. This reality is particularly acute for the Office of the Prosecutor and, as Chapter 4 argued, it has done the office few favours to pretend otherwise. Situated at the nexus of The Hague

---

[1000] Emily Haslam, 'Subjects and Objects: International Criminal Law and the Institutionalization of Civil Society', *International Journal of Transitional Justice* 5(2) (2011); see also Jelena Subotić, 'The Transformation of International Transitional Justice Advocacy', *International Journal of Transitional Justice* 6 (2012).

and situation countries, the Office of the Prosecutor (OTP) decision of whether and when to open preliminary examinations and investigations is arguably the defining question of whether the ICC's engagement can trigger domestic criminal proceedings. As this book has demonstrated, the OTP's use of preliminary examinations holds some promise for catalysing domestic accountability processes, but the conduct of these examinations is highly dependent on political context and timing, as the court's intervention in Kenya suggests. Investigations, which are similarly contingent on political context and cooperation, are also an important site where certain goals of 'positive' complementarity – knowledge transfer, technical assistance to national jurisdictions, strengthening domestic prosecutorial capacity – could be meaningfully enacted, but, to date, such an approach has been limited in practice and increasingly seen as outside the scope of the OTP's 'core mandate'. Fiscal austerity on the part of ICC member states has abetted these limitations, leading to a chronically underfunded office even as the situations competing for its attention multiply.

The developments traced here at a national level also make clear that the 'catalytic effect' of complementarity should be understood as part of a complex political process, rather than a singular desired outcome. Judged by the latter, the outcomes that ICC interventions, through the principle of complementarity, intended to catalyse – domestic prosecutions of international crimes – have only rarely and sporadically materialized. But the absence of criminal proceedings for ICC crimes has not meant that these states are inactive.[1001] Indeed, the court has been deeply alive in the political discourse and decision-making of all three countries: from Uganda, where it loomed large in the government's peace negotiations with the Lord's Resistance Army (LRA) and its subsequent (attempted) abandonment of amnesty; to Kenya, where it forged a political alliance united in opposition to The Hague; to the DRC, where the court's intervention has been skilfully weaponized by the Kabila government against its political opponents.

Furthermore, as the second part of the book illustrates, the ICC's intervention in situation countries has influenced the strategies and priorities of numerous NGOs and donor states. In the DRC, for example, civil society organizations have invoked complementarity not as an admissibility principle, but the idea that the ICC symbolically complements domestic

---

[1001] On dyadic tensions in the structuring of arguments, see Darryl Robinson, 'Inescapable Dyads: Why the International Criminal Court Cannot Win', *Leiden Journal of International Law* 28(2) (2015).

accountability efforts – to support important (if limited) prosecutions at the national level. In Kenya, advocates have similarly used the ICC's involvement as an axis around which to construct and engage in new forms of strategic litigation.

Finally, compliance with ICC standards and procedures belies the outsized influence of external constituencies as to what activities states undertake in the name of complementarity. Even in the absence of domestic proceedings, much attention has been focused on the creation (or proposed creation) of International Crimes Divisions (ICDs) in both Uganda and Kenya. As detailed in Chapters 6 and 7, while Uganda's ICD initially emerged out of a coercive relationship with the ICC's investigations ('classical' complementarity), this has shifted in recent years to complementarity in a literal sense. Now, it is less an alternative forum for domestic prosecution than a beneficiary of donor-driven interests for whom the trial of Thomas Kwoyelo must be seen to 'succeed'. The proposed Kenyan ICD was characterized in similar terms, as have the mobile courts in the DRC.

Moreover, these juridical bodies have frequently been portrayed as helping to strengthen domestic justice systems in the wake of conflict; however, as I have argued, there is a tension between the exceptionalism associated with their origin and functioning – particularly the donor agendas and patronage economies upon which many of them rely – and the desire to fortify 'ordinary' domestic systems. Indeed, in demonstrating an excessive homology with The Hague, such donor-driven projects can often (re)produce significant micro-tensions in the competition for attention and scarce resources. The effects of ICC interventions in each country thus underscore how 'international standards [do] not transcend the influence of local politics or the impact of global asymmetries'.[1002] Rather, these asymmetries, as well as the patronage networks they produce and sustain, are intimately entwined with the catalytic project.

The perceived duty to implement the Rome Statute in its identical form at the domestic level is another illustration of the relationship between the power of external constituencies and compliance. As Chapter 5 argued, it was less the threat or actuality of ICC intervention that catalysed the passage of national implementation legislation. In Uganda, the ICC had already been engaged for many years; in Kenya, the threat of its intervention was perceived to be remote at the time. Rather, domestic actors accelerated identical implementation of the Statute in order to 'perform' complementarity for predominantly international audiences.

[1002] Leebaw, 179.

In particular, the imminence of Uganda serving as host state for the Rome Statute Review Conference drove the passage of its 2010 legislation, while in Kenya, the recommendation of the Waki Commission was the catalyst for passage of Kenya's International Crimes Act (Kenya 2008) (ICA). Such 'performance' for the international community was significant in the DRC as well, insofar as the release of the 2010 United Nations (UN) Mapping Report served, at the time, to catalyse renewed proposals for the establishment of a special chambers/court and for passage of implementing legislation. A related concern is thus whether implementation of the Statute, when seen as something merely to be copied or transplanted, may in fact stymie the pursuit of other accountability efforts that could be more meaningful to affected communities.

2 Towards New Horizons

In the light of these complex histories, what paths might the ICC and criminal justice advocates chart in the years ahead? The trajectory traced here suggests that, while the court remains an important actor in the criminal justice landscape, increasingly it labours under the weight of too many expectations, too few resources and too little attention to the politics in which its interventions unfold. Furthermore, while advocates and norm entrepreneurs have continually summoned the symbolic power of the ICC and the polysemy of complementarity to serve a variety of reformist agendas, this strategy has not been without cost to other normative values like legal pluralism, local ownership and democratic deliberation. Below, I offer six broad areas for reflection.

Thinking Beyond Compliance

Compliance is the dominant currency in international law. This is evident in the framing of complementarity as a catalyst for compliance and is similarly reflected in the rise of private law firms that now cater to ICC-related services, such as a 'positive complementarity centre' and a 'resource center on complementarity monitoring'.[1003] Yet while compliance with the

---

[1003] See, e.g., Global Diligence, at www.globaldiligence.com (a 'for-profit legal advisory service engaged in public interest work', and specialized in 'international law and human rights compliance'); Global Rights Compliance, at www.globalrightscompliance.com ('an international legal partnership committed to enhancing compliance with international law, particularly international humanitarian law and human rights'). Amongst its services, the Nuremberg Academy has also inaugurated a 'Resource Centre on

Rome Statute's purported obligations has animated much of the interest in complementarity, ICC interventions themselves have rarely been the catalyst for domestic criminal proceedings, even as they precipitate developments that extend beyond the courthouse doors. Compliance is therefore too narrow a lens through which to capture the complex legal and political alchemy that ICC interventions produce or to understand the diverse ways in which actors have oriented their own objectives around the principle of complementarity. As Robert Howse and Ruti Teitel argue, rule compliance can lead 'to inadequate scrutiny and understanding of the diverse complex purposes and projects that multiple actors impose and transpose on international legality'.[1004] Thinking beyond compliance calls us to such deeper scrutiny.

In order to better appreciate the ICC's catalytic power, then, legalism – understood as compliance with a particular set of rules – cannot be the dominant framework. Indeed, the question that should be asked is not merely whether states comply with international norms or duties, but how and why they do so. Such an orientation can better capture not only what norms infiltrate a state in the process of an international judicial intervention, but if, how and why those norms are implemented in practice. As Subotic notes, 'Although international organizations may initiate international justice projects for all the noble reasons, their effects may be quite different when they are strategically adopted by local political actors in the context of domestic political contention and mobilization'.[1005] For these reasons, a deeper understanding of political context is essential.

But political understanding cannot extend only to how one assesses the effects of ICC engagement. Politics – the exercise of political

Complementarity Monitoring', which it describes as a 'goal-based assessment mechanism' to track developments relevant to complementarity in particular country contexts. See www.nurembergacademy.org/projects/detail/e28d08a0d5378c33316e4a26443d6892/resource-center-on-complementarity-monitoring-13/.

[1004] Robert Howse and Ruti Teitel, 'Beyond Compliance: Rethinking Why International Law Really Matters', *Global Policy* 1(2) (May 2010), 127. For an exploration of similar themes in another institutional context, see Par Engstrom (ed.), *The Inter-American Human Rights System: Impact Beyond Compliance* (Palgrave Macmillan, 2018).

[1005] Subotic, *Hijacked Justice*, 13; see also Lucy Hovil, 'Challenging International Justice: The Initial Years of the International Criminal Court's Intervention in Uganda', *Stability* 2(1) (2013), 1 ('Supported by the assumption that any intervention working to "end impunity" is somehow above reproach, there is an unwillingness to critically evaluate these well meaning, but sometimes unwanted and even harmful, interventions'.).

judgment – must also become a more explicit, acknowledged part of assessing the wisdom and conduct of ICC engagement as well.[1006] Legalism does a disservice to the need for such judgment because it insists on the myth that a world it imagines as rules-based is already (or might ever be) so. As a 'noble lie' this may occasionally serve useful ends, but, too often, it means that legal institutions conceive of themselves as functioning above political life, rather than in its midst.[1007] Such elevation of 'distant justice' is not unique to the ICC, but the court's performance failures – particularly the presumptions that informed how its early investigations in Uganda, Kenya and DRC were carried out – underscores the degree to which decisions about the ICC's institutional design and practice have failed to sufficiently appreciate international judicial intervention as not only a legal enterprise, but a deeply political one. Such interventions thus require a sharper, political assessment (by the prosecutor, but also by

---

[1006] For similar recommendations, see James A. Goldston, 'More Candour about Criteria: The Exercise of Discretion by the Prosecutor of the International Criminal Court', *Journal of International Criminal Justice* 8(2) (2010); Kenneth A. Rodman, 'Justice as a Dialogue between Law and Politics: Embedding the International Criminal Court within Conflict Management and Peacebuilding', 12 *Journal of International Criminal Justice* (2014); Marieke de Hoon, 'The Future of the International Criminal Court: On Critique, Legalism and Strengthening the ICC's Legitimacy', 17 *International Criminal Law Review* (2017) ('[W]hat the court needs to do is shake off its legalist feathers as it unhelpfully clouds the already difficult task of understanding how the court could best navigate the water, recognize its politics, explain and justify it choices, and engage openly in dialogue with those it tries to support and address'.); Nouwen and Werner, 942 (criticizing the depiction of politics 'as external to law, as something that needs to be overcome by independent organs acting on the basis of pre-given rules and principles'). It is worth noting that Pre-Trial Chamber II's opinion denying the prosecutor authorization to open an investigation in Afghanistan on the grounds of the 'interests of justice' is one of the court's first, explicit engagements with the political dimensions of its work; however, the decision has been rightly criticized for its superficial and unsatisfying treatment of the topic. See, e.g., Christian De Vos, 'No ICC Investigation in Afghanistan: A Bad Decision with Big Implications', International Justice Monitor (15 April 2019), at www.ijmonitor.org/2019/04/no-icc-investigation-in-afghanistan-a-bad-decision-with-big-implications/; Kai Ambos, 'Interests of Justice? The ICC urgently needs reforms', EJIL: *Talk!* (11 June 2019) (criticizing the decision for converting the 'clause into a mere, free floating policy factor which gives a chamber an unfettered discretion'), at www.ejiltalk.org/interests-of-justice-the-icc-urgently-needs-reforms/.

[1007] My use of 'noble lie' borrows from Moyn's elegant essay, in which he places Shklar's 'legalism' in conversation with developments in international criminal law, 494 ('Legalism, I suggest, not only does work but must work as a noble lie: philosophers, and perhaps associated guardians, know it is false but allow its many votaries to proceed as if it were true because only the myth makes their conduct possible'.).

ICC supporters generally) of the attendant advantages – and risks – they carry. As Shklar put it, this is legalism's 'great paradox': it 'is an ideology ... too inflexible to recognize [its] enormous potentialities ... as a creative policy, but exhausts itself in intoning traditional pieties and principles which are incapable of realization'.[1008] Intoning that the ICC could or should be a catalyst for 'compliance' is a piety that Shklar would likely have warned against.

The importance of embracing political judgment more clearly – and appreciating how ICC interventions spark a range of complex, frequently unexpected consequences – also requires greater scepticism about the strength of the court's coercive potential and of compliance as complementarity's principal mission. Although such an approach might yield results in certain situations, one lesson to draw from the ICC's early interventions is that the reputational cost of domestic inaction for certain states appears to be significantly lower than was first presumed, and that the court, ultimately, does not possess 'the type of primacy or finality akin to the ideal of sovereign coercive actors'.[1009] The wisdom of a predominantly disciplinary approach to complementarity, wherein domestic jurisdictions are encouraged to 'mirror' the standards and practices of the ICC, thus merits critical reflection. In particular, there is reason to be concerned that a mirror-based approach to complementarity has become an overly disciplinary exercise and, potentially, a futile one.[1010] It contributes to unrealizable expectations in most contexts; it flattens the breadth of what justice can or should mean in many contexts and it accommodates to state power, rather than challenging it, in certain contexts.

Given this, the OTP and the Assembly of States Parties (ASP) should consider anew a more robust investment in the cooperative dimensions of the principle, focusing on how the court itself can help strengthen domestic capacity and commitment, particularly in situations of

---

[1008] Shklar, 112.

[1009] Antonio Franceschet, 'The International Criminal Court's Provisional Authority to Coerce', *Ethics & International Affairs* 26(1) (Spring 2012), 100. See also David Bosco, *Rough Justice: The International Criminal Court in a World of Power Politics* (Oxford: Oxford University Press, 2014); Nouwen, *Complementarity in the Line of Fire*, 26 (concluding that 'even in countries where sovereignty and reputation costs are considered high, complementarity has not catalysed domestic proceedings because there are other costs that are even higher').

[1010] See, e.g., Zimmerman, *Global Norms with a Local Face*, 6 (arguing that the 'more precise' a norm, 'the less flexible the attitude of both external and domestic actors and the less substantial the ultimate localization').

concurrent jurisdiction.[1011] While there are legitimate concerns about the propriety (and financial cost) of an international court carrying such an assistance mandate, the circumscribed interactions between The Hague and national jurisdictions to date, and the fact that many national counterparts do look to the ICC for such assistance, suggest that this approach merits further examination as a potentially fertile role for the court to play. Particularly in the wake of the Bemba acquittal and the opening of a second ICC investigation in CAR, the newly established Special Criminal Court in the Central African Republic (SCC) offers an important opportunity for the court to proactively assist and partner with the SCC in ways that it has not done in other situation countries. Indeed, echoing a return to the language of cooperation and burden-sharing that characterized the ICC's early engagement with the DRC, the OTP has emphasized that collaboration should define the relationship between the ICC and CAR in the second unfolding investigation there, as well as the need 'to develop strong linkages between national judicial systems and the ICC'.[1012] This is likewise reflected in the office's post-2016 strategic priorities, though the degree to which it has been realized in practice remains far from clear.

Towards a Performance-Centred, Place-Based ICC

A shift away from a strict compliance framework would allow greater appreciation for the range of effects cast by the ICC's 'shadow'. At the same time, the court's performance challenges underscore the urgent need for its supporters and stakeholders to emphasize anew what must be the ICC's guiding lights: capable, ethical leadership grounded in the institution's mission; competent investigations and prosecutions; coherent, well-reasoned jurisprudence and the ability to be adequately responsive to the needs and

---

[1011] For a helpful, early assessment of the ICC's ability to serve as a 'supporting institution for national courts', see Jenia Iontcheva Turner, 'Nationalizing International Criminal Law', *Stanford Journal of International Law* 41(1) (2004), 30–37. For a more recent iteration, see Serge Brammertz, 'International Criminal Court: Now for Kony and Bashir', *The Guardian* (13 June 2012). This concept is explored further in Nicola Palmer's case study of the International Criminal Tribunal for Rwanda (ICTR), Rwandan national trials and *gacaca* proceedings; see *Courts in Conflict: Interpreting the Layers of Justice in Post-Genocide Rwanda* (Oxford University Press, 2015).

[1012] Statement by the prosecutor of the International Criminal Court, Fatou Bensouda, at the conclusion of her visit to the Central African Republic on Friday, 23 March: 'collaboration is key to closing the impunity gap' (27 March 2018), at www.icc-cpi.int/Pages/item.aspx?name=180327-otp-stat-car. A similar opportunity now exists in Myanmar, with the establishment of a UN-backed independent investigative mechanism and confirmation of the court's partial, overlapping jurisdiction.

demands of the victims and communities in whose names it seeks to act. 'Crisis' is often an overused phrase, meant to alarm rather than clarify; indeed, as many commentators would have it, the ICC has been in some form of crisis since before it opened its doors. The current moment, however, feels different, crystallized perhaps by the Trial Chamber's finding in 2018 that there was 'no case to answer' in the case against Gbagbo and Charles Blé Goudé, a determination that followed the Appeals Chamber's high-profile, fragmented acquittal of Bemba and the collapse of the Kenyan cases.[1013] Most controversially, the PTC's more recent opinion denying the prosecutor authorization to investigate in Afghanistan – after a nearly decade-long preliminary examination there – has alienated many of its strongest supporters.

As described herein, many of these performance woes owe to issues within the Office of the Prosecutor, which remains the engine of the ICC's work. But state and non-state actors alike have attached numerous expectations to the office and the ICC as a whole, without an attendant commitment of material resources and political support to either. From two unfunded UN Security Council referrals (Sudan and Libya), to continued non-cooperation in the arrest and transfer of suspects, the rhetorical commitments to Annan's 'promise of universal justice' have been overshadowed by the political and financial costs those commitments would entail.[1014] Such political assessments are stitched into the court's constitutional fabric, but the ICC's troubled history to date suggests that its current trajectory is unsustainable in the long term.[1015] Moreover, there is a growing picture of a judicial bench in disarray and of serious – possibly existential – governance deficiencies across the institution.[1016] In an effort

---

[1013] See, e.g., Joseph Powderly and Niamh Hayes, 'The Bemba Appeal: A Fragmented Appeals Chamber Destabilses the Law and Practice of the ICC' (26 June 2018), at http://humanrightsdoctorate.blogspot.com/2018/06/the-bemba-appeal-fragmented-appeals.html.

[1014] See Ambach and Rackwitz, 'A Model of International Judicial Administration? The Evolution of Managerial Practices at the International Criminal Court', 160. ('As desirable as the referral of yet another situation by the UN Security Council would be for the legitimacy, perception, and universal reach of the Court, if such a referral does not include a cost solution it will be potentially do more harm than good for the Court'.)

[1015] Stuart Ford, 'What Investigative Resources Does the International Criminal Court Need to Succeed?: A Gravity-Based Approach', *Washington University Global Studies Law Review* 16(1) (2017), 69 (concluding that 'significantly increasing the ICC's investigative resources would improve the ICC's success').

[1016] James Goldston, 'Amid US Attacks, Time to Reinvigorate the ICC', *Just Security* (14 December 2018), at www.justsecurity.org/61837/u-s-attacks-time-reinvigorate-icc/; Douglas Guilfoyle, 'This is not fine: The International Criminal Court in Trouble', EJIL: *Talk!* (March 2019), at www.ejiltalk.org/part-i-this-is-not-fine-the-international-criminal-court-in-trouble/.

to address these performance failures, four of the former ASP presidents took the extraordinary step of publicly calling for an independent expert assessment of the ICC, which, now constituted, could perhaps provide a blueprint for meaningful institutional reform.[1017]

But much of the ICC's uneven performance cannot be divorced from its lack of proximity to the situations that populate its docket. Presently, approximately 80 percent of the court's staff is based in The Hague, while only 20 percent are in situation countries. In many ways, 'intermediaries' were an effort by the OTP to outsource the lack of such expertise, but the dangers of doing so have been painfully illustrated.[1018] The Hague-centric approach to the conduct of preliminary examinations and investigations is but one clear illustration of an institutional reluctance to engage more deeply in the complicated, but necessary terrain of 'the field'. A senior court official working in a field office, whose previous assignments for both the ICC and International Criminal Tribunal for the Former Yugoslavia (ICTY) had been Hague-based, expressed the costs of this reluctance well:

> For the first time in many years, I see the benefit of a field office. I see that the court is here, not in The Hague. We have to deal with the impact here. The victims are here, not in The Hague. But we spend such time having to defend what we do … [for those] who don't realize the context in which we operate.[1019]

The court has taken small, tentative steps towards closer physical proximity with its situation countries, but despite much discussion of the possibility of in situ confirmations or trials, the practice is exceedingly thin and thus far confined only to brief judicial site visits.[1020] More recent judicial decisions in the context of victim participation (in Palestine) and jurisdiction

[1017] Prince Zeid Raad Al Huseein, Bruno Stagno Ugarte, Christian Wenaweser and Tiina Intelman, 'The International Criminal Court Needs Fixing', *Atlantic Council* (24 April 2019), at www.atlanticcouncil.org/blogs/new-atlanticist/the-international-criminal-court-needs-fixing. The ASP approved the establishment of an independent, expert review body in December 2019.

[1018] Approximate data based on ICC proposed budget for 2019, in particular staff figures for the Registry Division of External Operations. See ICC-ASP/17/20 Vol. II.

[1019] Interview with ICC outreach official (Nairobi, 27 November 2012). See also Adam Hochschild, 'The Trial of Thomas Lubanga', *The Atlantic* (1 December 2009); Benjamin Duerr, 'Come Up and See Me: Will There Ever Be an ICC Hearing in a Situation Country?', *International Justice Tribune* (29 March 2018).

[1020] See, e.g., Lino Owor Ogora, 'Community Members in Northern Uganda Elated by Visit of ICC Judges', International Justice Monitor (19 June 2018). For a useful recap of previous discussions around in situ proceeding for the ICC, see Sharon Nakandha, 'The Case of Dominc Ongwen: Possible Considerations for In Situ Proceedings', International Justice Monitor (10 February 2015).

(in Myanmar) have hinted at a more robust approach to outreach, with an emphasis on ensuring 'a system of public information and outreach activities among ... affected communities'.[1021] It remains to be seen, however, whether this more activist posture will exist in practice or ever extend to other critical phases of court proceedings, such as the confirmation of charges and trial, or indeed even preliminary examinations. In short, such a field-based orientation – ranging from more place-based (or proximally based) examinations and investigations, to more fulsome outreach programs, to greater use of in situ proceedings – would be a radical departure from how the court currently operates.[1022]

(Re)Defining Deference

In large measure, the ICC's complementarity jurisprudence endorses either an explicit or implicit homology with the OTP's charging practices, suggesting that failure to pursue the 'same conduct' as the prosecutor would per se render a case admissible. This approach, while consistent with the technically worded provisions of Article 17 has also tacitly furthered the idea of a 'mirror image' between The Hague and domestic jurisdictions. Arguably, it can also deter states that may be willing to pursue criminal investigations and prosecutions, but see little hope of successfully doing so. Put another way, through the court's current admissibility regime, states are perpetually seeking to 'catch up' with the ICC. In this vein, scholars like Drumbl have called for 'qualified deference' in the allocation of institutional authority, one that 'strikes a middle ground between subsidiarity and complementarity'.[1023]

As an orienting principle, subsidiarity recalls other deference doctrines such as the margin of appreciation, which originated in human

---

[1021] See *Situation in the State of Palestine*, Decision on Information and Outreach for Victims of the Situation, PTC I, ICC-01/18 (13 July 2018), para. 14. Equally, however, the decision could suggest yet another example of a growing 'turf battle' between the ICC bench and the OTP over how the latter conducts its work. Similar directives have been directed at the OTP, for instance, in the context of the authorized scope of its investigations and the time frame for preliminary examinations.

[1022] On the value of in situ proceedings, see Clark, 'Peace, Justice and the International Criminal Court', 532–535. Notably, the court has sought on numerous occasions to host portions of trials or confirmation proceeding in-country (in DRC and Kenya both, and most recently Uganda), but has not done so to date. See, e.g., Judge Sir Adrian Fulford, 'The Reflections of a Trial Judge', *Criminal Law Forum* 22 (2011), 215–223; David Kaye, 'What to Do with Qaddafi', *New York Times*, 31 August 2011.

[1023] Drumbl, *Atrocity, Punishment, and International Law*, 188.

rights adjudication, but have the potential to be fruitfully applied in the context of ICC admissibility determinations as well. As developed by the European Court of Human Rights, the doctrine is premised on an understanding that, while the European Convention binds all member states, they have substantial leeway as to the means by which those obligations are implemented. In this sense, the 'machinery of protection established by the convention is subsidiary to the national systems safeguarding human rights'.[1024] Subsidiarity then, like 'classical' complementarity, is a protective principle: it is rooted in the sovereignty of states.

As a prudential doctrine, a margin of appreciation could be usefully applied in the context of ICC admissibility determinations.[1025] Approaching complementarity in this way could free a space in which to think critically about its productive potential as part of a politically fraught and dynamic process. Such an approach might also better navigate the tensions between the legal test for complementarity, which is necessarily rooted in the degree of similarity between an ICC case and national jurisdictions, and its policy-based elements, wherein domestic proceedings are to be encouraged amidst a much larger 'universe of criminality'.[1026] In Drumbl's words, deference 'creates a rebuttable presumption in favour of local or national institutions that, unlike complementarity, does not search for procedural compatibility between their process and liberal criminal law and, unlike primacy, does not explicitly impose liberal criminal procedure'.[1027] Thus, rather than bearing the burden of proof to show evidence of 'concrete and progressive investigative steps', a rebuttable presumption would offer a more elastic threshold for indicia of investigative activity at the domestic level.

An approach that draws from subsidiarity would also avoid an outright jettisoning of the established 'same conduct' test, while tempering the incentives towards mimicry. The Appeals Chamber's endorsement of a 'substantially the same' approach to conduct would appear to be a

---

[1024] Handyside v. United Kingdom, European Court of Human Rights (1976), para. 48. For a thoughtful exploration of subsidiarity's relevance to international law and governance, see Paolo G. Carroza, 'Subsidiarity as a Structural Principle of International Human Rights Law', American Journal of International Law 97 (2003), 38–79.

[1025] For a similar argument in the context of international human rights courts, see Marisa Iglesias Vila, 'Subsidiarity, Margin of Appreciation and International Adjudication Within a Cooperative Conception of Human Rights', 15(2) International Journal of Constitutional Law (2017).

[1026] Rastan, 'Situation and Case: Defining the Parameters', 442.

[1027] Drumbl, Atrocity, Punishment, and International Law, 188.

small step in this direction, but, as noted, it remains a relatively restrictive standard that has been inconsistently applied. A more clearly articulated and consistent application of a deference principle – along the lines of that called for by Judge Ušacka in her dissents – could thus permit the court to maintain its current case-by-case approach to admissibility determinations without radically departing from the framing of admissibility challenges as to the accused person and alleged conduct.[1028] A margin of appreciation would, however, be incompatible with the excessively exacting 'same incident' approach to domestic proceedings, which, unlike the 'same conduct' test, finds no textual basis in the Statute. While the Appeals Chamber appeared to endorse such a test in the Gaddafi proceedings, lower chambers have said that incidents should not be determinative. The ICC should reconsider its approach in favour of the latter approach.

There has also been significant attention paid to the question of whether the ICC might play a more formal monitoring role over domestic proceedings, suggesting a form of 'qualified' or 'conditional' admissibility not unlike the 'reverse complementarity' approach that came to later define the ICTY and International Criminal Tribunal for Rwanda (ICTR) relationships with national jurisdictions. There would appear to be little support in the Statute for such a procedure; however, as Stahn has noted, 'If a chamber is entitled to make a final finding on admissibility, based on the criteria of Article 17, it must have the power to rule on the steps leading to that result'.[1029] Deference would thus constitute, in effect, an interim decision on inadmissibility, not unlike Article 18 rulings.[1030] Such an approach could perhaps have been usefully applied in the case of Simone Gbagbo, where domestic proceedings against the former first lady moved forward regardless of the ICC's finding that the case was admissible in The Hague. The Pre-Trial Chamber's decision to consider anew the admissibility of her case in 2018, four years after its first decision and well after Gbagbo's conviction (and subsequent release) in Abidjan, affirms that the ICC's admissibility determinations are not static, but it risks exposing them as something worse: irrelevant.

Still, it is far from certain that a conditional admissibility approach, particularly one that is judicially engineered, would not ultimately reinforce the primacy that qualified deference should guard against. It may

---

[1028] Stahn, 'Admissibility Challenges before the ICC', 258.
[1029] Ibid., 257.
[1030] Ibid.

also imperil the court's increasingly fragile political standing with member states. In short, the desire to catalyse domestic accountability broadly through the legal frame of case-specific admissibility proceedings may ultimately be irreconcilable. It asks Article 17 to solve a problem for which it was not built.

To that end, a more fruitful area of practice could be to make greater use of the Rome Statute's cooperation and dialogue regimes. Articles 89 and 94, for instance, provide for consultation between a state and the court in cases where an ICC request conflicts with domestic investigation of prosecution – that is to say, in relation to a different case – yet these provisions have received scant attention to date. As Darryl Robinson notes, 'The ICC has never rejected, nor has it ever received, a request for postponement from a state wishing to pursue a suspect for a different case'.[1031] Article 18(2) offers a similar opportunity in the context of the same case: the OTP could suspend or conditionally defer its investigation(s) (subject to re-initiation if domestic proceedings proved inadequate), while perhaps also undertaking a monitoring and/or advisory role in the process.[1032] Finally, as the OTP has already noted, case selection – wherein the onus would be on the office not to bring forward cases where the same or similar persons/conduct have already been addressed domestically – is another fertile space where a margin of appreciation approach may be fruitfully applied.

As to cooperation, the ICC's record in countries like the DRC, in particular, underscores the need for the court to readjust its relationship to national jurisdictions where there is an interest in domestic accountability. While the court's engagement with Germany in the FDLR cases stand out as a positive instance where cooperation materially advanced a domestic (third party) prosecution, the narrative of the ICC's relationship in a place like the DRC largely hangs between those in The Hague who 'repeatedly express reservations about sharing information', and those of Congolese counterparts who complain that cooperation with the ICC has been a 'one-way street'.[1033] The lack of domestic compliance with concerns over

---

[1031] Robinson, 'Three Theories of Complementarity', 182. On 'sequencing' in the context of Articles 89(4) and 94, see Carsten Stahn, 'Libya, the International Criminal Court and Complementarity: A Test for "Shared Responsibility"', *Journal of International Criminal Justice* 10(2) (2012).

[1032] Article 97, by way of analogy, may offer a similar opportunity for consultation in the context of a same case (although it relates to the court's cooperation regime rather than admissibility).

[1033] Patryk Labuda, 'Complementarity and Cooperation in the Congo', in Ronald Slye (ed.), *The Nuremberg Principles in Non-Western Societies: A Reflection on Their Universality, Legitimacy and Application* (International Nuremberg Principles Academy, 2016), 185.

witness protection and confidentiality has understandably led the court to be cautious, but, on the other hand, it has also hindered the prosecutor's early vision for a cooperative approach with national jurisdictions. In short, although Article 17 applications have been the crucible through which states have sought to accommodate their interaction with the ICC, they are a blunt instrument: the space they create for dialogue between states and organs of the court is exceedingly limited. Greater attention to the Statute's cooperation and consultation regimes is thus needed.[1034]

Finally, although the court's admissibility decisions in the Libyan cases were increasingly clear that mimetic conformity with ICC standards is not required for states undertaking domestic proceedings, this has mattered little in the broader meaning of the term, where compliance with 'international standards' and 'best practices' continues to command much of the accountability discourse. To that end, deference must also mean the necessary acceptance that the goal of accountability – whether sought alongside ICC proceedings, in the shadow of them or without them at all – is necessarily contingent on the numerous political, material and technical challenges that confront states. As Elena Baylis astutely writes of military courts in the DRC:

> [T]he goal in the Congo cannot be justice absolute, ideal and untarnished, but rather must be partial justice – justice for at least some victims, through imperfect processes, with the meagre but nonetheless ambitious aim of ending the certainty of impunity, rather than ending impunity itself.[1035]

This reality need not mean that the language of legal obligation should be relinquished, nor should it limit more abundant aspirations for justice. It should, however, temper them.

Geographies of Justice: Towards Regional and Local Experimentalism

At the same time that the ICC demands greater investment, another important approach would be to seek out other, potentially more creative

---

[1034] For a similar call, see Nicola Palmer, 'The Place of Consultation in the International Criminal Court's Approach to Complementarity and Cooperation', in Bekou and Birkett (eds.), *Cooperation and the International Criminal Court*, 223–224 (arguing that 'consultation, as included in the current cooperation clauses of the ICC Statute, offers the potential for domestic and international courts to reach shared understandings').

[1035] Baylis, 'Reassessing the Role of International Criminal Law', 9. For a similar argument in the context of transitional justice, see Lars Waldorf, 'Making do with "Good Enough" Transitional Justice: Rethinking the Concept', Oxford Transitional Justice Research Seminar Series (23 November 2016).

avenues for encouraging accountability at the international, regional, sub-regional, national and sub-national level.[1036] Judicial 'romanticism' for international criminal tribunals has too often invited and encouraged a mono-institutional approach to accountability.[1037] Indeed, as the experiences recounted herein suggest, the ICC has been regarded more often than not as the sole institutional locus of power or influence, even as it exists within a transnational network of institutions participating in and/ or supporting national proceedings. Such fundamentalism has resulted in a narrow approach towards the court's relationship with domestic jurisdictions that puts it too often above, rather than nested within, a broader network of accountability actors and processes. Moreover, as noted, ICC-centrism harbours a risk: it places a heavy performance burden on the court, one that the institution has struggled to meet.

Disproportionate focus on the court also overlooks other hybrid arrangements that, by their design, have a deeper relationship to national jurisdictions and may thus have a more lasting effect on strengthening domestic capacity. An instructive example is the work of Guatemala's International Commission against Impunity (CICIG), a novel institution that was created in late 2006, in the wake of Guatemala's long-running conflict, as a treaty-level agreement between the United Nations and the government. By mandate, CICIG operated as an independent body to support the Public Prosecutor's Office and the National Police, as well as other relevant state institutions, in the investigation and prosecution of crimes committed by organized criminal enterprises and engaged alongside state institutions in the dismantling of these groups' strong ties to the country's political and security sectors.

In its near ten-year existence, CICIG played a key role in strengthening state investigative and prosecutorial institutions (resulting in a number of high-level convictions against former senior state and military officials for corruption), improving prosecutorial capacity and establishing 'high risk' courts for the prosecution of organized crime and other complex cases.[1038] Indeed, it was one such court (and the

---

[1036] On the value of regional human rights courts as fora to advance domestic criminal accountability, see Alexandra Huneeus, 'International Criminal Law by Other Means: The Quasi-Criminal Jurisdiction of the Human Rights Bodies', *American Journal of International Law* 107 (January 2013), 1–44.

[1037] See McMahon and Forsythe, 'The ICTY's Impact on Serbia'.

[1038] For more on the impact of CICIG's work, see Open Society Justice Initiative, *Against the Odds: CICIG in Guatemala* (March 2016); Morris Panner and Adriana Beltrán, 'Battling Organized Crime in Guatemala', *Americas Quarterly* (Fall 2010).

extraordinary efforts of Guatemala's former attorney general, Claudia Paz y Paz) that led to the 2013 trial and conviction for genocide and crimes against humanity of Efraín Ríos Montt, Guatemala's former president.[1039] The Ríos Montt trial and, more recently, criminal proceedings against former President Perez Molina, are the most public in a series of important domestic investigations, but it was an outcome that owed to years of close, concerted work between the commission and national counterparts.

As a form of cooperation and assistance similar to that imagined for 'positive' complementarity, CICIG speaks to the importance of international(ized), yet nationally/locally situated, mechanisms that can work with judicial and political actors to seek accountability in ways that might resonate more meaningfully with domestic communities.[1040] Despite the commission's significant later contributions to international criminal justice, its work (and legitimacy) owes largely to its achievements in joining accountability with other crucial efforts in post-conflict Guatemala, such as investigating and prosecuting cases of corruption and other economic crimes that extend back to the country's authoritarian past.[1041] Similar experimentalism has animated other regional interventions in the Americas, including the Mission to Support the Fights against Corruption and Impunity in Honduras (known by the acronym MACCIH) and the International Advisory Group of Experts (*Grupo Asesor Internacional de Personas Expertas*, GAIPE), which was established by a powerful coalition of civil society actors and victims to investigate the murder of Honduran human rights activist Berta Cáceres in

---

[1039] For additional history of the Montt trial relevant to this point, see Elizabeth Oglesby and Amy Ross, 'Guatemala's Genocide Determination and the Spatial Politics of Justice', *Space and Polity* 13(1) (April 2009), 21–39; Susan Kemp, 'Guatemala Prosecutes former President Ríos Montt: New Perspectives on Genocide and Domestic Criminal Justice', *Journal of International Criminal Justice* 12(1) (March 2014), 133–156.

[1040] See, e.g., David A. Kaye, 'Justice Beyond The Hague: Supporting the Prosecution of International Crimes in Domestic Courts', Council on Foreign Relations (Council Special Report no. 61, June 2011). Kaye further notes that the 'compartmentalization of "accountability" and "rule of law" programming means that support for one does not benefit the other'. The two should be 'integrated as a central aspect of building rule of law in the wake of conflict', 15. The Open Society Justice Initiative has supported a similar approach. See, e.g., *International Crimes, Local Justice: A Handbook for Rule-of-Law Policymakers, Donors, and Implementers* (Open Society Foundations 2011).

[1041] See Ruben Carranza, 'Plunder and Pain: Should Transitional Justice Engage with Corruption and Economic Crimes?', *International Journal of Transitional Justice* 2(3) (2008), 310–330.

March 2016.[1042] Elsewhere, in Mexico, following the disappearance of 43 students from the state of Guerrero in 2014, the government entered into an agreement with the Inter-American Commission on Human Rights to create the Interdisciplinary Group of Independent Experts (GIEI), a five-panel body that was meant to bring 'technical assistance' to the state's investigation. Together, these approaches draw inspiration from the animating policy of 'positive' complementarity, but do so in ways that creatively expand the geographies of justice beyond The Hague.

Against the 'Justice Meme': Promoting Pluralism

An attendant phenomenon of ICC-centrism is mimicry. As interpreted by many norm entrepreneurs and advocates, the language of complementarity has increasingly been cast in the idiom of 'best practices' and 'international standards', while the ICC's jurisprudence suggests to national prosecutors that states should hew towards its procedures. This mirroring phenomenon is institutional as well as normative, ranging from what domestic courtrooms should look like, to the content of national implementation legislation.[1043] While such an interpretation of the Rome Statute is progressive in its reading of state obligations under complementarity, it is potentially regressive as well, insofar as those obligations can have the effect of calcifying the form and substance of justice at the national/local level. Indeed, just as the creation of special criminal divisions (as in Uganda) or the passage of national implementing legislation (as in Kenya) were 'fast tracked' for international audiences, so-called alternative justice measures – from enfeebled truth commissions to indolent 'transitional justice policies' – have been slow walked.

Here, too, the concept of margin of appreciation, as an orientation that seeks to 'develop a geographically and culturally plural notion of implementation', could be usefully applied.[1044] As Mégret notes, complementarity may be better understood as a 'device to accommodate diversity ... not only because this diversity exists, but because it has normative value in

---

[1042] For a helpful exploration of the idea of experimentalist governance theory in the context of international human rights regimes, see Gráinne de Búrca, 'Human Rights Experimentalism', *American Journal of International Law* 111(2) (2017), 277–316.

[1043] For another articulation of this view, see Sarah M. H. Nouwen and Wouter G. Werner, 'Monopolizing Global Justice: International Criminal Law as Challenge to Human Diversity', *Journal of International Criminal Justice* 13(1) (2015).

[1044] Frédéric Mégret, 'Nature of Obligations', in Daniel Moeckli, Sangeeta Shah and Sandesh Sivakumaran (eds.), *International Human Rights Law* (Oxford: Oxford University Press, 2010), 132.

itself'.[1045] Approaching complementarity in this way – as more than ceremonial fidelity to the Rome Statute – could free a space in which to think
critically about its productive potential as part of a politically fraught and
dynamic process. A different orientation towards international criminal
justice is needed, one that that welcomes it less as a matter of compliance
with a unitary set of rules than as a project of global legal pluralism.

Such a project would actively encourage thinking about the scope of
implementation legislation beyond the remit of the Rome Statute to prioritize, for example, the inclusion of other forms of criminal liability (for
corporations as well as natural persons) and/or criminal conduct (notably, economic and environmental crimes). Here, it is worth noting that
the Malabo Protocol (the recently adopted protocol on amendments to
the statute of the African Court of Justice and Human Rights) includes
jurisdiction over ICC crimes, as well as, inter alia, the crimes of corruption, money laundering and illicit exploitation of natural resources.[1046]
Most academic commentary has been negative about the court's proposed expanded jurisdiction, suggesting, for instance, that it is a 'rebel'
court keen to 'sabotage' the ICC and reducing it to a project solely birthed
as a result of the Kenyan government's efforts to neuter the court. As with
much commentary about the ICC, however, this view is inaccurate and
ahistorical.[1047] It also suggests a failure to appreciate how, rather than
merely mirroring the Rome Statute (which itself is not a complete reflection of customary international war crimes), the protocol could, in fact,

[1045] Mégret, 'Implementation and the Uses of Complementarity', 390. For further explo-
rations of this theme, see Greenawalt, 'The Pluralism of International Criminal Law';
Paul Schiff Berman, *Global Legal Pluralism: A Jurisprudence of Law Beyond Borders*
(Cambridge: Cambridge University Press, 2012).
[1046] See Protocol on Amendments to the Protocol on the Statute of the African Court of
Justice and Human Rights, Arts. 28A, 28E, 28I, 28I *Bis*, 28L Bis (on-file). More controversially, the protocol, unlike the Rome Statute, provides for immunity for heads of state
and government while they are in office.
[1047] For departures from this predominantly negative view, see Don Deya, 'Worth the Wait:
Pushing for the African Court to Exercise Jurisdiction for International Crimes'; Abel S.
Knottnerus and Eefje de Volder, 'International Criminal Justice and the Early Formation
of an African Criminal Court', in *Africa and the ICC: Perceptions of Justice*, 376–405
(arguing that 'the concerns that have been voiced about the intentions of African leaders and about possible jurisdictional battles with the ICC are exaggerated'); Theodor
Meron, 'Closing the Accountability Gap: Concrete Steps Towards Ending Impunity for
Atrocity Crimes', *American Journal of International Law* 112(3) (2018), 442–443 (contending that the 'establishment of regional bodies with jurisdiction to try cases related
to atrocity crimes is ... a welcome innovation that complements rather than distracts
from the aims underlying the Rome system').

encourage 'an alternative vision of regional criminal justice that perhaps is better suited to Africa's realities and aspirations'.[1048]

A pluralist orientation would also support and encourage the establishment of judicial arrangements that overlap, depart from or compete with the ICC's jurisdiction. In so doing, the vision of the ICC would no longer be driven by an insistence on its place atop a jurisdictional hierarchy, or by a desire to maintain its own institutional visibility and prestige, but more horizontally, i.e., as part of a broader global ecosystem. It would insist upon the dynamism and hybridity of international criminal law and canvass fora to seek civil and criminal redress at the international, regional, sub-regional, national and sub-national level. Such creative initiatives have already flourished well beyond The Hague, but receive too little attention.[1049]

In national courts, for instance, universal jurisdiction principles, rooted in the domestic ICC legislation of states, have been used to enforce ICC arrest warrants (as in Kenya, against President Al Bashir) and to press for national investigations of Rome Statute violators (as in South Africa, against members of the ruling Zimbabwe African National Union – Patriotic Front party, or ZANU-PF).[1050] The landmark

---

[1048] Matiangai Sirleaf, 'The African Justice Cascade and the Malabo Protocol', *International Journal of Transitional Justice* 11(1) (2017), 91. On the Rome Statute as a 'mere "artist's sketch" rather than a "faithful snapshot" of war crimes in general international law', see Georges Abi-Saab, 'The Concept of "War Crimes"', in Sienho Yee and Wang Tieya (eds.), *International Law in the Post-Cold War World: Essays in Memory of Lt Haopei* (Routledge, 2001), 118; see also Dapo Akande, 'Customary International Law and the Addition of New War Crimes to the Statute of the ICC', EJIL: Talk! (2 January 2018) at www.ejiltalk.org/customary-international-law-and-the-addition-of-new-war-crimes-to-the-statute-of-the-icc/ ('The general tenor of the Statute adopted at Rome was, if anything, to be under-inclusive of customary international law crimes, rather than over-inclusive'.).

[1049] Notably, recent NGO materials suggest a return towards the hybridity that once characterized the field. See, e.g., Dakar Guidelines on the Establishment of Hybrid Courts (2019). See also Carsten Stahn, 'Tribunals are Dead, Long Live Tribunals: MICT, the Kosovo Specialist Chambers and the Turn to New Hybridity', EJIL: *Talk!* (23 September 2016); Jennifer Trahan, 'Views of the Future of the Field of International Justice: A Scenarios Project Based on Expert Consultations', *American University International Law Review* 33(4) (2018), 837–941.

[1050] See, e.g., Southern African Litigation Centre and Zimbabwe Exiles Forum *v.* National Director of Public Prosecutions, High Court of South Africa (North Gauteng), Case no. 77150/09, Judgment (8 May 2012); Max du Plessis, 'The Zimbabwe torture docket decision and proactive complementarity', Institute for Security Studies Policy brief 81 (November 2015). Two scholars have argued that, far from a perceived decline in universal jurisdiction, the use of the doctrine has persistently expanded since the 1990s; indeed, 2016 saw eight completed universal jurisdiction trials, the largest number of any year to date. See Maximo

2017 conviction of former Chadian dictator, Hissène Habré, by the Extraordinary African Chambers in Senegal, as well as other significant decisions around corporate criminal liability in conflicts ranging from Liberia to Sudan to Syria (for conduct largely predating the Rome Statute's temporal limitations), serve as further reminders of the vital role of national jurisdictions in advancing accountability.[1051] Together, these efforts suggest that the empowerment of independent domestic judicial actors and the strengthening of ordinary domestic courts, especially outside of the European continent, deserve more attention than they have received to date.

Universal jurisdiction's 'quiet expansion' has likewise animated another important innovation in the wake of the failed referral of Syria to the ICC by the UN Security Council: the establishment by the UN General Assembly of an International, Impartial and Independent Mechanism (IIIM) for Syria.[1052] While not a prosecutorial body, the IIIM model promises to offer to prosecutors and/or investigators the kind of

Langer and Mackenzie Eason, 'The Quiet Expansion of Universal Jurisdiction', *European Journal of International Law* 30(1) (2019); Yuna Han, 'Rebirth of Universal Jurisdiction?', *Ethics & International Affairs* (May 2017), at www.ethicsandinternationalaffairs.org/2017/rebirth-universal-jurisdiction/.

[1051] The proceedings in Senegal, in turn, helped launch the prosecution of 20 Habré-era agents in Chad as well, where the government was ordered to pay millions in victim compensation. See Reed Brody, 'Victims Bring a Dictator to Justice: The Case of Hissène Habré (Bread for the World, February 2017), at www.brot-fuer-die-welt.de/fileadmin/mediapool/2_Downloads/Fachinformationen/Analyse/Analysis70-The_Habre_Case.pdf. On corporate accountability, important advancements include: a Dutch appellate court's 2017 conviction of Guus Kouwenhoven, a Dutch national, for illegal arms trafficking and complicity in war crimes in Liberia and Guinea between 2000 and 2003; indictments in France issued in 2018 against three high-ranking Syrian regime officials (in connection with the disappearance, torture and death of dual Syrian-French nationals) and, separately, against the French cement company Lafarge on charges of complicity in crimes against humanity; and a 2018 decision by the Swedish government to grant the public prosecutor's application to pursue criminal proceedings against two top executives of the Stockholm-based Lundin Oil company for assisting alleged crimes against humanity in Sudan between 1997 and 2003. See Dieneke De Vos, 'Dutch court convicts former "Timber baron" of war crimes in Liberia' (24 April 2017); 'Lafarge charged with complicity in Syria crimes against humanity', *The Guardian* (28 June 2018); Julia Crawford, 'Lundin Faces Prosecution for Sudan Oil War Abuses', Justiceinfo.net (26 October 2018).

[1052] UN General Assembly Resolution 71/248 (21 December 2016), establishing an international, impartial and independent mechanism to assist in the investigation and prosecution of persons responsible for the most serious crimes under international law committed in the Syrian Arab Republic since March 2011.

cooperation that 'positive' complementarity once envisioned by providing evidence and assistance to their domestic prosecutions (currently, almost ten states are currently prosecuting crimes in Syria through universal jurisdiction). It also offers a critical repository for the substantial documentation that has been gathered by Syrians themselves. Inspired by the Syrian experience – but avoiding the damaging time delay incurred by the failed ICC referral – the UN Human Rights Council, in September 2018, also established a IIIM for Myanmar. These decisions suggest a newfound willingness by some states not to allow the ICC's impotence to obstruct other avenues for accountability.

These developments, in turn, offer opportunities for further innovation. For one, the overlapping jurisdiction of the SCC and Myanmar IIIM with the ICC raises anew the potentially cooperative aspects of 'positive' complementarity, including the sort of assistance in evidence sharing envisaged by Article 93(10) or for 'burden-sharing' in the allocation of cases. Far from drawing the OTP from a narrowly defined 'core mandate' that the ASP typically defines, such policies could, in fact, serve the interests of efficiency and judicial economy. Emergent discussions about the wisdom of establishing a permanent, standing IIIM for new situations that may arise should also be supported.[1053] Such a body could potentially ease the burden on the ICC's OTP, securing evidence and initiating investigations at a much earlier point than the court is able and providing technical support to multiple jurisdictions.

A pluralist orientation would also encompass a deeper, more politically nuanced grappling with the relationship between criminal accountability and other transitional justice approaches, as the experience of South Africa's Truth and Reconciliation Commission once exemplified.[1054]

[1053] See, e.g., Polina Levina Mahnad, 'An Independent Mechanism for Myanmar: A Turning Point in the Pursuit of Accountability for International Crimes', EJIL: *Talk!* (1 October 2018) ('A standing IIIM … would also aid the International Criminal Court, both in taking on the bulk of the work in sifting through material to identify credible sources, but also in contributing to case selection through identifying where a critical mass of evidence leads'.); Kingsley Abbott and Saman Zia-Zarifi, 'Is It Time to Create a Standing Independent Investigative Mechanism (SIIM)?', Opinio Juris (10 and 11 April 2019).

[1054] For a compelling argument favouring this approach in the Ugandan context, see Erin Baines, 'Spirits and Social Reconstruction after Mass Violence: Rethinking Transitional Justice', *African Affairs* 109(436) (2010), 409–430; on amnesties, see Louise Mallinder and Kieran McEvoy, 'Rethinking Amnesties: Atrocity, Accountability and Impunity in Post-Conflict Societies', *Contemporary Social Science* 6(1) (2011), 107–128; on sentencing, see Nancy Armoury Combs, 'Seeking Inconsistency: Advancing Pluralism in International Criminal Sentencing', *The Yale Journal of International Law* 41(2) (2016), 1–49.

The 2016 peace agreement between the Colombian government and the FARC, which proposed a similar exchange of testimony in return for eligibility for a system of 'alternative justice', suggests a return to South Africa's pioneering admixture of accountability and truth, though much about that process remains in flux. The contributory influence of the ICC's extended preliminary examination in helping to shape the parameters of Colombia's transitional justice agreement is notable in this regard, though it appears increasingly that the terms of that agreement were negotiated not merely because of the OTP's involvement, but in conversation with it and other international actors.[1055] Seen in this way, it is precisely the hybridity of systems and processes – their contingency as well as their possibility – that allowed for a more dialogic space to emerge between Colombian authorities and the court.

Understood as a constellation of accountability efforts that orbit outside of the ICC, but that also contribute to an emergent, loosely integrated system of justice, these approaches recall what Mireille Delmas-Marty has referred to as 'ordering pluralism', wherein 'the process of integration rather than the results, the movement rather than the model' are the focus of a broader international justice project. In her words, 'In this new global world, we have to observe the different processes used for ordering pluralism by integrating the plural without reducing it to the identical'.[1056] Here the shifting, adaptive nature of complementarity is an asset that should, in fact, be marshalled. Depending on the political context, its logic can be invoked to displace the ICC; at other moments, its depiction as an extension of the ICC, meant to 'complement' and complete its work, offers a useful malleability.

From Management to Modesty

Although the ICC may be accused of having too quickly put itself at the centre of contentious accountability debates, many private actors and organizations have also helped put it there. An insistence by states and

[1055] See, e.g., Hillebrecht, Huneeus and Borda, 'The Judicialization of Peace', 329 ('[T]he terms of Colombia's peace were produced *through* – not *despite* – the international courts' ongoing deliberative engagement with the peace process'.); Marco Bocchese, 'El Coco Does Not Frighten Anymore: ICC Scrutiny and State Cooperation in Colombia' (on-file).

[1056] Mireille Delmas-Marty, *Ordering Pluralism: A Conceptual Framework for Understanding the Transnational Legal World* (Oxford and Portland: Hart, 2009). Drumbl likewise advances a philosophy of 'cosmopolitan pluralism' similar to the approach advocated here; see *Atrocity, Punishment, and International Law*, 181–186.

NGOs alike on the ICC's privileged place in the jurisdictional order too often led other worthy proposals – like a special court in the DRC, or a hybrid tribunal for Sudan – to labour under the suspicion that they were merely meant to undermine the court. Furthermore, as noted above, it is not clear that the political consequences of these legalist strategies were sufficiently thought through. Indeed, while the ICC Prosecutor or the court at large may be perceived as an ally by many in civil society, the consequences of its interventions for national-level advocates may ultimately do more harm than good. The near ubiquitous refrain amongst court officials and international NGOs of the need to 'manage the expectations' of victims and affected communities or that the ICC will 'deliver justice' suggests a similar phenomenon. At the same time, these same expectations often drive the ambitious faith in the ICC's ability to serve as a catalyst for compliance.

The instinct common amongst many lawyers and diplomats – at least until recently – to place the ICC at the centre of international criminal law's imagined hierarchy should thus be avoided. The ICC, as a number of interlocutors reminded me in my interviews, is subsidiary to domestic jurisdictions, not the other way around. 'If indeed it is a court of last resort, then let it act as one', said one Ugandan advocate. And yet the ICC is still typically invoked as the 'centrepiece of the international criminal justice system',[1057] while the Rome Statute is the international community's 'North Star', as one prominent figure in the field repeatedly noted at a 2016 conference.[1058] Such statements should be avoided; they invite the very indolence that Shklar warned against.

Rather than focusing on 'managing' the expectations of others, then, it would be wiser for ICC enthusiasts to temper their own. As the legal scholar Mirjan Damaska presciently cautioned, 'Disillusionment stemming from unfulfilled expectations and inconsistencies that spring from

---

[1057] See, e.g., 'Press Release by the Members of the Informal Ministerial Network for the International Criminal Court' (27 September 2018), at www.coalitionfortheicc.org/sites/default/files/cicc_documents/2018-9-27%20IMN%20annual%20breakfast%20-%20Press%20Release.pdf; see also 'Women, Peace and Security: Open Debate and Presidential Statement', What's in Blue (27 October 2014), at www.whatsinblue.org/2014/10/women-peace-and-security-open-debate-and-presidential-statement.php (noting debates within the UN Security Council to drop references to *ad hoc* and mixed tribunals 'since EU members of the Security Council would like to keep the focus on the ICC as the locus of international justice').

[1058] Comments made at War Crimes Research Office 20th Anniversary conference on 'Prosecuting Serious International Crimes: Exploring the Intersections between International and Domestic Justice Efforts' (30 March 2016, Washington, DC).

disorientation are harmful to any system of justice, and especially to an evolving one whose legitimacy in the communities affected by international crime is still as delicate as the wings of a butterfly'.[1059] The risk of disillusionment thus calls for more careful political consideration and sober reflection about the wisdom of soliciting the court's intervention in a country, before the scale of such ambitions is publicly tested by the 'delicate wings' of the ICC's doctrinal and/or institutional limits. In short, there is a need for greater modesty not only about what the ICC is able to achieve, but about what it is called to do in the first place.

Finally, as the case studies here suggest, the ICC is but one factor amongst many that influence and shape the choices of domestic political actors. Consistent with the more process-based approach that this book urges, then, court interventions can be more productively seen as one *tactic* that might, over time, alter a domestic political environment in favour of greater accountability. As Karen Alter suggests, 'The existence of an international legal remedy empowers those actors who have international law on their side, increasing their out of court political leverage'.[1060] Difficult as this may be to reconcile with legalism, it is this extra-legal leverage where the ICC's 'shadow' is likely to have its greatest effect and where law can play a constructive role, 'not above the political world but in its very midst'.[1061]

3   Une belle époque?

It is March 2015, and I am in Brussels for a high-level conference convened by the Belgian government. Entitled 'Implementation of the European Convention on Human Rights, our Shared Responsibility', the

---

[1059] Mirjan Damaška, 'What is the Point of International Criminal Justice?', *Chicago-Kent Law Review* 83(1) (2008), 365. More critical scholarship has also increasingly questioned the triumphalism surrounding international criminal law, as well as its own exclusions. See, e.g., Christine Schwöbel, *Critical Approaches to International Criminal Law: An Introduction* (Routledge, 2014); Tor Krever, 'Dispensing Global Justice', *New Left Review* 85 (January–February 2014).

[1060] Alter, *The New Terrain of International Law*, 19. For similar assessments see Hillebrecht, Huneeus with Borda, 'The Judicialization of Peace', 281 (arguing that the ICC's experience in Colombia can 'be viewed as the best-case scenario for international courts, helping us discern what international law and courts can achieve, and cannot achieve, under the most favourable conditions'); Philipp Kastner, 'Armed Conflicts and Referrals to the International Criminal Court: From Measuring Impact to Emerging Legal Obligations', *Journal of International Criminal Justice* 12(3) (2014), 471–490 (arguing that it 'would be more constructive to shift our attention from an elusive outcome – to a process-based analysis, and to view the increasingly frequent involvement of [international courts] … as an emerging and highly influential process-related commitment').

[1061] Shklar, 123.

conference marked the culmination of Belgium's six-month chairing of the Council of Europe, an alphabetically rotating honour that this small country will not hold for another twenty years. It is the year before Brexit and the election of Donald Trump, but already the stirrings of nationalist populism are apparent. Its trans-Atlantic spread is imminent. Amidst increasing fears of the United Kingdom withdrawing from the European Convention on Human Rights, and other, similar rumblings in countries throughout the Council, the conference was intended to reaffirm the 'deep and abiding commitment' of member states to the convention and to the 'full, effective and prompt execution' of the judgments of the European Court of Human Rights (ECHR).[1062] Negotiations on a text had been underway for the previous six months, and it was at the conference that the final 'Brussels Declaration' was to be adopted.

I attended the conference no longer as a researcher, but now as a norm entrepreneur myself, part of a community of legal advocates seeking to creatively expand the European Court's normative reach and influence. But being there was a bit how I imagined the summer of 1998 might have felt in Rome. As the conference began, there was still uncertainty as to whether agreement on a final text had been reached. Hushed conversations over coffee and croissants made clear that implementation was a concept that states were more comfortable with in theory than practice. And the parallels to the ICC were striking: another revered, but overburdened court; another bold experiment in the taming of sovereignty through law; another appeal to states, reminding them that it was their primary responsibility to protect and defend human rights at the national level. Rather than complementarity, the diplomats here spoke of subsidiarity, but the logic was the same: like The Hague, Strasbourg, too, was a place of last resort.

When the declaration was adopted at the end of the second day – after all states had expressed their support, and their reservations – everyone stood and applauded, flush with the ritual of political commitments renewed. As the delegates slowly drifted out for the final reception, I spoke casually with an old friend from Amnesty International's office in

---

[1062] Brussels Declaration (27 March 2015), at http://justice.belgium.be/fr/binaries/Declaration_EN_tcm421-265137.pdf. On similar anxieties in the context of regional human rights systems, see, e.g., Karen J. Alter, James T. Gathii and Laurence R. Helfer, 'Backlash Against International Courts in West, East, and Southern Africa: Causes and Consequences', *European Journal of International Law* 27(2) (2016); Mikael Rask Madsen, Pola Cebulak and Micha Wiebusch, 'Resistance to International Courts', *International Journal of Law in Context* 14 (2018), 193–196.

Brussels, for whom I had once worked (as an intern, on Belgium's domestic implementation of the Rome Statute) in 2001, but whom I had not seen since. Our meeting felt at once accidental and purposeful – as Adler says, 'communities of practice have no fixed membership; people "move in and out" of them' – but it was a pleasure to reconnect.[1063] Eventually joined by other colleagues, I listened as the group's conversation turned to the future of not only the ECHR, but other international institutions as well. They were clearly worried. There was a feeling that the human rights movement's best moments were perhaps behind it. They spoke nostalgically of Belgium's once pioneering universal jurisdiction law, of the signing of the Rome Statute in 1998 and of the remarkable legal door that was opened with the arrest of Augusto Pinochet that same year. *Ça c'était une belle époque*, said a member of the group to wistful nods.[1064]

My colleagues' sense of a progress narrative interrupted, as well as the circumstances that brought us together, touch upon a number of themes that this book has sought to surface. As their recollections attest, the role of international criminal law in global governance has grown ever larger, but, as I have suggested, these achievements have also unhelpfully narrowed into the face of one institution at the transnational top: the ICC. The court's performance woes have unfortunately complicated this phenomenon while dovetailing with a resurgent discourse of sovereignty, leaving many advocates to wonder, like those that had gathered in Brussels, whether the hard-won achievements of the international human rights movement may be eroding.[1065]

But while the ICC remains a significant actor in the international legal and political landscape, it is hardly the only one. Nor should it be. The mere fact that it now exists cannot be an invitation to indolence, as Shklar warned so many years ago. Furthermore, the close examinations offered

---

[1063] Adler, 'Communities of Practice in International Relations', 15.

[1064] My colleagues were not alone in this assessment. See, e.g., Stephen Hopgood, *The Endtimes of Human Rights* (Ithaca: Cornell University Press, 2013); David Luban, 'After the Honeymoon: Reflections on the Current State of International Criminal Justice', *Journal of International Criminal Justice* 11(3) (2013), 505–515. For an alternative view, see Kathryn Sikkink, *Evidence for Hope: Making Human Rights Work in the 21st Century* (Princeton University Press, 2017).

[1065] The title of a 2015 symposium in the *Journal of International Criminal Justice* 11(3) (July 2013) captures the sentiment well: 'Down the Drain or Down to Earth? International Criminal Justice under Pressure'. See also the February 2015 debate issued by the ICTJ, 'Is the International Community Abandoning the Fight Against Impunity?' at www.ictj.org/debate/impunity/opening-remarks.

here of Uganda, Kenya and the DRC illustrates that the ICC's practices on the ground, as well as the growing reality of its institutional limitations, provide good reason for sober reflection. Such inquiries from the proverbial 'field' may temper our faith in how catalytic a force the court itself or the principles summoned in its name can actually be, but this is a necessary reckoning. Our ambitions should be measured by more realistic expectations and continued reflection, while always seeking – and forging – new possibilities on the horizon.

SELECT BIBLIOGRAPHY

Books

Adler, Emanuel, *Communitarian International Relations: The Epistemic Foundations of International Relations* (London and New York: Routledge Press, 2005).

AfriMAP and Open Society Initiative for Southern Africa, *The Democratic Republic of Congo: Military Justice and Human Rights – An Urgent Need to Complete Reforms* (Rosebank: Open Society Foundations, 2010).

Allen, Tim, *Trial Justice: The International Criminal Court and the Lord's Resistance Army* (London: Zed Books, 2006).

Allen, Tim and Koen Vlassenroot (eds.), *The Lord's Resistance Army: Myth and Reality* (London: Zed Books, 2010).

Alter, Karen J., *The New Terrain of International Law: Courts, Politics, Rights* (Princeton: Princeton University Press, 2014).

Autesserre, Séverine, *The Trouble with the Congo: Local Violence and the Failure of International Peacebuilding* (Cambridge: Cambridge University Press, 2010).

Avocats Sans Frontières, *The Application of the Rome Statute of the International Criminal Court by the Courts of the Democratic Republic of Congo* (Brussels: Avocats Sans Frontières, 2009).

Babington-Ashaye, Adejoke, Aimee Comrie, and Akingbolahan Adeniran (eds.), *International Criminal Investigations: Law and Practice* (The Hague: Eleven International Publishing, 2018).

Barnett, Michael and Martha Finnemore, *Rules for the World: International Organizations in Global Politics* (Ithaca: Cornell University Press, 2004).

Bass, Gary Jonathan, *Stay the Hand of Vengeance: The Politics of War Crimes Tribunals* (Princeton: Princeton University Press, 2000).

Bekou,Olympia and Daley J.Birkett (eds.), *Cooperation and the International Criminal Court: Perspectives from Theory and Practice* (Leiden: Brill/ Martinus Nijhoff Publishers, 2016).

Benedetti, Fanny, Karine Bonneau, and John L.Washburn, *Negotiating the International Criminal Court: New York to Rome, 1994–1998* (Leiden: Martinus Nijhoff Publishers, 2014).

Bennett, Andrew and Jeffrey T. Checkel (eds.), *Process Tracing: From Metaphor to Analytic Tool* (Cambridge: Cambridge University Press, 2015).

Bergsmo, Morten, Cheah Wui Ling, Song Tianying, and Yi Ping (eds.), *Historical Origins of International Criminal Law: Volume 4* (Brussels: Torkel Opsahl Academic EPublisher, 2015).

Bergsmo, Morten, Klaus Rackwitz, and Song Tianying (eds.), *Historical Origins of International Criminal Law: Volume 5* (Brussels: Torkel Opsahl Academic EPublisher, 2017).

Bergsmo, Morten and Carsten Stahn (eds.), *Quality Control in Preliminary Examination, Vols. 1–2* (Bruseels: Torkel Opsahl Academic Epublisher, 2018).

Berman, Paul Schiff, *Global Legal Pluralism: A Jurisprudence of Law Beyond Borders* (Cambridge: Cambridge University Press, 2012).

Berwouts, Kris, *Congo's Violent Peace: Conflict and Struggle since the Great African War* (London: Zed Books, 2017).

Bogdandy, Armin von and Rüdiger Wolfrum (eds.), *Max Planck Yearbook of United Nations Law 7* (Leiden: Koninklijke Brill, 2003).

Bouvier, P. and F.Bomboko, *Le Dialogue intercongolais, anatomie d'une négociation à la lisière du chaos*, Cahiers africains No. 63–64 (Paris: L'Harmattan, 2004).

Branch, Adam, *Displacing Human Rights: War and Intervention in Northern Uganda* (Oxford: Oxford University Press, 2011).

Branch, Daniel, *Kenya: Between Hope and Despair, 1963–2011* (New Haven: Yale University Press, 2011).

Brass, Jennifer N., *Allies or Adversaries: NGOs and the State in Africa* (Cambridge: Cambridge University Press, 2017).

Broomhall, Bruce, *International Justice and the International Criminal Court: Between Sovereignty and the Rule of Law* (Oxford: Oxford University Press, 2003).

Brunnée, Jutta and Stephen J. Toope, *Legitimacy and Legality in International Law: An Interactional Account* (Cambridge: Cambridge University Press, 2010).

Carpenter, Charli, *'Lost' Causes: Agenda Vetting in Global Issue Networks and the Shaping of Human Security* (Cornell: Cornell University Press, 2014).

Christensen, Mikkel Jarle and Ron Levi (eds.), *International Practices of Criminal Justice: Social and Legal Perspectives* (London: Routledge Press, 2017).

Clark, John F. (ed.), *The African Stakes of the Congo War* (Kampala: Fountain Publishers, 2003).

Clark, Phil, *Distant Justice: The Impact of the International Criminal Court on African Politics* (Cambridge: Cambridge University Press, 2019).

Clarke, Kamari Maxine, *Fictions of Justice: The International Criminal Court and the Challenge of Legal Pluralism in Sub-Saharan Africa* (Cambridge: Cambridge University Press, 2009).

Clarke, Kamari Maxine, Abel S. Knottnerus, and Eefje de Volder (eds.), *Africa and the ICC: Perceptions of Justice* (Cambridge: Cambridge University Press, 2016).

Davis, Laura and Priscilla Hayner, *Difficult Peace, Limited Justice: Ten Years of Peacemaking in the DRC* (New York: International Center for Transitional Justice, 2009).

Dawkins, Richard, *The Selfish Gene* (Oxford: Oxford University Press, 2016, 4th ed.).

Deibert, Michael, *The Democratic Republic of Congo: Between Hope and Despair* (London and New York: Zed Books, 2013).

Delmas-Marty, Mireille, *Ordering Pluralism: A Conceptual Framework for Understanding the Transnational Legal World* (Oxford and Portland: Hart Publishing, 2009).

De Vos, Christian, Sara Kendall, and Carsten Stahn (eds.), *Contested Justice: The Politics and Practice of International Criminal Court Interventions* (Cambridge: Cambridge University Press, 2015).

Drumbl, Mark A., *Atrocity, Punishment, and International Law* (Cambridge: Cambridge University Press, 2007).

Dunoff, Jeffrey L. and Mark A. Pollack (eds.), *Interdisciplinary Perspectives on International Law and International Relations: The State of the Art* (Cambridge: Cambridge University Press, 2013).

Dutton, Yvonne, *Rules, Politics, and the International Criminal Court: Committing to the Court* (Oxon and New York: Routledge Press, 2013).

Ellis, Mark S., *Sovereignty and Justice: Balancing the Principle of Complementarity between International and Domestic War Crimes Tribunals* (Newcastle upon Tyne: Cambridge Scholars Publishing, 2014).

Engle, Karen, Zinaida Miller, and D.M. Davis (eds.), *Anti-Impunity and the Human Rights Agenda* (Cambridge: Cambridge University Press, 2016).

Ferdinandusse, Ward, *Direct Application of International Criminal Law in National Courts* (Leiden: Academisch Proefschrift, 2005).

Finnström, Sverker, *Living with Bad Surroundings: War, History, and Everyday Moments in Northern Uganda* (Durham: Duke University Press, 2008).

Gathii, James Thuo, *The Contested Empowerment of Kenya's Judiciary, 2010–2015: A Historical Institutional Analysis* (Nairobi: Sheria Publishing House, 2016).

Ghai, Yash Pal and Jill Cottrell Ghai, *Kenya's Constitution: An Instrument for Change* (Nairobi: Katiba Institute, 2011).

Glasius, Marlies, *The International Criminal Court: A Global Civil Society Achievement* (New York: Routledge Press, 2006).

Goodman, Ryan and Derek Jinks, *Socializing States: Promoting Human Rights Through International Law* (Oxford: Oxford University Press, 2013).

Green, Matthew, *The Wizard of the Nile: The Hunt for Arica's Most Wanted* (London: Portobello Books, 2009).

Gruszczynski, Lukasz and Wouter Werner (eds.), *Deference in International Courts and Tribunals: Standard of Review and Margin of Appreciation* (Oxford: Oxford University Press, 2014).

Haddad, Heidi Nichols, *The Hidden Hands of Justice: NGOs, Human Rights, and International Courts* (Cambridge: Cambridge University Press, 2018).

Hagan, John, *Justice in the Balkans: Prosecuting War Crimes in The Hague Tribunal* (Chicago: The University of Chicago Press, 2003).

Hayner, Priscilla, *The Peacemaker's Paradox: Pursuing Justice in the Shadow of Conflict* (New York: Routledge Press, 2018).

Hillebrecht, Courtney, *Domestic Politics and International Human Rights Tribunals: The Problem of Compliance* (Cambridge: Cambridge University Press, 2014).

Imoedemhe, Ovo Catherine, *The Complementarity Regime of the International Criminal Court: National Implementation in Africa* (Cham: Springer International Publishing, 2017).

Jalloh, Charles Chernor and Ilias Bantekas (eds.), *The International Criminal Court and Africa* (Oxford: Oxford University Press, 2017).

Jalloh, Charles Chernor, Kamari M. Clarke, and Vincent O.Nmehielle (eds.), *The African Court of Justice and Human and Peoples' Rights in Context: Development and Challenges* (Cambridge: Cambridge University Press, 2019).

Jurdi, Nidal Nabil, *The International Criminal Court and National Courts: A Contentious Relationship* (Farnham: Ashgate Publishing, 2011).

Keck, Margaret E. and Kathryn Sikkink, *Activists Beyond Borders: Advocacy Networks in International Politics* (Ithaca: Cornell University Press, 1998).

Kleffner, Jann K., *Complementarity in the Rome Statute and National Criminal Jurisdictions* (Oxford: Oxford University Press, 2008).

Kleffner, Jann K. and Gerben Kor (eds.), *Complementary Views on Complementarity: Proceedings of the International Roundtable on the Complementary Nature of the International Criminal Court, Amsterdam, 25/26 June 2004* (The Hague: TMC Asser Press, 2006).

Koskenniemi, Martti, *From Apology to Utopia: The Structure of International Legal Argument* (Cambridge: Cambridge University Press, 2006).

Krieger, Heike (ed.), *Inducing Compliance with International Human Rights Law: Lessons from the African Great Lakes Region* (Cambridge: Cambridge University Press, 2018).

Lake, Milli, *Strong NGOs and Weak States* (Cambridge: Cambridge University Press, 2018).

Leebaw, Bronwyn, *Judging State-Sponsored Violence, Imagining Political Change* (Cambridge: Cambridge University Press, 2011).

Lessa, Francesca and Leigh A. Payne (eds.), *Amnesty in the Age of Human Rights Accountability: Comparative and International Perspectives* (Cambridge: Cambridge University Press, 2012).

Lynch, Gabrielle, *I Say to You: Ethnic Politics and the Kalenjin in Kenya* (Chicago: University of Chicago Press, 2011).

Performances of Injustice: The Politics of Truth, Justice and Reconciliation in Kenya (Cambridge: Cambridge University Press, 2018).

Mahony, Chris, *The Justice Sector Afterthought: Witness Protection in Africa* (Pretoria: Institute for Security Studies, 2010).

Mari Tripp, Aili, *Museveni's Uganda: Paradoxes of Power in a Hybrid Regime* (Boulder: Lynne Rienner Publishers, 2010).

Materu, Sosteness Francis, *The Post-Election Violence in Kenya: Domestic and International Legal Responses* (The Hague: T.M.C. Asser Press, 2015).

Mazower, Mark, *Governing the World: The History of an Idea, 1815 to the Present* (New York: Penguin Books, 2012).

Mbokani, Jacques B., *Congolese Jurisprudence under International Criminal Law: An Analysis of Congolese Military Court Decisions Applying the Rome Statute – A Review by Open Society Initiative for South Africa (OSISA) OSISA-DRC* (New York: Open Society Foundations, 2016).

Mbote, Patricia Kameri and Migai Akech, *Kenya: Justice Sector and the Rule of Law – A review by AfriMAP and the Open Society Initiative for Eastern Africa* (Nairobi: Open Society Initiative for Eastern Africa, 2011).

McAuliffe, Padraig, *Transitional Justice and Rule of Law Reconstruction: A Contentious Relationship* (Abingdon: Routledge Press, 2013).

Merry, Sally Engle, *Human Rights and Gender Violence: Translating International Law into Local Justice* (Chicago: University of Chicago Press, 2006).

Michel, Verónica, *Prosecutorial Accountability and Victims' Rights in Latin America* (Cambridge: Cambridge University Press, 2018)

Mosse, David, *Cultivating Development: An Ethnography of Aid Policy and Practice* (London: Pluto Press, 2005).

Mpiana, Joseph Kazadi, *La Position du droit international dans l'ordre juridique congolais et l'application de ses norms* (Paris: Publibook, 2013).

Mutua, Makau, *Kenya's Quest for Democracy: Taming Leviathan* (Kampala: Fountain Publishers, 2008).

(ed.), *Human Rights NGOs in East Africa: Political and Normative Tensions* (Kampala: Fountain Publishers, 2009).

Nettelfield, Lara J., *Courting Democracy in Bosnia and Herzegovina: The Hague Tribunal's Impact in a Postwar State* (Cambridge: Cambridge University Press, 2010).

Nichols, Lionel, *The International Criminal Court and the End of Impunity in Kenya* (New York: Springer International Publishing, 2015).

Nouwen, Sarah M. H., *Complementarity in the Line of Fire: The Catalysing Effect of the International Criminal Court in Uganda and Sudan* (Cambridge: Cambridge University Press, 2013).

O'Connell, Mary Ellen, *The Power & Purpose of International Law: Insights from the Theory & Practice of Enforcement* (Oxford: Oxford University Press, 2011).

Olasolo, Hector, *The Triggering Procedure of the International Criminal Court* (Leiden: Martinus Nijhoff Publishers, 2005).

Open Society Justice Initiative, *International Crimes, Local Justice: A Handbook for Rule-of-Law Policymakers, Donors, and Implementers* (New York: Open Society Foundations, 2011).

Putting Complementarity into Practice: Domestic Justice for International Crimes in DRC, Uganda, and Kenya (New York: Open Society Foundations, 2011).

Orentlicher, Diane F., *Some Kind of Justice: The ICTY's Impact in Bosnia and Serbia* (New York: Oxford University Press, 2018).

Palmer, Nicola, *Courts in Conflict: Interpreting the Layers of Justice in Post-Genocide Rwanda* (New York: Oxford University Press, 2015).

Peskin, Victor, *International Justice in Rwanda and the Balkans: Virtual Trials and the Struggle for State Cooperation* (Cambridge: Cambridge University Press, 2008).

Pikis, Georghios M., *The Rome Statute for the International Criminal Court: Analysis of the Statute, the Rules of Procedure and Evidence, the Regulations of the Court and Supplementary Instruments* (Leiden: Martinus Nijhoff Publishers, 2010).

Reyntjens, Filip, *The Great African War: Congo and Regional Geopolitics, 1996–2006* (Cambridge: Cambridge University Press, 2009).

Riles, Annelise, *The Network Inside Out* (Ann Arbor: University of Michigan Press, 2001).

Risse, Thomas, Stephen C. Ropp, and Kathryn Sikkink (eds.), *The Persistent Power of Human Rights: From Commitment to Compliance* (Cambridge: Cambridge University Press, 2013).

The Power of Human Rights: International Norms and Domestic Change (Cambridge: Cambridge University Press, 1999).

Roht-Arriaza, Naomi, *The Pinochet Effect: Transnational Justice in the Age of Human Rights* (Philadelphia: University of Pennsylvania Press, 2005).

Sadat, Leila Nadya, *The International Criminal Court and the Transformation of International Law: Justice for the New Millennium* (Leiden: Martinus Nijhoff Publishers, 2002).

Schiff, Benjamin N., *Building the International Criminal Court* (Cambridge: Cambridge University Press, 2008).

Schwöbel, Christine (ed.), *Critical Approaches to International Criminal Law: An Introduction* (New York: Routledge Press, 2014).

Seils, Paul, *Handbook on Complementarity: An Introduction to the Role of National Courts and the ICC in Prosecuting International Crimes* (New York: International Center for Transitional Justice, 2016).

Shany, Yuval, *Assessing the Effectiveness of International Courts* (Oxford: Oxford University Press, 2014).

Regulating Jurisdictional Relations Between National and International Courts (Oxford: Oxford University Press, 2007).

Shklar, Judith N., *Legalism: Law, Morals, and Political Trials* (Cambridge: Cambridge University Press, 1964).

Sikkink, Kathryn, *The Justice Cascade: How Human Rights Prosecutions are Changing World Politics* (New York: W.W. Norton & Company, 2011).

Sila, Munyao, *Modern Law of Criminal Procedure in Kenya* (Johannesburg: Partridge Africa, 2014).

Simmons, Beth A., *Mobilizing for Human Rights: International Law in Domestic Politics* (Cambridge: Cambridge University Press, 2009).

Simpson, Gerry, *Law, War and Crime: War Crimes Trials and the Reinvention of International Law* (Cambridge: Polity Press, 2007).

Skouteris, Thomas, *The Notion of Progress in International Law Discourse* (Leiden: Proefschrift, 2008).

Slaughter, Anne-Marie, *A New World Order* (Princeton: Princeton University Press, 2004).

Slye, Ronald C., *The Kenyan TJRC: An Outsider's View from the Inside* (Cambridge: Cambridge University Press, 2018).

Songa, Nyabirungu mwene, *Droit International Pénal: Crimes contre la paix et la sécurité de l'humanité* (Kinshasa: Editions Droit et Société, 2013).

Squatrito, Theresa, Oran R. Young, Andreas Follesdal, and Geir Ulfstein (eds.), *The Performance of International Courts and Tribunals* (Cambridge: Cambridge University Press, 2018).

Stahn, Carsten (ed.), *The Law and Practice of the International Criminal Court* (Oxford: Oxford University Press, 2015).

Stahn, Carsten and Mohamed M. El Zeidy (eds.), *The International Criminal Court and Complementarity: From Theory to Practice* (Cambridge: Cambridge University Press, 2011).

Stearns, Jason K., *Dancing in the Glory of Monsters: The Collapse of the Congo and the Great War of Africa* (New York: PublicAffairs, 2011).

Stegmiller, Ignaz, *The Pre-Investigation Stage of the ICC* (Berlin: Duncker and Humblot, 2011).

Stigen, Jo, *The Relationship between the International Criminal Court and National Jurisdictions: The Principle of Complementarity* (Leiden: Martinus Nijhoff Publishers, 2008).

Stromseth, Jane, David Wippman, and Rosa Brooks, *Can Might Make Rights? Building the Rule of Law after Military Interventions* (Cambridge: Cambridge University Press, 2006).

Struett, Michael, *The Politics of Constructing the International Criminal Court: NGOs, Discourse, and Agency* (London: Palgrave Macmillan, 2008).

Subotić, Jelena, *Hijacked Justice: Dealing with the Past in the Balkans* (Ithaca: Cornell University Press, 2009).

Teitel, Ruti G., *Globalizing Transitional Justice: Contemporary Essays* (Oxford: Oxford University Press, 2014).

Humanity's Law (Oxford: Oxford University Press, 2011).

van den Herik, Larissa and Carsten Stahn (eds.), *The Diversification and Fragmentation of International Criminal Law* (Leiden: Martinus Nijhoff Publishers, 2012).

van der Merwe, Hugo, Victoria Baxter, and Audrey R.Chapman (eds.), *Assessing the Impact of Transitional Justice: Challenges for Empirical Research* (Washington, DC: USIP Press, 2009).

Van Reybrouck, David, *Congo: The Epic History of a People* (London: Fourth Estate, 2014).

Waddell, Nicholas and Phil Clark (eds.), *Courting Conflict? Justice, Peace and the ICC in Africa* (London: Royal African Society, 2008).

War Crimes Research Office, *Investigative Management, Strategies, and Techniques of the International Criminal Court's Office of the Prosecutor* (2012).

Wenger, Etienne, *Communities of Practice: Learning, Meaning, and Identity* (New York: Cambridge University Press, 1998).

Wrong, Michela, *It's Our Turn to Eat: The Story of a Kenyan Whistleblower* (London: Fourth Estate, 2009).

Zimmerman, Lisbeth, *Global Norms with a Local Face: Rule-of-Law Promotion and Norm Translation* (Cambridge: Cambridge University Press, 2017).

Articles and Chapters

Afako, Barney, 'Country Study V: Uganda', in M. du Plessis and J. Ford (eds.), *Unable or Unwilling? Case Studies on Domestic Implementation of the ICC Statute in Selected African Countries* (Pretoria: Institute for Security Studies, 2008).

Agirre Aranburu, Xabier, 'Methodology for the Criminal Investigation of International Crimes', in Alette Smeulers (ed.), *Collective Violence and International Criminal Justice: An Interdisciplinary Approach* (Antwerp: Intersentia, 2010).

Akhavan, Payam, 'Complementarity Conundrums: The ICC Clock in Transitional Times', *Journal of International Criminal Justice* 14(5) (2016).

'The Lord's Resistance Army Case: Uganda's Submission of the First State Referral to the International Criminal Court', *American Journal of International Law* 99(2) (2005).

'The Rome Statute's Missing Half: Towards an Express and Enforceable Obligation for the National Repression of International Crimes', *Journal of International Criminal Justice* 8(5) (2010).

Alter, Karen J., James T. Gathii, and Laurence R. Helfer, 'Backlash against International Courts in West, East, and Southern Africa: Causes and Consequences', *European Journal of International Law* 27(2) (2016).

Ambach, Philipp and Klaus U. Rackwitz, 'A Model of International Judicial Administration? The Evolution of Managerial Practices at the International Criminal Court', *Law and Contemporary Problems* 76(3–4) (2013).

Ambos, Kai and Ignaz Stegmiller, 'Prosecuting International Crimes at the International Criminal Court: Is There a Coherent and Comprehensive Prosecution Strategy?' *Crime, Law and Social Change* 58(4) (2012).

Anderson, Janet H., 'Ocampo's Shadow Still Hangs over the ICC', *International Justice Tribune* (18 June 2018).

Annan, Kofi, 'Advocating for an International Criminal Court', *Fordham International Law Journal* 21(2) (1997).

Apuuli, Kasaija Phillip, 'The ICC's Possible Deferral of the LRA Case to Uganda', *Journal of International Criminal Justice* 6(4) (2008).

Asaala, Evelyne Owiye, 'Prosecuting Crimes Related to the 2007 Post-election Violence in Kenyan Courts: Issues and Challenges', in H. J.van der Merwe and Gerhard Kemp (eds.), *International Criminal Justice in Africa: Issues, Challenges and Prospects* (Nairobi: Strathmore University Press and Konrad Adenauer Stiftung, 2016).

'The Deterrence Effect of the International Criminal Court: A Kenyan Perspective', in Jennifer Schense and Linda Carter (eds.), *Two Steps Forward, One Step Back: The Deterrent Effect of International Criminal Tribunals* (Nuremberg: International Nuremberg Principles Academy, 2016).

Askin, Kelly, 'Fizi Mobile Court: Rape Verdicts', *International Justice Tribune* (2 March 2011).

Autesserre, Séverine, 'Dangerous Tales: Dominant Narratives on the Congo and Their Unintended Consequences', *African Affairs* 111(443) (2012).

Baines, Erin, 'Spirits and Social Reconstruction after Mass Violence: Rethinking Transitional Justice', *African Affairs* 109(436) (2010).

Bassiouni, M. Cherif, 'The ICC–Quo Vadis?' *Journal of International Criminal Justice* 4(3) (2006).

Batros, Ben, 'The Judgment on the Katanga Admissibility Appeal: Judicial Restraint at the ICC', *Leiden Journal of International Law* 23(2) (2010).

Baylis, Elena, 'Function and Dysfunction in Post-conflict Judicial Networks and Communities', *Vanderbilt Journal of Transnational Law* 47(3) (2014).

'Outsourcing Investigations', *UCLA Journal of International Law and Foreign Affairs* 14 (2009).

'Reassessing the Role of International Criminal Law: Rebuilding National Courts through Transnational Networks', *Boston College Law Review* 50(1) (2009).

Bekou, Olympia, 'Crimes at Crossroads: Incorporating International Crimes at the National Level', *Journal of International Criminal Justice* 10(3) (2012).

Bellelli, Roberto, 'Obligation to Cooperate and Duty to Implement', in Roberto Bellelli (ed.), *International Criminal Justice: Law and Practice from the Rome Statute to Its Review* (Farnham: Ashgate, 2010).

Bensuoda, Fatou, 'Reflections from the International Criminal Court Prosecutor', *Case Western Reserve Journal of International Law* 45(1–2) (Fall 2012).

Bergsmo, Morten, Olympia Bekou, and Annika Jones, 'Complementarity after Kampala: Capacity Building and the ICC's Legal Tools', *Goettingen Journal of International Law* 2(2) (2010).

Bitti, Gilbert and Mohamed M. El Zeidy, 'The Katanga Trial Chamber Decision: Selected Issues', *Leiden Journal of International Law* 23(2) (2010).

Bjork, Christine and Juanita Goebertus, 'Complementarity in Action: The Role of Civil Society and the ICC in Rule of Law Strengthening in Kenya', *Yale Human Rights and Development Journal* 14(1) (2011).

Blumenson, Eric, 'The Challenge of a Global Standard of Justice: Peace, Pluralism, and Punishment at the International Criminal Court', *Columbia Journal of Transnational Law* 44(3) (2006).

Boesenecker, Aaron P. and Leslie Vinjamuri, 'Lost in Translation? Civil Society, Faith-Based Organizations and the Negotiation of International Norms', *International Journal of Transitional Justice* 5(3) (2011).

Bosco, David, 'Discretion and State Influence at the International Criminal Court: The Prosecutor's Preliminary Examinations', *American Journal of International Law* 111(2) (2017).

Bradfield, Paul, 'Reshaping Amnesty in Uganda: The Case of Thomas Kwoyelo', *Journal of International Criminal Justice* 15(4) (2017), 848.

Brighton, Clare, 'Avoiding Unwillingness: Addressing the Political Pitfalls Inherent in the Complementarity Regime of the International Criminal Court', *International Criminal Law Review* 12(4) (2012).

Brown, Stephen and Chandra Lekha Sriram, 'The Big Fish Won't Fry Themselves: Criminal Accountability for Post-Election Violence in Kenya', *African Affairs* 111(443) (2012).

Burke-White, William W., 'Complementarity in Practice: The International Criminal Court as Part of a System of Multi-level Global Governance in the Democratic Republic of Congo', *Leiden Journal of International Law* 18(3) (2005).

'Proactive Complementarity: The International Criminal Court and National Courts in the Rome System of International Justice', *Harvard International Law Journal* 49(1) (Winter 2008).

'The Domestic Influence of International Criminal Tribunals: The International Criminal Tribunal for the Former Yugoslavia and the Creation of the State Court of Bosnia & Herzegovina', *Columbia Journal of Transnational Law* 46(2) (2008).

Burke-White, William W. and Scott Kaplan, 'Shaping the Contours of Domestic Justice: The International Criminal Court and an Admissibility Challenge in the Uganda Situation', in *Carsten Stahn and Göran Sluiter, The Emerging Practice of the International Criminal Court* (Leiden: Brill/Martinus Nijhoff Publishers, 2008).

Carranza, Ruben, 'Plunder and Pain: Should Transitional Justice Engage with Corruption and Economic Crimes?' *International Journal of Transitional Justice* 2(3) (2008).

Carruthers, Bruce G. and Terence C. Halliday, 'Negotiating Globalization: Global Scripts and Intermediation in the Construction of Asian Insolvency Regimes', *Law & Social Inquiry* 31(3) (2006).

Cassese, Antonio, 'Is the ICC Still Having Teething Problems?' *Journal of International Criminal Justice* 4(3) (2006).

Charney, Jonathan, 'International Criminal Law and the Role of Domestic Courts', *American Journal of International Law* 95(1) (2001).

Chayes, Abram and Antonia Handler Chayes, 'On Compliance', *International Organization* 47(2) (1993).

Clark, Janine Natalya, 'Peace, Justice and the International Criminal Court: Limitations and Possibilities', *Journal of International Criminal Justice* 9(3) (2011).

Crawford, James, 'The ILC's Draft Statute for an International Criminal Tribunal', *American Journal of International Law* 88(1) (1994).

Cross, Matthew E. and Sarah Williams, 'Recent Developments at the ICC: Prosecutor v. Germain Katanga and Mathieu Ngudjolo Chui – A Boost for "Co-operative Complementarity"?' *Human Rights Law Review* 10(2) (2010).

Dai, Xinyuan, 'The Conditional Effects of International Human Rights Institutions', *Human Rights Quarterly* 36(3) (2014).

Damaška, Mirjan, 'What Is the Point of International Criminal Justice?' *Chicago-Kent Law Review* 83(1) (2008).

Dancy, Geoff and Verónica Michel, 'Human Rights Enforcement from Below: Private Actors and Prosecutorial Momentum in Latin American and Europe', *International Studies Quarterly* 60(1) (2016).

Dancy, Geoff and Florencia Montal, 'Unintended Positive Complementarity: Why International Criminal Court Investigations May Increase Domestic Human Rights Prosecutions', *American Journal of International Law* 111(3) (2017).

Davis, Laura, 'Power Shared and Justice Shelved: The Democratic Republic of Congo', *The International Journal of Human Rights* 17(2) (2013).

de Búrca, Gráinne, 'Human Rights Experimentalism', *American Journal of International Law* 111(2) (2017).

de Hoon, Marieke, 'The Future of the International Criminal Court: On Critique, Legalism and Strengthening the ICC's Legitimacy', *International Criminal Law Review* 17(4) (2017).

De Vos, Christian M., 'Investigating from Afar: The ICC's Evidence Problem', *Leiden Journal of International Law* 26(4) (December 2013).

'"Someone Who Comes between One Person and Another": Lubanga, Local Cooperation and the Right to a Fair Trial', *Melbourne Journal of International Law* 12(1) (June 2011).

Duerr, Benjamin, 'Come Up and See Me: Will There Ever Be an ICC Hearing in a Situation Country?' *International Justice Tribune* (29 March 2018).

Dutton, Yvonne and Tessa Alleblas, 'Unpacking the Deterrent Effect of the International Criminal Court: Lessons from Kenya', *St. John's Law Review* 91(1) (2017).

Ebobrah, Solomon T., 'Towards a Positive Application of Complementarity in the African Human Rights System: Issues of Functions and Relations', *European Journal of International Law* 22(3) (2011).

Ellis, Mark S., 'Beyond a Flawed Trial: ICC Failures to Ensure International Standards of Fairness in the Trials of Former Libyan Regime Members', *American University International Law Review* 33(1) (2017).

'International Justice and the Rule of Law: Strengthening the ICC through Domestic Prosecutions', *Hague Journal on the Rule of Law* 1(1) (2009).

'The International Criminal Court and Its Implication for Domestic Law and National Capacity Building', *Florida Journal of International Law* 15(2) (2002).

Finnemore, Martha and Duncan B. Hollis, 'Constructing Norms for Global Cybersecurity', *American Journal of International Law* 110 (3) (July 2016)

Finnemore, Martha and Kathryn Sikkink, 'International Norm Dynamics and Political Change', *International Organization* 52(4) (Autumn 1998).

Finnström, Sverker, 'Reconciliation Grown Bitter? War, Retribution, and Ritual Action in Northern Uganda', in Rosalind Shaw and Lars Waldorf, with Pierre Hazan (eds.), *Localizing Transitional Justice: Interventions and Priorities after Mass Violence* (Stanford: Stanford University Press, 2010).

Fisher, William, 'Doing Good? The Politics and Anti-Politics of NGO Practices', *Annual Review of Anthropology* 26 (1997).

Fletcher, George and Jens David Ohlin, 'Reclaiming Fundamental Principles of Criminal Law in the Darfur Case', *Journal of International Criminal Justice* 3(3) (2005).

Ford, Stuart, 'What Investigative Resources Does the International Criminal Court Needs to Succeed?: A Gravity-Based Approach', *Washington University Global Studies Law Review* 16(1) (2017).

Fourcade, Marion and Joachim J. Savelsberg, 'Global Processes, National Institutions, Local Bricolage: Shaping Law in an Era of Globalization', *Law & Social Inquiry* 31(3) (2006).

Franceschet, Antonio, 'The International Criminal Court's Provisional Authority to Coerce', *Ethics & International Affairs* 26(1) (Spring 2012).

Fry, Elinor, 'Between Show Trials and Sham Prosecutions: The Rome Statute's Potential Effects on Domestic Due Process Protections', *Criminal Law Forum* 23 (2012).

Fujiwara, Hiroto and Stephan Parmentier, 'Investigations', in Luc Reydams, Jan Wouteres, and Cedric Ryngaert (eds.), *International Prosecutors* (Oxford: Oxford University Press, 2012).

Fulford, Judge Sir Adrian, 'The Reflections of a Trial Judge', *Criminal Law Forum* 22(1) (2011).

Gioia, Federica, 'State Sovereignty, Jurisdiction, and "Modern" International Law: The Principle of Complementarity in the International Criminal Court', *Leiden Journal of International Law* 19(4) (2006).

Glasius, Marlies, '"We Ourselves, We Are Part of the Functioning": The ICC, Victims, and Civil Society in the Central African Republic', *African Affairs* 108(430) (2009).

'What Is Global Justice and Who Decides? Civil Society and Victim Responses to the International Criminal Court's First Investigations', *Human Rights Quarterly* 31(2) (2009).

Goldston, James A., 'More Candour about Criteria: The Exercise of Discretion by the Prosecutor of the International Criminal Court', *Journal of International Criminal Justice* 8(2) (2010).

Haas, Peter, 'Introduction: Epistemic Communities and International Policy Coordination', *International Organization* 46(1) (1992).

Haddad, Heidi Nichols, 'After the Norm Cascade: NGO Mission Expansion and the Coalition for the International Criminal Court', *Global Governance* 19(2) (2013).

Hansen, Thomas Obel, 'A Critical Review of the ICC's Recent Practice Concerning Admissibility Challenges and Complementarity', *Melbourne Journal of International Law* 13(1) (2012).

'Transitional Justice in Kenya? An Assessment of the Accountability Process in Light of Domestic Politics and Security Concerns', *California Western International Law Journal* 42(1) (2011).

Hansen, Thomas Obel and Chandra Lekha Sriram, 'Fighting for Justice (and Survival): Kenyan Civil Society Accountability Strategies and Their Enemies', *International Journal of Transitional Justice* 9(3) (2015).

Haslam, Emily, 'Subjects and Objects: International Criminal Law and the Institutionalization of Civil Society', *International Journal of Transitional Justice* 5(2) (2011).

Haslam, Emily and Rod Edmunds, 'Managing a New "Partnership": "Professionaliza-tion," Intermediaries and the International Criminal Court', *Criminal Law Forum* 24(1) (2013).

Helfer, Laurence R., 'Redesigning the European Court of Human Rights: Embeddedness as a Deep Structural Principle of the European Human Rights Regime', *The European Journal of International Law* 19(1) (2008).

Heller, Kevin Jon, 'A Sentence-Based Theory of Complementarity', *Harvard International Law Journal* 53(1) (2012).

'Radical Complementarity', *Journal of International Criminal Justice* 14(3) (2016).

'The Shadow Side of Complementarity: The Effect of Article 17 of the Rome Statute on National Due Process', *Criminal Law Forum* 17(3–4) (2006).

Hillebrecht, Courtney, Alexandra Huneeus, with Sandra Borda, 'The Judicialization of Peace', *Harvard International Law Journal* 59(2) (2018).

Hilpold, Peter, 'Intervening in the Name of Humanity: R2P and the Power of Ideas', *Journal of Conflict & Security Law* 17(1) (2012).

Hochschild, Adam, 'The Trial of Thomas Lubanga', *The Atlantic* (1 December 2009).

Holmes, J. T., 'The Principle of Complementarity', in R. Lee (ed.), *The International Criminal Court – The making of the Rome Statute* (The Hague: Kluwer Law International, 1999).

Horovitz, Sigall, 'How International Courts Shape Domestic Justice: Lessons from Rwanda and Sierra Leone', *Israel Law Review* 46(3) (2013).

Hovil, Lucy, 'Challenging International Justice: The Initial Years of the International Criminal Court's Intervention in Uganda', *Stability* 2(1) (2013).

Howse, Robert and Ruti Teitel, 'Beyond Compliance: Rethinking Why International Law Really Matters', *Global Policy* 1(2) (May 2010).

Huneeus, Alexandra, 'International Criminal Law by Other Means: The Quasi-Criminal Jurisdiction of the Human Rights Bodies', *American Journal of International Law* 107(1) (2013).

'Legitimacy and Jurisdictional Overlap: The ICC and the Inter-American Court in Colombia', in Nienke Grossman, Harlan Grant Cohen, Andreas Follesdal, and Geir Ulfstein (eds.), *Legitimacy and International Courts* (Cambridge: Cambridge University Press, 2018).

Iglesias Vila, Marisa, 'Subsidiarity, Margin of Appreciation and International Adjudication Within a Cooperative Conception of Human Rights', *International Journal of Constitutional Law* 15(2) (2017).

Inman, Derek and Pacifique Muhindo Magadju, 'Prosecuting International Crimes in the Democratic Republic of Congo: Using Victim Participation as a Tool to Enhance the Rule of Law and to Tackle Impunity', *African Human Rights Law Journal* 18(1) (2018).

Jalloh, Charles Cherner, 'Kenya vs. The ICC Prosecutor', *Harvard International Law Journal* 53 (August 2012).

James, John, 'Ivory Coast – Who's Next after Laurent Gbagbo?' *International Justice Tribune* (29 February 2012).

Jennings, Simon and Thomas Bwire, 'Kenyan Chief Justice Announces Special Court', *Institute for War & Peace Reporting* (10 December 2012).

Jessberger, Florian and Julia Geneuss, 'The Many Faces of the International Criminal Court', *Journal of International Criminal Justice* 10(5) (2012).

Jones, Louise, 'The Rape Trial of Colonel 106: A Test for Congo's Military Justice', *International Justice Tribune* (10 September 2014).

Jurdi, Nidal Nabil, 'Some Lessons on Complementarity for the International Criminal Court Review Conference', *South African Yearbook of International Law* 34(1) (2009).

'The Complementarity Regime of the International Criminal Court in Practice: Is It Truly Serving the Purpose? Some Lessons from Libya', *Leiden Journal of International Law* 30(1) (2017).

Kahombo, Balingene, 'The Principle of Complementarity in Practice: A Survey of Congolese Legislation Implementing the Rome Statute', in H. J. van der Merwe and Gerhard Kemp (eds.), *International Criminal Justice in Africa, 2016* (Nairobi: Strathmore University Press and Konrad Adenauer Stiftung, 2017).

Kambale, Pascal, 'Mix and Match: Is a Hybrid Court the Best Way for Congo to Prosecute International Crimes?' *Openspace* (February 2012).

Kapur, Amrita, 'The Value of International-National Interactions and Norm Interpretations in Catalysing National Prosecution of Sexual Violence', *Oñati Socio-Legal Series* 6(1) (2016).

Kastner, Philipp, 'Armed Conflicts and Referrals to the International Criminal Court: From Measuring Impact to Emerging Legal Obligations', *Journal of International Criminal Justice* 12(3) (2014).

Kaye, David, 'What to Do with Qaddafi', *New York Times* (31 August 2011).

'Who's Afraid of the International Criminal Court? Finding the Prosecutor Who Can Set It Straight', *Foreign Affairs* 90(3) (May/June 2011).

Kemp, Susan, 'Guatemala Prosecutes former President Ríos Montt: New Perspectives on Genocide and Domestic Criminal Justice', *Journal of International Criminal Justice* 12(1) (2014).

Kendall, Sara, 'Commodifying Global Justice: Economies of Accountability at the International Criminal Court', *Journal of International Criminal Justice* 13(1) (2015).

'"Constitutional Technicity": Displacing Politics through Expert Knowledge', *Law, Culture and the Humanities* 11(3) (2015).

'"UhuRuto" and Other Leviathans: The International Criminal Court and the Kenyan Political Order', *African Journal of Legal Studies* 7(3) (2014).

Kiai, Maina, 'Despised and Neglected, PEV Victims Are Now Being Abandoned by ICC', *Daily Nation* (8 June 2012).

Kleffner, Jann K., 'The Impact of Complementarity on National Implementation of Substantive International Criminal Law', *Journal of International Criminal Justice* 1(1) (2003).

Koller, David S., '… and New York and The Hague and Tokyo and Geneva and Nuremberg and…: The Geographies of International Law', *European Journal of International Law* 23(1) (2012).

'The Faith of the International Criminal Lawyer', *NYU Journal of International Law and Politics* 40(4) (2008).

Koskenniemi, Martti, 'Between Impunity and Show Trials', in J. A. Frowein and R.Wolfrum (eds.), *Max Planck Yearbook of United Nations Law, Volume 6* (The Hague, the Netherlands: Kluwer Law International, 2002).

Krever, Tor, 'Dispensing Global Justice', *New Left Review* 85 (January–February 2014).

Kulish, Nicholas, 'Legislators in Kenya Vote to Quit Global Court', *International Herald Tribune* (6 September 2013).

Labuda, Patryk, 'Complementarity and Cooperation in the Congo', in Ronald Slye (ed.), *The Nuremberg Principles in Non-Western Societies: A Reflection on Their Universality, Legitimacy and Application* (Nuremberg: International Nuremberg Principles Academy, 2016).

Lake, Milli, 'Building the Rule of War: Postconflict Institutions and the Micro-Dynamics of Conflict in Eastern DR Congo', *International Organization* 71(2) (2017).

'Ending Impunity for Sexual and Gender-Based Crimes: The International Criminal Court and Complementarity: From Theory to Practice in the Democratic Republic of Congo', *African Conflict & Peacebuilding Review* 4(1) (Spring 2014).

'Organizing Hypocrisy: Providing Legal Accountability for Human Rights Violations in Areas of Limited Statehood', *International Studies Quarterly* 58(3) (2014).

Langer, Maximo and Mackenzie Eason, 'The Quiet Expansion of Universal Jurisdiction', *European Journal of International Law* 30(1) (2019).

Laplante, Lisa J., 'Outlawing Amnesty: The Return of Criminal Justice in Transitional Justice Schemes', *Virginia Journal of International Law* 49(4) (2009).

'The Domestication of International Criminal Law: A Proposal for Expanding the International Criminal Court's Sphere of Influence', *The John Marshall Law Review* 43(3) (2010).

Lynch, Gabrielle, 'Electing the "Alliance of the Accused": The Success of the Jubilee Alliance in Kenya's Rift Valley', *Journal of Eastern African Studies* 8(1) (2014).

Macdonald, Anna, '"Somehow This Whole Process Became So Artificial": Exploring the Transitional Justice Implementation Gap in Uganda', *International Journal of Transitional Justice* 13(2) (2019).

Madsen, Mikael Rask, Pola Cebulak, and Micha Wiebusch, 'Special Issue – Resistance to International Courts', *International Journal of Law in Context* 14(2) (2018).

Mallinder, Louise and Kieran McEvoy, 'Rethinking Amnesties: Atrocity, Accountability and Impunity in Post-Conflict Societies', *Contemporary Social Science* 6(1) (2011).

Marcus, George E., 'Ethnography in/of the World System: The Emergence of Multi-Sited Ethnography', *Annual Review of Anthropology* 24 (1995).

Martineau, Anne Charlotte, 'The Rhetoric of Fragmentation: Fear and Faith in International Law', *Leiden Journal of International Law* 22(1) (2009).

Maya, Michael, 'Mobile Courts in the Democratic Republic of Congo: Complementarity in Action?' in Juan Carlos Botero, Ronald Janse, Sam Muller, and Christine Pratt (eds.), *Innovations in Rule of Law: A Compilation of Concise Essays* (HiiL and The World Justice Project, 2012) https://worldjusticeproject.org/sites/default/files/documents/wjp_hiil_compilation.pdf.

Mbazira, Christopher, 'Prosecuting International Crimes Committed by the Lord's Resistance Army in Uganda', in Chacha Murungu and Japhet Biegon (eds.), *Prosecuting International Crimes in Africa* (Pretoria: Pretoria University Law Press, 2011).

McAuliffe, Padraig, 'Bad Analogy: Why the Divergent Institutional Imperatives of the Ad Hoc Tribunals and the ICC Make the Lessons of Rule 11bis Inapplicable to the ICC's Complementarity Regime', *International Organizations Law Review* 11(2) (2014).

'From Watchdog to Workhorse: Explaining the Emergence of the ICC's Burden-Sharing Policy as an Example of Creeping Cosmopolitanism', *Chinese Journal of International Law* 13(2) (2014).

McEvoy, Kieran, 'Letting Go of Legalism: Developing a "Thicker" Version of Transitional Justice', in Kieran McEvoy and Lorna McGregor (eds.), *Transitional Justice from Below: Grassroots Activism and the Struggle for Change* (Portland: Hart Publishing, 2008).

McEvoy, Kieran and Louise Mallinder, 'Amnesties in Transition: Punishment, Restoration, and the Governance of Mercy', *Journal of Law and Society* 39(3) (2012).

McMahon, Patrice C. and David P. Forsythe, 'The ICTY's Impact on Serbia: Judicial Romanticism Meets Network Politics', *Human Rights Quarterly* 30 (2008).

Mégret, Frédéric, 'In Defense of Hybridity: Towards a Representational Theory of International Criminal Justice', *Cornell International Law Journal* 38(3) (2005).

'Three Dangers for the International Criminal Court: A Critical Look at a Consensual Project', in *Finnish Yearbook of International Law, Volume XII* (Leiden: Martinus Nijhoff Publishers, 2001).

Mégret, Frédéric and Marika Giles Samson, 'Holding the Line on Complementarity in Libya: The Case for Tolerating Flawed Domestic Trials', *Journal of International Criminal Justice* 11(3) (2013).

Meierhenrich, Jens, 'The Evolution of the Office of the Prosecutor at the International Criminal Court: Insights from Institutional Theory', in Martha Minow, C. Cora True-Frost, and Alex Whiting (eds.), *The First Global Prosecutor: Promise and Constraints* (Ann Arbor: University of Michigan Press, 2015).

Melman, Jesse, 'The Possibility of Transfer(?): A Comprehensive Approach to the International Criminal Tribunal for Rwanda's Rule 11bis to Permit Transfer to Rwandan Domestic Courts', *Fordham Law Review* 79(3) (2011).

Meron, Theodor, 'Closing the Accountability Gap: Concrete Steps Towards Ending Impunity for Atrocity Crimes', *American Journal of International Law* 112(3) (2018).

Merry, Sally Engle, 'Measuring the World: Indicators, Human Rights, and Global Governance', *Current Anthropology* 52(3) (April 2011).

Mertus, Julie, 'Considering Non-state Actors in the New Millennium: Toward Expanded Participation in Norm Generation and Norm Application', *NYU Journal of International Law and Politics* 32(2) (2000).

'From Legal Transplants to Transformative Justice: Human Rights and the Promise of Transnational Civil Society', *American University International Law Review* 14(5) (1999).

Meyersfeld, Bonita, 'Implementing the Rome Statute in Africa: Potential and Problems of the Prosecution of Gender Crimes in Africa in Accordance with the Rome Statute', in Kai Ambos and Ottilia A. Maunganidze (eds.), *Power and Prosecution: Challenges and Opportunities for International Criminal Justice in Sub-Saharan Africa* (Göttingen: Göttingen Studies in Criminal Law and Justice, 2012).

Michel, Verónica and Kathryn Sikkink, 'Human Rights Prosecutions and the Participation Rights of Victims in Latin America', *Law & Society Review* 47(4) (2013).

Moyn, Samuel, 'Judith Shklar versus the International Criminal Court', *Humanity* (Winter 2013).

Mubalama, Passy and Simon Jennings, 'Roving Courts in Eastern Congo', *Institute for War & Peace Reporting* (13 February 2013).

MuhindoMagadju, Pacifique, 'Législation congolaise de mise en oeuvre du Statut de Rome: Un pas en avant, un pas en arrière', in H. J. van der Merwe and Gerhard Kemp (eds.), *International Criminal Justice in Africa, 2016* (Nairobi: Strathmore University Press and Konrad Adenauer Stiftung, 2017).

Mureithi, Francis, 'How MPs Rejected the Proposed Special Tribunal for Kenya Bill', *The Star* (12 March 2011).

Musila, Godfrey M., 'Options for Transitional Justice in Kenya: Autonomy and the Challenge of External Prescriptions', *International Journal of Transitional Justice* 3(3) (2009).

Musua, Nzau, 'Kenya: Mutunga to Establish ICC Model Court', *The Star* (26 February 2013).

Mutua, Makau, 'Justice Under Siege: The Rule of Law and Judicial Subservience in Kenya', *Human Rights Quarterly* 23(1) (2001).

'Ruto, Uhuru Led Onslaught in Parliament against Local Tribunal', *The Standard* (7 April 2011).

Ndanyi, Mathews, 'Setbacks for Kenya's Special Court', *Institute for War & Peace Reporting* (23 December 2013).

Newton, Michael, 'The Complementarity Conundrum: Are We Watching Evolution or Evisceration?' *Santa Clara Journal of International Law* 8(1) (2010).

Nouwen, Sarah M. H. and Wouter G. Werner, 'Doing Justice to the Political: The International Criminal Court in Uganda and Sudan', *European Journal of International Law* 21(4) (2010).

'Monopolizing Global Justice: International Criminal Law as Challenge to Human Diversity', *Journal of International Criminal Justice* 13(1) (2015).

Oglesby, Elizabeth and Amy Ross, 'Guatemala's Genocide Determination and the Spatial Politics of Justice', *Space and Polity* 13(1) (April 2009).

Ogola, Florence, 'Uganda Victims Question ICC's Balance', *Institute for War & Peace Reporting* (14 June 2010).

Ogoola, Justice James, 'Lawfare: Where Justice Meets Peace', *Case Western Reserve Journal of International Law* 43(1) (2010).

Okafor, Obiora Chinedu and Uchechukwu Ngwaba, 'The International Criminal Court as a "Transitional Justice" Mechanism in Africa: Some Critical Reflections', *International Journal of Transitional Justice* 9(1) (2015).

Okeowo, Alexis, 'Thomas Kwoyelo's Troubling Trial', *The New Yorker* (21 July 2012).

Oketch, Bill, 'Rights Body to Assist Kwoyelo', *Daily Monitor* (2 January 2013).

'Uganda Set for First War Crime Trial', *Institute for War & Peace Reporting* (14 July 2010).

Okiror, Samuel Egadu, 'Ugandan Supreme Court Ruling Fuels Debate over Double Standards in War Crimes Prosecution', *International Justice Tribune* (21 April 2015).

Okuta, Antonina, 'National Legislation for Prosecution of International Crimes in Kenya', *Journal of International Criminal Justice* 7 (2009).

Olopade, Dayo, 'Who's Afraid of the International Criminal Court? In Kenya, the Answer Is No One At All', *New Republic* (9 March 2013).

Ongombe, Lievin Ngondji, 'RDC: la peine de mort, l'adoption de la loi de mise en oeuvre du statut du Rome', in Kai Ambos and Ottilia A. Maunganidze (eds.), *Power and Prosecution: Challenges and Opportunities for International Criminal Justice in Sub-Saharan Africa* (Göttingen: Göttingen Studies in Criminal Law and Justice, 2012).

Oola, Stephen, 'Will LRA Victims Get Justice?' *Saturday Monitor* (11 August 2015).

Opiyo, Peter, 'Isaac Ruto: Kenya Should Pull Out of ICC', *Standard Digital* (15 December 2010).

Orentlicher, Diane F., 'Settling Accounts: The Duty to Prosecute Human Rights Violations of a Prior Regime', *Yale Law Review* 100(8) (1991).

'"Settling Accounts" Revisited: Reconciling Global Norms with Local Agency', *International Journal of Transitional Justice* 1(1) (2007).

Palmer, Nicola, 'Transfer or Transformation: A Review of the Rule 11bis Decisions of the International Criminal Tribunal for Rwanda', *African Journal of International and Comparative Law* 20(1) (2012).

Pellet, Alain, 'Entry Into Force and Amendment of the Statute', in Antonio Cassese, Paola Gaeta, and John R. W. D. Jones (eds.), *The Rome Statute of the International Criminal Court: A Commentary, Vol. 1* (Oxford: Oxford University Press, 2002).

Pocar, Fausto, 'Completion or Continuation Strategy? Appraising Problems and Possible Developments in Building the Legacy of the ICTY', *Journal of International Criminal Justice* 6 (2008).

Rastan, Rod, 'Complementarity: Contest or Collaboration?' in Morten Bergsmo (ed.), *Complementarity and the Exercise of Universal Jurisdiction for Core International Crimes* (Oslo: Torkel Opsahl Academic EPublisher, 2010).

'What Is "Substantially the Same Conduct"? Unpacking the ICC's "First Limb" Complementarity Jurisprudence', *Journal of International Criminal Justice* 15(1) (2017).

Robinson, Darryl, 'Inescapable Dyads: Why the International Criminal Court Cannot Win', *Leiden Journal of International Law* 28(2) (2015).

'The Controversy over Territorial State Referrals and Reflections on ICL Discourse', *Journal of International Criminal Justice* 9(2) (2011).

'The Identity Crisis of International Law', *Leiden Journal of International Law* 21(4) (2008)

'The Mysterious Mysteriousness of Complementarity', *Criminal Law Forum* 21(1) (2010).

'Three Theories of Complementarity: Charge, Sentence, or Process?' *Harvard International Law Journal* 53 (April 2012).

Rodman, Kenneth A., 'Justice as a Dialogue between Law and Politics: Embedding the International Criminal Court within Conflict Management and Peacebuilding', *Journal of International Criminal Justice* 12(3) (2014).

Ronen, Yaël, 'The Impact of the ICTY on Atrocity-Related Prosecutions in the Courts of Bosnia and Herzegovina', *Penn State Journal of Law & International Affairs* 3(1) (2014).

Ruteere, Mutuma, 'Dr. Willy Mutunga: Why They Fear Him', *The Nairobi Law Monthly* 2(6) (June 2011).

SáCouto, Susana and Katherine Cleary, 'The Katanga Complementarity Decisions: Sound Law but Flawed Policy', *Leiden Journal of International Law* 23(2) (2003).

Schabas, William A., '"Complementarity in Practice": Some Uncomplimentary Thoughts', *Criminal Law Forum* 19(1) (2008).

'Prosecutorial Discretion v. Judicial Activism', *Journal of International Criminal Justice* 6(4) (2008).

Scheffer, David, 'International Judicial Intervention', *Foreign Policy* 102 (Spring 1996).

Shany, Yuval, 'How Can International Criminal Courts Have a Greater Impact on National Criminal Proceedings? Lessons from the First Two Decades of International Criminal Justice in Operation', *Israel Law Review* 46(3) (2013).

Sharp, Dustin N., 'Addressing Dilemmas of the Global and the Local in Transitional Justice', *Emory International Law Review* 29(1) (2014).

Sheng, Ada, 'Analyzing the International Criminal Court Complementarity Principle through a Federal Court Lens', *ILSA Journal of International and Comparative Law* 13(3) (2007).

Simpson, Gerry, '"Throwing a Little Remembering on the Past": The International Criminal Court and the Politics of Sovereignty', *University of California Davis Journal of International Law and Policy* 5(2) (1999).

Sirleaf, Matiangai, 'The African Justice Cascade and the Malabo Protocol', *International Journal of Transitional Justice* 11(1) (2017).

Slaughter, Anne-Marie and William Burke-White, 'The Future of International Law Is Domestic (or, the European Way of Law)', *Harvard International Law Journal* 47(2) (Summer 2006).

Slaughter, Anne-Marie, Andrew S. Tulumello, and Stepan Wood, 'International Law and International Relations Theory: A New Generation of Interdisciplinary Scholarship', *American Journal of International Law* 92(3) (1998).

Snyder, Jack and Leslie Vinjamuri, 'Trials and Errors: Principle and Pragmatism in Strategies of International Justice', *International Security* 28(3) (Winter 2003/2004).

Soares, Patricia Pinto, 'Positive Complementarity and the Law Enforcement Network: Drawing Lessons from the Ad Hoc Tribunals' Completion Strategy', *Israel Law Review* 46(3) (2013).

Sriram, Chandra and Stephen Brown, 'Kenya in the Shadow of the ICC: Complementarity, Gravity and Impact', *International Criminal Law Review* 12(2) (2012).

Stahn, Carsten, 'Complementarity: A Tale of Two Notions', *Criminal Law Forum* 19(1) (2008).

'How Is the Water? Light and Shadow in the First Years of the ICC', *Criminal Law Forum* 22(1–2) (2011).

'Libya, the International Criminal Court and Complementarity: A Test for "Shared Responsibility"', *Journal of International Criminal Justice* 10(2) (2012).

'One Step Forward, Two Steps Back? Second Thoughts on a "Sentence-Based" Theory of Complementarity', *Harvard International Law Journal* 53 (April 2012).

Starr, June and Mark Goodale, 'Introduction', in June Starr and Mark Goodale (eds.), *Practicing Ethnography in Law* (New York: Palgrave Macmillan, 2002).

Steer, Cassandra, 'Legal Transplants or Legal Patchworking? The Creation of International Criminal Law as a Pluralistic Body of Law', in Elies van Sliedregt and Sergey Vasiliev (eds.), *Pluralism in International Criminal Law* (Oxford: Oxford University Press, 2014).

Stromseth, Jane, 'Justice on the Ground: Can International Criminal Courts Strengthen Domestic Rule of Law in Post-Conflict Societies', *Hague Journal on the Rule of Law* 1 (2009).

Subotić, Jelena, 'The Transformation of International Transitional Justice Advocacy', *International Journal of Transitional Justice* 6(1) (2012).

Sunstein, Cass R., 'Social Norms and Social Roles', *Columbia Law Review* 96(4) (May 1996).

Tallgren, Immi, 'Completing the "International Criminal Order": The Rhetoric of International Repression and the Notion of Complementarity in the Draft Statute for an International Criminal Court', *Nordic Journal of International Law* 67 (1998).

'We Did It? The Vertigo of Law and Everyday Life at the Diplomatic Conference on the Establishment of an International Criminal Court', *Leiden Journal of International Law* 12(3) (1999).

Townsend, Gregory, 'Structure and Management', in Luc Reydams, Jan Wouters, and Cedric Ryngaert (eds.), *International Prosecutors* (Oxford: Oxford University Press, 2012).

Trahan, Jennifer, 'Views of the Future of the Field of International Justice: A Scenarios Project Based on Expert Consultations', *American University International Law Review* 33(4) (2018).

Trapani, Antonietta, 'Bringing National Courts in Line with International Norms: A Comparative Look at the Court of Bosnia and Herzegovina and the Military Court of the Democratic Republic of Congo', *Israel Law Review* 46(2) (July 2013).

Turner, Jenia Iontcheva, 'Nationalizing International Criminal Law', *Stanford Journal of International Law* 41(1) (2004).

Urueña, René, 'Prosecutorial Politics: The ICC's Influence in Colombian Peace Processes, 2003–2017', *American Journal of International Law* 111(1) (2017).

van den Berg, Stephanie, 'Praise for Historic Congo Rape Conviction', *International Justice Tribune* (11 December 2014).

van der Merwe, H. J., 'The Show Must Not Go On: Complementarity, the Due Process Thesis and Overzealous Domestic Prosecutions', *International Criminal Law Review* 15(1) (2015).

van der Wilt, Harmen and Sandra Lyngdorf, 'Procedural Obligations Under the European Convention of Human Rights: Useful Guidelines for the Assessment of "Unwillingness" and "Inability" in the Context of the Complementarity Principle', *International Criminal Law Review* 9(1) (2009).

Verini, James, 'The Prosecutor and the President', *The New York Times* (22 June 2016).

Vierucci, Luisa, 'National Implementation of the ICC Statute (Part II): Foreword', *Journal of International Criminal Justice* 5(2) (2007).

Waitherero, Betty, 'Can the International Crimes Division Prosecute Kenya's PEV Cases?' *The Nation* (8 February 2014).

Waldorf, Lars, '"A Mere Pretense of Justice": Complementarity, Sham Trials, and Victor's Justice at the Rwandan Tribunal', *Fordham International Law Journal* 33(4) (2011).

Wanyeki, L. Muthoni, 'Kenya: We Remember, and Have Evidence', *The East African* (9 November 2009).

Welch, Jr., Claude E. and Ashley F. Watkins, 'Extending Enforcement: The Coalition for the International Criminal Court', *Human Rights Quarterly* 33(4) (2011).

Wharton, Sara and Rosemary Grey, 'The Full Picture: Preliminary Examinations at the International Criminal Court', *The Canadian Yearbook of International Law* 56 (2019).

Whiting, Alex, 'Dynamic Investigative Practice at the International Criminal Court', *Law & Contemporary Problems* 76(3–4) (2013).

Williams, Sharon A. and William A. Schabas, 'Article 17: Issues of Admissibility', in Otto Triffterer (ed.), *Commentary on the Rome Statute of the International Criminal Court: Observers' Notes, Article by Article* (Portland: Hart Publishing, 2008).

Zeidy, Mohamed El, 'The Principle of Complementarity: A New Machinery to Implement International Criminal Law', *Michigan Journal of International Law* 23(4) (2002).

Reports

Amnesty Commission (Uganda), 'The Amnesty Act: An Act of Forgiveness' (on-file) (August 2009).

Amnesty International, 'Crying for Justice: Victims' Perspectives on Justice for the Post-election Violence in Kenya', AFR 32/001/2014 (15 July 2014) www.amnesty.org/en/documents/afr32/001/2014/en/.

'The International Criminal Court: Checklist for Effective Implementation', IOR 40/011/2000 (July 2000) www.amnesty.org/en/documents/IOR40/011/2000/en/.

'The Time for Justice Is Now: New Strategy Needed in the Democratic Republic of Congo: Summary', AFR 62/007/2011 (August 2011).

Carayon, Gaelle, 'Increased Use of Intermediaries: Increased Discontent', *ACCESS: Victims' Rights Working Group Bulletin* (Spring 2012).

Clark, Phil, '"All These Outsiders Shouted Louder than Us": Civil Society Engagement with Transitional Justice in Uganda', Security in Transition Working Paper, SiT/WP/03/15 (2015).

du Plessis, Max, Antoinette Low, and Ottilia Maunganidze, 'African Efforts to Close the Impunity Gap: Lessons for Complementarity from National and Regional Actions', *Institute for Security Studies Paper* No. 241 (November 2012).

Glassborow, Katy, 'ICC Investigative Strategy on Sexual Violence Crimes Under Fire', Institute for War & Peace Reporting (27 October 2008).

Human Rights Watch, 'Courting History: The Landmark International Criminal Court's First Years' (2008).

'DR Congo: Commentary on Draft Legislation to Establish Specialized Chambers for Prosecution of International Crimes' (11 March 2011).

'Etats Généraux of the Justice System in the Democratic Republic of Congo: Recommendations on the Fight Against Impunity for Grave International Crimes' (27 April 2015).

'ICC: Course Correction – Recommendations to the Prosecutor for a More Effective Approach to "Situations under Analysis"' (16 June 2011).

'Justice for Serious Crimes before National Courts: Uganda's International Crimes Division' (January 2012).

'Justice on Trial: Lessons from the Minova Rape Case in the Democratic Republic of Congo' (2015).

'Letter to the Executive Committee of the Prosecutor' (15 September 2008).

'Making Justice Work: Restoration of the Legal System in Ituri, DRC' (1 September 2004).

'Making the International Criminal Court Work: A Handbook for Implementing the Rome Statute' (September 2001).

'Pressure Point: The ICC's Impact on National Justice – Lessons from Colombia, Georgia, Guinea, and the United Kingdom' (2018).

'"Turning Pebbles": Evading Accountability for Post-Election Violence in Kenya' (December 2011).

'Unfinished Business: Closing Gaps in the Selection of ICC Cases' (September 2011).

International Bar Association, 'Rebuilding Courts and Trust: An Assessment of the Needs of the Justice System in the Democratic Republic of Congo', International Legal Assistance Consortium and IBA Human Rights Institute Report (August 2009).

International Center for Transitional Justice, 'The Future of International Justice: National Courts Supported by International Expertise' (22 April 2011).

'The ICC on the Ground: Complementarity at Work in Colombia and the DRC' (May 2010).

International Criminal Tribunal for Rwanda, 'Complementarity in Action: Lessons Learned from the ICTR Prosecutor's Referral of International Criminal Cases to National Jurisdictions for Trial' (February 2015).

International Crisis Group, 'Kenya: Impact of the ICC Proceedings', Africa Briefing No. 84 (9 January 2012).

'Northern Uganda: Seizing the Opportunity for Peace', Report No. 124 (April 2007).

International Law Commission, Conclusions of the Work of the Study Group on the Fragmentation of International Law, 'Difficulties Arising from the Diversification and Expansion of International Law', UN Doc. A/61/10 (2006).

International Refugee Rights Initiative, 'A Poisoned Chalice? Local Civil Society and the International Criminal Court's Engagement in Uganda' (October 2011).

International Refugee Rights Initiative and Aprodivi-ASBL, 'Steps Towards Justice, Frustrated Hopes: Some Reflections on the Experience of the International Criminal Court in Ituri' (January 2012).

JLOS, 'Annual Performance Report 2009/2010' (September 2010).

'Justice at Cross Roads? A Special Report on the Thomas Kwoyelo Trial' (2011).

'The Amnesty Law (2000) Issues Paper – Review by the Transitional Justice Working Group' (April 2012).

Judicial Service Commission, 'Report of the Committee of the Judicial Service Commission on the Establishment of an International Crimes Division in the High Court of Kenya' (30 October 2012).

Kambala wa Kambala, Olivier, 'International Criminal Court in Africa: "alea jacta est"', Oxford Transitional Justice Research Working Paper Series (12 July 2010).

Kaye, David A., 'Justice Beyond The Hague: Supporting the Prosecution of International Crimes in Domestic Courts', Council on Foreign Relations, Special Report No. 61 (June 2011).

Kenya National Human Rights Commission, 'On the Brink of the Precipice: A Human Rights Account of Kenya's Post-2007 Election Violence' (August 2008).

Kenyans for Peace with Truth and Justice, 'A Real Option for Justice? The International Crimes Division of the High Court of Kenya' (July 2014).

'Impunity Restored? Lessons Learned from the Failure of the Kenyan Cases at the International Criminal Court' (November 2016).

'Securing Justice: Establishing a Domestic Mechanism for the 2007/8 Post-election Violence in Kenya' (May 2013).

Khan, Tessa and Jim Wormington, 'Mobile Courts in the DRC: Lessons from Development for International Criminal Justice', Oxford Transitional Justice Research Working Paper Series (2011).

Manoba, Joseph A., 'First Trial before the War Crimes Division of the High Court in Uganda', VRWG Bulletin No. 17 (Winter 2010).

Muntazini Mukimapa, Colonel Toussaint, 'A Close-Up Look at the Fight against Impunity in the DRC', International Center for Transitional Justice (18 April 2016).

Musila, Godfrey M., 'Between Rhetoric and Action: The Politics, Processes and Practice of the ICC's Work in the DRC', Institute for Security Studies Monograph 164 (July 2009).

Okuta, Antonina, Accountability for International Crimes at the Domestic Level: Case Studies of Kenya, Uganda, and Cote d'Ivoire (University of Amsterdam, PhD Dissertation) (2016).

Ongeso, Aimee, 'An International Crimes Division in Kenya's High Court: Meaningful Justice or a White Elephant?' VRWG Bulletin No. 22 (Spring 2013).

Oola, Stephen, 'The Coalition for Reconciliation in Uganda: Important Lessons for Proactive Civil Society Engagement in Catalysing Transitional Justice Discourse', African Transitional Justice Research Network Workshop (30–31 August 2010).

Open Society Justice Initiative, Briefing Paper, 'SGBV Victims Seek Justice for Post-Election Violence' (February 2013).

Briefing Paper, 'Unfinished Business: Guatemala's International Commission against Impunity' (2015).

REDRESS, 'Ugandan International Crimes Division Rules 2016: Analysis on Victim Participation Framework, Final Version' (August 2016).

Refugee Law Project, 'Ambiguous Impacts: The Effects of the International Criminal Court Investigations in Northern Uganda', Working Paper No. 22 (October 2012).

Republic of Uganda, 'Report of the Committee on Defence and Internal Affairs on the Petition on the Lapsing of Part II of The Amnesty Act, 2000' (August 2013).

Southern African Litigation Centre, 'Positive Reinforcement: Advocating for International Criminal Justice in Africa' (May 2013).

Uganda Law Society, 'The International Crimes Division of the High Court of Uganda: Towards Greater Effectiveness' (2018).

United Nations Office of the High Commissioner for Human Rights, 'Judicial Workshop on Victim and Witness Protection in Uganda' (August 2011).

'Report of the Mapping Exercise documenting the most serious violations of human rights and international humanitarian law committed within the territory of the Democratic Republic of the Congo between March 1993 and June 2003' (August 2010).

'"The Dust Has Not Yet Settled": Victims' Views on the Right to Remedy and Reparation – A Report from the Greater North of Uganda' (Kampala, 2011).

Wanyeki, L. Muthoni, 'The International Criminal Court's Cases in Kenya: Origin and Impact', Institute for Security Studies Paper No. 237 (August 2012).

Parliamentary Debates

Kenya

Kenya National Assembly Official Record (Hansard), The International Crimes Bill, Second Reading (7 May 2008).

Kenya National Assembly Official Record (Hansard), The Constitution of Kenya (Amendment) Bill, Second Reading (3 February 2009).

Kenya National Assembly Official Report, The Constitution of Kenya (Amendment) Bill, Second Reading (2 December 2009).

Parliament of Kenya, Convening of Special Sitting of The Senate to Debate Motion on Withdrawal of Kenya from the Rome Statute, Official Record (Hansard) (10 September 2013).

Uganda

The Seventh Parliament of Uganda (Hansard), First Reading, The International Criminal Court Bill, 2004 (24 June 2004).

The Eighth Parliament of Uganda (Hansard), Second Reading, The International Criminal Court Bill, 2004 [sic] (10 March 2010).

The Eighth Parliament of Uganda (Hansard), Third Reading, The International Criminal Court Bill, 2006 (10 March 2010).

Republic of Uganda, Report of the Sessional Committee on Legal and Parliamentary Affairs on the International Criminal Court Bill, 2006 (March 2010).

ICC Documents

Report of the Ad Hoc Committee on the Establishment of an International Criminal Court, A/50/22 (1995).

Office of the Prosecutor, 'Informal expert paper: The principle of complementarity in practice', ICC-OTP (2003).

Office of the Prosecutor, 'Paper on some policy issues before the Office of the Prosecutor' (September 2003).

Office of the Prosecutor, 'Report on the activities performed during the first three years (June 2003–June 2006)' (12 September 2006).

Regulations of the Office of the Prosecutor, ICC-BD/05-01-09 (23 April 2009).

Agreed Minutes of Meeting of 3 July 2009 between the ICC Prosecutor and Delegation of the Kenyan Government (3 July 2009, The Hague).

Second Status Report on the Court's Investigations in to Efficiency Measures', ICC- ASP/8/30 (4 November 2009).

Kampala Declaration, RC/Decl.1; Resolution RC/Res.1 – Complementarity (adopted 8 June 2010).

Office of the Prosecutor, 'Prosecutorial Strategy 2009–2012' (1 February 2010).

Review Conference of the Rome Statute, 'Focal points' compilation of examples of projects aimed at strengthening domestic jurisdictions to deal with Rome Statute Crimes', RC/ST/CM/INF.2 (30 May 2010).

Assembly of States Parties, 'Proposed Programme Budget for 2012 of the International Criminal Court', ICC-ASP/10/10 (21 July 2011).

Draft Guidelines Governing the Relations between the Court and Intermediaries (August 2011).

Third Report of ICC Prosecutor to UN Security Council Pursuant to UNSCR 1970 (16 May 2012).

Assembly of States Parties, 'Report of the Court on Complementarity', ICC-ASP11/39 (16 October 2012).

Second Report on the Draft Guidelines [Governing the Relations between the Court and Intermediaries] (30 October 2013).

Office of the Prosecutor, 'Policy Paper on Preliminary Examinations' (November 2013).

Assembly of States Parties, 'Report of the Court on the Basic Size of the Office of the Prosecutor', ICC-ASP/14/21 (17 September 2015).

Speeches and Public Statements

Statement of the Prosecutor Luis Moreno-Ocampo to Diplomatic Corps (12 February 2004).

Third Session of the Assembly of States Parties to the Rome Statute of the International Criminal Court, Address by Prosecutor Luis Moreno-Ocampo (The Hague, 6 September 2004).

Remarks of the Honorable Minister of State and Deputy Attorney General at the UNDP Policy Dialogue on Complementarity' and Transitional Justice, 'The Role of Specialised Courts in Prosecuting International Crimes and Transitional Justice in Uganda' (12–13 October 2011).

Remarks by His Worship Asiimwe Tadeo, 'Effecting Complementarity: Challenges and Opportunities: A Case Study of the International Crimes Division of Uganda', paper presented at regional forum on international and transitional justice organized by ASF-Uganda Mission and the UCICC (20 July 2012).

Statement of the Prosecutor of the International Criminal Court, Fatou Bensouda, to the United Nations Security Council on the situation in Libya, pursuant to UNSCR 1970 (2011) (remarks delivered in New York, 14 November 2013).

Statement to the United Nations Security Council on the Situation in Darfur, pursuant to UNSCR 1593 (2005) (12 December 2014).

Press Releases

Amnesty International, 'Court's decision a setback for accountability for crimes committed in northern Uganda conflict', AFR 59/015/2011 (23 September 2011).

ICC, 'Election of the prosecutor, Statement by Mr. Moreno Ocampo', ICC-OTP-20030502-10 (22 April 2003).

CICC, 'Global Coalition Calls on Kenya to Ratify International Criminal Court' (11 January 2005).

UVF, 'Statement on the International Crimes Bill of 2009' (4 November 2009).

ICTJ, 'The Democratic Republic of Congo Must Adopt the Rome Statute Implementation Law' (April 2010).

PGA, 'La loi de mise en oeuvre du statut de Rome déclare recevable par l'Assemblée Nationale de la République Démocratique du Congo' (4 November 2010).

CICC, 'Global Justice Coalition Welcomes Advances in the Criminal Law Reform in the Democratic Republic of Congo', 9 November 2010; CN-CPI Press Release, 'The DRC coalition for the ICC welcomes the admission of the law proposal on the implementation of the Rome Statute' (5 November 2010).

Ligue pour la paix et les droits de l'homme, no. 006/CN/LIPADHO/2010, 'La majorité des députes s'opposent a l'abolition de peine capital' (18 November 2010).

No Peace Without Justice, 'Libya: NPWJ and NRPTT welcome ICC ruling on the Al- Senussi case' (24 July 2014).

Blog Posts

Elebe ma Elebe, Nick, 'Why DRC Lawmakers Again Rejected Special Chambers to Prosecute International Crimes' (23 May 2014).

Goldston, James, 'Amid US Attacks, Time to Reinvigorate the ICC', Just Security (14 December 2018).

Guilfoyle, Douglas, 'This Is Not Fine: The International Criminal Court in Trouble', EJIL: Talk! (March 2019).

International Center for Transitional Justice, 'Is the International Community Abandoning the Fight Against Impunity?'.

Jon Heller, Kevin, 'It's Time to Reconsider the Al-Senussi Case. But How?' (2 September 2014).

Kambale, Pascal, 'The ICC and Lubanga: Missed Opportunities' (16 March 2012).

Labuda, Patryk, 'The Democratic Republic of Congo's Failure to Address Impunity for International Crimes: A View from Inside the Legislative Process 2010–2011' (8 November 2011).

'Whither the Fight against Impunity in the Democratic Republic of Congo?' (24 June 2015).

Nakandha, Sharon, 'Supreme Court of Uganda Rules on the Application of the Amnesty Act' (16 April 2015).

'The Case of Dominc Ongwen: Possible Considerations for In Situ Proceedings', International Justice Monitor (10 February 2015).

Nanyuja, Brenda, 'The Thomas Kwoyelo Case at the ICD: Issues of Victim Participation', International Justice Monitor (13 March 2017).

O'Donohue, Jonathan and Sophie Rigney, 'The ICC Must Consider Fair Trial Concerns in Determining Libya's Application to Prosecute Saif al-Islam Gaddafi Nationally' (8 June 2012).

Ogora, Lino Owor, 'Community Members in Northern Uganda Elated by Visit of ICC Judges', International Justice Monitor (19 June 2018).

'Landmark Ruling on Victim Participation in the Case of Thomas Kwoyelo', International Justice Monitor (4 October 2016).

Ogora, Lino Owor and Beini Ye, 'To Participate or Not? Getting Victim Participation Right in the Kwoyelo Case', International Justice Monitor (18 October 2016).

Ogora, Lino Owor, 'Community Members in Northern Uganda Elated by Visit of ICC Judges', International Justice Monitor (19 June 2018).

Ravet, Romain, 'Thomas Kwoyelo in Uganda: Victims' Participation Brings Hope and Challenges', International Justice Monitor (17 October 2018).

Raymond-Jetté, Myriam, 'Small Gains on Large Crimes in DR Congo', Peace Insight (17 July 2015).

Stahn, Carsten, 'Tribunals Are Dead, Long Live Tribunals: MICT, the Kosovo Specialist Chambers and the Turn to New Hybridity', EJIL: Talk! (23 September 2016).

INDEX

328

Books in the Series

Lightning Source UK Ltd.
Milton Keynes UK
UKHW011510030622
403870UK00018B/438

9 781108 459723